Tolley's Pension F Handbook

Eighth Edition

Roger Self

LexisNexis™ UK

Members of the LexisNexis Group worldwide

United Kingdom	LexisNexis UK, a Division of Reed Elsevier (UK) Ltd, 2 Addiscombe Road, CROYDON CR9 5AF
Argentina	LexisNexis Argentina, BUENOS AIRES
Australia	LexisNexis Butterworths, CHATSWOOD, New South Wales
Austria	LexisNexis Verlag ARD Orac GmbH & Co KG, VIENNA
Canada	LexisNexis Butterworths, MARKHAM, Ontario
Chile	LexisNexis Chile Ltda, SANTIAGO DE CHILE
Czech Republic	Nakladatelství Orac sro, PRAGUE
France	Editions du Juris-Classeur SA, PARIS
Germany	LexisNexis Deutschland GmbH, FRANKFURT and MUNSTER
Hong Kong	LexisNexis Butterworths, HONG KONG
Hungary	HVG-Orac, BUDAPEST
India	LexisNexis Butterworths, NEW DELHI
Ireland	Butterworths (Ireland) Ltd, DUBLIN
Italy	Giuffrè Editore, MILAN
Malaysia	Malayan Law Journal Sdn Bhd, KUALA LUMPUR
New Zealand	LexisNexis Butterworths, WELLINGTON
Poland	Wydawnictwo Prawnicze LexisNexis, WARSAW
Singapore	LexisNexis Butterworths, SINGAPORE
South Africa	LexisNexis Butterworths, DURBAN
Switzerland	Stämpfli Verlag AG, BERNE USA LexisNexis, DAYTON, Ohio

© Reed Elsevier (UK) Ltd 2003

A CIP Catalogue record for this book is available from the British Library.

ISBN 0 75452 340 3

Typeset by Columns Design Ltd, Reading, England
Printed and bound in Great Britain by Hobbs the Printers Ltd, Totton, Hampshire

Visit LexisNexis UK at www.lexisnexis.co.uk

Preface

The purpose of this book, now in its eighth edition, is the same as at the time it was first published, namely to offer some help to the thousands of managers and employees who have taken on the role of serving as pension fund trustees.

The publication of this edition comes at a time of great difficulty for UK pension provision. A very large proportion of the country's final salary schemes have been closed to new entrants, and very many schemes are also now frozen so that no member is building up any further pensionable service. Where an alternative is being offered, this will usually take the form of a money purchase arrangement – perhaps still an occupational pension scheme run by trustees – but often a fully insured contractual arrangement not set up as a trust. There is nothing wrong with a money purchase scheme if the contributions are sufficient and investment returns are positive over the longer term. Yet in general those two conditions are not presently being met.

It is worth remembering that this book was first published also during troubled times. The revelations in 1991 that the occupational pension schemes of the Robert Maxwell group of companies had been systematically looted dominated national television news. A spate of other stories told of how many companies, experiencing financial difficulties in a long and severe recession, had turned to their pension funds for cash advances. The result? The company failed. The pension scheme was found to be underfunded. Employees lost not only their jobs, but also their pensions.

At that time, as now, the trust of many ordinary employees that their pensions were safe was severely tested.

Then, the House of Commons Select Committee on Social Security called for action. The Government set up the Pension Law Review Committee under Professor Goode which made 218 recommendations. The Government responded with a White Paper in June 1994 which by the summer of 1995 had become the *Pensions Act 1995*. Most of the Act's measures came into force on 6 April 1997.

Under this new legislative regime, it became clear that if occupational pension schemes were to survive, then much would depend on the continuing energy and integrity of the ordinary trustee. The *Pensions Act 1995* gave them new statutory powers. It also codified their duties and imposed tough sanctions in cases of non-compliance. Today it seems that pensions are even more subject to controversy than during those tumultuous months following the Maxwell affair. Pension fund investments have now registered three years of negative returns, employer costs are rising and, as mentioned above, the result is that many long-established final salary schemes have been closed to new members. More ominously, many final salary schemes are being put into wind up when they are severely underfunded. In these cases, many long-serving employees have found that only a fraction of their accrued benefits can be met by their trustees' pension fund.

It is not the job of this book to apportion blame for these problems, which for some individuals represent personal catastrophes. Nor does it seek to propose political solutions. Its purpose is rather to offer guidance to pension fund trustees so that they can carry out their duties.

Pension fund trustees themselves are also coming to terms with their new duties after the Government's endorsement of the recommendations issued in March 2001 by Paul Myners. These do not, it should be noted, require the 'professionalisation' of the lay trustee. Trustees are not suddenly required to become investment experts. They remain entitled to make use of the expertise of others. However, Paul Myners and the Government insist that pension fund trustees should have sufficient expertise to be able to evaluate whether the advice they receive is complete, up to date and based on appropriate assumptions. Importantly, trustees are reminded that they should exercise their own judgement when considering and acting upon advice – irrespective of the source of that advice. This is a reasonable expectation of any pension fund trustee. It is the aim of this book to help pension fund trustees realise this expectation.

In this book, I have always stressed two important points, and post-Myners and at a time when quality private pension provision is under threat, I believe that they are even more relevant today than when I first wrote them:

- Occupational pensions are an employee benefit. They do not exist in a vacuum but rather form part of the overall remuneration policy of the employer.

- Trustees should not expect to be pension experts. They must rely on a host of advisers whom they appoint. What is important is that they must understand the nature of their relationship with those advisers and be prepared to question them critically. If necessary, they should seek alternative advice.

The aim of this book has simply always been to give all pension fund trustees the confidence to undertake their appointed task of safeguarding the pension rights of their scheme's members.

I am grateful to the editor, Nigel Voak, who I have learnt is an even more patient and forbearing man than I gave him credit for in last year's preface. He has done a most excellent job.

Roger Self
May 2003

Contents

Contents

Contents

Table of Cases

Table of Statutes

Table of Statutory Instruments

Table of European Legislation

Chapter 1

Occupational pension schemes

Overview

1.1   This book is aimed at individuals who have been nominated either by their employer or by the general membership of an occupational pension scheme to serve as the scheme's trustees. The job of the trustees is to run the pension scheme.

Not all pension arrangements made by employers for the benefit of their employees are run by trustees:

- The public service pension schemes (run by central government) and the local authority schemes are governed by special statutes and are not set up as trusts.

- Private sector occupational pension schemes have to be set up as trusts if they are to receive the tax advantages that come with tax approval. There are, however, a number of private sector, unapproved, occupational pension schemes which are not set up as trusts. These cater almost exclusively for high earners.

- Many, mainly smaller, employers have chosen in recent years to provide pension cover for their employees by using personal pensions, which are individual contractual arrangements between each member and the pension provider – usually an insurance company. The employer may have facilitated what are known as group personal pension arrangements, a collection of what are still individual contracts between each member and the personal pension provider. Personal pensions are not governed by the requirements of trust law. The great majority of stakeholder pension schemes operate as a form of group personal pension arrangement and so are not run by trustees.

It is difficult to say exactly how many occupational pension schemes there are which are set up as trusts. The Pension Scheme Registry knew of 103,602 'live' private sector occupational pension schemes as at 31 March 2002. However, the great majority of these occupational pension schemes have very few members – typically just two or three directors of a small company. (The number of 'live' occupational pension schemes includes not only those which are open to new members but also closed schemes which new members cannot join, frozen schemes where members are no longer building up pension rights and frozen schemes which are also in the process of winding up.)

The Registry reports that as at 31 March 2002 there were 20,674 live occupational pension schemes with twelve or more members which are set up as trusts. These can range from a small, insured, money purchase scheme sponsored by a small company and covering a dozen or so members to the large, self-administered, final salary schemes with thousands of members sponsored by the UK's largest companies.

Below the terms just used to describe various kinds of pension scheme such as *insured, money purchase, self-administered, final salary* are explained. For all these schemes the job of the trustee is essentially the same – to run the pension scheme.

Types of occupational pension scheme

1.2   Occupational pension schemes can be divided into several different types. As a trustee, it is important to know what the differences are between various kinds of scheme, especially as it is possible for a scheme to change from one type to another and this will have important consequences for its members.

Approved, exempt approved and unapproved schemes

1.3   Approved, exempt approved and unapproved schemes are terms used by the Inland Revenue and are important because they define what kind of tax privileges, if any, will be granted to the scheme. It should, however, be pointed out that these terms may lose any meaning if the proposals put forward in December 2002 by the Treasury and Inland Revenue are put into effect. The proposals are set out in *Simplifying the Taxation of Pensions: Increasing Choice and Flexibility For All* and are summarised in **APPENDIX 2**.

An *approved scheme* must have rules limiting the benefits provided to members of the scheme. Approval is automatic if the benefits are limited as described in *section 590* of the *Income and Corporation Taxes Act 1988* (*ICTA 1988*). In contrast, schemes which apply the contribution and benefit limits set out in the Inland Revenue's Savings, Pensions, Share Schemes booklet IR12 can receive discretionary approval under *section 591* of the Act. However, if a pension scheme is just of approved status, the only tax relief is that employees will not be charged income tax on any employer contributions to the scheme (as specified in *section 596* of the Act). To qualify for further tax relief, a scheme must be one of a specified number of statutory public service schemes or be an *exempt approved scheme*.

An exempt approved scheme is an approved scheme which is established under irrevocable trusts. Establishment as an irrevocable trust means that the scheme's assets must be set aside to provide specified benefits to employees and must be held by under trust to ensure that, with certain exceptions, the assets are not available to the employer.

If the Inland Revenue accepts that an occupational pension scheme operates as an exempt approved scheme, then under *sections 592* and *596* of the Act:

- the employee is not taxed on any employer contributions to the scheme;

- income, once received from the scheme's investments, is free of income tax and gains realised on those investments are free of capital gains tax (but note that schemes can no longer claim back the tax deducted at source on dividend payments made by UK companies);

- premiums paid for life assurance are free of any tax charge;

- employer contributions are allowable as an expense;

- employee contributions up to a limit of 15% of annual pay are tax free.

It is only by means of an exempt approved scheme set up as an irrevocable trust that employers outside the public service can provide occupational pensions that enjoy all these very significant tax reliefs. This is the reason occupational pension schemes are set up as trusts under the stewardship of trustees.

Unapproved schemes

1.4 Before the *Finance Act 1989*, Inland Revenue approval would have been withdrawn from any existing exempt approved scheme if the employer provided an employee with benefits from both the exempt approved scheme and an *unapproved scheme*. Since 1989, this has no longer been the case and employees can be provided with retirement benefits up to the Inland Revenue limits from an exempt approved scheme and also with further top-up benefits provided by an unapproved scheme. Employers may find it necessary to do this because also from 1989 new employee members of approved schemes have been subject to the pensionable earnings cap. The cap sets a cash ceiling on the contributions and benefits payable in respect of high earners. This ceiling stood at £97,200 in 2002/03. Unapproved schemes are simply schemes or arrangements for paying retirement benefits to employees to which no special tax privileges are applied. Many funded unapproved schemes are set up as trusts.

Defined benefit and defined contribution schemes

1.5 A *defined benefit scheme* usually operates by linking the employee's eventual retirement benefit to his or her pay. They are often therefore called *salary related schemes*.

In most cases, the employee's pay at or near retirement is chosen so that the benefit promise is effectively inflation-proofed over the employee's working life. They are then commonly called *final salary schemes*. However, some schemes operate by calculating the average pay earned by the employee while a member of the scheme. The pay for each year is revalued to take account of either earnings or price inflation over the time until the pension is to be calculated. These are therefore called *average salary schemes*. Recently a new kind of defined benefit scheme known as a *cash balance scheme* has been introduced into the UK. In a cash balance scheme the employee's benefits are calculated as a defined percentage of pay but expressed as a lump sum amount.

3

1.5   *Occupational pension schemes*

A *defined contribution scheme* simply provides the employee with the pension which can be bought with the capital sum which that employee accumulates in an individualised retirement savings account. The capital sum is built up from regular defined contributions to the scheme made by the employer and usually also by the employee, plus any money transferred by the employee into the scheme from previous pension arrangements, plus the cumulative investment return net of any charges. Such schemes are also called *money purchase schemes*.

The advantage of a defined benefit scheme is that a greater degree of certainty is given to the employee's promised level of benefits. They can be used more flexibly, especially in cases of early retirement, to provide higher benefits than could be obtained by defined contribution schemes, where investment returns are very dependent on the length of time the money has been invested. With a defined benefit scheme, the investment risk is borne by the sponsoring employer who underwrites the benefit promise. The mortality risk, i e the risk of the pensioner living longer than expected, is also borne by the sponsoring employer in the case of a final salary or average salary scheme, but in the case of the third type of defined benefit scheme mentioned, the cash balance scheme, the mortality risk is borne by the pensioner.

The advantage of a defined contribution scheme is that it appears to be more easily understandable. If contribution levels are high enough, they can provide good benefits even if the actual level of the benefit cannot be known in advance. Each employee has an individual account so early leavers from the scheme do not subsidise those who stay to retirement as can happen in schemes which operate simply on the defined benefit basis. One problem is that the level of retirement benefit has been often extraordinarily dependent on the investment conditions prevailing at the time of the employee's retirement (although 'lifestyle' funds are designed to lock in earlier gains from riskier investments by switching the member's fund progressively into safer investments in the run up to the member's planned retirement age). Also, the regular stream of payments in retirement is often secured by purchasing an annuity. The amount of pension that can be secured by any given capital sum will vary over time because annuity rates depend on the medium-term outlook for inflation. With a defined contribution scheme both the investment risk and the mortality risk is borne by the employee.

The distinction between defined benefit and defined contribution schemes is not as great as is often claimed. Final salary schemes are funded by contributions to produce the targeted benefit. Money purchase schemes can be funded to produce the same targeted benefit. The key difference is simply that the employer is seen to underwrite the target in a final salary scheme.

Some schemes also combine the two approaches in what is known as a *money purchase underpin* or a *final salary underpin*. In a money purchase underpin employees are guaranteed that their benefits, either on transferring benefits from the scheme or at retirement, will be calculated as the greater of the amount obtained using the defined benefit and the defined contribution

4

method. This will be so whether the employees are early leavers from the scheme who have preserved their pension rights in the scheme or have remained active members of the scheme up to the time they began to draw their pension.

In a final salary underpin an employee receives money-purchase-style benefits but these are guaranteed never to be less than a defined minimum amount.

Insured and self-administered schemes

1.6   In an *insured scheme* all the benefits are provided by an insurance company with whom the trustees have taken out a contract to pay regular premiums. The pensions administration and investment strategy are invariably the responsibility of the insurance company. Over 95% of all occupational pension schemes are insured. There are many thousands of *executive pension plans*, often with only one member, which are special insured schemes designed for senior employees.

In a *self-administered scheme*, the trustees are responsible for the overall investment strategy and can decide who will administer the scheme. Although there are far fewer self-administered schemes than insured schemes, they are on average far larger. Benefits of scale mean that once a pension fund has grown to, say, £20m, it is usually more cost effective for the fund to operate on a self-administered basis rather than to remain insured.

There are also a very large number of *small self-administered schemes*. Such schemes have fewer than 12 members and, in most cases, all the members are senior directors of the sponsoring company. Small self-administered schemes are subject to especially strict Inland Revenue monitoring because, like executive pension schemes, they can be used to provide loans to, and invest in the assets of, the sponsoring company.

Contracted-in and contracted-out schemes

1.7   Occupational pension schemes that are *contracted in* provide employees with a pension which is additional to the one they accrue at the same time in the State Earnings Related Pension Scheme (SERPS) or State Second Pension (S2P) – see **APPENDIX 5**. Employees and the employer pay National Insurance contributions at the not-contracted-out rate. Technically such schemes are known as *participating schemes* or *not-contracted-out schemes*.

Occupational pension schemes that are *contracted out* provide employees with a pension that replaces the *additional pension* that they would otherwise have accrued in SERPS or S2P during that same period of employment. In return for the reduced amount of state retirement pension, the employee and the employer are liable to pay National Insurance contributions at a lower rate than would be the case if the employee were either a member of a contracted-in occupational pension scheme or not a member of any occupational pension scheme at all.

It is not true to say, however, that the contracted-out pension the employees receive when they reach state pension age will always *completely* replace their additional pension from SERPS or from S2P. First of all, the Government calculates employees' additional pension entitlement from SERPS with reference to any periods of contracted-out employment between 6 April 1978, when SERPS first began, and 5 April 1997, when the links between contracted-out employment and SERPS were broken, as if those employees had not been contracted out at all. This preliminary calculation gives the employees' *notional* additional pension entitlement from SERPS. However, this notional entitlement is then offset by an amount known as a *contracted-out deduction* (COD). The COD is equal to the value of the *guaranteed minimum pension* (GMP) that the employees are taken to have accrued during their periods of contracted-out employment. After the offset is applied, the resulting figure is the employees' *net* additional pension entitlement.

The net additional pension paid from SERPS after the COD offset, and which covers any period of contracted-out employment before 6 April 1997, may or may not initially be a zero amount. (Non-zero amounts may be payable because the employee ceased being an active member of the scheme and became an *early leaver*. As a result his or her GMP may have been revalued by the scheme at a different rate from that used by the state to revalue SERPS.) However, once in payment, employees' entitlement to increases on their notional additional pension payable by the state through SERPS may overtake the amount of the GMP after taking into account the more limited increases payable on GMPs by the occupational pension scheme.

The long and short of this explanation is that a pensioner who was contracted out from SERPS before 6 April 1997 will often also receive some additional pension from SERPS covering those periods of contracted-out employment.

For pension rights built up between 6 April 1997 and 6 April 2002, the date S2P began (see **APPENDIX 5**), these residual links with additional pension provided by SERPS have been broken. During this period employees were either contracted in and built up rights to SERPS or they were contracted out and built up no further rights to additional pension.

Secondly, now that S2P has come into operation, an employee who is contracted out through membership of an occupational pension scheme may also build up rights to additional pension. A top-up additional pension is provided by S2P to any employees earning above the National Insurance lower earnings limit but who earn less than £25,600 in 2003/04 during any period they are contracted out by an occupational pension scheme (**APPENDIX 5** gives more details). The introduction of S2P restores the links between contracted-out employment and the state additional pension. Apart from pension rights built up in the last five years of SERPS, many employees in membership of contracted-out pension schemes have enjoyed, and now once again enjoy, residual rights under the state additional pension.

Contracting-out tests

1.8 Until 6 April 1997, an occupational pension scheme could be contracted out by the *guaranteed minimum pension* (GMP) test. The employee becomes entitled to the payment of a defined benefit called the GMP which is payable at state pension age. As explained above, the amount of the individual's accrued GMP is deducted at state pension age from the employee's additional pension entitlement under SERPS. Once in payment GMPs have to be increased each year in line with the rise in prices. For GMPs built up from 6 April 1988 until 5 April 1997 part of the increase is paid by their scheme (the first 3%) and the state provides any further increase necessary to match the rise in inflation. For GMPs built up before 6 April 1988, the state pays all of the annual increase.

Alternatively, an occupational pension scheme may be contracted out by the *protected rights* test. Statutory defined minimum payments have to be made each month by the employer into the member's scheme account where they are invested. This capital sum is known as the member's protected rights fund and is used at retirement from age 60 to buy a pension. The amount of pension built up from the protected rights fund before 6 April 1997 is treated by the Government to be equal in value to the notional GMP the employee would have accrued if he or she had been contracted out by the GMP test. The employee's SERPS pension is reduced by the COD offset explained above by the amount of this notional GMP even though in practice the amount of pension actually bought by the protected rights will undoubtedly be either greater or less than the notional GMP. Once in payment, any pension bought with the protected rights fund built up before 6 April 1997 must increase each year in line with inflation up to a ceiling of 3% in any one year. The state pays for any further increase necessary to match the annual rise in inflation.

Since 6 April 1997 new contracting-out tests have replaced the tests described in the previous paragraphs. From that date a member of a contracted-out scheme ceased to build up any rights to additional pension from SERPS. All pensions built up from 6 April 1997 provided by an occupational pension scheme (whether contracted out or not) have to increase as a statutory minimum each year in line with prices up to a ceiling of 5% in any one year. If inflation is higher than 5%, the state is not responsible for any further increase. (There are some exceptions to this rule in the case of rights under a defined contribution scheme which are used to purchase an investment-linked annuity at retirement that cannot guarantee increases, but this relaxation does not apply to any protected rights pension built up from contracted-out employment.)

A scheme is able to contract out employees if it satisfies an overall quality test known as the *reference scheme* test. In return for the loss of future SERPS or S2P benefits, the employee and employer together pay National Insurance contributions at a lower contracted-out rate. Alternatively, under a revised protected rights test, a scheme may contract employees out of SERPS or S2P if the employer pays a flat-rate percentage of earnings (known as *minimum payments*) each month to the scheme to build up a protected rights fund for each contracted-out employee. The National Insurance contributions payable by the employer and employee are reduced by an amount equal to the minimum payments, but this is less than the total reduction gained from the reference scheme test. After the end of the tax year, the Inland Revenue's National Insurance Contributions Office pays over to the scheme an age-related percentage as a top-up in respect of each contracted-out employee. The percentage rises according to the age of the employee.

Since 6 April 2002 the saving to the employer is 3.5% of earnings between the National Insurance lower and upper earnings limits in the case of the reference scheme test and 1.0% in the case of the protected rights test. For both these contracting-out tests the National Insurance saving for the employee is 1.6% of earnings between the two limits.

The level of National Insurance contributions payable by employers and employees where the employees are contracted out from S2P by an occupational pension scheme reflects the fact that a top-up amount of additional pension is still payable for those earning above the National Insurance lower earnings limit but less than £25,600 (2003/04). In short, employees who earn below this limit but above the National Insurance lower earnings limit and who are members of a contracted-out occupational pension scheme will nevertheless build up some entitlement to additional pension from S2P.

A description of both SERPS and S2P is set out in **APPENDIX 5**.

Contributory and non-contributory schemes

1.9   If the employees are required as a condition of membership to make contributions to the occupational pension scheme out of their pay, the scheme is termed a contributory scheme. If no such requirement is made, it is termed a non-contributory scheme. In both cases, it is a general condition of social security law that employees have the right to make additional voluntary contributions. Employees who have earned no more than £30,000 in any of the previous five tax years (not counting any tax year before 2000/01) may also contribute up to £3,600 to a personal or stakeholder pension scheme (see **2.15**).

Funded and unfunded

1.10   If the occupational pension scheme builds up assets which are invested, it is termed a *funded scheme*. If benefits are provided from income on a pay-as-you-go basis, it is termed an *unfunded scheme*. In practice all private sector, exempt approved occupational pension schemes are funded. On the other hand, many of the public service schemes are unfunded, but not all: for example, the local government scheme is funded. Top-up schemes designed to provide unapproved benefits to those who earn above the level of the pensionable earnings cap may be *unfunded unapproved retirement benefit schemes* (UURBS) or *funded unapproved retirement benefit schemes* (FURBS).

Pensions as an employee benefit

1.11   It is very important not to lose sight of the fact that occupational pensions exist first and foremost because they have been seen by the sponsoring employers as a necessary element of the remuneration package, needed to attract, retain and motivate employees.

They have also been vital in allowing employers to react flexibly to the need to allow employees to retire but in a way which can avoid financial hardship.

Although death, and ill-health benefits can be provided by other insured benefit provisions, they form part and parcel of the benefit package of most occupational pension schemes.

In practice, and over the long term, the average defined benefit occupational pension scheme probably costs employers around 20% of pensionable payroll. The figure will obviously be a little lower in contributory schemes where there is an employee contribution than in a non-contributory scheme. However, because of the effect of higher investment returns in the late 1980s, surpluses arose which helped to lower the average employer contribution rate. During the 1990s these surpluses began to be run down, with the consequence that employer contribution rates to defined benefit schemes have begun to rise to their long-term norm. Furthermore, the early years of this century have witnessed:

- a sustained fall in the world's stockmarkets, and the prospect of only modest long-term prospects for investment returns in general; and

- in the UK, revised demographic data which show that the average 60-year old who had retired in 1999 could expect to live as much as one-third as long again compared to a 60-year old who had retired in 1970.

The result is that employer contribution rates to defined benefit schemes have begun to climb very sharply. Many employers are seeking to control their pension costs, and by the early months of 2003 the term 'pensions crisis' has become the phrase on everyone's lips.

Surveys show that over half of defined benefit schemes have been closed to new entrants, although existing members can continue to build up pension rights as before. Yet such a move does not reduce employer costs very quickly.

On reviewing the options, employers are seeking to change the nature of future pension provision for existing members, to look at ways of deterring early retirement and to persuade employees to bear more of the pension cost and/or risk. Pensions have begun to be the cause of industrial relations unrest as employees have become angry that the 'pension promise' which they believed had been made to them is being broken.

One common approach in the recent past has been to close the defined benefit scheme to new entrants and offer instead a defined contribution arrangement.

This may be in the form of a separate defined contribution, trust-based occupational pension scheme, or as a new defined contribution section within the same trust fund as the closed defined benefit scheme. Alternatively, new employees may be offered a contract-based defined contribution arrangement such as is described in **CHAPTER 2**.

In a defined contribution scheme the employer contribution will be determined either by collective or individual bargaining or by the employer's decision on what is needed and what is affordable.

Pensions are, therefore, part of the employee remuneration package. Trustees of occupational pension schemes have very particular concerns which are specified by trust law and Acts of Parliament. They do not normally negotiate on pensions. Yet, trustees should remember that occupational pensions are provided as an employee benefit and they form part of the industrial relations life of the organisation for which they work.

The law relating to occupational pension schemes

1.12   Occupational pension schemes are governed by two distinct strands of law: statutory law and trust law.

Statutory law

1.13   Statutory law is set by Acts of Parliament, which are the primary legislation, and associated Statutory Instruments, which are the secondary legislation.

The main statutes governing occupational pension schemes originate from the Department for Work and Pensions which frames social security law and from the Treasury/Inland Revenue which is responsible for taxation law. A guide to the major pieces of legislation from these two government departments which is of concern to trustees of occupational pension schemes is given in **APPENDIX 3**.

Occupational pension schemes are also affected by other statutory law including:

- the *Equal Pay Act 1970*;
- the *Race Relations Act 1975*;
- the *Sex Discrimination Act 1976*;
- the *Disability Discrimination Act 1995*;
- the *Employment Rights Act 1996*;
- the *Industrial Tribunals Act 1996*; and
- the *Data Protection Act 1998*.

European law

1.14   European Community law is important in any consideration of occupational pensions. Directives issued by the EU are incorporated into new UK statutory legislation and in some cases can be relied upon by individual citizens seeking redress through the courts. The European Court of Justice (ECJ) has the final authority on the interpretation of the European Treaty and its judgments are binding.

In fact, it was precisely in the area of occupational pensions that European law first impacted significantly on the lives of ordinary UK citizens. The *Barber* judgment (see **9.3**) enforced equal treatment for men and women in the setting of normal pension ages under pension scheme rules. This was so even though there was no UK legislation in place to effect this change until the relevant sections of the *Pensions Act 1995* came into force. Similarly, pension rights for part-time employees were largely initially stimulated by case law from the ECJ. Later, anti-discrimination requirements against part-time employees were confirmed by a directive issued by the European Commission and incorporated into UK employment law. A similar process is now in place to protect the pension interests of fixed-term workers. In the near future, anti-discrimination provisions will also protect employees against discrimination on the grounds of age and sexual orientation.

Yet European law's impact on pensions is not just concerned with discrimination issues. It acts to protect the employment benefits of workers whose employer changes when businesses are sold and, although there is an exemption for occupational pensions, the recent case of *Beckmann v Dynamco Whicheloe Macfarlane Ltd [2002] All ER (D) 05, [2002] 64 PBLR* issued by the ECJ shows that this exemption is quite narrowly limited to 'old-age benefits' and not necessarily, say, to enhanced early retirement pensions. The protection of employees' pension rights upon the insolvency of their employer is also an area covered by European law – see **23.6**.

European law will increasingly be used to prevent member states from imposing unnecessary barriers to the free movement of workers by disallowing tax relief on pension contributions to schemes established in other member states, or to the freedom on pension service providers to operate across internal EU borders.

Trust law

1.15   As explained above, most UK occupational pension schemes are established as *irrevocable trusts* because the Inland Revenue imposes this as a condition for the granting of full tax relief.

Trusts have a very long history. Essentially they have been used to protect the financial interests of persons who have been unable to look after themselves or their affairs.

A standard definition of a trust has been given in the book *Law of Trusts and Trustees* by Sir Arthur Underhill:

> 'A trust is an equitable obligation imposing upon a person (who is called a trustee) the duty of dealing with property over which he has control (which is called the trust property) for the benefit of persons (who are called beneficiaries ...) of whom he may himself be one; and any one of whom may enforce the obligation. Any act or neglect on the part of a trustee which is not authorised or excused by the terms of the trust instrument, or by law, is called a "breach of trust".'

Property is not to be taken in its usual sense. It refers to any financial assets held by the trust. *Equitable* refers to the special system of law called *equity* which is founded on principles of *natural justice* and *fair conduct*. It supplements the common law (i e case law made by judges) and tends to be more flexible. *Trust instrument* means the trust deed and rules.

Under trust law, the assets of an occupational pension scheme are placed under the legal ownership of the scheme's trustees. Yet the beneficiaries (active members, early leavers who have preserved their pension in the scheme, pensioners, surviving dependants of former members and the employer) also own the assets according to the principles of equity.

Supporters of trust law claim that such a system has unrivalled flexibility. However, trust law has long had critics who do not see it as a suitable body of law to regulate occupational pension schemes. Following the revelations in the Maxwell case, the House of Commons Social Security Committee wrote in its report:

> 'We are in no doubt, as a Committee, about the urgent need to reform the law as it applies to pension funds. We believe that trust law gives an inadequate legal underpinning to occupational pension schemes.'

Nevertheless, the Pension Law Review Committee (set up by the Government under Professor Goode to review the framework of law and regulation within which occupational pension schemes operate) confirmed the role of trust law to regulate occupational pension schemes. The Goode Committee reported that:

> 'Trust law in itself is broadly satisfactory and should continue to provide the foundation for interests, rights and duties arising in relation to pension schemes. But some of the principles of trust law require modification in their application to pensions.'

The Government accepted this recommendation. In fact, the *Pensions Act 1995* can be seen as an affirmation of the role of trust law, especially in the importance it places on the central role of pension fund trustees.

The present Government has also affirmed the importance of the principle of occupational pension schemes being governed by trustees. However, there are still counter currents. Stakeholder pension schemes, for example, may be set up as personal pension schemes governed by individual contracts between the pension provider and each member. In the early days the emphasis was much more on stakeholder pension schemes being run by trustees. In the event, although both forms of governance are permitted most stakeholder pension schemes are set up under the individual contract model. In part, it has been in the interests of the stakeholder pension providers that this should be so but in fact there has been no demand from employers generally to bring stakeholder pensions under the trust-based model.

A further counter current is represented by those who have doubts that trustees prove effective stewards of their scheme's investments. The most important voice to express such doubts has been that of Paul Myners, who was asked by the Government to carry out a review of institutional investment. The results of that review, which was published in March 2001, are likely to be profound. This matter is explored further in CHAPTER 17.

Checklist 1

- As a trustee of an occupational pension scheme that is *exempt approved* by the Inland Revenue you should understand the very significant tax advantages that arise from this tax status and should ensure that no action is taken which might endanger those privileges.

- It is important to know whether your occupational pension scheme provides pensions essentially on a *defined benefit* basis or a *defined contribution* basis as this determines whether the employer or the employees bear the investment risk.

- If your scheme is *self-administered*, you as trustees are responsible for the scheme's overall investment strategy.

- Whether the scheme is to be contracted in or contracted out is a decision for the employer (who must consult with employees and recognised trade unions) but the trustees will have to ensure that the scheme provides the minimum levels of benefit that are a condition of contracting out and meets the administrative standards required by the National Insurance Contributions Office.

- Whether employees make contributions to the scheme from their pay or whether all the contributions are made by the employer makes no difference to the general statutory and trust law rights of employees as members of an occupational pension scheme and which you as trustee must uphold.

- Pensions are an employee benefit and therefore form part of the employees' remuneration package. As a trustee you should be aware of this but it is not the job of trustees generally to negotiate on levels of pension provision with employee representatives or the employer. This should be left to other industrial relations forums.

- As a trustee, you must ensure that your scheme is run in accordance with UK statutory law and you may face penalties if you fail to take all reasonable steps to ensure that the law is upheld.

- As a trustee, you have a duty to all concerned to ensure that the scheme is run in accordance with the terms of its *trust deed and rules*. If you deliberately betray that duty, you could be found by the courts to have committed a breach of trust.

- The *Pensions Act 1995* has confirmed the prime importance of your role as a trustee in the running of an occupational pension scheme.

- The trust-based model of pension provision, as typified by the exempt-approved occupational pension scheme is, however, now facing stiff competition from contract-based pension provision.

Chapter 2

Trust-based and contract-based pensions

Two approaches

2.1   There are two basic approaches to the governance of private pension provision in the UK outside the public sector. The pension scheme may either be set up as a trust and be run by trustees or it may be set up on a contract basis between each individual member and the pension provider. By and large, occupational pension schemes outside the public sector are set up as trusts but most personal pensions are contract-based. Stakeholder pension schemes, which became available for the first time on 6 April 2001, may either be trust-based or contract-based although in practice most are contract-based.

There are two essential differences between trust-based and contract-based pension provision. The most obvious of these differences is that in the case of a trust-based scheme the scheme is governed by a trustee, or body of trustees, who are obliged to act in accordance with the general principles of trust law. These principles are set out in **CHAPTER 5**. These principles do not apply outside trust-based arrangements. Personal pensions, and most stakeholder pension schemes are governed in the main by the terms of the written contract made between the individual member and the pension provider.

This first difference leads directly to the second essential difference. In a trust-based scheme there is a body of people, the trustees, who can stand in between the individual members of the scheme and the pension service providers. The relationship between the individual members and the trustees is governed by an important principle, that of the trustees acting in the best interests of the members. The relationship between the trustees and the pension providers is governed by the law of contract.

This second difference has an immediate practical effect. Subject to the contractual obligations between the trustees and the providers, the trustees can decide to replace a pension provider, say the scheme administrator if it is giving poor service, or the investment manager if its investment performance is below expectations. But if they do so, the members may remain in the same pension scheme and subject to the same entitlements. This is not usually the case in a contract-based scheme. If the individual members are dissatisfied with the service given by their pension provider, their main option is to bring that contract to a close and seek to become a member of another pension scheme. This difference may not amount to much on its own if the terms of the contract between the individual member and the original service provider will permit a penalty-free exit from the pension scheme – as is the case with all stakeholder pension schemes.

Yet it could be argued that a group of trustees who are committed to carrying out their duty to act in the best interests of their members can negotiate the very best terms for the management of the scheme and the investment of its assets. These advantages stemming from benefits of scale will naturally be greatest in the case of a large trust-based self-administered occupational scheme.

This book's aim is essentially to point out to pension fund trustees how they can carry out their duty to act in the best interests of their members. The only prior requirement of the trustees in order to carry out this duty is their own commitment to do so. The practical expertise needed to do so can be provided by the advisers whom the trustees have appointed, although it is clear that, especially as regards investment, trustees will need to become familiar with the issues for which they are responsible. If trustees carry out this duty, they will bring far more expertise to bear in acting in the best interests of their members than any one individual member in a contract-based scheme would be likely to be able to muster.

Personal pension schemes

2.2   Retirement annuity contracts, sometimes known as *section 226 contracts*, were the precursor of the modern personal pension. Until 30 June 1988 they were available to employees who were not members of an occupational pension scheme and to the self-employed. Although no new retirement annuity contracts have been set for individuals since 1 July 1988, anyone who already held a contract before that day is still permitted to contribute to it.

Personal pensions themselves first became available on 1 July 1988. They are all established as defined contribution arrangements (see **1.5**) and have been able to receive contributions from individual employees and their employers and from the self-employed. An employee may choose a special kind of personal pension known as an *appropriate personal pension*, to contract himself or herself out of SERPS or S2P. (see **APPENDIX 5**).

A personal pension must have received approval from the Inland Revenue if the members are to benefit from the tax advantages. This entails compliance with the relevant tax legislation. The tax rules governing personal pension schemes changed on 6 April 2001 and the new rules are described at **2.15**.

Because personal pension schemes are classified as *controlled investments* they must be marketed and sold only by a person authorised to do so under the requirements of the *Financial Services and Markets Act 2000*.

The Association of British Insurers estimates that there were over 21 million personal pensions and retirement annuity contract policies in force at the end of 2000, and the Inland Revenue estimates that 9.41m members were making contributions to their personal pensions in the 2001/02 tax year, of which 1.8m were in employer-sponsored arrangements.

Contributions may be paid to a personal pension in two distinct ways. Under the first method, the individual (and possibly the individual's employer) may contract with the personal pension provider to pay in a specified sum on a regular basis. Individual members will normally do this by setting up a direct debit or standing order arrangement through their bank. If this regular stream of payments continues over the term of the contract, the accumulated capital sum arising from the investment roll-up on the contributions, less deductions for charges, will be available to provide the member with his or her pension benefits. If, however, the member ceases to pay contributions during the term of the contract (and the contract is not continued by the operation of some waiver of contribution insurance policy), the personal pension contract will normally become 'paid up'. Depending on the terms of the contract, some of the charges that fell due to be deducted over the intended term of the contract may be deducted immediately from the accumulated capital up until the date the contributions were suspended.

To avoid a continuing commitment to make contributions to a single personal pension, the individual may prefer to use the alternative method of paying contributions, which is solely to make a commitment to pay a single premium lump sum payment to the personal pension contract. There will then be no commitment on the individual to make any further payments although the contract will usually permit him or her to do so.

Criticisms of personal pensions

2.3   The greatest criticism of personal pensions is that the charging structure of many personal pensions has made them unsuitable saving products for those on low or even moderate earnings. This has been especially the case when the individual member has been unable to continue making contributions for the full term of the contract. There is evidence to suggest that the advent of stakeholder pension schemes, with their controlled charging structure, has had a beneficial knock-on effect in relation to personal pensions more generally.

Mis-selling of personal pensions

2.4   Personal pensions impacted on the attention of the trustees of occupational pension schemes during the late 1980s and early 1990s because very large numbers of them were sold in contravention of the rules made under the financial services legislation.

A very large number of employees who could have joined their employers' occupational pension scheme were persuaded instead by independent financial advisers, insurance company representatives and other tied agents to buy a personal pension contract. In other cases, existing active members of an occupational pension scheme were persuaded to opt out of that scheme and take out a personal pension. Many of this group were also persuaded to transfer their accrued occupational pension scheme rights out of the scheme and over to their personal pension. Other individuals who retained deferred pension rights in an occupational pension scheme run by their former employer and who were then approaching retirement were also persuaded to transfer their accrued rights to a personal pension.

Because employers contribute to an occupational pension schemes and because occupational pension schemes nearly always provide more generous ill-health benefits and death benefits than personal pension schemes, such personal pension sales were usually non-compliant with the duty on the sales person to provide best advice. The mis-selling of personal pensions has undoubtedly been one of the biggest financial scandals of recent years and has caused a great deal of misery to the individuals affected and their families. It severely damaged the reputation of the insurance industry and also has cost billions of pounds in reinstatement or compensation costs.

The chief cause of the mis-selling scandal was ineffective regulation of a market that was largely driven by commission-based sales.

Legal basis

2.5   Most personal pensions are insurance contracts made between an individual and an insurance company. They are usually established by a *deed poll*. This is a legal document that establishes the personal pension scheme and is important because it allows any dependant of the member to enforce any obligations assumed by the personal pension provider to pay benefits to that dependant. Without the deed poll mechanism, a contract can only be enforced by the parties who actually entered into that contract. However, a deed poll does not establish a trust such as described at **1.15**. The contributions paid by the member to the personal pension provider become the property of that personal pension provider. Some personal pensions adopt a limited form of trust known as a *trust of policy* which can be used to mitigate inheritance tax considerations upon the death of a member. Some, but not many, personal pensions are, however, set up as full trusts.

Group personal pension arrangements

2.6   Group personal pension (GPP) arrangements are collections of individual personal pension contracts taken out with the same personal pension provider and which are sold by independent financial advisers, insurance company representatives and other tied agents to the employees of a particular employer. The employer in effect facilitates the sale of the individual personal pensions by offering access to the personal pension provider's representative or an independent financial adviser. The employer may also offer a payroll check-off facility through which employees may pass on their personal pension contributions to the personal pension provider. The employer may, moreover, choose to make its own contributions on behalf of all or some of the employees direct to the personal pension provider. If so, it is likely that the employer's contribution will be a term of the contract of employment between the employer and the employee concerned.

In any case, the benefits of scale arising from the fact that a number of personal pension sales have been made on a collective basis often means that the contractual terms for the investment of contributions are more favourable than would be the case if the personal pension had been bought individually outside the GPP arrangement. This collective basis can mitigate the criticism mentioned above that the charging structure of personal pensions has often in the past made them unsuitable as savings vehicles, particularly for those on low or modest earnings.

GPP arrangements have become very popular especially amongst smaller employers. The GPP arrangement can often be 'badged' with the employer's name and so to all intents and purposes it takes on the outward appearance of a defined contribution occupational pension scheme.

GPPs have become popular with employers in many ways because they have not involved the establishment of a trust and they are not subject therefore to the requirements of trust law nor to the statutory requirements set out in the *Pensions Act 1995* which apply in the main only to occupational pension schemes.

Direct payment arrangements

2.7   It should be noted, however, that since 6 April 2001, certain requirements of the *Welfare Reform and Pensions Act 1999* have come into force which have helped level the playing field between defined contribution occupational pension schemes and GPP arrangements. The requirements also apply to individual personal pension contracts outside any GPP arrangements.

The requirements relate to the monitoring of employers' payments into a personal pension scheme and operate whenever a *direct payment arrangement* is found to exist between an employer and any employee and where that employee is a member of a personal pension scheme. Here a *direct payment arrangement* is defined as an arrangement where contributions fall to be paid by or on behalf of the employer to the employee's personal pension either:

- on the employer's own account but in respect of the employee; or

- on behalf of the employee out of deductions made from the employee's earnings.

In such circumstances the employer is required to prepare, maintain and from time to time revise a record of its direct payment arrangements which shows the rates and due dates of contributions payable under those arrangements. The employer is required to send to the personal pension provider a copy of this record, and of any subsequent revisions made to it. The *Personal Pension Schemes (Payments by Employers) Regulations 2000 (SI 2000/2692)* stipulate that the copy of the record must be sent so that it is likely that it becomes available to the personal pension provider no later than the date upon which the first contribution payable by reference to the record falls due for payment.

If any contribution shown on the record is subsequently not paid on or before its due date, the personal pension provider must report that default to Opra within a period of 30 days beginning with the day following the due date. If the payment still remains outstanding after the end of a period of 60 days beginning with the day following the due date, the personal pension provider must inform the employees concerned before the end of a period of 90 days beginning with the day following the due date.

In the case of contributions which have been deducted from the employee's earnings, the due date is set by regulations as the 19th day of the tax month following the month in which the deduction was made, as is also the case with occupational pension schemes. The only circumstances in which the personal pension provider is relieved of the duty to report a failure by the employer to pass over contributions listed on the record of amounts and due dates for payment under a particular direct payment arrangement is when it has been informed by Opra that it need no longer do so. Opra might wish to do this when an endemic problem has been identified. If this can be rectified, Opra can instruct the personal pension provider to recommence its monitoring of that direct payment arrangement. The personal pension provider must send to the employee regular statements setting out the amounts and dates of payments actually made under the direct payment arrangement over the previous period. Regulations set out how often the statements must be sent out and what period they must cover.

Opra has produced a valuable guide *Direct Payment Arrangements to Personal Pension and Stakeholder Pension Schemes (Opra Note 8)* setting out the legislative requirements as well as giving advice on how to comply. Copies can be obtained free of charge from the Opra helpdesk on tel. 01273 627600.

Penalties for non-compliance

2.8   Opra has been armed with the right to impose severe penalties on employers and personal pension providers who do not comply with these requirements. Opra has the power to impose a fine directly on the employer if the employer fails:

- to prepare a record of its direct payment arrangements; or

- to send the record to the personal pension provider within the prescribed timescale; or

- to pay contributions by the due dates.

If the personal pension provider fails:

- to inform Opra within the prescribed timescale of the employer's failure to make the payments on time as set out in the record of the direct payment arrangement; or

- to send the employee the regular statements setting out the amount and date of the actual payments made;

then Opra has power to impose fines directly on the personal pension provider. If the personal pension scheme were registered as a trust-based stakeholder pension scheme, Opra could also prohibit the current trustees from continuing to act for the scheme.

The maximum fine imposable by Opra on either an employer or a personal pension provider is £50,000 in the case of a corporate body and £5,000 in the case of an individual.

Opra has also been given powers to require any person to provide it with relevant documents if it believes that person has information relating to non-compliance with the new requirements. It also has the ability to send inspectors to the personal pension provider's and the employer's premises to investigate any possible non-compliance.

Any employer or other person who is knowingly concerned in a fraudulent evasion of the direct payment arrangements in respect of contributions which have been deducted from the employee's earnings will be guilty of a criminal offence.

Unbundled GPP arrangements

2.9   It is possible to reproduce in a GPP arrangement some of the advantages of benefits of scale and independent advice that is available to trust-based occupational pension schemes. This works by the employer establishing a management committee which includes an external pension consultant. There is a set of overall contracts between each individual member and the personal pension provider. Yet this provider simply puts in place the overall legal documentation. The day-to-day administration of these contracts and the investment management of the underlying assets can be carried out by other organisations appointed, and possibly from time to time replaced in case of unsatisfactory performance, by the management committee. This is termed an *unbundled* arrangement because the administration and investment functions are no longer bundled together with the underlying personal pension contracts. Since no trust has been set up, the members of the management committee are not likely to be seen as trustees.

Free-standing additional voluntary contributions

2.10   All members of an occupational pension scheme must be given an opportunity to boost their eventual pension by making *additional voluntary contributions* (AVCs). The trustees of the occupational pension scheme are charged with selecting any external AVC providers used to fulfil this obligation and to ensure that they continue to provide a reasonable investment return. There will be therefore a contractual arrangement between the trustees and the external AVC providers (see **16.27** for further discussion of this area). However, members are also allowed to choose to make AVCs by taking out an individual contractual arrangement with a provider of a *free-standing additional voluntary contribution* (FSAVC) scheme. A FSAVC scheme resembles a personal pension, therefore, in that it is entirely an individual contractual member between each member and the FSAVC provider. The contractual arrangement can, however, be entered into only by those who are active members of an occupational pension scheme.

Under the Inland Revenue rules, the maximum contribution that an individual member can make to a FSAVC scheme is the same as applies to an AVC scheme provided through the trustees. This limit is set so that the total employee contribution made by the member to the main scheme, plus any AVCs, plus any FSAVCs should not exceed 15% of the employee's remuneration. The employer is prevented from directly contributing to a member's FSAVC scheme.

Similarly the total benefits to be provided by the main scheme, plus any AVCs, plus any FSAVCs must not exceed the Inland Revenue limits set out in **APPENDIX 2**. The employee's contributions will, if they exceed £2,400 in a year, need to be tested to ensure that they do not exceed an amount necessary to secure any headroom between the benefits under the main scheme and the maximum Inland Revenue limits.

Surplus AVCs, i e where they have produced benefits which mean that the Inland Revenue benefit levels are exceeded, will have to be repaid. Where the member has paid no AVCs but has paid FSAVCs it falls to the FSAVC provider to monitor this Inland Revenue requirement; but it falls to the trustees if the member has paid both AVCs and FSAVCs.

AVC schemes offered by external providers and all FSAVC schemes will impose management charges. However, AVCs are usually completely free of any commission charges and this gives them a competitive edge over FSAVC schemes where the individual member must bear the commission charge. Nevertheless, a great number of FSAVC contracts have been sold and many occupational pension scheme trustees are of the opinion that this has amounted to mis-selling. Indeed, the Financial Services Authority has recently completed a limited review into sales of FSAVC schemes and nearly 85,000 FSAVC policyholders have received a total of £250m in compensation. It should be admitted, however, that some trustees have not always given a high priority to AVC schemes and offered a poor choice of indifferently performing schemes.

Sales of FSAVC and AVC schemes are likely to have been affected by the right of employees in membership of an occupational pension scheme, who have earned no more than £30,000 in any of the previous five tax years (not counting any tax year before 2000/01), to contribute up to £3,600 (including tax relief at the basic rate) to a stakeholder pension scheme (see **2.15** below). The stakeholder pension is likely to be more advantageous because part of the final fund can be taken as a tax-free lump sum.

Stakeholder pension schemes

2.11   Stakeholder pension schemes first became available on 6 April 2001, having been established by the *Welfare Reform and Pensions Act 1999*. Essentially, stakeholder pensions are defined contribution schemes which are:

(*a*)   legally established either as an occupational pension scheme or as a personal pension scheme; and

(*b*)   legally governed either by trustees and therefore set up as a trust, or set up as an individual contract between the individual member and the stakeholder pension provider.

In practice there are three kinds of stakeholder pension schemes. These are stakeholder pension schemes which are:

- trust-based occupational pension schemes which are established by employers, or groups of employers, or by other affinity groups such as trade unions;

- trust-based personal pension schemes which operate in the form of group personal pension arrangements established by personal pension providers and governed by trustees appointed by employers, or groups of employers, or by other affinity groups such as trade unions;

- contract-based personal pension schemes governed uniquely by contracts between the individual members and the stakeholder manager employed by the personal pension provider.

The key characteristic of any stakeholder pension scheme is that it must be registered by Opra and, to be so registered, the scheme must comply with a set of minimum standards laid down in the legislation:

- the scheme must be tax approved by the Inland Revenue;

- any charges made from each member's pension account must not exceed 1/36,500 of the value of that member's pension account for each day the member remains in the scheme, although extra charges can be made if they are for additional services which are completely optional and provided under a separate contract;

- the scheme must offer a default investment option available to members who do not wish to choose between a number of different investment options;

- the scheme must comply with detailed disclosure requirements;

- members must be free to make contributions of any amount, provided it is not less than £20, at any frequency they wish although when employers are deducting employee contributions from their pay the employer can impose limitations on how often the employees can vary the amount that is to be deducted for each pay period. Restrictions can be placed, however, on the payment by members of contributions by means of cash or credit card;

- the scheme must not only provide transfer values as with any occupational or personal pension scheme but must also accept any transfer payment coming from another tax-approved pension arrangement;

- if the scheme ever ceases to be registered with Opra, it cannot accept any further contributions and must immediately begin to wind up and complete its winding up normally within twelve months by making transfer payments to a registered stakeholder pension scheme or by complying with a request from a member for a transfer to another tax-approved pension arrangement.

The access requirement

2.12   Since 8 October 2001 all employers with more than four employees have been required to designate a stakeholder pension scheme and offer access to that scheme to any 'relevant employees'. Here 'relevant employees' means any employee who is either employed in this country or employed abroad by an employer resident or incorporated in this country and who both earns in excess of the National Insurance lower earnings limit and is not entitled to membership of an occupational pension scheme.

However, the following groups of employees will not be regarded as 'relevant employees'. They are those:

- who will become eligible for membership of an occupational pension scheme after an initial waiting period of no more than twelve months from the time they started in that employment;

- who are temporarily excluded from membership of an occupational pension scheme because they are currently aged under 18;

- who are excluded from membership of an occupational pension scheme because they started in that employment when they were aged less then five years below the scheme's normal pension age;

- who, had they wished to join an occupational pension of the employer at some time in the past, would have qualified for membership of the scheme, but who, in the event, are now excluded from the scheme because they did not join the scheme at that earlier opportunity;

- who were once members of an occupational pension scheme of the employer but chose to opt out of membership and are now as a result excluded from membership of that scheme;

- who have been employed by the employer for less than three months;

- whose earnings have not equalled or exceeded the National Insurance lower earnings limit in any week within the last three months;

- who are ineligible under UK tax law to make contributions to a stakeholder pension scheme (e g employees working abroad who do not satisfy the residency conditions).

There is, however, an exemption for one group of employers from the requirement to designate a stakeholder pension scheme even if some of the employees fall into the category of 'relevant employees'. An employer does not need to comply with the access requirement if it is a term of the contract of employment of every 'relevant employee', other than those who have not yet reached age 18, that the employer will make contributions to a personal pension for that employee and, if requested to do so by that employee, offer a payroll deduction service so that contributions will be deducted from the employee's pay and passed directly to the personal pension provider. The employer must pay at a rate of not less than 3% of the employee's basic pay (i e excluding overtime, bonuses and the like) but this can be made conditional on the employee making a contribution to the same scheme at a specified rate.

If the arrangement was already in place on 8 October 2001, the employer's contribution rate must equal or exceed that of the employee but if the condition that the employee must pay a contribution at a specified rate did not come into effect until on or after 8 October 2001, or if the employer's contribution rate ceases to be equal to or exceed that of the employee after that date, the employee cannot be required to make any contribution in excess of 3% of basic pay.

This exemption only applies if the personal pension does not impose any exit charges on the member, i e the personal pension cannot impose any penalty on members who cease contributing to the scheme or transfer their funds out of the scheme.

Where the access requirement applies, the employer must designate at least one stakeholder pension scheme which is registered by Opra and which offers membership to all the employer's 'relevant employees'. Before designating a stakeholder pension scheme, the employer must consult with its relevant employees or any organisations representing them.

If a stakeholder scheme designated by the employer subsequently ceases to be registered with Opra, that scheme must also cease to be the employer's designated stakeholder scheme.

The employer must supply all relevant employees with the name and address of the designated stakeholder scheme, or schemes, and also allow representatives of the designated scheme, or schemes, reasonable access to all the relevant employees so that they can supply them with further information. The selling and marketing of stakeholder pension schemes is regulated by the Financial Services Authority.

There had been concern that employers might be held legally responsible if they designated a stakeholder pension scheme which turned out to perform badly. However, the legislation specifies that an employer, in designating a stakeholder pension scheme, is under no duty to investigate or monitor, or make any judgment as to the past, present or future performance of the scheme.

The employer, if requested to do so by a relevant employee who has become a member of a scheme which the employer has designated, is required to:

- deduct the employee's chosen contributions to the scheme from the employee's pay; and

- pay them to the stakeholder scheme within the specified time.

Because a stakeholder pension is legally either an occupational pension scheme or a personal pension scheme, contribution schedules will have to be drawn up for stakeholder pension schemes. These schedules are subject to the same requirements as apply to occupational and personal pension schemes in general. Furthermore, similar sanctions also apply in cases of failure to comply with these requirements.

There are certain limitations on the freedom of employees to change the rate and frequency of their own contributions which they have asked the employer to deduct from their pay. First, the rules of the stakeholder pension scheme are able to stipulate that the provider can refuse to accept any contribution which is less than £20. Conversely, any contribution of £20 or more up to the Inland Revenue limits must therefore be accepted, whether this is a regular or a one-off payment. For these purposes any tax relief, any contracting-out minimum payments and any age-related rebate payments will not count towards the £20 minimum level.

Second, the employer may decide that an employee not be permitted to change the amount of his or her contributions deducted via the payroll more than once every six months. The employer must, however, stop making any deductions and paying them over to the stakeholder scheme as soon as practicable when requested to do so by the employee. If this happens, the employer, if asked to do so by the employee, is not obliged to restart any further payroll stakeholder deductions from that employee's pay for a further six months.

Trust-based stakeholder schemes

2.13   Where a stakeholder pension scheme is set up as a trust, whether that scheme is legally an occupational or a personal pension scheme, the trustees of that scheme will be subject broadly to the same requirements that are placed by statute and trust law on the trustees of a defined contribution occupational pension scheme. *Section 6* of the *Welfare Reform and Pensions Act 1999*, together with *Schedule 1* to that Act, achieves this effect. Unless otherwise stated, any duty described in this book as falling on the trustees of an occupational pension scheme should be taken as also falling on the trustees of any trust-based stakeholder pension scheme unless that duty relates only to a defined benefit occupational pension scheme.

In addition, Opra has the power to prohibit anyone from acting as a trustee of a stakeholder pension scheme and to fine the trustee if he or she fails to take reasonable steps to secure that the scheme complies with all the minimum standards set out in **2.11** above.

At least one trustee and at least one third of the total number of trustees of a trust-based stakeholder pension scheme must be independent. That is to say, this minimum number of trustees must be neither connected with, nor an associate of, any person providing services to the scheme or otherwise managing the scheme (other than as a trustee). If there is a corporate trustee (see **3.3** and **3.4**) and no individual trustees of the stakeholder pension scheme, at least one of the directors of the corporate trustee and at least one-third of the total number of directors must also be independent as defined immediately above.

The trust documentation must not require the trustees of a stakeholder pension scheme to need the consent of any other person before making any decision about investments. Nor must the trust documentation prevent the trustees, unless required to do by an Act of Parliament, from amending the trust documentation to provide for different investments to be held.

Personal pension, contract-based, stakeholder schemes

2.14   Essentially, stakeholder pension schemes that are legally established as a personal pension, and which are set up under contract, are just the same as personal pension schemes with the importance difference that the minimum standards set out in **2.1** above must apply – in particular the minimum charges that can be imposed.

The DC tax regime

2.15   Personal pensions and all stakeholder pension schemes are subject to a new tax regime informally known as the *DC tax regime* which was established by the *Finance Act 2000* and which came into force on 6 April 2001. If the trustees of a defined contribution occupational pension scheme so choose, then provided certain Inland Revenue conditions are met, that scheme may also become subject to the DC tax regime. All defined benefit occupational pension schemes and those defined contribution occupational pension schemes not subject to the DC tax regime remain subject to the Inland Revenue rules on maximum levels of contributions and benefits which are set out in **APPENDIX 2**. It should, however, be noted that the proposals set out by the Treasury and Inland Revenue in December 2002 would create a new unified tax regime governing all pension arrangements. These simplifying proposals are also set out in **APPENDIX 2**.

The overall DC tax regime is summarised below.

Employees may be members of a scheme operating under the DC tax regime provided they are not, during the same tax year, also a member of an occupational pension scheme that is not subject to the DC tax regime. However, if such an occupational pension scheme member earns no more than £30,000, that member has been permitted since 6 April 2001 to be a concurrent member of any scheme subject to the DC tax regime and to contribute up to £3,600 a year to that scheme. The test relates to the employee's P60 earnings but that figure, provided it is no more than £30,000, permits the employee also to contribute to a stakeholder pension scheme up to the stated limit in each of the following five tax years.

The self employed are also eligible to join stakeholder schemes and personal pension schemes operating under the DC regime. Individuals without earnings may become a member of a scheme subject to the DC tax regime provided they satisfy a general residency test.

Contributions of up to £3,600 p a can be paid into any scheme subject to the DC tax regime irrespective of the person's age or earnings (this amount includes any tax relief that is payable but does not include any contracting-out rebates).

Contributions of more than £3,600 p a can be paid within an age-related and earnings-related scale regulating contributions to personal pensions. This scale is given in the following table:

Age on 6 April	*% of net relevant earnings* *
35 or less	17.5%
36–45	20%
46–50	25%
51–55	30%
56–60	35%
61 or more	40%

* *NB net relevant earnings are subject to the ceiling imposed by the current level of the pensionable earnings cap (£97,200 in 2002/03 and £99,000 in 2003/04).*

As an example, take an employee aged 47 who earns £20,000 a year. Her employer has agreed to pay 5% of her earnings into a stakeholder pension. She is not taxed on the value of this employer contribution. The maximum she can contribute to the stakeholder pension out of her taxed earnings during the tax year is £3,120. This is because the overall limit on contributions payable in respect of this employee is the higher of £3,600 and 25% of £20,000: i e £5,000. This total must include £1,000 from the employer, £3,120 from the employee's taxed pay and tax relief at the basic rate (assumed to be at 22%) from the Inland Revenue of £880.

Within the overall contribution limits, up to 10% of the amount which is paid as a pension contribution can be used to provide life assurance cover but personal pension contracts made before 6 April 2001 can continue to be subject to the former limit set at 5% of the policyholder's earnings.

Earnings paid in one year, the *basis year*, can cover pension contributions above the £3,600 p a limit for the following five tax years. Members can nominate a subsequent year as the basis year, which can be any one of the five tax years after the initial basis year, if they wish to increase their rate of pension contributions and their earnings have increased. The Inland Revenue will require information about the member's level of earnings in the basis year if contributions above £3,600 p a are to be paid. It should be observed that the basis year need not be a year of assessment in which the individual concerned was a member of the personal or stakeholder pension scheme.

Note that in any situation where the member's *net relevant earnings* are in practice limited by the pensionable earnings cap, the level of the cap used is that in force during the tax year in which the contributions are paid, and not the level of the cap that had been in force in the basis year used to fix the employee's net relevant earnings.

If a member has no actual net relevant earnings in a tax year, known as the *break year*, but had net relevant earnings in the tax year before, known as the *cessation year*, and was also entitled to pay contributions above the £3,600 limit in any one or more of the six tax years before the break year, known as the *reference years*, then the basis year may be any one of the reference years for which the member has provided the required information on earnings. The effect of this is to allow a member to continue to contribute more than £3,600 p a for five tax years after he or she has ceased to have any relevant earnings. If the member starts earning once again during this five-year period, contributions must be based on those earnings.

The overall effect is that it is always presumed that, for each of the five tax years following the basis year, the member's earnings remain level. A member could therefore choose to pay for up to five tax years contributions higher than £3,600 p a from savings even though his or her earnings had ceased altogether immediately after the end of the basis year, which might have been eleven years earlier.

An individual who pays a contribution before the 31 January in any tax year beginning 2001/02 may at that time elect to have that contribution, or part of it, treated as if it were paid in the preceding tax year. This is a modified version of the old personal pension 'carry back' provisions. On the other hand, the old personal pension provisions whereby unused tax relief can be carried forward for up to six tax years was abolished from 6 April 2001.

When the pension becomes payable, one quarter of the member's fund can be taken as a tax-free lump sum. If the scheme has been used to contract the member out of SERPS or S2P, none of the protected rights built up from the age-related contributions paid into the scheme by the National Insurance Contributions Office, or otherwise transferred into the personal or stakeholder pension scheme, can be taken in lump sum form. The remaining balance of the member's fund can be taken to buy an annuity or the annuity purchase can be deferred, up to a maximum age of 75, and instead the member can draw down income from the fund which remains actively invested attracting investment returns.

Financial services regulation

2.16   All contract-based schemes (personal pensions, free-standing additional voluntary contribution schemes) and all stakeholder pension schemes, including those legally established as occupational pension schemes, are subject to regulation under the financial services legislation in the manner they are promoted to potential members. Occupational pension schemes and additional voluntary contribution schemes taken out by the trustees of an occupational pension scheme are not, though, subject to financial services regulation in the manner that they are promoted to potential members.

The day-to-day investment management of an occupational pension scheme's assets and of the assets of an AVC scheme, however, just as with all pension assets held in contract-based schemes, must be generally carried out by those who are authorised to do so under the financial services legislation (see **16.5** below).

Reduction in yields

2.17   Where a commercial body provides any form of pension scheme it quite legitimately needs to cover its operational costs, the costs of investing contributions and managing the scheme's assets as well as generating a surplus either for further investment in operations or, in the case of a company, for distribution to its shareholders. The costs of operations will also include the costs of promoting the scheme to potential members and this may include commission payments made to third parties such as independent financial advisers.

Where there is the involvement of an employer, these costs will generally be less than in the case of individual arrangements.

The overall effect of these costs is that the commercial pension providers will either charge their client a fee or they will not pass on the full investment return earned on the scheme's assets to the client in the form of pension benefits. In the latter case, there will be a measurable annual 'reduction in yield' (RIY) that will bring down the investment return from that actually achieved.

As an example, take an individual who pays £1,000 as a single premium into a personal pension scheme and draws a pension after 25 years. If the scheme's investment return over that entire period is a 7% p a nominal return ('nominal' means without taking inflation into account) that will produce a capital sum of about £5,427. If however the scheme's charging structure has the net result of an annual RIY of 1.1%, the nominal return is reduced to 5.9% p a with the result that the end capital sum is about £4,192. In other words, in the example, the capital sum is about 77% of what it would have been without the charges.

The annual RIY will vary widely between different providers. It may also vary according to:

- the way in which the pension arrangement was sold;

- the amount of contributions paid into the scheme;

- the overall size of the fund; and

- the length of the term of the contract.

However, if these factors are held constant, a comparison of the annual RIY associated with each provider gives an objective ranking of the providers in terms of their charges.

The Financial Services Authority (FSA) maintains on its website an interactive set of tables which show the monetary effect of the RIY resulting from the charging structures of UK personal pension schemes and stakeholder pension schemes. The FSA assumes that the contributions will attract a 7% p a nominal investment return over the entire term of the contract.

The tables may be found at http://www.fsa.gov.uk/tables and, because they are interactive, they allow the viewer to choose the appropriate contribution rate and contract term for each of the providers listed. In each case the tables for each named scheme show the monetary amount of explicit charges and deductions that will be deducted over the term of the policy to the chosen retirement date. In other words, the capital fund that would have been built up on the contributions paid at the chosen rate over the entire term of the contract up to the chosen retirement date will be reduced by the amount shown in the 'charges & deductions' column of the tables.

In addition, the tables show the 'charges deducted in the early years'. This is the monetary amount that would have been deducted if, instead of continuing with the policy for the intended term, the individual ceased making contributions after the first three years.

We accessed the tables on 1 March 2003 and specified an interest in personal and stakeholder pension schemes into which a 30-year old, who planned to retire at age 65, would pay regular premiums of £200 per month. The table lists 86 individual personal or stakeholder pension schemes but two providers (Skandia Life and St James Place) did not participate in the survey and so no details of the effect of their charges was given.

Among the 84 participating schemes:

- the lowest figure for charges and deductions was £32,388;

- the mean figure for charges and deductions was £80,213;

- the median figure for charges and deductions was £84,207;

- the highest figure for charges and deductions was £104,809;

- the lowest figure for charges in the early years was £14;

- the mean figure for charges in the early years was £285;

- the median figure for charges in the early years was £162;

- the highest figure for charges in the early years was £4,640.

As explained above, any charges made from each member's stakeholder pension account must not exceed 1/36,500 of the value of that member's pension account for each day the member remains in the scheme. This may be thought of as a maximum 1% annual charge (i e 365/36,500 = 1%) although technically the annual RIY comes out at 1.0057%.

Checklist 2

- Pension schemes may be trust-based or contract-based.

- Personal pension schemes are generally contract-based individual arrangements between the member and the personal pension provider.

- Personal pensions can be very effective vehicles for saving for retirement but in the past many have been mis-sold. In some cases, their charging structures has made them unsuitable for low or moderate earners.

- Group personal pensions can mimic the appearance of defined contribution occupational pension schemes.

- New *direct payment arrangements* have been enforced by Opra since 6 April 2001 in cases where an employer has agreed to make payments to an employee's personal pension.

- Free-standing AVC schemes are similar to personal pensions but can only be sold to those in membership of an occupational pension scheme. They compete with the AVC schemes run by the trustees of the occupational pension scheme, and since 6 April 2001, for employees earning no more than £30,000 p a, with both concurrent personal and stakeholder pension schemes.

- Stakeholder pension schemes became available on 6 April 2001 and can be legally established as occupational pension schemes or as personal pension schemes. Employers of 'relevant employees' have been required to offer those employees access to a stakeholder pension since 8 October 2001.

- Since 6 April 2001 a new DC tax regime has governed personal pension schemes, all stakeholder pension schemes (including those legally established as occupational pension schemes) and those defined contribution occupational pension schemes where the trustees have opted to convert from the present tax regime to the new DC regime.

- The effect of charges and deductions in reducing the overall yield obtained by investment returns on contributions still varies markedly between different personal and stakeholder pension scheme providers.

Chapter 3

The trustee body

Different structures

3.1 How a trustee body, charged with the care of an occupational pension scheme, is structured will be set out in the *trust deed and rules*, the legal document which constitutes the scheme.

From the point of view of trust law, the structure of the trustee body does not in any way change the overall legal obligations which are placed on the trustees. The trustee body will still have the same job to do.

Occupational pension schemes vary enormously. Consider some examples:

- a small scheme for three or four directors in a small family firm;

- a scheme administered by an insurance company for fifty employees working for a small service company based in one small town;

- a large scheme with three thousand employees in ten different sites throughout the UK.

Each of these very different occupational pension schemes will be under the care of a trustee body. In the first example all the members can themselves be trustees and will be intimately connected. In the second example, it is likely that all the trustees will know all the members, and probably will have met their families. Yet some will be senior managers, some will be office staff, some will be part of the sales force.

In the third example, the trustees will know only a very small proportion of the total number of members. Only personnel records will indicate whether a member is married. A member may have a financially dependent, physically handicapped child but this may not be known to the trustees. The pensions department may be located at company headquarters in London, three hundred miles from the most distant company site. The ten sites could vary enormously in size and character: for example, one site could have a thousand industrial staff in the Midlands and be highly unionised while another site might be a formerly independent, small company in Wales with fifty employees and which is fiercely proud of its own identity.

It is no wonder that different structures for trustee bodies have evolved to cope with such varied situations.

Individual trustees

3.2   The trust deed and rules may commonly provide for trustees to be appointed as individuals. In some cases a minimum number and a maximum number will also be specified. Just how individuals are appointed, how long a time they serve as trustees and how they can be replaced will also be defined in the trust deed and rules. These areas are dealt with more fully in **CHAPTER 4**.

Individual trustees, other than professional, independent trustees hired for their expertise, are still generally unpaid, although, of course, they may recover their expenses and those who are employees of an employer participating in the scheme continue to receive their normal wage or salary. This general practice of relying on unpaid lay trustees was challenged by Paul Myners in his review of institutional investment. One of his recommendations is that lay trustees should be paid. For more details see *Principle 1* in **17.4** and **17.5**.

One advantage of individuals serving as trustees is that they provide the human touch in what may be a large occupational pension scheme, with its own bureaucracy and form-filling. The trustees may be well known by the members and be on hand, both formally and informally, to listen to problems and give advice, although there are certain pitfalls in this area – see **CHAPTER 9**.

One problem that arises is that the trust deed will need to be amended whenever a trustee resigns and a new replacement is appointed. Also, any change in who are the trustees has to be notified to the Inland Revenue, to the National Insurance Contributions Office and to the Pension Schemes Registry. Because of these, and certain other reasons, many occupational pension schemes make use of a corporate trustee.

Corporate trustees

3.3   Instead of individual men and women serving as trustees, the trust deed and rules may specify that there is a single *corporate trustee*. This simply means that a company acts as the trustee body. The company will usually be a specially named and constituted subsidiary company of the main company that employs the workforce. Yet this does not necessarily mean that the trustee body becomes totally institutionalised.

What happens is that the various possible processes for the selection and appointment of individual trustees are mirrored exactly in the selection and appointment of the directors of the corporate trustee. They are usually termed *trustee directors* and they have, in general, the same role as individual trustees.

Throughout this book, whenever we use the term 'trustees', we generally mean to include 'trustee directors'.

One procedural advantage is that there is no need to change the trust deed whenever an individual trustee director resigns and a replacement is appointed.

From a legal point of view, the trustee body remains unchanged as the same corporate trustee.

A second advantage stems from possible extra legal protection for the individuals who serve as trustee directors; the theory being that the corporate trustee is sued not the individual directors. See **CHAPTER 22** for more details.

There may also be advantages concerning VAT if a corporate trustee is used because the trustee company may be included in a group VAT registration with the employer. The employer can then deduct the VAT on supplies of certain goods and services made to the trustee which would not otherwise be deductible.

It is quite useful to have a corporate trustee rather than individual trustees if the pension scheme includes land as one of its investments. This is because under the *Trustee Act 1925* no more than four individual trustees can be involved in a settlement for the sale of land. On the other hand, also under the *Trustee Act 1925*, a sole trustee (unless it is also a trust corporation – see **3.4** below) cannot give a valid receipt for the proceeds of a sale of land by the trust so there would be a need to appoint a separate trustee for this purpose. All of this may seem pretty arcane and the scheme's lawyer should be able to devise a solution in either case!

It should be remembered that, since a corporate trustee is a company, it will have to comply with all the requirements of the *Companies Acts*. This may include the need both to appoint auditors and to have the accounts of the corporate trustee audited. It also includes the requirement that the private address of each director of the corporate trustee must be held by the Registrar of Companies. It should be noted that a director of a corporate trustee should be made automatically to resign if he or she individually becomes disqualified from acting as a trustee. This would be the case, for example, if the director became personally bankrupt. If the director were not to resign, the corporate trustee itself would be disqualified from acting as a trustee.

Trust corporation

3.4   The trust deed may give the sponsoring employer power to appoint a trust corporation. A trust corporation is a company set up to provide trustee services as a commercial business. Many banks and insurance companies, for example, have established trust corporations.

A trust corporation is therefore a corporate trustee but not one that is a subsidiary of the sponsoring employer. Trust corporations are staffed by professionals who are delivering a service in return for a fee. They do not have any intimate connection with the membership.

A trust corporation has to be established under the law of one of the member states of the European Union and usually be registered under the UK *Companies Acts*, or their equivalent in another member state of the European

Union. Generally speaking, it must also have capital of not less than £250,000 of which not less than £100,000 has been paid up (i e the shareholders have actually paid this amount to hold the shares).

Many are in membership of The Association of Corporate Trustees (TACT):

> TACT
> 3 Brackerne Close
> Cooden
> Bexhill on Sea
> East Sussex
> TN39 3BT
> Tel: 01424 844144
> Fax: 01424 844144
> email: tact@cooden.fsbusiness.co.uk
> Website: http://www.trustees.org.uk

It is generally accepted that the courts will impose a higher duty of care on a trust corporation than on an individual trustee or trustee director of an 'ordinary' corporate trustee. It was held in a famous case that:

> '... a professional corporate trustee is liable for breach of trust if loss is caused to the trust fund because it neglects to exercise the special care and skill which it professes to have.' (*Bartlett v Barclays Trust Co Ltd [1980] 1 All ER 139.*)

This distinction has been maintained in the proposals issued by the Government in February 2002 for new legislation to require trustees who undertake investment duties to be familiar with the issues with which they are concerned. These proposals arise out of the review of institutional investment by Paul Myners. For more details see **17.7**.

Independent trustee

3.5   An *independent trustee* means a trustee who has no connection with the employer and is neither a member nor a beneficiary of the occupational pension scheme. The term is usually applied to specialist corporate trustees or trust corporations who offer professional trustee services in return for a fee but may also refer to an individual who is unconnected with the employer or membership.

A number of larger pension schemes in recent years have appointed independent trustees to be members of their trustee boards. In some cases the trust deed and rules have been amended to give the independent trustee reserve powers and so have a veto over certain kinds of changes – often with a view to safeguarding the existing members' interests in the event of a hostile takeover. A typical set of requirements embedded in the trust deed and rules might be that:

- there must always be an independent trustee so that, although the present independent trustee could be removed, this could only be done if another independent trustee were found as a replacement;

- the independent trustee has power to veto any proposal that it considers would prejudicially affect the accrued rights of beneficiaries;

- the independent trustee can close the scheme to new entrants or effect a wind up to protect accrued rights;

- if the independent trustee is removed it has the right to advise all beneficiaries in writing of the reasons for its removal.

In other cases, the independent trustee is not 'embedded' in the trust deed and rules and has exactly the same powers and duties as the other trustees. In practice the independent trustee may be seen to be more strongly placed since it can draw on its corporate and professional resources.

In certain circumstances the independent trustee is statutorily appointed. Under the provisions of *sections 22–26* of the *Pensions Act 1995*, an independent trustee must be appointed to the trustee body of a defined benefit scheme, if one is not already in place, if the employer becomes insolvent. The requirement does not apply to defined contribution (money purchase) schemes, and there are certain other exemptions. The legislation specifies further requirements that the independent trustee has to satisfy in such circumstances – see **19.7**. Also, since 6 April 1997, the Occupational Pensions Regulatory Authority (Opra) has had power to appoint an independent trustee in certain circumstances – see **4.4**.

While the integrity of the main providers of independent trustee services is not doubted, the statutory legislation itself in the past has not prohibited independent trustees from exercising trustee powers for their own benefit. For example, in a case where an independent trustee has been appointed to an occupational pension scheme of a company which has gone into receivership, it was possible that a company associated with the independent trustee could place the scheme's assets with an insurance company in return for a substantial commission payment. It would seem that such an action would nevertheless have been a breach of trust. The legislation now prohibits the appointment of any independent trustee upon an employer's insolvency if that independent trustee is connected or associated with anyone who has an interest in the assets either of the scheme, or of the employer, other than as a trustee of the scheme.

An important disadvantage of having an independent trustee, especially for smaller schemes, is the cost of the fees, while others judge that the membership ought to be able to rely on a combination of member-nominated and employer-nominated trustees, supported by their external professional advisers, without drawing on outsiders to act as trustees.

The issue of fees that may be charged by independent trustees who are appointed to wind up a defined benefit scheme of an insolvent employer is proving to be highly controversial. OPAS, the Pensions Advisory Service, has drawn attention to the lack of control over the activities of such independent trustees and the sometimes 'extortionate' charges they levy. OPAS is calling for greater accountability for the costs in winding up a pension scheme and believes that independent trustees, who have sole control over the whole wind-up process, have such an important role they should be licensed. OPAS has stated:

> 'At present, anyone or any organisation can set themselves up in business as an independent trustee without needing any authorisation. No standards of knowledge, ability or resources are required. Regulation of this sector of the market would be in the interests of the many trustees who are competent and responsible.'

There is a considerable amount of sympathy with the stance being taken by OPAS. The Government has not taken any action, however, mainly because the pensions representative bodies in recent years have decried what they perceive as over-regulation of UK private pension provision.

One possible solution is to legislate so that an independent trustee appointed by an insolvency practitioner to wind up a defined benefit scheme would have to follow the same guidance as already applies to independent trustees appointed by Opra (see **4.4**). Such trustees must follow the guidelines set out in **APPENDIX 5** which ensure that they do not spend money or time unnecessarily and so deplete the scheme's funds beyond the amount needed to carry out the action.

Management committees

3.6   The term *committee of management* or *management committee* tends to be used in a variety of senses.

A management committee may provide a local forum for active members, especially in a large occupational pension scheme where the active members are spread over many sites. As such it serves as a *pensions consultative committee*.

Similarly, some employers negotiate with trade unions and employee representatives on pensions. This may be through the standard negotiation machinery or through special pension negotiating committees, and the term *management committee* might be used in this context.

However, if either of these kinds of bodies under the terms of the trust deed and rules have any trustee duties, powers and discretions delegated to them, the members of such management committees are trustees. Their actions will be governed by trust law.

It is common to find in a large multi-site company that the trust deed and rules specify that certain discretionary powers are not exercised by the main trustee body. Rather they are delegated to local management committees. These may be discretionary powers such as deciding who should receive a dependant's pension after a member has died and to whom any lump sum should be paid. The argument is that it is better that such decisions are taken at local level. For a fuller discussion see **5.4**.

Sometimes the term *management committee* is reserved for another central body operating alongside the main trustee body – the trustee board itself. A standard division of labour might give the trustee board responsibility for investment matters, for holding the scheme assets, strategic issues such as powers of amendment to the trust deed and powers exercisable when the occupational pension scheme is wound up, while the management committee oversees day-to-day administration.

Pensioneer trustee

3.7   *Pensioneer trustee* is a term uniquely associated with *small self-administered schemes*. These are occupational pension schemes which have less than twelve members. They usually provide benefits to directors of small companies. The key element is that the trustee body controls the investment strategy. Small self-administered schemes have important tax privileges, including the ability to make loans to the sponsoring company and invest in its assets. The Inland Revenue therefore needs to maintain tight supervision over such schemes to prevent tax abuse and so insists that each small self-administered scheme has a special independent trustee, known as a pensioneer trustee, appointed to the trustee body. Inland Revenue approval has to be obtained before anyone can act as a pensioneer trustee. Pensioneer trustee services are provided on a fee-payment basis usually by insurance companies and specialist consultancies.

Many, but far from all, pensioneer trustees are in membership of the Association of Pensioneer Trustees (APT):

> APT
> c/o Punter Southall & Co
> Charlotte House
> 2 South Charlotte Street
> Edinburgh
> EH2 4AW
> Tel: 0131 225 1155
> Fax: 0131 220 3828
> email: linda.clark@puntersouthall.com
> Website: http://www.pensioneers.org

The Inland Revenue maintains a list for inspection of all approved pensioneer trustees. This may be viewed on the following web address: http://www.inlandrevenue.gov.uk/pensionschemes/apt-list.htm.

Custodian trustee

3.8   The term *custodian trustee* is sometimes used. Quite simply, the custodian trustee's job is to hold financial assets. In the strict sense, a custodian trustee has to be a trust corporation and can only be removed by a court order. Such a custodian trustee in fact is hardly ever used by occupational pension schemes. The term is sometimes applied to what is properly known as a *holding trustee* who is appointed and removed under the terms of the trust deed and rules. However, most usually the term refers to a nominee custodian. A nominee custodian is usually engaged by the investment manager and is not actually a trustee of the scheme at all. Their role is discussed at **16.23**.

Checklist 3

- The structure of the trustee body will in part reflect the size of the sponsoring employer and whether or not employment sites are geographically widespread, but this does not change the nature of the trustees' duties.

- The trustee body may be made up of *individuals acting as trustees* or there may be a *corporate trustee* with individual *trustee directors*. There are technical differences between the two sorts of trustee boards but trustees and trustee directors have essentially the same duties.

- Professional trustees, often constituted as trust corporations, can serve as *independent trustees* alongside individual trustees or a corporate trustee with trustee directors. They charge a fee for their services.

- An *independent trustee* must be appointed in specific circumstances (e g in the case of most defined benefit schemes, when the employer becomes insolvent).

- If members of a *management committee* are charged with carrying out any trustee duty, they are acting as trustees and are subject to trust law.

- Special trustee arrangements apply to *small self-administered schemes.*

- It is not usual for the *custodian* of an occupational pension scheme's assets to be a trustee.

Chapter 4

How trustees are chosen

Appointment and removal

4.1   Until the coming into force on 6 April 1997 of certain sections of the *Pensions Act 1995*, the appointment and removal of trustees had been governed solely by the trust deed and rules, and also, in the case of a corporate trustee, the articles of association. If the trust deed and rules do not say how the trustees should be appointed or removed, then *sections 36–39* of the *Trustee Act 1925* provide a set of default rules. In cases of dispute or difficulty, the courts can interpret the trust deed and rules in the light of general principles of trust law. In the case of a corporate trustee, how the trustee directors are appointed and removed will also be subject to company law. Until the coming into force of the relevant measures in the *Pensions Act 1995*, the power to appoint and to remove trustees in most cases lay exclusively with the employer.

Those disqualified from acting as trustees

4.2   Again, until the coming into force of certain sections of the *Pensions Act 1995*, anyone was eligible to act as a trustee with the exceptions of minors, those certified as insane and those declared bankrupt. However, since 6 April 1997, the following are specifically excluded from acting as a trustee of an occupational pension scheme:

(*a*)   the scheme's actuary;

(*b*)   the scheme's auditor;

(*c*)   anyone who has been prohibited by an order made by the Occupational Pensions Regulatory Authority (Opra);

(*d*)   anyone disqualified by Opra or who has already been removed as a trustee of another scheme by the courts on the grounds of misconduct or mismanagement;

(*e*)   anyone who has been temporarily suspended from acting as a trustee by an order made by Opra;

(*f*)   anyone who has been convicted of an offence involving dishonesty or deception (unless the conviction has become spent under the *Rehabilitation of Offenders Act 1974*);

(*g*)   anyone who is an undischarged bankrupt;

(*h*)   anyone who has made an undischarged arrangement with his or her creditors;

(*i*)   anyone who has failed to make a payment as required under the terms of a county court administration order;

(*j*)   anyone disqualified by Opra on the grounds of mental disorder;

(*k*)   any director of a company which itself has been disqualified from acting as a trustee (also applies to a partner in a Scottish partnership);

(*l*)   anyone who has been disqualified from acting as a company director; and

(*m*)   a company disqualified by Opra because it has gone into liquidation.

If any of the above ignores the ban from acting as a scheme trustee, they are guilty of an offence and liable, if convicted, to a fine and imprisonment.

However, anything done as a trustee by someone who was in fact disqualified will not automatically become invalid.

Except in the case of the scheme actuary and auditor, Opra has the power to waive the disqualification or to revoke its own disqualifying order.

These exclusions also apply in the case of trustees of a stakeholder pension scheme.

Register of disqualified persons

4.3   Opra maintains a register of those it has disqualified from acting as a trustee under points (*c*), (*d*), (*j*) and (*m*) above.

Under measures contained in the *Child Support, Pensions and Social Security Act 2000* Opra is required to make the register available for inspection by the public. Opra is also permitted to publish, in a medium of its choosing and so including therefore on its website, a list of those whose names appear on the register. The full name, including initials and titles, and date of birth must be listed if Opra has a record of these details, even if these details are not recorded on the register itself. The pension schemes themselves are, however, not named.

Opra's register of disqualified trustees may be viewed at the following web address: http://www.opra.gov.uk/general/trustdis.shtml.

In summary, therefore, the lists show those trustees whom Opra has disqualified from acting as trustees because:

●   it has prohibited them from acting as a trustee of a trust scheme under *section 3* of the *Pensions Act 1995*, or the High Court or Court of Session has removed them on the grounds of misconduct or mismanagement of the scheme, and in both cases Opra considers that they should not act as the trustee of any trust scheme;

●   it considers them to be incapable of acting as a trustee due to mental disorder; or

- the trustee is a company (a corporate trustee) which has gone into liquidation.

The legislation requires Opra to show this summary in three lists:

(*a*)   those trustees who are disqualified in respect of all trust schemes;

(*b*)   those trustees who are disqualified in respect of only one scheme; and

(*c*)   those trustees who are disqualified in respect of two or more schemes, but not in respect of all trust schemes.

The legislation does not allow Opra to give any other information than is shown in this summary.

Opra points out that individuals may be automatically disqualified from acting as a trustee for other reasons, such as bankruptcy or conviction of an offence involving dishonesty or deception, but that Opra's register of disqualified trustees does not include the names of such trustees. The only way one can find out whether a person has a conviction is to ask that person, but one can find out whether someone is an undischarged bankrupt by contacting the following address:

> Officer in Charge
> Bankruptcy Public Search Room
> 2nd Floor
> Ladywood House
> 45/6 Stephenson Street
> Birmingham
> B2 4UZ
> Tel: 0121 698 4000

The Government hopes the legislation will provide easier access to the register for those responsible for appointing trustees and that it will reduce the risk of disqualified persons being appointed as trustees. To prevent inequity, Opra will not publish a person's name until either the time limits for appeals and for applications to review the disqualification decision are passed, or when it is unlikely that there will be an appeal or application for review, or when an appeal or review is pending.

Opra appointed trustees

4.4   Once it has removed an existing trustee Opra has the power to appoint a replacement trustee who will act in the same way as an independent trustee appointed by an insolvency practitioner (see **19.7**). Such a trustee may be given restricted powers only or the right to exercise certain of the trust powers exclusively.

In fact Opra has a general power to appoint a trustee to an occupational pension scheme if it is satisfied that it is necessary to do so in order to make sure that:

- the trustees as a whole have, or exercise, the necessary knowledge and skill for the proper administration of the scheme;

- there are enough trustees to:

    - do the job properly; or

    - look after the scheme's assets properly.

Any such trustee would in practice be an independent trustee whose fees and expenses would have to be paid out of the scheme's resources. The appointment could be on a temporary basis. Opra has published guidance for the use of the independent, professional trustees it appoints in such circumstances. The aim of the guidance (see **APPENDIX 5**) is to ensure that professional trustees do not spend money or time unnecessarily and so deplete the scheme's funds beyond the amount needed to carry out the action required.

Member-nominated trustees

4.5   A trust law purist may say that it does not matter how trustees are chosen since in all circumstances they must conscientiously carry out their various trustee duties impartially and not represent sectional interests.

Following the Maxwell imbroglio which broke in 1991, and other revelations, considerable doubts were expressed by some commentators about the wisdom of exclusively relying on trustees drawn from the senior management of the sponsoring employer, or even, in some rare instances, relying on the sponsoring company itself serving as the sole trustee. It was felt that the scope for a breach of trust in such circumstances was too great, especially in circumstances where the company was experiencing financial difficulty. While some commentators went so far as to say that directors of the company should be debarred from being trustees, others countered by arguing that employers would withdraw their support from occupational pension funds if they did not have a direct input in their trustee bodies.

In the event the Pension Law Review Committee recommended that:

(*a*)   employers should not have the sole power to appoint trustees, and should not be able to veto a trustee selected by the scheme members;

(*b*)   schemes should be able to retain their present arrangements for the appointment of trustees, unless the members exercise their right to make appointments.

Following extensive consultation, the Government introduced measures in the *Pensions Act 1995* and the *Occupational Pension Schemes (Member-nominated Trustees and Directors) Regulations 1996 (SI 1996/1216)* which offered employers, trustees and scheme members the following choices with effect from 6 October 1996:

- The employer is permitted to propose *alternative arrangements* that do not give the members the right to nominate and select at least a third of their scheme's trustees, or which curtail the powers of any member-nominated trustees, or which give the employer a right to remove member-nominated trustees; and provided that it is not rejected by the membership under the *statutory consultation procedure* this alternative arrangement will stand for a period of up to six years.

- If the employer does not propose an alternative arrangement, or the employer's alternative arrangement is rejected by the members, the existing trustees must implement the general requirement of the *Pensions Act 1995* and implement arrangements which meet the general requirements set out in the Act (e g to give the members the right to nominate and select one third of their scheme's trustees, with a minimum of two trustees or a minimum of one trustee if the scheme has less than 100 members). These general requirements are set out in full below. The existing trustees implement these arrangements by proposing *appropriate rules*. These appropriate rules will stand for a period of up to six years provided they are not rejected by the membership under the statutory consultation procedure.

- In the case of an impasse, the trustees can implement a set of *prescribed rules* for the nomination and selection of member-nominated trustees. Alternatively this set of default rules can be adopted from the outset.

We set out below the relatively complex requirements in force at the time of writing relating to the general requirements for member-nominated trustees, the right of employers to propose alternative arrangements, the requirements relating to appropriate rules proposed by the scheme trustees, the statutory consultation procedure for testing the acceptability of the proposed arrangements for appointing trustees, and the fall-back set of prescribed rules set out in the regulations.

In its December 1998 Green Paper *A New Contract for Welfare: Partnership in Pensions* and in a separate consultation paper issued at the same time, the Government did announce that it intended to reform the legislation governing the nomination and selection of member trustees. These reforms are now contained in the *Child Support, Pensions and Social Security Act 2000* but have not yet been brought into force. The reforms, which are explained at **4.29** below, were to have applied to an occupational pension scheme when its current arrangements expired at the six-year time limit. However, in February 2002, the Government announced that it would be delaying the implementation of the new legislation. The reason cited by the Government was that it wished to await the results of a review of all private pension legislation, which reported in July 2002. The review, headed by Alan Pickering, had been asked to produce a package of options for a radical simplification of the pensions legislation.

In the event, amending regulations introduced on 6 October 2002 automatically extended the duration of existing alternative arrangements and appropriate rules for the nomination and selection of member-nominated trustees or trustee directors for a further four years. The amending regulations in question are the *Occupational Pension Schemes (Member-nominated Trustees and Directors) Amendment Regulations 2002 (SI 2002/2327)*. As a result, alternative arrangements and appropriate rules that were endorsed via the statutory consultation procedure before 6 October 2002 automatically continue for a total period of ten years. No action is required by either the employer or the trustees to begin another statutory consultation procedure. Revised rules apply, however, in the case of new arrangements or appropriate rules made on or after 6 October 2002, and these are explained at **4.14** and **4.15** respectively.

The member-nominated trustee requirements do not apply to trust-based stakeholder pension schemes. However, at least one trustee and at least one-third of the total number of trustees of a trust-based stakeholder pension scheme must be independent as explained at **2.13** above.

General requirements before proposed changes

4.6   The *Pensions Act 1995* makes the following general requirements of any arrangements for the nomination and selection of trustees. These requirements, however, do not apply to any *alternative arrangement* proposed by the employer.

Right to be nominated

4.7   Any person who has been nominated and selected in accordance with the *appropriate rules* proposed by the existing trustees and approved under the *statutory consultation procedure* automatically becomes a trustee. However, if the employer so wishes, the appropriate rules must give the sponsoring employer the right to veto any person who is not a scheme member (i e the person is neither an active member, nor a deferred pensioner nor a pensioner). For example, a trade union official who is not a scheme member can be nominated and selected as a member-nominated trustee provided the employer does not object.

Removal of member-nominated trustees

4.8   A member-nominated trustee can only be removed with the agreement of all the other trustees. Member-nominated trustees who were employees but cease to be employees will not lose their right to continue as trustees provided they have become either deferred pensioners or pensioners. Any member-nominated trustee who was a scheme member when appointed (i e was either an active member, deferred pensioner or pensioner) must, however, cease to be a trustee if he or she ceases to be a scheme member.

Treatment of vacancies

4.9   Where a vacancy for a member-nominated trustee is not filled because insufficient nominations are received, the arrangements must provide for the filling of the vacancy, or for the vacancy to remain, until the end of the next period in which persons may be nominated and selected. This period must be defined in the appropriate rules but must end at the time the trustees' period of office ends.

Period of office

4.10   The arrangements must provide for the period of office of any member-nominated trustees to be for a minimum of three years and a maximum of six years.

Minimum number of member-nominated trustees

4.11   The arrangements must ensure that the members nominate and select at least one-third of the total number of trustees, with a minimum of at least two such member-nominated trustees (unless the scheme has in total less than 100 members in which case the minimum is one member-nominated trustee). The selection arrangements may provide that more than the statutory minimum number of trustees can be nominated by the members, provided that the sponsoring employer has consented.

Status of member-nominated trustees

4.12   The arrangements must not allow the functions of member-nominated individual trustees to differ from those of any other trustees. Therefore, member-nominated individual trustees could not systematically be excluded from sitting on any investment sub-committee. However, this rule does not apply to trustee directors in the case of a corporate trustee although the requirements of the *Companies Act* are relevant. (Exceptions are also made in the case of the special statutory powers that can be given to a trustee appointed by Opra or by an insolvency practitioner).

Schemes excepted from the general requirements

4.13   The general requirements outlined above apply both to defined benefit and defined contribution schemes. There are, however, specific kinds of scheme which are excepted from the general member-nominated trustee requirements. They include:

● small self-administered schemes;

● schemes which have in place an independent trustee appointed by the insolvency practitioner to the sponsoring employer (see **19.7**);

● schemes which have less than two members;

● unapproved schemes;

● schemes providing only death benefits;

● industry-wide schemes where the sponsoring employers are unassociated and where one-third of the trustees can be classed as independent;

- schemes where the employer is the sole corporate trustee and all the members are either current or former directors of the company provided that at least one-third of the members are current directors;

- insured schemes where no further contributions are payable;

- schemes which have been modified under the *Coal Industry Act 1994* and certain other statutory schemes; and

- wholly insured schemes where the insurance company and the sole corporate trustee are connected, provided the insurance company is neither the employer nor connected to the employer.

Employer's alternative arrangements

4.14   Initially, in the case of existing schemes, the employer had the right to propose *alternative arrangements* at any time during the period from 6 October 1996 to 5 May 1997, except that if the employer gave the existing trustees a written notice stating that it would not be proposing any alternative arrangement at any time during this period, that decision could not then be revoked during the same period. If the employer did tell the existing trustees that it did not wish to propose alternative arrangements, the trustees could then go ahead and propose their own *appropriate rules*. If the employer had not announced that it would be proposing alternative arrangements by 5 May 1997, the employer has normally become prevented from doing so during the following six years, i e to 6 April 2003. In the case of a new scheme, an employer has one month in which to propose alternative arrangements. If it does not, it is normally precluded from doing so for the next six years. (However, note the effect of the four-year extension mentioned at **4.5** above and further discussed below.)

In any case where the employer does decide to propose alternative arrangements, the employer, rather than the existing trustees, becomes responsible for carrying out the *statutory consultation procedure* which is explained at **4.17** below. If, before 6 May 1997, the employer did propose alternative arrangements, the employer had six months, or by 5 October 1997 if earlier, in which to gain acceptance from the membership. If under the statutory consultation procedure approval was gained, the existing trustees then were obliged to implement the alternative arrangements. If approval was for the existing arrangements to continue, they were immediately in place, otherwise the existing trustees had six months in which to implement the alternative arrangements. Once in place, an alternative arrangement was to operate for a maximum of six years. After this time the mandate given by the members via the statutory consultation procedure was to lapse and a new statutory consultation procedure had to be undertaken. However, as explained at **4.5**, alternative arrangements that had received approval via the statutory consultation procedure by 6 October 2002 can now continue for a further four years.

If an employer wishes to propose a new alternative arrangement on or after 6 October 2002, and this proposal is accepted under the statutory consultation procedure, approval is given for a maximum period of four years. Provided that the trustees give their consent, the employer may propose a new alternative arrangement at any time.

If the trustees do not give their consent, the employer may still propose a new alternative arrangement at any time on or after 6 October 2002 provided that it is to replace an existing alternative arrangement already in place. On the other hand, if there is no alternative arrangement in place in relation to the scheme, and the employer last proposed an alternative arrangement before 6 October 2002, the employer is prevented from proposing a new alternative arrangement until the end of a period of ten years from the date of its last proposal for putting in place a new alternative arrangement. Similarly, if there is no alternative arrangement in place but the employer, without the trustees' consent, wishes to propose an alternative arrangement on or after 6 October 2002, it can do so, but if the proposal fails to be accepted under the statutory consultation procedure the employer is prevented from making a further such proposal for a further four years.

Note that all the above time limits relate to the period of validity of the alternative arrangement itself, not to the maximum term of office of member-nominated trustees or trustee directors themselves. The term of office of member-nominated trustees or trustee directors continues to be defined by the rules made by the alternative arrangement.

Employers have only proposed alternative arrangements if they wished to have in place nomination and selection procedures for the trustees that, in one or more ways, did not fulfil all the general requirements set out from **4.6** to **4.12** above. Examples might include alternative arrangements in which there are either no 'member' (i e non-management) trustees or fewer than a third; where the status of member trustees differs from that of management trustees; where the power of selection and removal of all trustees is exercised by the employer; and where member trustees can remain in office for more than six years. In many cases there were existing arrangements that had been negotiated between the employer and recognised trade unions that did not meet the general requirements set out above. If such an arrangement were to continue to operate, the employer had to propose them as an alternative arrangement and gain approval for it via the statutory consultation procedure.

Appropriate rules

4.15   Once the existing trustees knew that the employer would not be proposing *alternative arrangements*, which for existing schemes in the first instance was 6 October 1996 at the earliest and 5 May 1997 at the latest, they had six months in which to propose *appropriate rules* and have put in place the eventual arrangements for the nomination and selection of member-nominated trustees. If the employer announced that it would be proposing alternative arrangements but in the event those proposals were rejected under the *statutory consultation procedure* explained below, the trustees always had six months from the date of the opt-out failure to implement the requirements for member-nominated trustees. Since the latest date for an opt-out failure during the introduction of the new procedures was 5 October 1997, the latest date for implementation of appropriate rules was 6 April 1998.

All appropriate rules must meet the general requirements for member-nominated trustees set out above. In addition the appropriate rules:

- must determine the procedure for the nomination and selection of a person to fill a vacancy as a member-nominated trustee;

- may determine, or provide for the determination of, the conditions required of a person for filling such a vacancy;

- must provide for a member-nominated trustee to be eligible for re-selection at the end of his or her period of office;

- must specify, in the case where a vacancy for a member-nominated trustee is not filled because insufficient nominations have been received, the start date of the next period in which persons may be nominated and selected (the end of this period must coincide with the end of the trustees' period of office); and

- must provide that, where the employer so requires, a person who is not a member of the scheme must have the employer's approval to qualify for selection as a member-nominated trustee.

There was considerable scope for the trustees to propose appropriate rules which were designed to meet the circumstances of their scheme. For example, if there were, say, four sites in which the sponsoring company operates in the UK, the trustees may have decided that active members at each site should nominate and select one trustee and that the pensioners should nominate and select a fifth trustee. There would then be five constituencies each selecting one member-nominated trustee. In such circumstances, five separate ballots could have taken place and the candidate in each ballot with the highest number of votes would have been selected. The trustees may also have proposed that in order to be put forward as a candidate, any person should have received, say, ten nominations from other members of that constituency.

As another example, a company may employ a large number of distinct employee groups and have only recently established an occupational pension scheme. The trustees may have wished to keep the trustee board to a maximum of five, of whom two will be nominated by the active members. The trustees may also have decided that pensioners should not be involved in the nomination and selection process. Because they expected a large number of nominations, the trustees may then have proposed that selection should be by ballot of the active members using the single transferable vote system which would favour the selection of a universal second choice compromise candidate who was broadly acceptable to all active members.

Once in place, the *appropriate rules* were to have operated for a maximum of six years. After this time the mandate given by the members via the statutory consultation procedure was to have lapsed and a new statutory consultation procedure would have had to be undertaken, but as explained at **4.5** appropriate rules which had received approval via the statutory consultation procedure by 6 October 2002 can now continue for a further four years.

In the case where trustees propose new appropriate rules on or after 6 October 2002 and this proposal is accepted under the statutory consultation procedure, approval is given for a maximum period of ten years. Note that this differs from the case of new alternative arrangements proposed on or after 6 October 2002 which, if approved under the statutory consultation procedure, only have four years' validity. The reason for the difference is that any appropriate rules automatically will comply with the proposed new requirements for all schemes to have a minimum one-third of member-nominated trustees or trustee directors as described at **4.29** below.

Relevant events

4.16   As explained above, once, via the *statutory consultation procedure*, an *alternative arrangement* proposed by the employer, or an arrangement governed by *appropriate rules* proposed by the previous trustee body, is in place, the authority for that arrangement was to have lapsed after a maximum of six years, but this period has now been extended by a further four years as set out at **4.5** above.

However, the regulations stipulate that in certain situations the trustees must consider whether it would be detrimental for the approval of the appropriate rules or of the alternative arrangement to continue to have effect before this time limit is reached. The situations envisaged in the regulations are the occurrence of a *relevant event*, that is:

- a bulk transfer of members into or out of the scheme where the individual consent of each member has not been obtained;

- a new employer becoming a participating employer;

- an existing employer ceasing to be a participating employer; or

- an employer becoming a wholly owned subsidiary of another employer and that other employer not employing members of the scheme.

In the wake of any of the above relevant events, if the trustees consider that the continuation of the existing arrangement would be detrimental to the interests of the members, they may give notice to the employer that the existing alternative arrangement or appropriate rules will cease to have effect. In this case, the employer has one month in which to give the trustees notice that it intends to propose an alternative arrangement under the statutory consultation procedure. The employer then has six months in which to gain acceptance for the alternative arrangement. If the employer does not propose an alternative arrangement, or if the employer's alternative arrangement is rejected, then the trustees must propose appropriate rules under the statutory consultation procedure. The trustees have six months in which to gain acceptance for the proposed *appropriate rules*.

In the case of a new scheme, the requirement to implement the member-nominated trustee requirements (ending the statutory consultation procedure) must come into play within six months of the date the scheme received Inland Revenue approval.

Statutory consultation procedure

4.17   The *statutory consultation procedure* is the detailed set of procedures for obtaining the views of members of occupational pension schemes as set out in *Schedule 1* to the *Occupational Pension Schemes (Member-nominated Trustees and Directors) Regulations 1996 (SI 1996/1216)*. Some details of the statutory consultation procedure differ according to whether it is the employer who has proposed *alternative arrangements* or the existing trustees who have proposed *appropriate rules*. Other details are common to both situations.

The employer proposes alternative rules

4.18   The employer must send a notice to each active member, each pensioner (i e each retired active member; not widows, widowers or dependants), and any deferred pensioners whom the existing trustees have decided should also be consulted. This notice must contain a general statement which explains that if the *alternative arrangements* proposed by the employer are not approved, the trustees will put in place arrangements for the nomination and selection of member-nominated trustees that comply with the general requirements which we have outlined above (see **4.6** to **4.13**).

The employer's notice must contain details of the alternative arrangements proposed which must include:

(*a*)   the proposed total number of trustees for the scheme;

(*b*)   the procedure proposed to be adopted for the selection of trustees;

(*c*)   the period proposed as their period of office;

(*d*)   if it is proposed that the functions of any trustees should differ from those of other trustees, the differences in those functions (and in the case of trustee directors, whether any special rules for decisions to be made by particular directors are proposed and, if so, what they are); and

(*e*)   whether it is proposed that, if at the time the arrangements come into force the trustees already include member-nominated trustees, they should continue or cease to be trustees and, if they are to cease, the time when they are to do so.

The existing trustees propose appropriate rules

4.19   The existing trustees must send a notice to each active member, each pensioner (i e each retired active member; not widows, widowers or dependants) and any deferred pensioner whom they have decided to consult. This notice must contain a general statement that the existing trustees are required to put in place arrangements for the selection of member-nominated trustees and to implement *appropriate rules* to regulate those arrangements.

The trustees' notice must contain details of the appropriate rules proposed. Those details must include the following particulars:

(*a*)   the total number of trustees for the scheme;

(*b*)   the number of trustees to be selected by the members;

(*c*)   the number of trustees to be selected by the employer;

(*d*)   whether, if a vacancy for a member-nominated trustee is not filled because insufficient nominations are received, the vacancy is to be filled or to remain and, if it is to be filled, the procedure proposed to be followed;

(*e*)   the period for which selection as a member-nominated trustee is to have effect (not being less than three but not more than six years).

Common procedures

4.20   Any notice sent out by either an employer proposing *alternative arrangements* or by the trustees proposing *appropriate rules* must also include details of:

(*a*)   whether any, and if so what conditions are proposed for persons to be considered as eligible for nomination;

(*b*)   the number of members of the scheme proposed to be required to make a nomination;

(*c*)   in cases where a vacancy is not filled because insufficient nominations are received, the period proposed as the next period in which persons may be nominated and selected; and

(*d*)   the procedure proposed for selection where the number of persons nominated to fill vacancies exceeds the number of vacancies.

In addition, the notice must explain that all the active members, all the pensioners (i e each retired active member; not widows, widowers or dependants) and, if the trustees have so decided, any deferred pensioners that the trustees have included in those to be consulted, either:

•   are being given a period within which they may object to the proposals and may be balloted if at least 10% of the total number of members consulted (or 10,000 members if less) have objected within the period; or

•   are being balloted directly.

In either case, if the trustees have decided that some deferred pensioners should be consulted, the notice must explain the 'effect of that determination'.

In the case where the members must register objections, the notice must explain that if the required number of objections are not received within the stated period the proposals will be treated as approved, but that if at least the required number of objections are received within the notice period then a ballot will be held of all the members to be consulted. The notice must also explain:

- the manner in which objections may be made;

- the length of the objection period which must last at least one month beginning from the date the notice is given to the members; and

- the number of members who can vote (provided that the objection period ends before the beginning of the first scheme year).

Whenever the members are being balloted, the notice must explain that the proposals must be approved by a ballot of all the members to be consulted.

The notice must also:

- explain the procedure to be used for the ballot, including whether it is to be conducted so that those voting can do so in secret; and

- give the last date on which votes may be cast which must be at least one month after the date on which the notice is given.

Where a ballot is to be held, the following rules apply:

- the result must be obtained by a simple majority of those voting;

- if the employer undertook the *statutory consultation procedure*, the employer must inform the trustees of the result as soon as it is known;

- if the existing trustees undertook the statutory consultation procedure, the existing trustees must inform the employer of the result as soon as it is known;

- if approval is given by the ballot, the proposals shall be treated as approved from the date the result of the ballot is known.

The statutory consultation procedure will not be invalidated if it is subsequently discovered that the procedures followed meant that members did not have the opportunity to make objections to the proposals, provided that the number of potential objections would not have made a material difference to the result.

Prescribed rules

4.21   The *prescribed rules* may be seen as a default set of rules for the appointment of member-nominated trustees, to be used when all proposals put to the members under the *statutory consultation procedure* have been rejected. Alternatively, they may be seen by existing trustees and employer alike as an attractive option in their own right, in which case they can be adopted at the outset without the need for any statutory consultation procedure. It should be noted, however, that any ballot held under the prescribed rules for the selection of member-nominated trustees will involve only the active members. They are not suitable, therefore, for adoption if the trustees wish, or feel they have a duty to involve pensioners, or even deferred pensioners, in the selection process.

The existing trustees must invite nominations for the filling of vacancies by giving notice in writing to the active members specifying the last date on which nominations may be made, which must not be earlier than one month after the date on which the notice is given. The notice must set out the terms for the arrangements that the trustees are making to comply with the general requirements that would apply under the *Pensions Act 1995* to any set of *appropriate rules*, e g to have in place at least one-third of the trustees as member-nominated trustees (see **4.6** to **4.13**).

The notice must also give the following details:

(*a*)   the total number of trustees for the scheme;

(*b*)   the number of trustees to be selected by the members;

(*c*)   the number of trustees to be selected by the employer;

(*d*)   whether, if a vacancy for a member-nominated trustee is not filled because insufficient nominations are received, the vacancy is to be filled or to remain and, if it is to be filled, the procedure proposed to be followed; and

(*e*)   the period for which selection as a member-nominated trustee is to have effect (not being less than three but not more than six years).

Any person may be nominated to be a member-nominated trustee (including any of the existing trustees) subject to the sponsoring employer being able to veto the nomination of any person who is not an active member, deferred pensioner or pensioner of the scheme. Any nomination must be made in writing by an active member of the scheme and be supported by at least one other member. Nominees must give their written consent to the nomination.

If the number of valid nominations does not exceed the number of vacancies, those persons become member-nominated trustees. If the number of valid nominations exceeds the number of vacancies, those vacancies must be filled by those nominees elected by a ballot of the active members.

No later than 14 days after the last date on which nominations can be made, the existing trustees must give notice in writing to all the active members specifying:

• the procedure to be used for the ballot (including whether it is to be conducted so that those voting can do so in secret);

• the last date on which votes may be cast (being a date not less than 14 days nor more than one month after the date on which the notice is given); and

• the arrangements to be made for overseeing the conduct of the ballot, and for the counting of the votes and the declaration of the result.

In the ballot itself each active member may vote only for one nominee in respect of each vacancy. The vacancy or vacancies will be filled by the nominee or nominees for whom the most votes are cast. Any tie must be resolved by drawing lots.

The existing trustees may decide that in the event of insufficient nominations any remaining vacancy will be filled by the first valid nomination received during the period for which selection as a member-nominated trustee is to have effect. Alternatively, if the existing trustees have decided that in the event of insufficient nominations any vacancy will remain and further nominations will be sought, the next period in which persons may be nominated and selected to fill that vacancy is the period beginning either:

●   if the new trustees consent, the day after the last day specified in the notice inviting nominations; or

●   the day when nominations could be made to select a new member-nominated trustee if the vacancy had been filled and the member-nominated trustee had completed the period of office.

Enforcement of the member-nominated trustee requirements

4.22   Any employer who proposes an *alternative arrangement* but fails to give effect to the *statutory consultation procedure* would be liable to be fined by Opra. Trustees also face possible prohibition orders and fines if they fail to take all reasonable steps to secure compliance with the requirements to make arrangements for persons selected by members of the scheme to be trustees and to implement those arrangements and the *appropriate rules* or *prescribed rules*.

Employer-nominated trustees

4.23   The sponsoring employer will usually appoint some senior company managers as trustees. It is likely that certain company executives or managers (including one or more of the following positions: company secretary, managing director, finance director, human resources director or personnel manager) would be appointed trustees *ex officio*. Of the company officers, the role of the finance director might seem to be especially critical and a useful presence on the trustee board. Certain members of the employing company's board, such as the chairman, might serve as employer-nominated trustees.

Trust law requires that, when acting as trustees, senior managers must, in the case of any conflict of interest, carry out their duties as trustees in preference to the interests of the company. It is wrong, however, to suppose that all matters will give rise to a conflict of interest. After all, it is generally in the interests of the scheme members that the sponsoring employer flourishes and that the pension scheme serves to attract, retain and motivate the employees without imposing unmanageable costs on the employer. Nevertheless, conflicts can and do arise and employer-nominated trustees will be aware that, just as with member-nominated trustees, they owe a duty to put the interests of the pension scheme members above all other considerations.

It is currently possible for the employer alone to select all the trustees, or for member-nominated trustees drawn from the membership to be appointed subject to the employer's approval. However, such an arrangement would mean that the members of the scheme would have foregone their right to nominate at least one-third of the trustees through the *statutory consultation procedure*.

Duration of appointment, removal and retirement of trustees

4.24   In the case of individual trustees, the appointment of a new trustee is normally made by the execution of a deed amending the trust deed and rules. The formal power of appointment is specified in the trust deed and is usually given to the employer. In the case of a corporate trustee, the trustee directors will normally be appointed under the articles of association of the corporate trustee.

Member-nominated trustees

4.25   Special conditions set down in the *Pensions Act 1995* govern the duration of appointment, removal and retirement of member-nominated trustees (unless such member-nominated trustees have been nominated and selected by the members under the rules governing an *alternative arrangement* proposed by the employer). As explained above:

- Selection as a member-nominated trustee must be for a period of at least three years but not more than six years.

- The appropriate rules adopted by a scheme to govern the arrangements for nominating and selecting member-nominated trustees must provide for a member-nominated trustee to be eligible for reselection at the end of his or her period of service.

- A member-nominated trustee cannot normally be removed from the trustee board without the agreement of all the other trustees.

- If a person was a member-nominated trustee when appointed but subsequently ceases to be either an active member, a deferred pensioner or a pensioner of the scheme, he or she automatically ceases to be a trustee. (Note that member-nominated trustees who lose their jobs with the sponsoring employer can currently continue to act as trustees provided they do not decide to transfer their pension rights out of the scheme, and it is this provision which persuaded many employers to choose to propose an alternative arrangement.)

- If a member-nominated trustee resigns, a replacement member-nominated trustee should be selected, probably within six months.

Employer-nominated trustees

4.26   The trust deed and rules, or articles of association in the case of a corporate trustee, will normally specify how long trustees serve on the trustee body, how they may be removed or simply retire.

Individuals who have been nominated by the employer will normally stop being trustees if they leave their employment. In the case of management trustees appointed *ex officio* they may cease to be trustees if they no longer hold that specific post.

It should be noted, however, that the appointment of an individual trustee does not automatically end if the trustee leaves the employment or ceases to be a member of the scheme. The procedure laid down in the trust deed and rules must be followed (but if the trust deed and rules are defective, trust law lays down a procedure of last resort). In the case of individual trustees, a trustee can normally only retire if an appropriate deed is executed by a solicitor. In the case of a trustee director, the corporate trustee as such does not change in such circumstances, but a new trustee director has to be appointed none the less.

Removal because of disagreement

4.27   The *Pensions Act 1995* permits the decisions of the trustees to be taken by agreement of a majority unless the trust deed and rules specify otherwise. In practice, at most trustee meetings a consensus approach is sought. Yet a serious disagreement may arise and this might involve an attempt by the employer to remove 'troublesome' trustees (provided that the trust deed and rules stipulate that the power of removal is held by the employer). In the case of an attempt to remove any member-nominated trustee (unless nominated and selected under an *alternative arrangement* proposed by the employer), since 6 April 1997 the agreement of **all** the other trustees is required. The vacancy would then have to be filled in accordance with the *appropriate rules* which had been approved by the *statutory consultation procedure*.

It should be remembered that the power granted to an employer to remove trustees is generally thought to be exercisable only on a *fiduciary* basis. That is to say, the employer must use it as would a trustee acting in the best interests of the beneficiaries as a whole. Some pension lawyers disagree and argue that the removal of a trustee by the employer is not necessarily bound by any *fiduciary* duty and that at least in some cases the employer may look to its own interests when exercising any power it has to remove a trustee. However, in any case, if the threatened trustees believe that the employer's attempt to remove them is improper, they should report the matter to Opra. They may also resist through the courts or through the Pensions Ombudsman (see **20.7**).

If a trustee or a small group of trustees disagrees with the decision that the majority of the trustees propose to take, but a breach of trust is not involved (see **21.4**), the conflict may in the end result in that trustee or small group of trustees resigning. It would then be obvious to the members that any consensus had broken down. In the case of member-nominated trustees, this would give rise to a vacancy or vacancies that would then have to be filled in accordance with the appropriate rules.

Practice since 1997

4.28   Survey evidence overwhelmingly shows that, since the requirements of the *Pensions Act 1995* came into force, the great majority of employers who sponsor self-administered occupational pension schemes have exercised their right to propose *alternative arrangements*. That is to say these employers have opted out of the statutory, member-nominated trustee requirements. Furthermore, the great majority of statutory consultation exercises resulted in only a handful of members in each scheme raising objections. The objection route, with its hurdle of needing 10% of those consulted to object (or 10,000 if lower), is a stiff target in the absence of any widespread, organised opposition to an employer's proposal.

The 1997 annual survey carried out by the National Association of Pension Funds (NAPF) found that among 531 private sector pension schemes:

- 83% had adopted an *alternative arrangement* proposed by the employer;

- 11% had adopted *appropriate rules* proposed by the trustees; and

- 5% had adopted the *prescribed rules* set out in the legislation.

In the main, the few serious challenges made to proposals for alternative arrangements took place when the employer's proposal made no specific provision to ensure that there was a scheme pensioner among the trustees and there happened to be a powerful and organised pensioners' action group that could mobilise opposition. In some cases, an employer's proposal met organised opposition from trade union members in the scheme but this seemed to be relatively rare. In many cases, the employer's proposal was for the maintenance of the pre-existing arrangements for the nomination and selection of trustees. If there was a recognised trade union already involved in the nomination and/or selection of some trustees, this would mean that the trade union would tend to support the employer's opt-out proposal.

There are a number of important points to be made about current practice. Although employers' proposals for schemes to opt out of the statutory member-nominated trustee requirements have usually succeeded, it is still very common:

(*a*)   for there to be trustees drawn from the general membership; and

(*b*)   for the general membership to be involved in the formal process of appointing these member trustees.

The NAPF found that, among private sector final salary schemes, the appointment of member trustees:

- in 75% of schemes involved the active scheme members; and

- in 43% of schemes involved pensioners.

In some 16% of schemes trade unions were formally involved in some way in appointing member trustees.

Therefore it is not uncommon to find that in a scheme where an employer's alternative arrangement is in place (and so the formal general requirements set out at **4.6** to **4.12** above do not have to apply), up to one half of the trustees will have been appointed following a ballot of the active members and pensioners. This fact begs the question therefore why an alternative arrangement was proposed. In some cases the answer lies in the employer anticipating problems in not being able to remove member-nominated trustees appointed according to appropriate rules. Also an employer may prefer not to have deferred pensioners, now working for another employer, acting as trustees of the pension scheme.

Research carried out by Incomes Data Services and published in April 1998 indicated that where member trustees are in post, their term of office is very often three years. Towards the end of the trustee's term, a fresh nomination and selection procedure is carried out so that a new member trustee is ready to take the place of the resigning member trustee. In some schemes the existing member is immediately able to seek re-nomination. In others this is forbidden and the trustee must always stand down, although he or she could seek a further nomination at the end of the next term. Vacancies are often filled from a reserve list of shortlisted nominees from the last nomination and selection process or by the person who received the next highest number of votes in a ballot. A replacement member trustee will usually serve the rest of the former trustee's term of office and will then usually be eligible for re-nomination and re-selection.

Reform of nomination and selection of member trustees

4.29   As signalled at **4.5** above, the Government indicated in its 1998 Green Paper *A New Contract for Welfare: Partnership in Pensions* and in a separate consultation paper issued at the same time, that it intended to reform the legislation governing the nomination and selection of member trustees. The Government stated:

'We believe that all funded schemes set up under trust should have member-nominated trustees. That is the way to give members a proper feeling of ownership of and commitment to their scheme. We also believe that schemes with significant numbers of pensioners must be given the chance to elect a pensioner trustee. The present provisions do not always achieve either. They are also very complicated both to understand and to operate. We therefore propose changes which will not only provide considerable simplification, but will also ensure that the member-nominated trustee provisions actually deliver member-nominated trustees. They will mean that schemes must have trustees who are nominated and elected by members and that there should be provision for a pensioner trustee in large mature schemes.'

In October 1999 the then DSS issued a further consultation document setting out the Government's current proposals on changes to the member-nominated trustee requirements following responses to the December 1998 Green Paper. The proposals were in fact devised by a working group made of DSS officials, representatives of various pensions organisations, the TUC and Opra. Under these revised proposals all trust-based occupational pension schemes (save for the existing exceptions) would be required to have at least one-third member-nominated trustees but the requirement that mature schemes should always have a pensioner among the trustees was dropped.

The proposals are now enacted in the *Child Support, Pensions and Social Security Act 2000* but have not been brought into force.

Under these measures, there would be two different ways to nominate and select member-nominated trustees:

- a statutory route – where the trustees will be responsible for implementing nomination and selection procedures as set out in legislation; and

- a scheme-specific route – where the employer will be able to propose nomination and selection procedures to suit the scheme. At least one-third of the trustees must be nominated by members, but the nomination and selection procedure can be whatever the employer chooses. The arrangements will have to be approved by scheme members under a *statutory consultation procedure.*

However, as signalled at **4.5** above, in February 2002 the Government announced that the measures contained in the *Child Support, Pensions and Social Security Act 2000* would be delayed until the results of the simplification review being carried out by Alan Pickering had been studied. Alternative proposals were then subsequently put forward in the December 2002 pensions Green Paper – see **4.33** below.

Statutory route

4.30   Under the statutory route, the existing trustees would be responsible for implementing nomination and selection procedures as set out in legislation. The legislation, as currently framed, allows trustees some flexibility to tailor the procedures to suit the circumstances of the scheme. Trustees would be required to put in place arrangements which ensured that at least one-third of the trustees were nominated and selected by members of the scheme (unless the employer had gained approval for scheme-specific nomination and selection arrangements). There would be no requirement to obtain members' approval of the statutory proposals, but trustees would be required to document the procedures and make them available to scheme members on request. They would also be required to set out the procedures in their annual report.

A trustee who had been nominated and selected by members under the statutory route would be defined in regulations in such a way as to:

- ensure that all active, deferred and pensioner members were free to stand for selection, although the employer would have to approve the nomination of a person who was not a scheme member;

- ensure that all active and pensioner members were invited to make nominations;

- allow the trustees to determine whether deferred members were to be included in the nomination process;

- specify the times by which the arrangements had to be in place, and trustees selected in accordance with the arrangements – these deadlines would be broadly the same as now where trustees generally have six months to comply; and

- exempt schemes of a particular class or description – again the existing exemptions would continue to apply, although the Government stated that it was prepared to look at the case for exempting further types of scheme.

The Government also proposed to give trustees some flexibility over the selection process. Regulations could set out a straightforward selection process (probably based on one member, one vote). But they would also have the discretion to devise an alternative process, if they thought it appropriate given the circumstances of the scheme. This flexibility would include giving trustees the power to decide whether to include deferred members in the selection process, whether to split the electorate into constituencies (for example on a geographical basis, or for a separate pensioner constituency) and whether to make provision for selection panels (although the Government would limit this to selection panels where the majority were scheme members or member representatives). The precise details would be in regulations, and would be subject to further consultation.

There would be no time limit for expiry of the nomination and selection procedures under the statutory route. Trustees would be free to revise the procedures at any time, provided they continued to meet the statutory requirements, and any trustees appointed under the old procedures could continue to the end of their term.

The scheme-specific route

4.31   The scheme-specific route would provide an alternative to the statutory route if the employer wished to use it. The employer would be able to propose scheme-specific arrangements for nominating and selecting the trustees of the scheme. But the arrangements would still have to provide for at least one-third of the trustees to be nominated by members, with at least two member-nominated trustees in schemes with 100 or more members and at least one in schemes with less than 100 members.

The employer's proposals would be able to provide different arrangements for the nomination and selection of trustees by the member from those laid down under the statutory route described at **4.30** above. For example, the employer would be able to propose that nominations for trustees were made by organisations representing members (such as trade unions or a pensioner group) rather than directly by the members themselves.

Employer-devised nomination and selection arrangements would have to be approved by the scheme members under a statutory consultation procedure. This would be broadly the same as now, where approval is deemed if less than 10% of the members object or a simple majority approve in the event of a ballot. For these purposes 'members' means active and pensioner members (the trustees would be free to determine whether deferred members should also be included).

The Government stated that it was aware of concerns that the current statutory consultation procedure was capable of being abused, and would look at ways of increasing confidence in the process. Examples of how this might be done are:

- requiring the notice to members to be separate from any other communication;

- requiring a standard format or form of words for the notice, including an explanation of what involvement each category of member (active, pensioner, deferred) has in the process;

- requiring the employer to attach or enclose a reply slip;

- prohibiting the employer from requiring members to give reasons for an objection (although the Government wants members to have the opportunity to comment if they wish);

- requiring objections to be sent to the trustees rather than to the employer;

- requiring the trustees or employer to declare the result of the exercise; and

- requiring secret returns/ballots and/or independent scrutiny.

Common features

4.32   As with the current requirements, the arrangements would have to:

- provide for there to be at least two member-nominated trustees in schemes with 100 or more members and at least one in schemes with less than 100 members. Arrangements which provide for more than the minimum would require the employer's agreement;

- provide for member-nominated trustees to be in post for between hree and six years;

- provide for member-nominated trustees to be free to stand for re-election on expiry of their term of office;

- provide for all the trustees to have the same power; and

- explain what would happen where vacancies for member-nominated trustees remain unfilled because insufficient nominations had been received.

At the moment, a member-nominated trustee can only be removed if all the other trustees agree. As explained above, a member-nominated trustee who stopped being an active member of the scheme but instead became a deferred pensioner would not be required to stand down. This would change under the proposed new measures since they contain provision in the arrangements for a member-nominated trustee to be removed if he or she ever changes category of membership, i e from being an active member to a deferred pensioner, or from an active member to a pensioner.

The 2002 Green Paper

4.33   After the publication of Alan Pickering's *A Simpler Way to Better Pensions* in July 2002, the Government published a further Green Paper, *Simplicity, Security and Choice: Working and Saving for Retirement*, in December 2002. The Government's current thinking on member-nominated trustees was, however, set out in an accompanying technical consultation paper. The paper invited views on the possibility of introducing legislation that provides for all schemes to have a minimum of one-third of the trustees (or directors of a corporate trustee) nominated and selected by scheme members. This legislation would then be backed up with guidance issued by the pensions regulator on good practice for nomination and selection arrangements.

The paper sought views on two options:

(*a*)   the option put forward in Alan Pickering's review which provides for only a minimum requirement in the legislation itself – namely, that schemes must have at least one-third member-nominated trustees or trustee directors; or

(*b*)   an option which qualifies this minimum requirement with a further condition in the legislation that arrangements for nominating and selecting member-nominated trustees or trustee directors should be 'fair and open'.

The paper makes it clear that in each case the legislation would also make the following provisions:

● exemptions from the requirement to have member-nominated trustees (the Department for Work and Pensions anticipates similar exemptions to those contained in the existing regulations – see **4.13**);

● ensuring that arrangements adopted under the legislation override scheme rules where there is a conflict between the two;

● restrictions on trustees so that they cannot unilaterally impose more than the minimum of one-third member-nominated trustees;

● protection to ensure that member-nominated trustees cannot be removed except with the agreement of all the other trustees;

● protection to ensure that member-nominated cannot be excluded from certain trustee functions; and

- where no members were willing to stand as trustees, protection for the existing trustees from being in breach of the requirement to implement the minimum legislative requirement.

The paper discusses what having the pensions regulator decide good practice would involve, and also under the second option how the pensions regulator would have to define what 'fair and open' would mean and then adjudicate in disputes. The paper makes the following comment:

> 'These possible new arrangements would attempt to simplify what many pension practitioners cite as some of the most complex of all pension legislation for what is, essentially, a straightforward objective – to allow scheme members to nominate some of their scheme's trustees. The reason the legislation is so complex is because, in attempting to achieve fairness, it prescribes how schemes should conduct their nomination and selection arrangements.'

The choice is therefore between the option of a simple requirement for a one-third minimum proportion of member-nominated trustees with the pensions regulator issuing guidance, and the option of ensuring that the pensions regulator would also adjudicate in cases where the scheme's existing trustees had to demonstrate that their procedures for satisfying this minimum requirement were also open and fair.

Checklist 4

- The Occupational Pensions Regulatory Authority (Opra) has the power to prohibit, suspend or disqualify a person from acting as a trustee of a particular scheme, and the list of categories of persons who are automatically disqualified from acting as a trustee has been extended.

- Opra has the power to install a replacement trustee if it judges it to be necessary.

- The *Pensions Act 1995* has introduced statutory rules for the nomination and selection of member-nominated trustees although the employer has the right to propose alternative arrangements which will stand provided they are not rejected by the membership under a statutory consultation procedure. If they are not rejected, the existing trustees must implement the employer's proposals. This alternative arrangement was then to stand for a maximum of six years when it automatically would have lapsed, but in 2002 a four-year extension was granted for alternative arrangements in place before 6 October 2002.

- If the employer does not propose an alternative arrangement, the existing trustees must either propose appropriate rules for an arrangement for the nomination and selection of member-nominated trustees in accordance with the general requirements of the *Pensions Act 1995* or adopt a default set of prescribed rules. If the existing

---

trustees propose appropriate rules, these rules will stand provided they are not rejected by the membership under a statutory consultation procedure. If they are not rejected, the existing trustees must implement their proposals. The appropriate rules were then to stand for a maximum of six years when they automatically would have lapsed, but again a four-year extension has been granted for appropriate rules put in place before 6 October 2002.

- On or after 6 October 2002, the same arrangements apply to new schemes, but an alternative arrangement will be valid for only four years while a scheme adopting the appropriate rules will be valid for ten years.

- In case of an impasse, the prescribed rules governing the nomination and selection of member-nominated trustees can be adopted without going through a statutory consultation procedure.

- In proposing appropriate rules, the existing trustees must follow the general requirements of the *Pensions Act 1995,* but also, as trustees, be guided by their fiduciary duty to all classes of the membership.

- In the statutory consultation process, the existing trustees must decide whether some of the deferred pensioners (e g those for whom they hold a current address) should be included with the active members and pensioners among those to be consulted.

- Under the rules, those pensioners to be consulted under the statutory consultation procedure do not include widows, widowers and dependants.

- If a *relevant event* occurs (e g a bulk transfer, or a new participating employer), the trustees have a statutory duty to consider whether they should give notice that either the current alternative arrangement or the appropriate rules should cease to have effect and be replaced.

- The employer, under the terms of the trust deed and rules, will usually remain solely responsible for the selection, appointment and removal of the other trustees.

- A member-nominated trustee, selected under either the appropriate or prescribed rules, who is still an active member, a deferred pensioner or a pensioner cannot be removed by the employer and can only be removed during his or her period of office with the agreement of all the other trustees, or by Opra.

- Any trustee who is removed and has reasonable grounds for fearing that his or her removal is to facilitate a breach of trust should report the matter to Opra.

- The *Child Support, Pensions and Social Security Act 2000* proposes revised requirements for the nomination and selection of trustees by the members. These are designed to offer reasonable flexibility to employers but always to ensure that at least one-third of the trustees are always member nominated. However, earlier proposals to guarantee a pensioner place among the member-nominated trustees in cases where pensioners formed a substantial proportion of the membership were dropped. However, this legislation may never be brought into force.

- Following the publication of Alan Pickering's simplification review in July 2002, the Government published new proposals in December 2002 for the implementation of a simple minimum legislative requirement that schemes, unless exempt, should all have one-third of their trustees or trustee directors nominated and selected by the members, with the pensions regulator issuing good practice guidance. Consultation was begun on the issue of whether this minimum legislative requirement should be qualified by an additional 'fair and open' legislative test to be adjudicated by the regulator.

Chapter 5

Trustee duties, powers and discretions

General principles

5.1   As explained in **CHAPTER 1**, trustees must carry out all their responsibilities mindful of both the statutory law and trust law under which they operate. A certain number of general principles derive from trust law.

The Occupational Pensions Board, the governmental body responsible for supervising occupational pension schemes until 6 April 1997, issued a booklet entitled *Pension Trust Principles* for all trustees. Addressing trustees directly, *Pension Trust Principles* summarises the general duties of all trustees of occupational pension schemes in five points:

(*a*)   to act in accordance with the trust deed and rules of the scheme, within the framework of the law;

(*b*)   to act prudently, conscientiously and honestly and with the utmost good faith;

(*c*)   to act in the best interests of the beneficiaries and strike a fair balance between the interests of different classes of beneficiary;

(*d*)   to take advice on technical matters and any other matters which you do not understand; and

(*e*)   to invest the funds.

Traditionally, the responsibilities of trustees are divided into three categories: duties, powers and discretionary powers. *Duties* are usually very specific tasks which the trustee must ensure are carried out. *Powers* are rights which the trust deed and rules give to trustees. *Discretionary powers* are those powers given to trustees by the trust deed and rules which permit a choice to be made. (Note that the trust deed and rules are likely to give duties, powers and discretionary powers to the employer as well as to the trustees.)

The duties placed on the trustees by the trust deed and rules are not the only duties that trustees must carry out. Statutory duties are also placed on the trustees by the legislation, notably by the *Pensions Act 1995*.

The Occupational Pensions Regulatory Authority (Opra) has published a guide to help trustees understand their various duties and responsibilities. *A Guide for Pension Scheme Trustees* is available from Opra's helpdesk on tel. 01273 627600 (individual copies are free of charge) or from their website at http://www.opra.gov.uk/pdf/trusteeguide.pdf. Rather than summarise it here, we simply urge the reader to obtain a copy and read it directly.

It is accepted that trustees, in carrying out their duties, must exercise a proper care when investing trust funds and that the standard of care required of trustees in general has been that as first set out back in 1883 in the case of *Speight v Gaunt [1883] 9 App Cas 1*. The judge held that:

> '[A] trustee sufficiently discharges his duty if he takes in managing trust affairs all those precautions which an ordinary prudent man of business would take in managing similar affairs of his own.'

As noted at **3.4** a higher standard of care is expected from professional, paid trustees, but as a government consultation paper issued in February 2002 stated in quoting the well-known legal maxim:

> 'In contrast, unpaid, non-professional trustees are required to take such care as an ordinary prudent man would take, if he were minded to make an investment for the benefit of other people, for whom he felt morally bound to provide.'

Despite the use of terms such as 'man', 'he' and 'his', it is not the case that this standard is nowadays only expected of men and not of women.

Following the review of institutional investment carried out in 2001 by Paul Myners, this general standard of care has been challenged, at least in relation to the exercise by pension fund trustees of their duty to invest the fund. In its February 2002 paper, the Government proposed to amend the legislation so that lay pension fund trustees will be required to exercise an enhanced standard of care in carrying out their duties in relation to investment functions. Broadly, the proposed requirement is that pension fund trustees should be 'familiar with the issues concerned'. These developments are explored in more detail at **17.7**.

Main trustee duties

5.2   The five general duties identified above form the core of any trustee's duties. One further general duty often quoted is that a trustee should not profit from the assets of the fund. This does not mean of course that a trustee cannot also be a scheme member who will eventually draw a pension in the usual way. Indeed the *Pensions Act 1995* also clarified trust law by specifically authorising member trustees to exercise discretionary powers even if they may benefit as members of the scheme. Rather, the general duty not to profit from the assets of the fund means that it is absolutely forbidden for a trustee to deal in investments with the pension fund.

Other specific duties will be specified in any trust deed and rules and will usually be distinguished by the phrase *'The trustees shall … '*.

In practice, trustees can delegate many of these duties to the professional administrators employed in the pensions department, whether the administration is provided by an insurance company, or contracted out to a third party administrator, or whether it is an in-house administration team employed either by the pension fund or the company. Such duties are often simply part of the day-to-day administration and management of the occupational pension scheme. See **CHAPTER 11** for a general discussion of this topic.

The ultimate responsibility for ensuring that these duties are carried out, nevertheless, remains with the trustees.

Main trustee powers

5.3   One of the main powers given in the trust deed and rules is the power to delegate. This is vital since it is impossible for part-time lay trustees to carry out all the duties of a large, modern occupational pension scheme. A related power is the ability to employ agents to carry out these duties (e g the appointment of an investment manager to look after the funds). Other powers that may be included in the trust deed and rules include the power to open bank accounts, to borrow money, to order accounts and audits and to buy annuity contracts (contracts with insurance companies to provide members with regular pensions). This list is far from exhaustive.

Main discretionary powers

5.4   One of the advantages that supporters of trust law argue in its favour is its flexibility. A prime example is the use of discretionary powers by trustees. Certain benefits can be awarded if circumstances permit even if all those circumstances are not codified in the trust deed and rules. The exercise by trustees of their discretionary powers must be reasonable. The trustees' exercise of a discretionary power would probably be challenged if it seemed to be capricious or irrational. In short, the trustees must consider the circumstances carefully before exercising any discretionary power and in so doing bear in mind the five general principles outlined in **5.1** above.

In exercising any discretionary power, it is unlikely that the decision of the trustees would be overturned by the courts or by the Pensions Ombudsman if the trustees follow the rules (first applied in a context outside trust law) which are known as the *Wednesbury Principles*:

- The trustees must ask themselves the correct questions.

- They must direct themselves correctly in law; in particular they must adopt a correct construction of the trust deed and rules.

- They must not arrive at a perverse decision, i e a decision to which no reasonable body of trustees could arrive, and they must take into account all relevant, but no irrelevant, factors.

Powers which are discretionary in one scheme may not be so in another. Nevertheless, there are some which are almost always discretionary, such as who should receive the death-in-service lump sum.

Discretionary powers that affect all benefits rather than those of one individual will almost certainly only be exercisable with the consent of the employer – an example is the level of any discretionary pension increase.

In a very large organisation, the pension manager is likely to present the bulk of individual discretionary decisions to the trustees for their consideration with a bare minimum of detail – unless there are particular complications. In some instances, where undue delay would be caused by waiting until the next trustee meeting (such as in the payment of a death-in-service lump sum) it is the practice in many schemes for the pensions administrator to contact just two or three trustees for a decision. It is important that the trustee body as a whole has properly delegated the discretionary power to the sub-committee of trustees in such circumstances.

The major discretionary powers that trustees usually exercise without needing the specific consent of the employer are considered below.

Death-in-service lump sum

5.5   If a member dies while still in employment as an active member of the scheme most occupational pension schemes pay out a lump sum. The maximum that is allowed by the Inland Revenue for an approved scheme is four times salary (the salary is limited in some cases to the current level of the pensionable earnings cap) plus a refund of the employee's own contributions with reasonable interest. The recipient pays no income tax on the lump sum and, provided the lump sum is not paid into the deceased employee's estate, it is free of inheritance tax.

The lump sum amount that the trustees can pay is not discretionary since it is specified in the trust deed and rules. Rather, the discretionary power lies in deciding who receives the money.

The Inland Revenue says:

> 'The lump sum may be paid to the employee's legal personal representatives or a nominated beneficiary, or distributed at the discretion of the trustees/administrator: it is not necessary to limit nomination or distribution to dependants. The money may continue to be held under the rules of the pension scheme for a period not exceeding 2 years if this is necessary for the trustees/administrator to determine who is to benefit … '.

Standard practice is to encourage all employees on joining the pension scheme to complete an expression of wish declaration whereon the employee states who should receive any such lump sum. This declaration may be placed in a sealed envelope or, alternatively, confidentially recorded so that the details appear on that individual's benefit statement each year. This way the employee will be prompted to revise the declaration if circumstances have changed.

Trustees should take account of this expression of wish but are not bound by it.

The following factors may come into play:

●   The trust deed and rules may define the category of potential beneficiary more narrowly than the Inland Revenue.

- The member may inadvertently not have completed an expression of wish form, or it may be very out of date, being written, for example, before he or she was married.

- The nominee may have pre-deceased the member.

- The trustees may find it *unreasonable*. For instance, the member may have recently nominated as the beneficiary a brain-washing religious cult who advised extreme fasting and the member's spouse, having the care of their three young children, may be left in straightened circumstances, about to lose the family home.

- The member may have left the money to a proscribed military or political group.

- The member may have recently split with his partner without being divorced and moved in with a new partner. The member may have recently changed the nomination or not. Of the ex-partner and new partner, one may be rich, the other poor; one or the other or both may have care of the employee's children.

The trust deed and rules will typically allow the trustees to split any lump sum between different beneficiaries and this gives more scope in dealing with difficult decisions. It might be, for example, in the case of a split marriage, that the trustees would ensure that any children would directly benefit from the lump sum by setting up a suitable trust.

However, the trustees may find that they are bound by a court order that requires them to pay the death-in-service lump sum payment to a divorced member's former spouse – see **9.24**.

There are two further possible complications. Firstly, the member may have copied the expression of wish declaration to the beneficiary. Secondly, the *Occupational Pension Schemes (Disclosure of Information) Regulations 1996 (SI 1996/1655)* specify that where a member or a beneficiary of a scheme has died and rights or options are available to a person in consequence, the information on any survivor's rights or options must be provided automatically to that person within two months after the trustees have been notified of the death and, on request, to any personal representative of the deceased person or anyone authorised to act on behalf of the survivor within two months of the request. (Note, however, that any person may be limited to making one request only during a three-year period.)

There are those who argue that not to act according to the member's wishes because the trustees think it unreasonable smacks of paternalism. Others see a way out if inheritance tax were ever to cease to be relevant to most estates and in such conditions, as a change in practice, they urge that the sum should be paid to the member's estate so that it is disposed of in accordance with the member's will – if there is a will!

In many large schemes, the exercise of this particular power of discretion may be taken by trustees in local management committees. Some feel this is better because they are closer to the people concerned. Others might feel this is precisely the wrong approach and members would be happier if they knew the decision would be taken by those who were more remote and so less likely to be prejudiced.

When trustees have taken a decision, the facts and the decision itself should be clearly minuted. It should be clear that the trustees considered their decision properly but the reasoning that led to the decision should not be recorded in the minutes. The theory is that the Pensions Ombudsman or the courts will not reverse an exercise of discretion unless it can be shown that it was taken in error or through prejudice. In other words, the trustees' decision should abide by the *Wednesbury Principles* set out at **5.4** above. The issue of how the trustees' decision should be recorded in the minutes of the trustees' meeting, and in what situations the minutes of this meeting should be disclosed to interested parties, the court or to the Pensions Ombudsman, are both examined at **18.5**.

Other lump sum payments

5.6   In many schemes, lump sum payments are also made in the case of early leavers who die before drawing their deferred pension and in the case of pensioners who die within the first five years of retirement. Many of the remarks made above for death-in-service pensions will apply in these cases.

Survivors' pensions

5.7   The trust deed and rules may give the trustees some discretionary powers in respect of pensions to widows, widowers and dependants. Some scheme rules stipulate that only widows' and widowers' pensions are provided. Others will give the trustees discretion to pay pensions to other dependants.

Statutory law imposes certain markers:

(*a*)   if the member had entitlement under the scheme to a guaranteed minimum pension (GMP), the scheme must pay a widow's or widower's GMP (WGMP) to the widow or widower for any period during which a category B retirement pension, or a widowed mother's allowance, widowed parent's allowance, widow's pension or bereavement allowance is payable to the member by the state (see **APPENDIX 5**). If the widow or widower stopped being entitled to widowed parent's allowance or bereavement allowance from the state when aged over 45, the occupational pension scheme must nevertheless continue to pay a WGMP. However, WGMPs do not have to be paid under the legislation if the recipient is under state pension age and cohabiting with a person of the opposite sex (in which case the WGMP could be suspended) or has remarried (in which case it could be ended altogether). The scheme rules may, however, be more generous. Note that in the case of a widower a WGMP is payable only in relation to pensionable service since April 1988. The term legal widow or widower means the person to whom the member was married at the time of death, but this includes partners in a *marriage by habit and repute* in Scotland. Similar requirements apply under the contracting-out legislation to protected rights pensions and the rights payable to a widow or widower under a scheme contracted out by the reference scheme test after 5 April 1997. Note that a divorced person under the law does not become a widow or widower of their former spouse upon that person's death.

(b)   The total amount of all survivors' pensions is limited by Inland Revenue rules.

(c)   A survivor's pension may be paid to a dependant and this term may be defined in the scheme's trust deed and rules but, if the scheme is exempt approved, it cannot be used in a wider sense than as defined by the Inland Revenue. In June 1996, the Revenue revised its definition of 'dependant' as follows:

> 'Dependant means a person who is financially dependent on the employee or dependent on the employee because of disability or who was so dependent at the time of the employee's death or retirement. An ex-spouse of the employee who was in receipt of payments from the employee up to his or her death in respect of, for example, a financial provision order under the *Matrimonial Causes Act 1973* may be regarded as financially dependent on the employee.

> An adult relative who is or was not supported by that employee is not that employee's dependant. Subject to the following paragraphs a pension paid to an adult dependant who qualifies on grounds of financial dependency or disability may continue indefinitely.

> Natural or adopted children of the employee may automatically be regarded as dependent on the employee if at the time of his or her death they were:

> (i)   under 18;

> (ii) over 18 but continuing to receive full-time education or vocational training;

> (iii) dependent on the employee because of disability.

> Any pensions paid by reason of (i) or (ii) should cease when age 18 is reached or full-time education or vocational training ceases* whichever is later. A pension paid by reason of (iii) may continue indefinitely.

> Other children (i e neither natural nor adopted children of the employee) may qualify as dependants only if they were financially dependent on the employee, or dependent on the employee by reason of disability. Any pensions paid to such children on grounds of financial dependence should cease when age 18 is reached or full-time education or vocational training ceases* whichever is the later. This ensures parity of treatment between offspring and other minor dependants. A pension paid because of dependency by reason of disability may continue indefinitely.

It is not necessary to show financial dependency for a person dependent on the employee because of disability or in the case of widows or widowers. The latter automatically qualify for survivors' benefits on the basis that partners in a legal marriage may always be assumed to be financially dependent on one another. But an unmarried partner, whether of the same or opposite sex, can qualify for a survivors' pension only if he or she were financially dependent on the employee. Financial interdependence of the employee and his or her partner would be an acceptable criterion, e g where the partner relied upon a second income to maintain a standard of living which had depended on joint income prior to the employee's death.

Decisions on whether or not a person is a dependant are a matter for the scheme trustees. The [Inland Revenue] would not challenge the trustees' judgment provided they had acted in accordance with the scheme rules.

* A break of not more than an academic year between leaving school and taking up a confirmed place in full-time education or vocational training will not be regarded as a cessation for this purpose, but it is for the trustees to decide whether the pension should be paid during the break.'

(The 1996 definition remains in place but was revised after the pensions sharing on divorce measures were introduced on 1 December 2000, so that references to a dependant of the employee would also include a dependant of the 'ex-spouse', i e a person who has received a pension credit under the scheme as a result of a pension sharing order.)

Within these constraints, and acting in accordance with the trust deed and rules, trustees might therefore use their discretion to:

- pay part of the survivor's pension to a former spouse and part to the spouse at the date of the member's death. However, the need for the use of trustee discretion in the matter of pensions and divorce may be circumscribed by mandatory court orders earmarking pension rights and, from 1 December 2000, by the sharing out of pension rights between the divorcing parties by the courts at the time of divorce itself – see **9.24**. However, the use of trustee discretion in cases where there has been no marriage, and so no divorce, may remain. For example, the trustees may discover that an unmarried member had a relationship with two partners and had recently parented a child in each family unit. The trustees might decide, if permitted by their trust deed and rules, to split the survivor's pension equally between the two partners.

- pay a dependant's pension to a gay or lesbian partner, elderly parent or disabled friend provided that the Inland Revenue would accept that the person and the member have been financially interdependent.

Trustees who have such discretionary powers will need a substantial amount of detailed information on the circumstances of both the deceased scheme member and the survivor.

Ill-health pensions

5.8   Perhaps one of the most tricky decisions for trustees in the use of their discretionary powers can be whether or not to award a member an enhanced early retirement pension on the grounds of ill-health. The decision may be at the discretion of the trustees but inevitably takes place within an employment context. It may be that the employer wishes to secure the early departure of an employee and has 'promised' an ill-health early retirement pension as a way of avoiding an unfair dismissal claim. However, such considerations cannot be allowed to bind the trustees in how they decide to use their discretion since they have a responsibility to safeguard the fund from improper use in the wider interest of all the members. On the other hand, the employee may have been dismissed and awarded only a deferred pension and it is not apparent that the trustees ought to have considered an enhanced early retirement pension on the grounds of ill-health. This is especially the case where it only becomes apparent later that the employee had been suffering from an undiagnosed illness which had in fact been the cause of the employee being unable to carry out his or her job. In such cases, the trustees may well consider they can revisit their earlier decision.

This last point does not conflict with the principle that has been reasonably clear since the Court of Appeal judgment in the case of *Re McClorry* (1998, unreported). This is that the date at which an employee ceases to be employed is the date at which the test of incapacity set by the scheme's trust documentation must be applied.

There are important guidelines for trustees in considering whether or not to grant ill-health pensions:

- the trustees should obtain medical information from the employee and the employer, and where they consider it necessary, from an independent source;

- the trustees should consider and follow the requirements of the trust deed and rules – in many cases the rules will specify that members may receive a higher benefit if they are totally unable to perform any work and a lower benefit if they are prevented by illness from performing their own job but capable of working in another job;

- the trustees should try to set consistent standards and treat the claim fairly;

- the trustees should ignore the industrial relations context;

- if the trustees decide that an enhanced early retirement pension on the grounds of ill-health should be payable, the trustees should consider whether they ought to obtain periodic medical reports on the member's health (at least until the member reaches the normal pension age for the scheme) to ensure that pension funds are not being misappropriated – the scheme auditors may be consulted on the best method. The trustees would not want to be heavy-handed in carrying out this duty and so cause a genuinely sick member any anxiety. It may be that a pensioner welfare service is available to assist.

One particular case decided by the Court of Appeal that may be of use to trustees who are having to decide whether an ill-health early retirement pension may be payable is that of *Harris v Lord Shuttleworth [1995] OPLR 79.* Here the Court of Appeal decided that the phrase 'retirement from the service by reason of incapacity' meant that the member had left the employer's service at some date before reaching normal pension age by reason of some physical or mental disability or ill-health so serious that, at the time of leaving service, it was probable that the member would be unable by reason of disability to follow his or her present or similar employment with the employer or any other employer during any part of the period before reaching normal pension age.

It should, however, always be remembered that any court decision will normally depend on the specific circumstances of that case and in particular what the scheme's own trust deed and rules require.

Late joiners

5.9   If an employee declines to join the pension scheme on first becoming eligible to do so, or if an existing member decides to opt out, the trustees will often have discretion over whether that employee, having changed his or her mind, may later join the scheme. The trust deed and rules may lay down certain conditions that have to be met, such as a satisfactory medical examination, but in many cases the final decision will rest with the trustees. This issue has in the recent past taken on importance in view of guidance from the former Securities and Investments Board (now the Financial Services Authority). This guidance recommended that those who had been mis-sold personal pensions rather than joining or maintaining their membership of occupational pension schemes should ideally, at least if they were still employees of an employer who participated in the scheme, be allowed to join or rejoin the pension scheme both for future and past service upon payment of a suitable transfer value.

New statutory powers and duties

5.10   The *Pensions Act 1995* sets out a large number of new statutory powers and duties that complement pre-existing powers and duties made under earlier legislation or other quasi-statutory powers and duties imposed by authorities such as the Inland Revenue. These powers and duties are explained at the appropriate point in this Handbook.

Checklist 5

- Traditionally, trustees have five main duties:
    - to act in accordance with the trust deed and rules, within the framework of the law;
    - to act prudently, conscientiously and honestly and with the utmost good faith;

- – to act in the interests of the beneficiaries and strike a fair balance between the interests of different classes of beneficiary;

- – to take advice; and

- – to invest the funds.

- The standard of care required by a lay trustee has been that of the 'ordinary prudent man or woman of business' but an enhanced standard is now proposed in relation to investment issues which would require 'familiarity with the issues concerned'.

- Trustees have various powers given to them by the trust deed and rules, including the power to delegate.

- Trustees have discretionary powers given them by the trust deed and rules, some of which must be exercised only with the agreement of the employer and some of which should be exercised by the trustees acting on their own.

- The use of the trustees of their discretionary powers will not normally be questioned by the courts or by the Pensions Ombudsman provided the trustees have:

  - – asked themselves the correct questions;

  - – directed themselves correctly in law, in particular by adopting a correct construction of the trust deed and rules; and

  - – not arrived at a perverse decision (i e one at which no reasonable body of trustees could arrive) and have taken into account all relevant, but no irrelevant, factors.

Chapter 6

Trust deed and rules

Overview

6.1   For all practical purposes, an occupational pension scheme set up under a trust arrangement must operate under a signed and delivered document called the *trust deed*. The actual rules of the scheme are usually set out in a schedule or in an attached document.

Often in the past, in order to set up an occupational pension scheme quickly, a short *interim deed* usually established the scheme. An interim deed contains the basic material needed to operate the scheme as a trust and so could act as a sufficient legal basis for the Inland Revenue to grant tax relief on a temporary basis. Confirmation of the tax relief then had to wait until the definitive trust deed and rules were signed and delivered. It is important to note that a definitive deed cannot make fundamental changes to the interim deed.

If after a period of two years the interim deed had not been replaced by a definitive trust deed, the Inland Revenue could demand that all the tax reliefs granted on a provisional basis should be repaid.

However, since 6 April 2002, this interim authorisation procedure has been withdrawn except for new schemes set up as a result of a *corporate reorganisation* – i e where:

●   the new scheme is set up to receive a bulk transfer from another pension schemes of funds and/or employees; and

●   the bulk transfer has been brought about by a change, or intended change of:

–   ownership of an employer; or

–   ownership of all or part of an employer's trade or business.

Unless these conditions are met, applications for the tax approval of an occupational pension scheme from 6 April 2002 can no longer be made if that scheme's definitive documentation is not yet operative.

The employer, the trustees and the Inland Revenue are all involved in the approval process.

National Insurance contributions are levied on employer contributions paid to any pension scheme which has not received tax approval from the Inland Revenue. An exception to this rule has been made for certain schemes provided that an application for approval has been made to the Inland Revenue and that this application has not been rejected. A valid application for approval for a scheme set up under interim documentation, where this is still permitted by the Inland Revenue, can count for this purpose. The rules of the scheme concerned, however, must also satisfy certain other conditions. If these conditions are not met, National Insurance contributions must be paid on any employer contributions paid to the scheme. If the scheme is subsequently approved, any National Insurance contributions paid by employer and employees can be recouped.

Trust deeds vary enormously from one scheme to another and some prove defective when it comes to important changes, such as on a takeover of the sponsoring company. In recent times there were calls for legislation that would impose a basic standard trust deed and rules with optional variations. Others (especially solicitors) argued that the necessary degree of flexibility required to suit the needs of different companies and different workforces could only be delivered by a tailor-made trust deed and rules.

Announcement, undertakings and overriding legislation

6.2   The trustees or the employer may have made formal announcements to the members which describe changes to contribution levels and benefits. However, the formal trust deed and rules may not have been amended to reflect these changes. Such formal announcements remain valid and are binding on the trustees so new trustees reading the trust deed and rules should ensure that any formal announcements to members have also been appended.

When Parliament creates pensions law, the new measures may need to be incorporated into each trust deed and rules before they become operative or they may be *overriding*. The operation of overriding legislation means that the new measures must be applied even if the existing trust deed and rules make no equivalent measure or even contradict it. Most new legislation is not incorporated into the trust deed and rules and so a reading of the latter will not give a complete picture.

The Pension Law Review Committee set up under Professor Goode recognised that this was a problem. However complicated the definitive trust deed and rules are to read, they at least ought to be the final word. The Committee urged that scheme authorities should be encouraged to consolidate their trust deeds and rules at least every five years. The Government accepted the recommendation but said that this was a measure to be dealt with by best practice and not by legislation.

A recent example of the effect of new legislation on the trust deed and rules is given by the pension sharing on divorce requirements brought in by the *Finance Act 1999*. In this example, if a new scheme had not gained Inland Revenue approval by 10 May 2000, the new pension sharing provisions must be included in trust deed and rules. Even if an application for approval had been made before that date, the trust deed and rules would have had to be resubmitted with the new pension sharing provisions included. On the other hand for all schemes already approved before 10 May 2000, and which continued to be approved on and after 1 December 2000, when the pension sharing provisions actually came into force, these provisions will be applied by statutory override. Yet the Inland Revenue makes it clear that pension schemes are not expected to rely on overriding provisions indefinitely. In this case, the trustees should ensure that the pension sharing provisions are incorporated into the trust deed and rules at the earliest 'convenient opportunity' – this is defined as the next occasion on or after 1 December 2000 when the trust deed and rules are being amended other than in a trivial way.

Power of amendment

6.3 The clause usually seen as the most important clause in the trust deed and rules is the *power of amendment clause*. It is usually very widely drawn because it is virtually impossible to amend an amending clause. Indeed, the amending clause in the definitive deed must be the same as in any interim deed. It is usually possible to use the power of amendment to amend a trust deed and rules retrospectively. Nevertheless, any amendment will ordinarily require the consent of the trustees who cannot abandon their fiduciary duty to protect the interests of the beneficiaries.

Section 67 of the *Pensions Act 1995* introduced new overriding legislation from 6 April 1997. This states that any power to modify a pension scheme cannot be exercised in a manner which would reduce any existing entitlements or accrued rights to pension of any member unless the trustees themselves have approved of the modification and the consent of each individual member has been obtained for the reduction in his or her accrued rights. Indeed, no modification of the pension scheme is allowed at all until the trustees are satisfied, after taking professional actuarial advice, that the modification would not reduce any existing entitlement or accrued rights or, if it would do so, that the members have given their consent.

Ordinarily a term such as *accrued rights* does not refer to future pension rights that the members would accrue if they continued in membership and the rules of the scheme were unchanged.

Alan Pickering in his July 2002 review argued that *section 67*, as currently constructed, prevented many wholly proper amendments which were justifiable in terms of members' interests and which were essential to enable a scheme to adapt to changing circumstances. He argued that its current requirements should be replaced by an *equivalence value* test which would enable trustees and employers to change members' past service rights without their consent so long as the overall value of the replacement benefits are expected, but are not guaranteed, to be equivalent in value.

In its December 2002 Green Paper and accompanying technical paper, the Government argued that such a proposal went too far because it would permit employers and trustees to change fundamentally the terms of the pension scheme in respect of a member's past service. The Government offered further to clarify the wording of *section 67* and allow changes to be made provided that the actuarial value of the change did not exceed, say, 5% of any member's total accrued rights and also that the rights foregone were replaced with other rights of an actuarially equivalent value.

It should be noted that, unless the proposed legislation is overriding, a scheme's existing power of amendment clause might still prevent such *de minimis* changes to members' accrued rights.

The *Pension Schemes Act 1993* and the *Pensions Act 1995* give trustees the power to modify the trust deed and rules to achieve any of a specified list of purposes. Most of the purposes are to allow the trustees to modify their schemes so that they comply with various legislative requirements.

The Occupational Pensions Regulatory Authority (Opra), like its predecessor the Occupational Pensions Board (OPB), has direct power to modify the trust deed and rules of an occupational pension scheme for specific purposes set out in the legislation. In some cases, the trustees could approach the court to see if they can be granted authority to amend the trust deed and rules, and in some cases the court itself can directly amend the trust deed and rules.

Checklist 6

- As a trustee of an occupational pension scheme that is *exempt approved* by the Inland Revenue you should understand the very significant tax advantages that arise from this tax status and should ensure that no action is taken which might endanger those privileges.

- The trustees must observe the trust deed and rules.

- A trust deed and rules can be overridden by Acts of Parliament, and sometimes by announcements that have been made in the name of the trustees to the members – all of which the trustees must take into account when reading their trust deed and rules.

- The trustees should periodically ensure that their trust deed and rules are consolidated and brought up to date.

- It is virtually impossible to amend the power of amendment clause but, provided the terms of the power of amendment clause are respected, the trust deed and rules can be amended.

- *Section 67* of the *Pensions Act 1995* prevents scheme amendments that result in the retrospective worsening of an individual's already accrued pension rights, and a similar provision is often made by the trust documentation of individual schemes.

- Opra, the courts and the *Pensions Acts* can help trustees to amend their trust deed and rules for specified purposes if the power of amendment clause does not give them the ability to do so. The courts

---

can give the trustees authority to make an amendment if the trustees have any doubts about whether they have a right to do so.

- Any amendment to the trust deed and rules must not diminish the rights that members have already accrued by virtue of pensionable service before the date of amendment.

Chapter 7

Pensions in the context of industrial relations

View that trustees cannot negotiate

7.1   The following advice is crystal clear:

> 'As a trustee you are not a representative of the group or interest from which you are drawn: your duty is to serve all the different classes of beneficiary impartially. Nor, by the same token, are you a negotiator. There may well be negotiations on pension benefits between representatives of the employer and the workforce, but the trustees' meeting is not the arena for these.'

Source: former Occupational Pensions Board publication *Pension Trust Principles*.

For those who are trustees, their only responsibility, at least while they are wearing their trustee hats in a trustee meeting, is to ensure that the obligations imposed by the trust deed and rules and any overriding legislation are met.

Member trustees nominated through a process involving a recognised trade union sometimes feel frustrated by the fact that they should not normally seek improvements in benefit provision in trustee meetings.

Member trustees might try to table an agenda item asking, for example, that pensionable pay be based on all earnings rather than just earnings above the current National Insurance lower earnings limit. The trustee chairing the meeting may refuse the item properly pointing out that the trustee meeting is not a negotiating forum. Subsequently, the company may inform the trustees that, owing to a favourable actuarial report and valuation (nowadays a much rarer occurrence than in the past), it wants to bring in this particular improvement, especially as the improvement disproportionately benefits lower paid members. The trustees would almost certainly agree to the proposed rule change provided they felt that other classes of beneficiaries would not be disadvantaged, for example if the current pensioners were granted a reasonable annual increase. However, to the member trustees it would appear that the issue does not appear on the agenda if they propose it, but does appear if the company proposes it.

Nevertheless, the trust deed and rules may give trustees some discretionary powers which they can exercise with the consent of the employer. An example might be the level of increase granted to pensions in payment. Clearly, in such circumstances the trustees will be operating within the terms of the trust deed and rules if they approach the employer to suggest a figure.

It is recognised that pensions are subject to negotiations in an industrial relations context. And, indeed, advice from the former Occupational Pensions Board on the ways it would assist a scheme to modify its trust deed and rules so that a payment of a pension fund surplus may be taken by the employer (see **CHAPTER 19**) implied that pension negotiations would have taken place beforehand.

It is also clear from recent court cases that in certain circumstances it is correct for the trustees to negotiate with the sponsoring employer. For example, Justice Knox in the case of *Hillsdown Holdings v Pensions Ombudsman [1997] 1 All ER 862, [1996] OPLR 291* reports the opinion of another judge, Justice Millet who:

' … contemplates as perfectly proper a process of bargaining between trustees of a pension fund and the employer in the context of a desire by an employer to obtain payment of at least part of a surplus and a desire by the trustees to secure increased benefits for their members.'

The reference to Justice Millet in fact comes from the well-known case of *Re Courage's Group Pension Schemes [1987] 1 All ER 528* in which he said that:

'Where the employer seeks repayment, the trustees … can be expected to press for generous treatment of employees and pensioners and the employer to be influenced by the desire to maintain good industrial relations with its workforce.'

In these kinds of cases, it is perfectly proper for the trustees to negotiate with the employer but the acid test, as Justice Knox points out in the *Hillsdown* case, is that both the trustees and the employer should both have a legitimate interest to preserve, and here 'legitimate interest' means acting in accordance with the trust deed and rules. The trustees should not through negotiation consent to any course of action which is specifically forbidden by the trust deed and rules.

The kind of negotiation between trustees and the employer which the courts have noted with approval is a bargaining situation where each side has something to give or withhold by way of necessary consent and there is no absolute bar on what is sought to be achieved, e g a change in the trust deed and rules that can be made using the power of amendment clause.

The trustees must always act in the best interests of the members but it is acknowledged that those best interests are likely to be well served by consultation with the employer, with a view to ensuring that pension fund trustees take a decision which fits in, so far as practicable and permissible, with an employer's business strategy.

Although the use of surpluses has in the past usually been at the centre of such trustee/employer consultation, it may be that investment strategies will also become an important item on the agenda in discussions between the employer and the trustees. As explained at **16.6** and **16.8**, since the coming into force of the *Pensions Act 1995*, the trustees have absolute responsibility for the investment strategy, as set out in the scheme's Statement of Investment Principles. The employer is not allowed to have any reserve powers to veto the trustees' approach but the trustees must consult the employer. Clearly this makes sense for the trustees of a defined benefit scheme where the employer bears the investment risk. It would be counterproductive for the trustees to set out on an investment strategy that implied a rate of funding which the employer was either unwilling or unable to support.

The point also to bear in mind is that in these situations the trustees, as a whole, are negotiating with the employer: the bargaining forum is not a trustee meeting but a meeting between the trustees and the employer. At a trustee meeting, there can be no bargaining because, quite simply, the employer is not present.

The case of *South West Trains v Wightman [1997] OPLR 249* heard by Justice Neuberger in December 1997 is of particular interest because it looks at whether a collective agreement negotiated between an employer and a trade union can affect the terms of a pension scheme's trust deed and rules. Justice Neuberger held that all the aspects of a restructuring proposal that had been satisfactorily negotiated in an industrial relations joint working group and had been agreed by the employer and the trade union, including some re-negotiated pension rights, acted to bind the employer and the employees concerned contractually on an individual basis.

One group of employees had argued that the provisions of the scheme's trust deed and rules would provide them with more favourable benefits and objected to a proposed amendment to the scheme which would take in the changes that had been negotiated. However, because of the contractual agreement, Justice Neuberger held that it was arguable that the trustee of the pension scheme concerned could in any case refuse to pay the employees concerned a pension at a higher rate than that agreed with the employer. However, the correctness of the arguments put forward did not have to be decided in this case because Justice Neuberger had already held that the employer could enforce the binding pensions agreement by restraining any employee claiming a pension on a more generous basis than that agreed under the binding agreement.

In general, however, it would seem a good idea to make sure that the trust deed and rules are properly amended before a change is implemented. Furthermore, it should be noted that *section 67* of the *Pensions Act 1995* prevents changes that reduce a member's already accrued rights unless each member potentially affected consents to the change (see **6.3** above).

Many pension lawyers share the opinion that there is in fact a contractual relationship between the employer and the trustees which the trustees can, and probably should, enforce if the employer fails to comply with the terms of the trust. Speaking at the 2001 conference of the Association of Pension Lawyers, Duncan Buchanan pointed out that deeds of adherence admitting new employers as participating employers in an occupational pension scheme often contain an express covenant that the employer will comply with the terms and conditions of the scheme. He said:

'Of course, in practice it is rare that the trustees need to enforce these contractual provisions because the employer complies with the terms and conditions of the scheme. That said, I believe that there is a clear contractual relationship between the employer and trustees.'

In June 2001, the Central Arbitration Committee (CAC) delivered its decision in the case of *UNIFI v Union Bank of Nigeria [2001] IRLR 712, [2001] PLR 239.* The issue to be decided was whether negotiation on matters relating to pensions came under the ambit of 'pay' in the sense in which that word is used in the Schedule and Model Method set out in the *Trade Union Recognition (Method of Collective Bargaining) Order 2000 (SI 2000/1300).* The decision of the CAC also contains a very useful summary of the wider issue of whether pension rights are generally included as part of an employee's 'pay' outside the area of equal treatment, where it is already clearly established that pensions represent 'deferred pay'.

The CAC's deliberations acknowledged that, after the judgment of the Privy Council in the case of *Air Jamaica Ltd v Charlton [1999] OPLR 11, [1999] PLR 247,* it is now generally accepted that the rights of employees in relation to their membership of an occupational pension scheme derive from their contracts of employment and 'are not inappropriately described as "deferred pay"'. The particular details of this case concerned the employer's contributions to a money purchase arrangement and the CAC concluded on the facts that the obligation on the Bank of Nigeria to negotiate with UNIFI on 'pay' included all matters relating to the levels or amount of employer's pension contributions.

The CAC also distinguished the issues of whether employer contributions to a defined contribution arrangement and to a defined benefit scheme are both 'pay'. The implication of the CAC's decision is that in general employer contributions to a defined contribution arrangement are 'pay', but in the case of a defined benefit scheme it is the benefit payable, rather than the employer's contributions, which can be considered 'pay'. The CAC stated:

'Having considered the relevant authorities and sought to establish whether guidance can be obtained from the Parliamentary debate, we next consider what assistance can be gained by bringing to bear our industrial relations experience on whether pay includes any, and if so which aspects, of the term 'pensions' in the collective bargaining context and any relevant case law. Our conclusion is that employer pension contributions (in a defined contribution scheme) and the benefits payable (in a defined benefit scheme) are now seen as an integral and important part of a worker's pay and the two aspects of a worker's financial reward for his or her services are intertwined.'

Pension negotiations

7.2   Although the ownership of the pension fund and, specifically (at least theoretically), of surpluses that arise in the fund, can be a matter of dispute, it is much more generally accepted that the eventual pension itself can be seen as a form of *deferred pay* for the employee. Such conclusions can be drawn from judgments of the European Court of Justice.

If pensions are part of the overall remuneration package offered by an employer to employees, then it is clear that individual employees, staff associations and trade unions will seek to negotiate with the employer over pensions.

Pensions can have effects on pay negotiations. In the mid-1980s one company found it had a surplus in the pension fund and a temporary cut in the employee pension contribution level was negotiated. After the ending of the employee contribution holiday, it proved very difficult to restore employee contributions to their original level. Especially resistant were young employees who had joined the company during the contribution holiday. The matter was resolved by restoring the contribution levels at the same time as granting a slightly higher than expected pay increase.

Similarly, a company, finding that the pension fund was enjoying a surplus, while it, itself, needed to control costs, succeeded in negotiating a lower pay-round increase with its employees by simultaneously agreeing that the pension scheme would become non-contributory.

The greater general awareness of pensions issues among employees and the general public in recent years encouraged many trade unions during the 1980s until the late 1990s to seek benefit improvements in their members' pension schemes. The process had also been helped by the codification by the Inland Revenue of how pension fund surpluses should be reduced – see **19.1**. In many ways, the Chancellor of the Exchequer in the *Finance Act 1986* placed pension fund surpluses on negotiating tables across the land.

Similarly, the ending of the ability of employers to make membership of the pension scheme a condition of employment, the measures introduced during the 1980s on disclosure of information and the encouragement of membership of personal pensions – all measures introduced by the Government of the day as part of its pension reform programme – led to greater emphasis on improved pension communications.

Employers and trade unions were drawn into alliances to protect occupational pension schemes. One result was that pensions moved up the negotiating agenda.

By 2003, pension negotiations once again have risen to near the top of the negotiating agenda between employers and organised labour, with the trustees often sitting uncomfortably in the middle. By now, however, the cause is not how to divide up a surplus, but how to proceed when falling stockmarkets, greater pensioner longevity and the prospect of only moderate, single-digit investment returns in future have together revealed a large deficit in many formerly well-funded schemes.

Many final salary schemes have been closed to new entrants. In many cases trade unions and other forms of staff representative bodies have been unable to prevent this from happening, mainly because employees who were existing members of the scheme were not threatened.

In other cases, employers have approached the membership, via their representatives, to seek ways of reducing pension costs relating to existing members. Such proposals have included moving for future service from a 1/60th to a 1/80th accrual rate, removing enhanced early retirement provisions and often also increasing the employee contribution rate. It must be said that any plan to resist such proposals by the trade unions is likely to be hindered if in early years the final salary scheme has been closed to new entrants, who have themselves been offered cheaper alternative provision. The new entrants would wonder why they are being asked to contemplate industrial action to support their fellow workers in the more generous scheme when they themselves have already been denied that provision with the passive acceptance of the trade unions.

Some of those in the personnel and human resources field are also becoming concerned about the longer term implications of different pension arrangements depending on the date an employee joins the company. One can have two colleagues with the same experience and responsibilities who joined the employer within a week of each other. Yet one will be building up a defined benefit in a 1/60th final salary scheme; the other may be in a defined contribution scheme receiving a 5% employer contribution. After a few years, the cost of the two remuneration packages, all else being equal, will differ markedly and this can cause resentment.

It should be noted, however, that by the summer of 2002, some employers had proposed closing final salary schemes for all further accrual. In one notable case, Caparo Industries, this provoked industrial action and the withdrawal of that proposal.

Relationship between trustees and negotiators

7.3   Although the trustees will not negotiate on pensions in meetings of the trustee body, it is quite likely that as individuals they will be involved in the negotiations either directly or indirectly.

When the negotiations are concluded, the employer will invite the trustees to agree any necessary changes to the trust deed and rules. Normally, this should not present any problems since it is unlikely that the package negotiated will involve any diminution in benefits for any scheme members.

However, the trustees might want to consider that they are still acting in the interests of *all* beneficiaries. For example, if a pension fund surplus has been completely used to grant the employer a contribution holiday and to improve the accrual rate for all current members, the trustees might have a problem since existing and deferred pensioners would have been excluded from the benefit improvements. (It should be noted in this respect that the *Pensions Act 1995* has made annual pension increases up to a cap of 5% in any one year a compulsory minimum provision on all pension rights accrued after 5 April 1997. It was already a legislative requirement that if a payment out of surplus is being made to the employer all pension rights have to increase in line with this limited price indexation formula.)

In February 1999, the Pensions Ombudsman criticised the corporate trustee of one scheme for leaving benefit improvements to negotiations between the employer and the trade unions. The Pensions Ombudsman held that the trustee had failed in its fiduciary duty to the beneficiaries by not considering making recommendations in respect of the disposal of a surplus – particularly in respect of those members whose interests may not be properly considered in the collective bargaining process. The language was precise. The trustee did *not* have a duty to make recommendations: rather it had a duty to *consider* making recommendations for benefit improvements.

Pensions and contractual obligations to members

7.4   The case of *South West Trains v Wightman [1997] OPLR 249* (discussed at **7.1**) shows that there can be a complex interaction between, on the one hand, the employment rights of an employee as set out in the employee's contract of employment, and, on the other hand, the provisions of the pension scheme's trust deed and rules. The case of *Trustees of the NUS Officials and Employees Superannuation Fund v Pensions Ombudsman [2001] All ER (D) 439 (Oct)* concerned the treatment of an element of the remuneration of one employee. The employee had been offered an increase in salary by his employer, but on condition that the increase would not count as pensionable earnings. The rules of the member's pension scheme, however, in effect provided that salary increases were pensionable. The employee had raised an objection to this condition at the time the offer was made, although he had accepted the increased salary.

In the High Court, Justice Lightman held that the employer had offered a non-pensionable increase and that, in accepting the increase, the employee had also accepted that the increase was non-pensionable. It was, said the judge, not open to the employee to accept one element of the employer's offer but not the other. Although not stated explicitly, the result of the judgment seems to confirm the judgment in *South West Trains v Wightman* that the terms of the employee's contract, provided it is clear that they have been accepted by both parties, can override the provisions of the trust deed and rules.

More generally, consideration in recent times has turned to the question of whether employees may, in particular circumstances, have a contractual right to continue to accrue pension rights while employed under the terms of their employment contract. Would it breach the terms of employees' contracts of employment if, say, the employer closed an occupational pension scheme so that existing employees ceased to build up pensionable service under the scheme from a specified date?

Alternatively, could there be circumstances where, say, the employer closes a defined benefit scheme for future service for all employees but offers them instead membership of a defined contribution scheme, with the result that the employees could successfully claim a breach of their employment contract because they were being offered inferior benefits?

The decisions are much discussed at the time of writing. In any particular case, of course, the outcome will depend not only on the actual terms of the employment contract itself but also on the terms of any other statements that have been made by the employer to the employees concerned. The outcome will also depend on whether the employees concerned can be seen to have accepted or rejected the variation in the terms of their employment contract.

However, this is a question of employment law that centres on the employer and the employees as the two parties involved. It might be thought that the trustees themselves might not be directly involved although, of course, the resolution of any such employment law question would be of significant importance to the trustees concerned.

It may also be the case, as pointed out by Duncan Buchanan at the Association of Pension Lawyers 2001 annual conference, that contractual rights may exist between the scheme members and the trustees. Such contractual rights are distinct from the fiduciary rights that members can enforce against the trustees and which arise from the terms of the trust deed and rules.

An example is contained in the case of *Nicol & Andrew v Brinkley [1996] OPLR 361* where, following the sale of a business between two employers, an employee was offered, in return for transferring his accrued pensionable service to a new scheme established by his new employer, a transfer credit of seven years' pensionable service. However, various errors meant that the transfer credit had been too low and the trustees of the scheme tried to rectify matters by reducing the service credits. In giving judgment, Sir John Vinelott held that the offer of the service credit of seven years, which had been accepted by the member, had clearly given rise to a contract and that it was absurd to suppose that the terms of that contract could now be altered.

Checklist 7

- It is accepted that those serving as a scheme's trustees, while acting in the capacity of trustees, do not generally seek to negotiate on pension provision with the employer.

- A trustee meeting, where only the trustees, their secretary and advisers are present, is not a negotiating forum between the employer and trade unions.

- In the exercise of those discretionary powers where the trustees must seek the agreement of the employer, the trustees would not normally be seen as negotiating with the employer.

- There are, however, circumstances where the trustees would be expected by the courts to negotiate with the employer, such as when the employer seeks to persuade the trustees to take a course of action which is not forbidden by the trust deed and rules.

- In many organisations, trade unions or staff representatives negotiate on pension provision with the employer and it has now long been recognised that pensions are a form of deferred pay.

- The decision of the Central Arbitration Committee in the case of *UNIFI v Union Bank of Nigeria* has clarified the question of whether negotiation between an employer and employee representatives on matters relating to pensions come under the ambit of 'pay' in the sense in which that word is used in the Schedule and Model Method set out in the *Trade Union Recognition (Method of Collective Bargaining) Order 2000*.

- If the employer and trade unions have negotiated changes to the pension scheme rules, the trustees will normally accept the changes to the trust deed and rules provided no class of beneficiary has been disadvantaged by the changes.

- It might be the case that employees already in membership of an occupational pension scheme could have a contractual right to accrue future pensionable service under the terms of the contract of employment.

- Contractual obligations can arise between the trustees and the employer, and between the trustees and the members, that are distinct from the fiduciary relationship that arises under trust law.

Chapter 8

Trustees and the employer

The employer as settlor of the trust

8.1   The person who creates the trust is known as the *settlor* of the trust and in the case of most occupational pension schemes this will be the employer.

In the report issued by the Occupational Pensions Board way back in 1982, the view of the Board members was that:

> 'The concepts developed in trust law become rather strained when applied to a modern pension scheme. Under trust law the employer is considered to be the "settlor" who endows the trust from which the members or "beneficiaries" draw their pensions, overlooking the fact that the members as well as the employer often contribute to the scheme and the employer's contributions can scarcely be considered as an act of unilateral benevolence.
>
> Trust laws seem to pre-suppose that the two interests (of the settlor and the beneficiaries) will be co-incident but in pension schemes there is a potential source of conflict between the interests of employer and the interests of members.'

The law of trusts has in the past developed in the context of ordinary family trusts where the settlor does not have a continuing financial interest in the trust: this is not the situation with an employer and an occupational pension scheme.

The employer is not only the settlor of the trust, but also a potential beneficiary under the trust deed and rules. For example, surpluses can be reduced by making a payment to the employer (see **19.1**) and the trust deed and rules may specify that any surplus remaining after the winding up of the scheme may be given to the employer, although the making of such payments is now subject to rigorous conditions.

The employer, therefore, as settlor of the trust, decides what the provisions of the trust deed and rules will be. The trustees are then under a duty to carry out the provisions of that trust documentation. As mentioned in **7.1** the trustees and the employer probably have a contractual relationship so that the trustees could enforce the terms of the trust against the employer. If on the other hand the trustees failed to carry out their duties under the trust, then the employer probably would seek to remove those trustees under the powers granted to it by the trust deed and rules.

Employers, however, establish occupational pension schemes under trust mainly because the Inland Revenue sets that as a condition for the granting of tax relief.

Among the reasons commonly cited by employers for the inclusion of occupational pensions as an element of the overall employee remuneration package are that:

- they offer a means of effecting a smooth transition for older employees from employment to retirement;

- they can be designed to offer the employer a degree of control over when employees retire, which in particular can reflect changing demands on the job market;

- they can be the vehicle for provision of life insurance benefits allowing the employer to assume a degree of social responsibility by being able to protect the employee's family more economically than the employee could do so on an individual basis;

- they are seen as an essential element in a competitive remuneration policy necessary for attracting, motivating and retaining skilled employees; and (somewhat less positively)

- they have simply been inherited by the current management.

The reality is that an occupational pension forms part of the employee remuneration package offered by most employers of any size. In many cases, they are an integral part of the normal industrial relations regime in the company. That said, in the recent past there has been a trend among some employers away from occupational pension schemes and over to contract-based personal or stakeholder pension schemes.

Powers of the employer

8.2   The employer as settlor of the trust has very substantial powers.

Many of the discretionary powers under the terms of the trust deed and rules can be exercised by the trustees only with the consent of the employer.

The power of amendment contained in the trust deed and rules will allow the employer to make extensive changes to how the scheme operates and the benefits it offers. The trustees will, however, usually have to agree to these changes. The power is also circumscribed by the *Pensions Act 1995* as explained at **6.3** above to avoid reducing the already accrued rights of scheme members.

The employer will normally be able to wind up the scheme at any time. Prior to the coming into force of the requirements governing member-nominated trustees the employer also usually had the sole power to appoint and remove the trustees. Although an employer can, if approval is gained through the statutory consultation procedure explained at **4.17**, currently retain the unique power to appoint all the trustees, the Government's policy is that schemes will generally in future always have among their trustees a proportion who have been nominated directly or indirectly by the scheme members – see **4.33**. The employer naturally will retain the unique power to appoint and remove employer-nominated trustees.

The trust deed and rules will normally assign certain powers to be exercised only by the employer. It may be that some of those powers can be seen as *fiduciary powers* which simply means that the employer must act in a trustee-like way when exercising those powers. If the power in question is a fiduciary power, the employer would need to exercise that power by taking into account only the interests of the members and to disregard its own interest. Many of the powers given to the employer, however, will not be fiduciary powers. Such powers are given absolutely to the employer and so when exercising those powers the employer may first and foremost have regard to its own interest.

Trust law also defines the principle of a *fraud on a power*, meaning simply that a person who has a limited power must exercise that power in good faith for the end designed, otherwise the exercise will be void.

In an important development in 1990, in the case of *Imperial Group Pension Trust Ltd v Imperial Tobacco Ltd [1991] 2 All ER 597, [1990] PLR 263*, the then Vice Chancellor (the senior judge in the Chancery Division which hears pension law cases) Sir Nicolas Browne-Wilkinson, held that an employer must exercise any powers given to it by the trust deed and rules subject to an *implied duty of good faith*.

The phrase 'implied duty of good faith' is a kind of legal shorthand used to refer to the employment law concept that in contracts of employment there is an implied obligation that:

> '… the employers will not, without reasonable and proper cause, conduct themselves in a manner calculated or likely to destroy or seriously damage the relationship of confidence and trust between employer and employee'.

In other words, since the *Imperial case* it has been accepted that this general obligation of an employer applies as much to the exercise of its rights and powers under a pension scheme as it does to the other rights and powers that exist under employment law.

Payment of pension contributions

8.3   It is a general condition of tax approval that the employer contributes to the occupational pension scheme. However, employer contributions can be suspended under the *Finance Act 1986* as one of the authorised methods of reducing a pension fund surplus – see **19.2**.

It had always been the duty of the trustees to check that any contributions due from the employer were properly paid over to the scheme. The auditor's report which must appear in the trustees' annual report previously had to contain a statement of whether or not contributions payable to the scheme during the scheme year had been paid in accordance with the rules and, in the case of defined benefit schemes, with the recommendation of the actuary. Now, where the scheme is required to have in place a *schedule of contributions* (see **8.5** below) or a *payment schedule* (see **8.6** below), the auditor's statement must state whether, in the auditor's opinion, contributions have been paid in accordance with that schedule.

Schemes that are contracted out have always had to satisfy further requirements: in particular, employers with contracted-out money purchase schemes have always had to forward the minimum payments within 14 days of the end of each tax month to the scheme's trustees.

Where employee and employer contributions have not been paid when due, there have been instances where the contributions have been made good by the National Insurance fund – see **23.5**.

The law governing the payment of pension contributions was radically altered by the *Pensions Act 1995* and we describe below the requirements made by that Act, and the associated regulations, regarding employee contributions in general, the schedule of contributions applying to schemes subject to the minimum funding requirement and the payment schedule applying to money purchase schemes. The *Welfare Reform and Pensions Act 1999* substantially modified the legislation made in the *Pensions Act 1995* on the payment of contributions, as well as introducing a new requirement on employers in respect of any contributions that they have agreed to pass on or make directly to a personal pension or stakeholder pension scheme held by an employee – see **2.7**.

Employee contributions

8.4   The *Pensions Act 1995* and the *Occupational Pension Schemes (Scheme Administration) Regulations 1996 (SI 1996/1715)* specifically require that any employee contributions deducted from employees' earnings must be paid over to the scheme within a specified deadline. Under the changes made by the *Welfare Reform and Pensions Act 1999* it falls to the trustees to report to the Occupational Pensions Regulatory Authority (Opra) any infringement of this requirement on the employer to pass on contributions that have been deducted from any employee's pay before the stated deadline.

Following an easement in the reporting requirement that was brought into effect on 3 April 2000, the trustees are required to report the failure by the employer to pass over the employee contributions by the 19th day of the calendar month following the month in which they were deducted from employees' pay unless:

(*a*)   the employer has paid the employee contributions before the end of the period of ten days beginning with the 20th day of the calendar month following the month in which they were deducted from employees' pay; and (*b*)   this default by the employer to meet the deadline of the 19th day of the following calendar month is only the first or second such default in the period of twelve months ending with that 19th day.

The trustees are required to report any failure by the employer to meet this requirement to Opra before the end of a period of 30 days, beginning with the day following the 20th day of the calendar month following the month in which the contributions were deducted from the employee's pay.

If the employee contributions are still outstanding at the end of the period of 60 days beginning with the 20th day of the following calendar month, the trustees must also report the employer's default to the members concerned. These reports must be made by the end of the period of 90 days beginning with the 20th day of that calendar month.

At present, this reporting requirement does not apply in the case of additional voluntary contributions (AVCs) that are not paid on time although there is still a legal requirement on the employer to pay over AVCs by the same deadline. It is likely that the reporting requirement will be extended to cover AVCs and trustees would probably feel bound to report the failure in any case.

If the trustees do not take all reasonable steps to carry out these reporting requirements, they are liable to be fined by Opra and prohibited from acting any longer as trustees. Any employer who fails to pass over the contributions deducted from employees' pay by the deadline risks being fined by Opra.

If the trustees fail to carry out this reporting requirement, Opra is able to prohibit any person from continuing to act as a trustee of that scheme and impose a fine not exceeding £50,000 on a corporate trustee, and not exceeding £5,000 on an individual trustee.

In addition, Opra can impose a fine on the same scale on the employer for failure to pay over within the time limit any contributions that have been deducted from the employees' pay.

Before 3 April 2000, if the employer deducted contributions from employees' pay but failed to pay them over to the trustees within the previous time limit without a reasonable excuse, the employer was guilty of a criminal offence and, on summary conviction, was liable to a fine and on conviction on indictment, was liable to imprisonment or a fine, or both. However, for Opra, this criminal penalty provided a problem of enforcement. In order to secure a conviction for a criminal act, a much higher standard of proof is required than applies where a civil penalty can be imposed. In order to enforce the requirement on a practicable basis, Opra argued for the changes that have now been brought into force. However, of course, a criminal sanction still remains in any case where there is sufficient evidence of a fraudulent evasion of the obligation to pay over the contributions deducted from any employee's pay.

Opra warns that the greater flexibility offered by the new civil penalty will mean that it will be much more effective in policing the requirement. Opra has issued a booklet *Paying Pension Contributions on Time – A Guide for Employers with Occupational Pension Schemes* which sets out the requirements and how it is enforcing them (see 'Guidance from the Occupational Pensions Regulatory Authority' in APPENDIX 3).

In the spring of 1998, one year after the coming into force of the *Pensions Act 1995*, non-compliance with this requirement accounted for over one-third of the over seven thousand cases that had been opened by Opra. John Hayes, Chairman of Opra, emphasised that failure by employers to pay over their employees' pension contributions in the time allotted by Parliament was the largest single issue facing the new regulator. He added:

> 'Cock-ups and isolated embarrassments are one thing, but the practice of routinely hanging on to money that is not yours to keep is only a few steps away from fraud'.

The high level of non-compliance in passing on employee contributions in a timely fashion seems to stem from two main factors. There is a core problem among a relatively small minority of employers who regard employee pension contributions as a temporary, unsecured, interest-free loan. This may be regarded as in part a cultural problem.

But Opra says that most of the problems have arisen simply from poor administration. As might be suspected, delays in passing employee contributions are most common with small employers. Not all the blame should be directed to such employers. If they run an occupational scheme at all, it is highly likely it will be a fully insured scheme. The bulk of the administration is carried out by the insurance company itself. However, while some insurance companies have been very helpful to their clients, putting resources into support services, explanatory material and advice lines, others have not. (In fact many insurers have sought to 'convert' their occupational pension schemes business by persuading their clients to switch to group personal pension schemes where the writ of the *Pensions Act 1995* does not run. However, the reforms of the *Welfare Reform and Pensions Act 1999* took effect on 6 April 2001 and there is now a level playing field in this respect between occupational, personal and stakeholder pension schemes – see **2.7**.)

Yet, in the case of an insured occupational pension scheme, at the bottom line it is the employer, not the insurance company, which is responsible for complying with the *Pensions Act 1995*. Indeed, it may even be the insurance company which has reported to Opra the employer's non-compliance in failing to pass employee contributions over to the scheme within the time limit.

Employer contributions – schedule of contributions

8.5   Since 6 April 1997, trustees of schemes that are subject to the minimum funding requirement or MFR (i e most defined benefit schemes) have had a duty to prepare and maintain a *schedule of contributions* following the scheme's first MFR valuation. For a discussion of the MFR itself, see **13.9–13.12** below. The schedule of contributions is the central mechanism for delivering the MFR and enables trustees to check that contributions are paid into the scheme promptly and at an appropriate rate. It also ensures that non-payment of contributions is quickly identified so that action to enforce payment can be initiated promptly.

The schedule should separately identify employer and employee contributions and the due dates for payment. (Employees' AVC payments also have to be shown separately.) Any schedule of contributions that is certified by the scheme actuary on or after 19 March 2002 must also show separately any extra contributions that the employer must pay in order to bring the scheme's funding up to the 90% level. The trustees and the employer should agree the rates of contributions to be entered on the schedule, subject to the requirement that they can be certified by the scheme's actuary to be adequate to meet the MFR. There is some flexibility to revise the schedule during inter-valuation periods provided the revised rates can be certified by the actuary as still satisfying the MFR. In the event of the employer and trustees being unable to agree what the long-term funding rate for the scheme should be, the trustees must set the contributions at a rate adequate to secure that the scheme complies with the MFR.

The schedule of contributions must be drawn up following the first MFR actuarial valuation after 5 April 1997. From that point on, the schedule must be revised after every subsequent actuarial valuation in order to take into account any change in the funding position of the scheme. The schedule has to be in place within twelve weeks after the actuary has signed the valuation report.

The trustees are required to notify Opra if the employer fails to pay over on time the correct amount of contributions as listed in the schedule of contributions. The requirements were modified with effect from 30 December 1999 so that from that date the trustees must notify Opra if the employer fails to pay the contributions by the due date listed in the schedule. However, an exception is made so that no notification need be given if:

- the required payment was made before the end of a period of ten days beginning with the due date; and

- the default in missing the due date was only the first or the second such default in the period of twelve months ending on and including the due date.

When notification to Opra is required, the notification must be given before the end of the period of 30 days beginning with the due date.

The trustees must also take action to notify the members if the employer has still failed to pay the required contributions by the end of the period of 60 days after the due date. In this event, the trustees must notify the members before the end of the period of 90 days beginning with the due date.

These detailed requirements are set out in the *Occupational Pension Schemes (Minimum Funding Requirement and Actuarial Valuations) Regulations 1996 (SI 1996/1536).*

8.5   *Trustees and the employer*

In practice, it often makes sense for the 'due dates' that are to be specified in the schedule of contributions to be set at the 19th day of each month in view of the separate requirements applying to the payment of contributions that have been deducted from employees' pay. At the same time, since this date is the statutory long-stop, it also makes sense for the trustees and employer to agree in practice to process the payments much earlier. In an example schedule used by Opra, the due date is set as the 19th day of the month but a written statement is made to the effect that the employer has agreed to aim to pay the contributions by the 7th day of each month.

Any outstanding unpaid contributions due according to the schedule are a statutory debt on the employer which can be enforced by the trustees through the courts. It is a matter for the trustees to decide whether or when to take action to enforce a debt arising because of unpaid contributions. Opra itself has powers to warn employers of the potential consequences of non-payment of contributions.

Opra has the power to fine any trustee up to £5,000 in the case of an individual or £50,000 in case of a corporate trustee for:

- failing to prepare or revise a schedule of contributions within the specified time; or

- failing to report to Opra and to the membership any non-payment of contributions by the employer in the circumstances set out in the legislation.

Ultimately, Opra has power to remove trustees who fail to comply with their statutory duties to enforce the MFR.

Furthermore, as explained at **8.4** above, an employer who fails to pass on employee contributions could face a fine imposed by Opra, or in cases of fraudulent evasion, a criminal prosecution.

Some defined benefit schemes are not subject to the MFR and so their trustees do not have to put in place a schedule of contributions. Such schemes include those with only one member, those which only provide death benefits and certain schemes which only provide lump-sum retirement benefits. Unapproved schemes are not caught by the MFR provisions.

Employer contributions – money purchase schemes

8.6   Late arrival of the contributions, whether employee or employer contributions, is especially important with defined contribution (money purchase) occupational schemes since the delay translates directly into lost investment opportunities. The same observation can be made of contributions that have been deducted from employees' earnings by the employer's payroll but not speedily passed onto a personal or stakeholder pension scheme. Since 6 April 1997, the trustees of most defined contribution occupational pension schemes have been required to prepare, maintain and revise a *payment schedule* showing:

- the rates of contributions payable to the scheme by the employer and separately by the active members;

- any amounts payable to the scheme by the employer to cover expenses that are likely to be incurred during the scheme year; and

- the due dates on or before which the contributions and other payments must be made.

The payment schedule must contain separate entries for the rates and the due dates of contributions payable to the scheme by the employer (and if there is more than one employer, rates and due dates for each employer's contributions must be shown) and by the active members of the scheme. (Note that AVCs do not have to be listed.)

However, where an insurance premium is payable, the payment schedule does not have to contain separate entries for identifying the contributions making up that premium that are payable by the employer and the active members.

The trustees are required to report to Opra and the members according to the same deadlines as apply to the schedule of contributions in a scheme subject to the MFR (see **8.5** above): the appropriate changes to the requirements were made with effect from 30 December 1999. In the case of a payment schedule, the detailed requirements are set out in the *Occupational Pension Schemes (Scheme Administration) Regulations 1996 (SI 1996/1715)* mentioned at **8.4** above.

So, therefore, the trustees must notify Opra if the employer fails to pay the correct level of payments as required in the payment schedule. They must also notify Opra if the employer fails to make these payments by the due date listed in the schedule. An exception is again made so that no notification need be given if the required payment was made before the end of a period of ten days beginning with the due date and that default was only the first or second such default in the period of twelve months ending on and including the due date. When notification is required to Opra, the notification must be given before the end of the period of 30 days beginning with the due date.

The trustees must also take action to notify the members if the employer has still failed to pay the required payments by the end of the period of 60 days from the due date. In this event, the trustees must notify the members before the end of the period of 90 days from the due date.

If the trustees fail to take all reasonable steps to put in place, maintain and revise a payment schedule, or to carry out these reporting requirements, Opra has the power to prohibit a person from acting as a trustee of the scheme and to impose a fine not exceeding £50,000 on a corporate trustee, and not exceeding £5,000 on an individual trustee.

Any amounts shown on the payment schedule that remain unpaid after the due date, whether payable by the employer or not, will automatically be treated as a debt from the employer to the trustees. Opra has the power under the *Pensions Act 1995* to fine any employer if any amount payable on the employer's own account in accordance with the payment schedule has not been paid by the due date. The fine on the employer is one of up to £50,000 in the case of a corporate employer, and up to £5,000 in the case of an individual. As explained in **8.4** above, an employer who fails to pass on contributions deducted from employees' earnings could face a fine under the separate provisions introduced on 3 April 2000 by the *Welfare Reform and Pensions Act 1999*. Any fraudulent evasion by the employer in passing over employee contributions could result in a criminal prosecution.

A number of kinds of defined contribution schemes are exempt from the requirement to operate a payment schedule. They include small self-administered schemes and certain kinds of executive pension plans, provided that in both kinds of scheme all the members are trustees and every member has to agree each decision. Also excluded are schemes with only one member, schemes that provide death benefits only and unapproved schemes.

Just as in the case of schedules of contributions, trustees and employers usually agree that the 19th day of each month is the most practicable choice of due date because of the separate requirements applying to the payment of contributions that have been deducted from employees' pay. Because this is the statutory long-stop with no room for error, the trustees and employers will usually arrange to aim to pay the contributions by, say, the 7th day of each month but keep the 19th day of the month as the official due date.

Payments to personal pension schemes

8.7   The *Welfare Reform and Pensions Act 1999* introduced a new requirement for the monitoring of employers' payments to personal pension schemes. The requirement came into force on 6 April 2001.

The aim of the new legislation was in part to redress an imbalance in the regulatory safeguards dealing with the payment of pension contributions that have emerged between:

- those employees who are members of an occupational pension scheme; and

- those employees who are members of a personal pension into which their employer has agreed to make a direct contribution or simply to offer a payroll deduction facility to pass on employee contributions to the personal pension provider on a net-of-tax basis.

The many regulatory requirements to pay contributions on time placed on employers who sponsor occupational pension schemes, whether of the defined benefit or the defined contribution variety, had persuaded many employers who wished to make pension provision for their employees to prefer the use of personal pensions, which were then subject to a much lighter regulatory touch. The imbalance in the regulatory requirements had therefore created a distorting effect which has fed through to employers' choice of pension provision.

Also, from 6 April 2001 stakeholder pension schemes became available. As explained in **2.11** above, stakeholder pensions may be legally established as occupational pension schemes, in which case the rules relating to employee contributions described at **8.4** above and the rules relating to payment schedules used in money purchase occupational pension schemes described at **8.6** above both apply.

However, stakeholder pension schemes may also be legally established as personal pensions. In order for there to be a level playing field between these two types of stakeholder pension schemes, similar legislation to protect the members of personal pension-based stakeholder pension schemes against non-payment, incorrect payment and delayed payment of contributions was needed. The decision was taken to extend the scope of this legislation to all personal pensions.

If the personal pension-based stakeholder pension scheme is set under trust, the trustees will be responsible for implementing the new requirements.

The detail of these requirements relating to a *direct payment arrangement* between an employer and a personal pension scheme provider are set out in **2.7** above.

Time off for trustees

8.8   Since 6 April 1997, the *Employment Rights Act 1996* requires an employer who sponsors an occupational pension scheme to give any employee who serves as a trustee to that scheme paid time off during working hours to perform trustee duties and to undergo relevant training. There is, however, no mandatory requirement on the employer to provide training. (This requirement was originally contained in the *Pensions Act 1995*.)

There was an error in the original legislation with the result that this right to paid time off work applied to employees who were 'trustees' but not employees who were 'trustee directors'. It is notable that there were reports of this drafting error being exploited. Amendments made by the *Welfare Reform and Pensions Act 1999* ensure that the requirement applies to employees who are directors of a trust company in the same way as they do to employees who are individual trustees.

The amount of time that an employee is permitted to take to perform trustee duties or undergo relevant training, the timing of this paid time off, and any conditions subject to which the time off may be taken will be those which are:

'reasonable in all the circumstances having regard in particular to:

(*a*) how much time off is required for the performance of the duties of a trustee of the scheme and the undergoing of relevant training, and how

107

much time off is required for performing the particular duty, or, as the case may be, for undergoing the particular training; and

(*b*) the circumstances of the employer's business and the effect of the employee's absence on the running of that business'.

The employee trustees should receive the pay they would normally have received if they were working normally for the time they were engaged in performing trustee duties or relevant training. If payment varies with the amount of work done, the amount payable should be calculated by reference to the average hourly earnings for that work for the employee trustee concerned. The right to be paid an amount under these rules does not affect any right of employees to pay under their contract of employment, but the amount of pay due and the amount of contractual pay due can be mutually offset.

Where a dispute arises, the trustee can present a complaint to an employment tribunal if he or she feels that the employer has refused paid time off unreasonably. The trustee should present the complaint within three months of the refusal.

Before the introduction of this legislation in 1997, the issue of paid time off to carry out trustee duties had been the subject of some tribunal cases, notably the case of *STC Submarine Systems v Piper [1994] OPLR 13, [1993] PLR 185* where the Employment Appeal Tribunal ruled that the trustee, who was also a trade union branch secretary, had been entitled to paid time off work to attend training on developments in equal treatment in relation to pensions.

Employment protection rights

8.9   The *Pensions Act 1995* introduced some new measures of employment protection for all employee trustees irrespective of how long they have served as employees. These new measures are now contained in the *Employment Rights Act 1996*. The Act provides that:

'... an employee has the right not to be subjected to any detriment by any act, or any deliberate failure to act, by his employer done on the ground that, being a trustee of a trust scheme which relates to his employment, the employee performed (or proposed to perform) any functions as such a trustee.'

The dismissal of an employee will be treated as an unfair dismissal under the *Employment Rights Act 1996* if the reason, or the principal reason, for the employee's dismissal or redundancy is connected to the employee's activities as a trustee.

The employee trustee must normally present a complaint of detriment in employment or unfair dismissal to an employment tribunal within three months of the event.

It should be remembered that it will not automatically follow in all cases that, if an individual is dismissed as an employee, he or she will also cease to be a trustee of the scheme, although in practice this is usually the result. The *Welfare Reform and Pensions Act 1999* ensures that these employee protection measures apply in the same way to employees who are directors of a trust company as they do to employees who are individual trustees.

Protection as a whistle blower

8.10   If an employee trustee (or any other employee involved in the administration of the pension scheme) has reasonable cause to believe that any duty relevant to the administration of the scheme is not being complied with and that this failure is likely to be of material significance, that employee may *blow the whistle* to Opra. If the employee does so, the disclosure will not be treated as a breach of any duty of confidence to the employer and so the employee could not be sued by the employer for breach of a term of the contract of employment. This protection is given by *section 48* of the *Pensions Act 1995*. However, it must be said that this is a very limited form of protection.

In February 2000 Opra published *Opra Note 6 – The Right to Report Problems to Opra* which deals with 'voluntary reporting', i e reports to Opra by those who have the right and benefit from the limited protection against being sued for breach of contract but not including those who already have a statutory duty to report problems, meaning in practice the scheme actuary and scheme auditor. This is useful reading for any pension fund trustee.

It is important to note that the limited legal protection granted by *section 48* of the *Pensions Act 1995* does not apply to those who are seen as being involved in managing or administering the scheme. There is no legal protection given by the *Pensions Act 1995* to ordinary scheme members (unless they are trustees) or to any employees not appointed by the trustees to provide services to the scheme. So, for example, employees working in the payroll department of the employer would not normally be appointed by the trustees to provide services to the scheme and so would not be covered. Furthermore, the protection is only granted if the whistle blower makes the report to Opra rather than to any other body.

The *Public Interest Disclosure Act 1998*, however, has extended the protection given to employees who blow the whistle. It amends the *Employment Rights Act 1996* to give individuals the right to take a complaint to an employment tribunal if they feel they have suffered unfair dismissal or other detriment because:

• they have reported a failure to another person with a statutory duty to report the failure to the proper authorities; or

• they have reported the failure directly to a public body such as Opra.

Provision of information

8.11   Regulations made under the *Pensions Act 1995* require the employer to provide trustees with information relevant to a defined benefit scheme's funding position (which in turn the trustees must provide to the scheme actuary whom they have appointed). The *Occupational Pension Schemes (Scheme Administration) Regulations 1996 (SI 1996/1715)* require the employer (and any actuary or auditor acting for the employer) to disclose within one month of its occurrence any event which there is reasonable cause to believe will be of material significance in the exercise by the trustees or professional advisers of any of their functions.

In addition, these Regulations require the employer to disclose on request to the trustees such information as is reasonably required for the performance of their duties or those of the professional advisers. In this way, the onus is placed on the trustees to establish a suitable arrangement with the employer that will ensure that they have access to relevant information and are kept informed as changes take place and events occur.

Under employment law, the House of Lords has ruled in the case of *Scally v Southern Health and Social Services Board [1991] 4 All ER 563, [1991] PLR 195* that the implied duty of mutual trust and confidence in the employment relationship means that an employer must take reasonable steps to bring the existence of a valuable right (such as that relating to an occupational pension scheme) to the attention of the employee. However, in giving this judgment Lord Bridge set conditions limiting the extent of this duty on the employer. The following conditions must apply:

- the terms of the contract of employment have not been negotiated with the individual employee but result from negotiation with a representative body or are otherwise incorporated by reference;

- a particular term of the contract makes available to the employee a valuable right contingent upon action being taken by the employee;

- the employee cannot, in all the circumstances, reasonably be expected to be aware of the term unless it is drawn to his or her attention.

This means that the employer's duty to provide information does not abrogate pension scheme members of all responsibility for any decision they may take regarding options they are free to take under the scheme. If the employee has access to accurate and complete information describing the scheme, the employer is entitled to assume that the employee will exercise any option granted under the scheme knowing the implications of doing so. This point has been made by Mr Justice Hart in the case of *University of Nottingham v Eyett [1999] 2 All ER 445, [1999] OPLR 55* where he held that the employer had not breached the implied duty of mutual trust and confidence. In that case, the employer had simply not taken action positively to alert the employee that by delaying his voluntary early retirement by one month, his pension would be a greater amount because of the way final pensionable earnings were calculated under the scheme rules.

The same general issue came before the Court of Appeal in April 2000 in the case of *Outram v Academy Plastics [2000] OPLR 321, [2000] PLR 283*. It was suggested in this case that an appellant alleging that an employer had failed to carry out any duty to give advice on pensions would generally often need to show that such a duty to do so arose out of the contract of employment, rather than more generally looking for a test for liability for causing economic loss to another person. Lord Justice Chadwick, one of the appeal judges hearing this case, gave credence to the view that:

> 'the duties owed by an employer, or former employer, in relation to its employees were in a state of development, particularly in the field of economic loss suffered by an employee as a result of action or omission by the employer ancillary to the performance of the contract of employment itself.'

However, this aspect of the case could not be tried by the Court of Appeal because the appellant's barrister had expressly rejected the suggestion that the claim could be put on a contractual basis.

Employer provides the administration services

8.12   The trustees are responsible and will be held accountable for the proper running of their occupational pension scheme but generally the task of the day-to-day administration of the scheme is delegated by the trustees to a pensions administration department – see **CHAPTER 11**. However, in the *Occupational Pension Schemes (Scheme Administration) Regulations 1996 (SI 1996/1715)*, it is recognised that if the trustees are to be held responsible for ensuring proper administration, then the trustees must be perfectly clear about the terms on which administrative services are provided. Accordingly, the Regulations include a requirement that where it is the employer who makes provision for the administration of the scheme, it must disclose to the trustees the terms on which these services are provided. In particular, this should mean that the trustees will be clear about whether the administrators owe a duty of confidentiality primarily to the employer or to them as trustees.

Checklist 8

- The employer is the settlor of the trust and so can devise a trust deed and rules which will serve its purpose of providing pensions that fit in with its overall remuneration policy.

- The trust deed and rules will give the employer specific powers to amend the scheme, but usually the trustees will have to agree to the changes and no retrospective worsening of members' accrued rights is permitted under the *Pensions Act 1995* – unless all members give their consent.

- In certain cases the employer must exercise powers given to it by the trust deed and rules in line with fiduciary principles.

- Under employment law, the employer must exercise powers subject to an implied duty of good faith.

- It was formerly a criminal offence if an employer, without reasonable excuse, failed to pay over contributions that had been deducted from employees' earnings within the prescribed time limit. For practical reasons, the penalty was changed to a civil penalty but fraudulent evasion remains a criminal act.

- The trustees are responsible for enforcing a schedule of contributions (schemes subject to the minimum funding requirement) or payment schedule (defined contribution schemes) and for ensuring that the employer makes the correct contributions or payments to the scheme within the specified time limits. Similar duties now apply when an employer makes payments to a personal or stakeholder pension scheme.

- Any employee trustee must be given paid time off work to attend to trustee duties.

- An employee trustee is given special employment rights protection against unjust treatment and unfair dismissal by the employer.

- An employee trustee or employee involved in administration of the pensions scheme who blows the whistle on the employer cannot be sued by the employer for breach of confidence.

- The employer must inform the trustees whenever material events take place and must disclose on request to the trustees information that they reasonably require.

- If the employer provides the pension administration services, the employer must disclose to the trustees the terms on which the services are provided.

Chapter 9

Trustees and the pension fund members

Duty to act fairly between differing groups

9.1   Under trust law, it has always been held that trustees should act in the best interest of all the scheme's beneficiaries and strike a fair balance between the different classes of beneficiary. This is also embodied in social security law where, for example, early leavers who preserve their pensions in the scheme are protected against unfair curtailment of benefit. Naturally, trustees must observe the general law, such as the *Race Relations Act 1975* and the *Disability Discrimination Act 1995*.

The Occupational Pensions Regulatory Authority (Opra) in its *Guide for Pension Scheme Trustees* lists the various classes of beneficiary of an occupational pension scheme as possibly including all the following:

• active members (current employees);

• pensioner members;

• deferred pensioners;

• prospective members;

• widows and widowers of members;

• dependants and future dependants of members; and

• the employer.

Opra comments that the trustees must consider the interests of all these classes of beneficiary, striking a balance so that an appropriate weight is given to the interests of each class, depending on the issue being considered. Opra then makes an important point – giving due consideration to each class 'does not necessarily mean treating all classes equally'.

The Vice Chancellor, Sir Richard Scott, senior judge in the Chancery Division, the division of the High Court that hears pensions law, discussed the issue of whether trustees could favour one class of beneficiaries over another in a judgment where he overturned an earlier Determination of the Pensions Ombudsman. The Pensions Ombudsman had found that the trustees of a pension scheme had committed maladministration because they breached their duty to act impartially between the different classes of beneficiaries when considering how to use a pension fund surplus.

In particular, in his Determination, the Pensions Ombudsman had said:

'The trustees' duty to act impartially between the different beneficiaries does not equate with a duty to exercise their discretion on all occasions in such a way to produce equal benefits of equal value to all beneficiaries. Nor does it even require that all beneficiaries receive some benefit from an exercise of a discretion. It is permissible to exercise a discretion in such a manner as to omit particular beneficiaries, or a class thereof. But the discretion to exclude those beneficiaries must not be the result of undue partiality towards the interests of the preferred beneficiaries.'

In the appeal in the case of *Edge v Pensions Ombudsman [1998] 2 All ER 547, [1998] OPLR 51,* heard in December 1997, the Vice Chancellor said that he agreed with all of the above bar the final sentence and in particular the phrase 'undue partiality'. The Vice Chancellor said:

'The trustees are entitled to be partial. They are entitled to exclude some beneficiaries from particular benefits and to prefer others. If what is meant by 'undue partiality' is that trustees have taken into account irrelevant or improper or irrational factors, their exercise of discretion may be flawed. But it is not flawed simply because someone else, whether or not a judge, regards their partiality as 'undue'. It is the trustees' discretion that is to be exercised. Except in a case in which the discretion has been surrendered to the court, it is not for a judge to exercise the discretion. The judge may disagree with the manner in which the trustees have exercised their discretion but, unless they can be seen to have taken into account irrelevant, improper or irrational factors, or unless their decision can be said to be one that no reasonable body of trustees properly directing themselves could have reached, the judge cannot interfere. In particular he cannot interfere simply on the ground that the partiality shown to the preferred beneficiaries was in his opinion undue.'

This is a very robust defence of the right of trustees to exercise the discretionary powers given to them by the trust deed and rules as they see fit. There is the exception that the trustees must not take into account 'irrelevant, improper or irrational factors' etc – the *Wednesbury principles* discussed at **5.4** above – but otherwise the Vice Chancellor has upheld the principle that the courts should not reverse the decision of properly appointed trustees who are carrying out their duties and exercising their powers in accordance with their trust deed and rules. There is, however, a clear tension between the view of the Pensions Ombudsman and the Vice Chancellor over exactly what 'striking a fair balance between the various classes of beneficiaries' actually means.

In July 1999, the Court of Appeal heard the Pensions Ombudsman's appeal against the Vice Chancellor's High Court judgment in *Edge v Pensions Ombudsman [1999] 4 All ER 546, [1999] OPLR 179).* The Pensions Ombudsman argued that the Vice Chancellor was wrong to hold that, in the exercise of their discretionary power to amend the rules, the trustees were not subject to a duty to act impartially as between individual classes of beneficiaries. He also argued that it was wrong to hold that the trustees were themselves the judges of whether their exercise of the power was fair between included and excluded beneficiaries.

The Court of Appeal held that the beneficiaries concerned had no right to insist on an increase in benefits as a means of reducing the scheme surplus but in the words of Lord Justice Chadwick: 'Their right was to have the matter properly considered'. He added that: 'the trustees must, in deciding whether or not to increase benefits (and, if so, which benefits), act in a way which appears to them fair and equitable in all the circumstances;'

In coming to such a fair and equitable decision the trustees would need to consider the circumstances in which the surplus had arisen, but that did not mean that they would be bound to take any particular course as a result of that consideration. The main purpose of the scheme was to provide retirement and other benefits for employees of the participating employers, and the trustees 'must consider the effect that any course which they are minded to take will have on the financial ability of the employers to make the contributions which that course will entail'.

In the end the Court of Appeal affirmed the *Wednesbury Principles* explained at **5.4** above as being appropriate guidance for trustees in exercising discretionary powers. Lord Justice Chadwick held that if the trustees follow those principles 'they cannot be criticised if they reach a decision which appears to prefer the claims of one interest – whether that of the employers, current employees or pensioners – over others. The preference will be the result of a proper exercise of the discretionary power.'

The *Wednesbury Principles* emphasise that the trustees' decision must not be perverse. It must be a decision at which a reasonable body of trustees could arrive. As an absurd example, suppose the trustees decided under a discretionary power that no pension increases would be payable to pensioners with red hair. This would be unreasonable. It could also be attacked because the trustees were taking into account irrelevant matters. It is so unreasonable that it might be described as being done in bad faith. Other examples might occur to readers. Suppose that the trust deed and rules gave the trustees the discretionary power to award a dependant's pension to any financial dependant of an employee and member of the scheme who had died. What if the trustees were prepared to do so for an opposite-sex partner but not for a same-sex partner where in both cases there was incontrovertible evidence of financial dependency? The same arguments apply as in the case with denying pension increases to those with red hair.

Equal treatment

9.2   European law has been the driving force in achieving equal treatment for men and women in the matter of:

- access to occupational pension schemes; and

- the contributions and benefit provisions of occupational pension schemes.

It should be remembered that judgments of the European Court of Justice (ECJ) in its interpretation of the European Treaty are the supreme authority under UK law. The key to equal treatment and pensions questions lies in a series of judgments of the ECJ made over the years in connection with its interpretation of Article 119 of the EEC Treaty, the Equal Pay Article. (Note that Articles 117 to 120 of the EEC Treaty have now been replaced by Articles 136 EC to 143 EC and Article 119 has now become Article 141 EC). The ECJ has ruled that pension benefits count as pay for all purposes of Article 141 EC. If pensions are pay, then pension rights have to respect the principle of equal treatment for men and women. In one of the judgments (*Coloroll Pension Trustees v Russell [1995] All ER (EC) 23, [1994] OPLR 179*) given in 1994, the ECJ made two important rulings of importance to trustees.

'The direct effect of Article 119 of the EEC Treaty may be relied on by both employees and their dependants against the trustees of an occupational pension scheme who are bound, in the exercise of their powers and performance of their obligations as laid down in the trust deed, to observe the principle of equal treatment.'

'In so far as national law prohibits employers and trustees from acting beyond the scope of their respective powers or in disregard of the provisions of the trust deed, they are bound to use all the means available under domestic law, such as recourse to the national courts, in order to eliminate all discrimination in the matter of pay.'

It is quite clear therefore that trustees have a direct responsibility under the law to ensure that their pension scheme observes the principle of equal treatment. The *Pensions Act 1995* sets out an equal treatment rule that states in effect that where a member is employed to perform work of equal value to that performed by a member of the other sex, any terms treating the member less favourably will be treated as modified to remove the inequality. In a legal defence it will be for the trustees (rather than the employer) to prove to the court that any difference in treatment of men and women is due to a material factor which is not sex-related.

Trustees may not be able to make alterations to the trust deed and rules because they do not have the power to do so, or if the procedure is unduly complex, protracted or involves gaining consents which cannot be obtained or can only be obtained with great difficulty. In this case they are helped by the equal treatment provisions contained in the *Pensions Act 1995* that give trustees the ability to modify the trust deed and rules by simple resolution to ensure that the scheme conforms with the equal treatment rule set out in the Act.

Interpretation and exceptions

9.3   The ECJ has given certain derogations to trustees regarding equal treatment. The law can become complex but the following summary will serve as a basic pointer:

● Periods of pensionable service before 17 May 1990 (i e the date of the *Barber* judgment by the ECJ) do not have to give rise to equal benefits and any attempt to equalise benefits retrospectively that involves a worsening of benefits could conflict with UK trust law.

- Periods of pensionable service on or after 17 May 1990 but before the scheme rules were changed to eliminate discrimination between men and women must give rise to equal benefits by granting to the disadvantaged sex the same advantages as those enjoyed by the advantaged sex.

- Equal treatment for periods of pensionable service after the date the scheme rules were changed can generally be achieved by reducing the advantages which the advantaged sex used to enjoy.

- In defined benefit schemes there is no requirement that unisex actuarial factors must be used, so that commutation rates for retirement lump sums, for example, do not have to be equal.

- In all schemes, the amount of any employee contributions must be on a sex-equal basis. In defined benefit schemes, it is the pension that has to be on a sex-equal basis and so any difference in the employer's funding level due to different actuarial factors for men and women is permitted. It is not entirely clear what the requirement is for defined contribution (money purchase) schemes but some lawyers hold that, provided both employee and employer contributions are calculated on a sex-equal basis, it does not matter that non-unisex annuity rates will produce unequal pension amounts. (Note that the UK contracting-out legislation insists that any protected rights fund (see **1.8**) when used to secure an annuity must be used to do so using unisex annuity rates.)

- Bridging pensions payable to pensioners to compensate for the current inequality in state pension ages may be payable to men and not women between the ages of 60 and 65. But as the state pension age for women begins to rise in 2010, bridging pensions, if paid to men over 60, will also have to be paid to women over 60 until they reach state pension age.

- The Pensions Ombudsman in January 2000 issued a decision in which he held that guaranteed minimum pensions (GMPs) built up from 17 May 1990 until 5 April 1997 under the contracting-out legislation had to be equalised as a separate element of a member's pension. However, the High Court quashed his direction but only on the argument that the Ombudsman did not have jurisdiction to determine the question. The judge did not refer the question to the ECJ for a preliminary ruling.

- Where a transfer value has been based on unequal benefits for pensionable service on or after 17 May 1990 and is lower than if it had been based on equal benefits, the receiving scheme must increase the benefits to the level that could have been bought by the higher transfer value.

- The exclusion from the pension scheme of part-time employees, or any other category of employees, has constituted indirect discrimination if there is no objective justification for the exclusion unrelated to the sex of the members and if the exclusion affects a far greater number of one sex than the other. However, since 1 July 2000, new legislation – the *Part-time Workers (Prevention of Less Favourable Treatment) Regulations 2000 (SI 2000/1551)* – ensures that, unless there is an objective justification, it has become unlawful in any case to discriminate in pension terms and conditions against part-time employees irrespective of sex discrimination issues.

- National rules relating to time limits for bringing actions under national law may be relied on against employees who assert their right to join an occupational pension scheme, provided that they are not less favourable for that type of legal action than for similar actions of a domestic nature, and that they do not render the exercise of rights conferred by Community law impossible in practice. In May 2000, the ECJ in the case of *Preston v Wolverhampton Healthcare [2001] UKHL/5, [2001] 3 All ER 947, [2001] OPLR 1* upheld the UK time limit that prevented a claim being valid if it was made more than six months after the employee had left the employment concerned. However, it rejected the UK legislation that limited to no more than two years any backdating of scheme membership in restitution for unlawful denial of scheme access. The House of Lords later decided that in such cases membership could be backdated to the date the employee was first unlawfully excluded from membership – although this could not be earlier than 8 April 1976, the date of the judgment in *Defrenne v Sabena [1976] ICR 547* when the ECJ first demonstrated that Article 119 EEC (now Article 141 EC) could be relied upon in legal claims.

Women on maternity leave

9.4   The legislation provides for special treatment of women members who are taking maternity leave. *Schedule 5* to the *Social Security Act 1989* provides that any period of *paid* maternity leave must be pensionable. Paid maternity leave will involve receipt of either statutory maternity pay or contractual maternity pay. During periods of *paid* maternity leave the member:

- must continue to accrue pensionable service;

- must still be covered by death-in-service benefits;

- need only pay any employee contributions calculated on the actual maternity pay she is receiving; and

- must have any benefits that fall to be calculated based on the pensionable earnings she would have received if she had been working normally.

In the case of a member of a defined contribution (money purchase) scheme during any period of *paid* maternity leave, any contribution the employee is required to make is calculated on the actual maternity pay she is receiving, while the employer makes its contributions based on the pay she would have received if she had been working normally. But this will result in a shortfall and so the employee will not receive the same pension benefits as if she had been working normally. Some lawyers believe that the employer should also pay during any period of *paid* maternity leave a top-up payment equal to the difference between the employee's actual contributions and the contributions she would have paid if she had been working normally.

Any member taking her minimum 26 weeks' 'ordinary maternity leave' must continue to accrue pension rights even if, unusually, her period of employment has been so short that she does not qualify for statutory maternity pay. Note that the *Employment Act 2002*, in extending the statutory maternity pay period from 18 to 26 weeks, also equalised the duration of the statutory maternity pay period and the ordinary maternity leave period.

A period of *unpaid* maternity leave that falls after the period of ordinary maternity leave or any period of paid maternity leave does not have to be pensionable, but the period of pensionable service before and after this period of unpaid maternity leave must be treated as continuous. The rules of the scheme may specify that the period is pensionable or that the employee is able to make additional contributions to make this period pensionable. In some schemes, periods of unpaid maternity leave will become pensionable automatically, provided the member returns to work for a minimum period.

It should be noted that *Schedule 5* to the *Social Security Act 1989* introduced legislation not only to prevent 'unfair maternity provisions' but also 'unfair family leave provisions', and that these existing provisions have force in conjunction with the paternity, adoption and maternity leave provisions introduced by the *Employment Act 2002* and the secondary legislation introduced under that Act.

Other forms of discrimination

9.5   Under the provision of *Race Relations Act 1975* it would clearly be unlawful to deny access to pension schemes or provide inferior pension benefits on the ground of race or ethnicity. The pensions aspects of discrimination on other grounds are not always so clear. There are at present a number of developments at a European and UK level to prevent unlawful discrimination against particular groups of people in society, other than in the areas of sex discrimination and discrimination against part-time employees which have been discussed immediately above.

Disability discrimination

The *Disability Discrimination Act 1995* prohibits any employer from discriminating against disabled people in terms of offering access to a pension scheme. *Section 17* of the 1995 Act inserts into every occupational pension scheme a 'non-discrimination' rule which prevents the trustees or managers of the scheme from taking any action which would amount to disability discrimination if the same action were carried out by the employer.

However, the *Disability Discrimination (Employment) Regulations 1996 (SI 1996/1456)* allows discrimination against a disabled person if, as a result of the disabled person's disability, the cost of providing benefits under an occupational pension scheme is likely to be substantially greater than it would be for a comparable person without that disability. This justification for discrimination against a disabled person can normally only be applied at the time that consideration is being given to admitting the disabled person into membership. These regulations also permit the scheme rules to set a uniform rate of employee contributions so that a disabled employee can be asked to pay the required contribution even if that disabled person is not eligible to receive all the benefits that are provided by the scheme, or to receive them at a lower rate.

The Government is at the time of writing consulting on how the UK will adopt the provisions prohibiting indirect or direct discrimination against disabled employees without objective justification as set out in the European Council Directive 2000/78/EC. These measures should be in place by 2 December 2006.

Age discrimination

European Council Directive 2000/78/EC states as general policy that any direct or indirect discrimination in employment based on age should be prohibited throughout the Community and sets 2 December 2006 as the latest date for implementation. Nevertheless, it allows occupational pension schemes to fix ages for admission or entitlement to retirement or invalidity benefits (including the fixing under those schemes of different ages for employees or groups or categories of employees, and the use of age criteria in actuarial calculations) without that amounting to discrimination on the grounds of age, provided this does not result in discrimination on the grounds of sex.

The key issue to be decided is whether the future legislation will remove the existing ability of an employer to dismiss an employee who has reached normal retiring age without that employee have recourse to making a claim for unfair dismissal to an employment tribunal. Some commentators argue that the current situation where employees lose the right to take a complaint for unfair dismissal to an employment tribunal once they have reached their normal retiring age is incompatible with the requirements of the Directive. This, however, is an employment law question and not one that directly affects trustees of pension schemes.

Questions that may be relevant to many schemes, however, include for example whether a defined contribution scheme that has a contribution structure that means that higher employer contributions are paid to older employees than to younger employees would fall foul of the age discrimination provisions, or whether it would come under the exceptions noted above.

Fixed-term workers

European Council Directive 1999/70/EC applies the principle of non-discrimination to those in fixed-term employment through the European

Union. The UK Government introduced measures in the *Employment Act 2000* and the *Fixed-term Employees (Prevention of Less Favourable Treatment) Regulations 2002 (SI 2002/2034)* to prevent discrimination against such employees. The regulations require employers to offer fixed-term employees access to occupational pension schemes on the same basis as offered to permanent employees unless different treatment can be objectively justified. However, the regulations also make it clear that a difference in the pension provision offered to fixed-term employees and to permanent employees can be objectively justified if the terms of a fixed-term employee's contract of employment, taken as a whole, are at least as favourable as the terms of the comparable permanent employee's contract.

Guidance issued by the Department of Trade and Industry at the time the regulations were laid before Parliament explained that where a fixed-term contract was for a period less than the vesting period applied by the rules of an occupational pension schemes, any move to allow the fixed-term employee access to the scheme might lead to a disproportionate cost with no benefit to the employee. Nevertheless, it should be noted in this context that the December 2002 Green Paper and accompanying technical paper explored proposals for the immediate vesting of occupational pension scheme rights. The implications of such a change would be the same for those employees on short fixed-term contracts as for employees on permanent contracts who nevertheless leave their employer after a short period.

Sexual orientation

European Council Directive 2000/78/EC states as general policy in relation to employment that any direct or indirect discrimination based on sexual orientation should be prohibited throughout the Community and sets 2 December 2003 as the latest date for implementation. The new requirements are likely to impact where benefits are payable to a surviving partner on the death of the scheme member if benefits are in practice not paid to same-sex partners but are paid to opposite-sex partners. The Directive will still permit the scheme rules to restrict survivors' benefits to the legal widows and widowers because the Directive is expressed to be 'without prejudice to national laws on marital status and the benefits dependent thereon'.

Early retirement programmes

9.6   As a result of a downsizing operation, the employer may propose that especially attractive early retirement terms are offered to older employees. Trustees should seek actuarial costings of the operation and ask whether a cash injection from the employer is necessary to finance the extra cost – which can be quite considerable. It may be that the early retirement programme is offered to all employees over a certain age. Or it may be that the employer's consent will also be needed and certain employees with vital skills will not be offered the favourable early retirement option. Trustees should ensure that they are being fair among members.

It is not to say that the occupational pension scheme should not be involved in financing an early retirement programme. Perhaps a surplus is available and the trustees reason that favourable early retirement terms on a temporary basis are as reasonable as an employer contribution holiday, although such surplus and contribution holidays are rarer now than in earlier times. If the early retirement programme *and* an employer contribution holiday is proposed, trustees should consider whether the interests of other classes of beneficiaries (younger members, early leavers and pensioners) are being sacrificed. In cases of redundancies, the trust deed and rules may often specify that the employer must bear the cost of providing unreduced or enhanced early retirement pensions. As ever, the key in deciding what policy the trustees should adopt is to see what the trust deed and rules say.

Augmentation of benefits to senior executives

9.7   It is boardroom practice very often to offer an *augmented* (i e increased) pension to a senior director who joined the company and contributed greatly to steering it through difficult times. The employer may offer the maximum approvable pension to this executive. The trust deed and rules should be checked to see if there is a power to augment benefits, and, if so, whether the extra cost, as determined by the scheme actuary, of providing the enhanced benefits should be met by the employer making a special contribution. At the end of the day, the trustees should not seek to define the employer's remuneration policy. Conversely, the trustees do owe a duty to strike a balance between the interests of the different classes of beneficiary. Augmentation became more common as an interim measure for dealing with the effects of the pensionable earnings cap.

Treatment on bulk transfers

9.8   Trustees of the main occupational pension scheme must be alert to the situation of the employer who wishes to transfer members of, for example, a separate senior executive scheme into the main scheme. Such schemes will have few members and are therefore subject to wild fluctuations in their funding level. The executive scheme could be underfunded, and a top-up payment may be due from the employer. If, as part of some harmonisation exercise, these members are to be transferred into the main pension scheme but in a separate section which provides superior benefits, trustees must take independent actuarial advice to ensure that a fair bulk transfer payment is made to cover the new liability.

Not to do so could unfairly damage the interests of existing beneficiaries and be a breach of trust. The employer might point to a current scheme surplus and argue that it should be used to cover the new liability. Again, the trustees must question whether this strikes a fair balance between the different groups of beneficiaries. It may be that the trustees feel the balance is fair and that no other group will suffer as a result: for example, the surplus is also sufficient to pay the usual discretionary increases on pensions-in-payment over the foreseeable future. However, it would still be expected that the bulk transfer payment would be sufficient to cover the past service liabilities of the transferring employees.

Similar situations can arise as a result of a merger or takeover – see **19.5**.

Trustees and active members

New employees

9.9   Trustees should be concerned that newly recruited employees who are eligible to join the occupational pension scheme are encouraged to do so.

To this end, effective communications have been important and are considered below. Many schemes have also decided to abandon lengthy waiting periods or minimum age requirements in their eligibility criteria to encourage membership.

Many schemes also have adopted the process of *automatic membership*: new employees are automatically entered into the scheme unless they positively decide to opt out.

On the other hand, the widespread perception of a 'pensions crisis' that became apparent during 2002 may mean that there is less need to sell the idea of membership of a good scheme.

Pensionable earnings cap

9.10   Trustees should ensure that the employer and personnel staff involved in recruiting senior staff are aware that all new employees are caught by the pensionable earnings cap. Details of the pensionable earnings cap should be included in the handbook describing the scheme. The problem is the employer's, not the trustees', since an approved scheme is prevented from providing benefits on earnings over the cash ceiling set by the cap. (It is possible, though, that the employer will set up a separate trust to provide unapproved top-up benefits to those caught by the pensionable earnings cap.) Nevertheless, trustees will not want senior executives who are members of the scheme to be unaware of the limitation.

Benefit redesign

9.11   Benefit redesign may offer a way of making the occupational pension scheme more attractive to employees. For example, the introduction of a *money purchase underpin* will mean that early leavers are not going to lose out. Younger employees might prefer a *starter defined benefit scheme* with low employee contribution rates and a slower accrual rate or one that is money purchase based, although to achieve the same effect it would now be much more common to offer a stakeholder pension scheme with a matched employer contribution up to a defined limit. Some schemes have successfully brought in *age-related employee contributions*. For instance, younger employees may

123

need to maximise take-home pay but will be willing to contribute 2.5% of salary; older employees will be motivated to pay 6.0%. Benefit redesign is, however, the responsibility of the employer, although trustees will need to be consulted and involved. It must also be admitted that benefit redesign issues relating to final salary schemes since 2002 in the vast majority of cases have become centred on the employer's perceived need to control costs rather than attract new entrants. Indeed, the commonest benefit redesign has precisely been to close the scheme to new entrants, offering them instead access to some other form of pension provision.

Opting out

9.12   Trustees should also consider what their attitude is towards those who remain in employment but opt out of the pension scheme. Much, as always, may depend on the trust deed and rules but in many cases trustees may have discretion to decide their policy. Will the employer continue to cover these employees for death-in-service lump sums? And if so, will it do so at the same or a lower level than for pension scheme members? Will those who request a transfer have their transfer value restricted to benefits that were accrued since 6 April 1988, as is allowed by the legislation, or will all their pensionable service count?

If an employee opts out, or refuses to join when first eligible, but then seeks to join or rejoin the scheme, will the trustees impose a medical examination to avoid selection against the pension scheme? (A medical examination may well be required by any insurer who has been engaged to provide death-in-service lump sum benefits.) Will a maximum re-entry age be set in such a case?

Similar issues have arisen in the recent past as a result of the mis-selling of personal pensions during the late 1980s and early 1990s. Employers and trustees had to decide whether those who had been mis-sold personal pensions were to be allowed to restore the missed past service upon receipt by the scheme of an adequate transfer value, and whether there would be a different policy on re-entry for those who were no longer employees, i e would they be re-instated as deferred pensioners.

Personal pensions

9.13   Whatever policy is adopted towards employees who have personal pensions, it would be wise to ensure that it is consistent. It should be remembered that many new employees may already have personal pensions set up several years ago and face severe upfront paid-up charges under these older contracts if they stop their contributions in order to join the occupational pension scheme. However, it is no longer always the case that an employee needs to stop contributing to a personal pension scheme in order to become a member of an occupational pension scheme. Concurrency is an option for those whose earnings have not exceeded £30,000 in any of the previous five tax years (but not counting any year before 2000/01 – see **2.15**).

Trustees should be aware of whether the employer is willing to contribute directly to an employee's personal pension.

Trustees and early leavers

9.14   The rights of the early leaver may not always be uppermost in the trustees' considerations. Trustees may think that those who have left the company should take a back seat. Even if understandable, such an approach is not honourable. In a contributory scheme, the early leavers will have paid contributions to the scheme during their time as employees and, if they have chosen to defer a preserved pension with the scheme, thereby becoming deferred pensioners, they will have shown good faith and confidence in the scheme. The great majority of the UK working population are early leavers after all.

The *Social Security Act 1973* introduced the preservation requirements for early leavers. Before that time, an employee could lose all pension rights if he or she left employment before normal pension age, even after 39 years service! The *Social Security Act 1985* introduced the revaluation and transfer legislation which is now to be found in the *Pension Schemes Act 1993*. Before that time, an early leaver's pension could be compulsorily frozen in the scheme without any increases except those applying to any Guaranteed Minimum Pension. It is now generally acknowledged that the pension industry's hostility to the situation of the early leaver caused much resentment and lost occupational pension schemes much support.

General principle

9.15   In the legislation, the pension entitlement of the early leaver is known as *Short Service Benefit (SSB)* as opposed to the *Long Service Benefit (LSB)* of those who stay until retirement. The *Pension Schemes Act 1993* states:

> 'A scheme must not contain any rule which results, or can result, in a member being treated less favourably for any purpose relating to short service benefit than he is, or entitled to be, treated for the corresponding purpose relating to long service benefit.'

The above rule, however, does not apply to benefit improvements made after the member has left employment.

It should be noted that if the scheme has equalised pension ages at, say, 65 but members have the right without the need to gain consent to retire at, say, 60 on an unreduced pension, age 60 has become the normal pension age for future early leavers (and this will increase the size of any transfer payment for an early leaver).

It is not uncommon to find that the payment of an unreduced early retirement pension is subject under the scheme rules to the exercise of a discretionary power in any particular case. The power may be exercisable by the trustees or the employer. In such a situation it is quite possible that an active member is offered an unreduced early retirement pension at say, age 55, while a deferred pensioner of the same age who contacts the scheme to ask if he or she can be paid an immediate pension is offered an early retirement pension with the normal actuarial reduction applied.

Trustees must also decide whether deferred pensioners should be consulted about the nomination and selection rules for member-nominated trustees (see **4.18**).

Trustees should not forget deferred pensioners when considering the use of any discretionary powers that they are free to exercise under the provisions of the trust deed and rules.

Revaluation of deferred pensions

9.16   For defined benefit schemes, there are a number of points in relation to the revaluation of the deferred pensions (in excess of any GMP which is in effect revalued in line with national average earnings):

- For those employees who left before 1 January 1986 there does not have to be any revaluation at all.

- Deferred pension rights that were accrued on or after 1 January 1985 for those who left on or after 1 January 1986 but before 1 January 1991 have to be revalued at a minimum over the period of deferment in line with the rise in prices or at 5% compound per annum if this is less.

- For those who have left on or after 1 January 1991 all deferred pensions rights have to be revalued at a minimum over the period of deferment in line with the rise in prices or at 5% compound per annum if this is less.

Around one quarter of the larger private sector final salary schemes give trustees discretionary power to revalue deferred pensions by more than the statutory amount. In many cases, the rise-in-prices-or-5%-compound formula (known as Limited Price Indexation or LPI) is used irrespective of the date the member actually left the scheme.

Average salary schemes must revalue the deferred pensioners against the same index as is used to calculate the pensions of those retiring from active service.

GMPs have been abolished for pensionable service after 5 April 1997. All the pension rights of early leavers from defined benefit schemes which have accrued from that date are revalued using the LPI formula and no element of the deferred pension has to be revalued in line with national average earnings.

Deferred pensions preserved in defined contribution (money purchase) schemes will simply continue to participate in the fund's investment growth less, where applicable, any administrative charge levied by an insurance company.

Transfer payments

9.17   An actuary will calculate transfer values for early leavers who wish to take their pension out of the scheme in accordance with the legislation, in particular the *Occupational Pension Schemes (Transfer Values) Regulations 1996 (SI 1996/1847)*. The legislation requires that transfer values should normally reflect any customary discretionary benefits that are paid.

A discretionary increase on pensions-in-payment is the main example and, of course, the transfer value will be larger if it reflects these increases. The legislation does, though, permit trustees specifically to forbid the actuary to take account of such discretionary increases so that the transfer value is kept low. However, under the *Occupational Pension Schemes (Transfer Values) Regulations 1996* the trustees must not instruct the actuary to ignore discretionary increases unless they have consulted him or her, and have obtained a written report on the implications for the state of the scheme funding if they go ahead and indeed instruct him or her to ignore discretionary increases. The report must include the actuary's opinion as to whether or not there would be any adverse implications for the funding of the scheme if the trustees did not instruct the actuary to ignore discretionary increases. Members requesting transfer values have a right to see this report. In other words, it is now theoretically harder for trustees to justify not allowing the actuary to take into account discretionary benefits when calculating transfer values if the actuary's report makes it clear that it would not have difficult funding implications for the scheme.

Under the requirements of the *Occupational Pension Schemes (Disclosure of Information) Regulations 1996 (SI 1996/1655)* members must be told as part of the information given on the basic benefits provided by the scheme whether discretionary increases are taken into account in calculating transfer values.

In the case of defined benefit schemes, a member's right to a quoted transfer value must, since 6 April 1997, normally be guaranteed for a minimum period of three months. Furthermore, since that date such schemes gradually became subject to the *minimum funding requirement* (MFR) (see **13.7**) and the Transfer Values Regulations require in such cases that the transfer value is calculated on a basis which is no less favourable to the early leaver than that used in assessing the actuarial valuation of the liabilities under the MFR.

If the trustees fail without reasonable excuse to pay the member's transfer value within six months, the transfer value must be increased with interest in accordance with the requirements of the Transfer Values Regulations. It might also be the case that the Pensions Ombudsman, if involved, would find that the trustees were guilty of maladministration.

In January 2003, the Department for Work and Pensions circulated for comment draft amending regulations which are to change the requirements of the Transfer Values Regulations. The change will allow the trustees of defined benefit schemes to reduce transfer values by reference to factors other than the MFR funding position at the time of the last MFR valuation. The resulting amount must still not be less than the MFR minimum. The aim is to ensure that early leavers wishing to transfer their rights out of the scheme do not take more than the due proportion of the fund at the expense of the other members remaining in the scheme. The investment market conditions that had developed at this time indicated that under the old rules there was a danger that the interests of the remaining members could be damaged in this way.

The legislative requirement that a transfer value from a defined benefit scheme, once quoted, is guaranteed for three months has not been changed – at least not for schemes that do not go into wind up during this intervening period. Therefore, in February 2003, the pensions regulator Opra exercised its right not to penalise trustees who decide to delay the issue of such guaranteed statements of entitlement until the amending regulations are put into effect.

Death before retirement

9.18   Many schemes will provide an immediate widow's, widower's or dependant's pension to the survivor of a deferred pensioner in the event of his or her death before pension age. Some schemes will also pay a discretionary lump sum to a nominated survivor. The trust deed and rules will determine what pension, if any, is paid and trustees may have discretionary powers to determine who should receive it – see **5.4**. Problems may arise if the survivors of a deferred pensioner are unaware of their rights although, in the case of contracted-out schemes, the scheme administrator will be informed by the National Insurance Contributions Office if a widow's or widower's contracted-out pension is payable.

Trustees and pensioners

9.19   During the early 1990s, there were a number of groups of pensioners exercising pressure on their occupational pension schemes and persuading the trustees to pay them due regard. It seemed likely that such examples would be part of a continuing trend and indeed pensioner groups have continued to be active in lobbying trustees to pay due attention to the interests of pensioner members, not only in regard to the issue of pension increases but in other more general areas such as arguing against payments from surplus to be paid to the sponsoring employer. It must be said, however, that in present years the closure of underfunded defined benefit schemes has often left pensioners in a relatively privileged position compared to active members since pensions in payment are awarded a higher priority than many other benefits when a scheme is wound up – see **19.11**.

There are repeated calls from pensioner action groups to be represented on the trustee body and pensioners have to be involved in the nomination and selection rules for member-nominated trustees. Following strong opposition, however, the Government in 1999 backed away from a proposal it had made that large mature schemes should have a reserved place on the trustee board for a pensioner member. Whether pensioners are able to nominate candidates for selection as member-nominated trustees, and whether active members, in cases where they can nominate member trustees, could nominate pensioners are questions that are determined by the scheme rules governing trustee selection (see **CHAPTER 4**). Where pensioner trustees are in place, their input has generally been very highly regarded. It is often suggested that pensioner trustees can be more single-minded in carrying out their trustee duties because they have no conflicts arising from any employment contract with the sponsoring employer.

Pension increases

9.20   A key concern of pensioners, if not of all scheme members, is the ability of the occupational pension scheme to grant annual increases to pensions-in-payment so that their value is preserved in real terms.

The trust deed and rules will specify how pensions-in-payment will be increased. On 6 April 1997, legislation contained in the *Pensions Act 1995* introduced Limited Price Indexation (LPI). This means that pension rights accrued from that date have to give rise to pensions which, once in payment, as a minimum, have to rise each year in line with the rise in prices up to a ceiling of 5%.

The introduction of compulsory LPI on pension rights built up from 6 April 1997 may compensate members of schemes contracted out by the GMP test for the loss of future GMP rights from the same date. GMPs, once in payment, are in effect increased in line with the full rise in prices.

This LPI formula does not necessarily apply to pensioners who have retired, other than on the grounds of ill-health, before age 55. Once a pensioner, who retired before age 55, reaches age 55 the whole amount of the missed pension increases then become payable and the pension must be uprated normally thereafter.

Any discretionary increases above the LPI formula can be offset against the following year's LPI increase.

AVC contributions do not have to give rise to increasing pensions. Also, the Government allows members of defined contribution (money purchase) schemes the choice of buying an investment-linked annuity which does not guarantee increases, instead of a conventional annuity that would guarantee the LPI increase on post-5 April 1997 pension rights (although this choice is not open to those who need to secure protected rights built up in a contracted-out scheme).

9.21

Most of the larger occupational pension schemes in the private sector have granted increases which have restored, or nearly restored, the original purchasing power of pensions-in-payment.

Full annual increases in line with the retail prices index (RPI) are hardly ever given as a right under the rules of private sector schemes. The norm among the larger schemes is to have a rule that will raise each year all pensions-in-payment in line with the RPI up to the LPI limit of 5% and then give the trustees discretionary powers to grant an additional increase. Note that this goes beyond the statutory requirement which requires LPI increases only on pension rights earned after 5 April 1997.

Very often, during a period of high inflation, the pension increase is lower than the RPI. Then, a few years later, special targeted increases are made to groups of pensioners over a specified age in a series of 'catching-up' exercises.

Trustees who have discretionary powers to award pension increases, which will almost always involve the need to obtain the consent of the employer, may feel in a very exposed position. Yet the decision of the employer, the advice of the scheme actuary and the history of custom and practice may mean that in the event there is very little scope for discretion and a figure will emerge.

When general benefit improvements are being considered, perhaps as a result of the distribution of a surplus, pensioners would undoubtedly challenge a decision not to award a reasonable increase, with perhaps special weighting for those who have been retired the longest.

Some smaller schemes simply grant a fixed increase of 3% a year (although they are obliged to offer the LPI formula on post-5 April 1997 service as explained above). When inflation was high members' pensions provided by these schemes would have declined in *real* value.

Example

An employee has a pension of £100 p m. If inflation is, say, 7% , the pension will need to be increased by 7% to retain its *real* value, i e increased to £107 p m. The 7% increase is said to be a *nominal* increase as it just preserves the *real* value of the pension. If the scheme actually grants 3% fixed pension increases only, the pension is increased to £103 p m. Because 103/107 x 100 comes out at 96.26%, we can say that the pension has declined in *real* value by 3.74%.

Some other schemes did not grant any increase at all prior to the new legislation coming into force, other than the statutory increase on any GMP if the scheme had been contracted out. Therefore a scheme offering a fixed increase was seen as generous in comparison.

Ironically, at a time of low inflation those schemes which promise 3% fixed increases are often providing a more generous increase than those which promise full price inflation.

Example

An employee has a pension of £100 p m. If inflation is, say, 1% , the pension would need to be increased by 1% to retain its *real* value, i e increased to £101 p m. As before, this increase is said to be a *nominal* increase as it just preserves the *real* value of the pension. If the scheme actually grants 3% fixed increases only, the pension is increased to £103 p m. Because 103/101 x 100 comes out at 101.98%, we can say that the pension has increased in *real* value by 1.98%.

Under such conditions, a 3% fixed increase can become a very costly benefit provision. Removal of a right to a fixed 3% increase, however, except in relation to pension rights built up after the date of any rule change, is very likely to be challenged for falling foul of *section 67* of the *Pensions Act 1995*. This is the measure that prevents the worsening of any accrued rights without the consent of all the members affected (see **6.3**).

Even schemes which do not promise a fixed increase could find that that they are meeting the cost of granting *real* increases if there were ever to be a period of deflation – that is when the retail prices index becomes negative. This is because the trust deed and rules of pension schemes allow for pensions to be *increased* to take account of inflation, but do not permit them to be *reduced* in *nominal* terms during a period of deflation.

Example

An employee has a pension of £100 p m. If inflation was, say, −1% (i e deflation of 1%), the pension would need to be reduced by 1% to retain its *real* value, i e reduced to £99 p.m. As before, this reduction is said to be a *nominal* reduction as it just preserves the *real* value of the pension. However, the trust deed and rules of the scheme are likely to preclude such a reduction and in practice the pension would remain at £100 p m. Because 100/99 x 100 comes out at 101.01%, we can say that the pension has increased in *real* value by 1.01%.

Other aspects

9.22   Trustees may also be involved in pensioner welfare activities, or the pensions administration may employ an officer with special responsibilities for pensioner welfare. Visits to the homes of pensioners may be made by volunteers and annual events organised, especially if the employer is established in a particular part of the country. As a matter of good practice, pensioners should be circulated with any pension newsletter that is produced.

Trustees and surviving dependants

9.23   Trustees may be called on to exercise discretionary powers under the trust deed and rules in deciding whether a person qualifies as a dependant of the bereaved pensioner, current active member or deferred pensioner. For more details see **5.4**.

It is quite common in the rules governing private sector schemes to find a provision stating that a spouse's pension will be reduced if he or she is more than a certain number of years younger (often ten) than the deceased. This is in part an attempt to safeguard against the so-called 'death-bed marriages' in which an elderly pensioner marries a young man or woman solely so that the latter can be provided with a pension for life. Many of the stories are probably apocryphal.

It is now rare for scheme rules to withdraw a survivor's pension in cases of the survivor later remarrying, although the practice is widespread in the public sector. Even rarer would be any private sector scheme which would suspend a survivor's pension during any period when the recipient was cohabiting. In both cases, there could be great difficulties in monitoring compliance with such a rule.

Trustees and divorced partners

9.24   The *Pensions Act 1995* gave the courts the power to make orders that will direct the trustees to pay part of a divorced member's pension rights, once they have come into payment, direct to that member's former spouse. This process is known as *earmarking* the benefit. Once the trustees receive the order they will have to inform the parties concerned of the changed circumstances and give information about the value of the pension benefits. Trustees are able to recover administrative expenses for the scheme.

The court may order the member to commute the whole or part of his or her benefit and the order will extend to the lump sum payment. As explained at **5.5**, all or part of any death-in-service lump sum may have to be paid to the ex-spouse. Earmarking orders, however, cannot be used to earmark survivors' pensions payable on the member's death. Once an earmarked pension has come into payment it will cease on the member's death. If the ex-spouse dies first, the earmarked pension may cease, be paid to the ex-spouse's estate, or revert to the member.

Once a court order is in force, it will transfer automatically if the member subsequently transfers all his or her pension rights out of the scheme to another pension arrangement.

These provisions only apply where the petition for divorce was presented to the court on or after 1 July 1996.

The Welfare Reform and Pensions Act 1999 and the *Finance Act 1999* have introduced *pensions sharing* on divorce provisions available to divorces granted on or after 1 December 2000. Pensions sharing on divorce operates as an alternative to earmarking orders, and indeed also as an alternative to the long-established practice of the courts in devising financial settlements that offset pension rights against other assets. Pension sharing has the important advantage over earmarking in that it works on the 'clean break' principle and the divorced spouse does not have to wait until the ex-partner decides to draw the pension rights before being able to receive any pension benefit.

Broadly, pension sharing works as follows. Spouses A and B were a married couple until their divorce. Spouse A is a member of either an occupational or a personal pension scheme. If there is a pensions share, there is a reduction in spouse A's pension rights known as the 'pension debit' and a corresponding allocation of rights to spouse B known as the 'pension credit'. Spouse A's SERPS/S2P entitlement can also be debited and a corresponding credit granted to Spouse B. In the case of an occupational pension scheme spouse B becomes a special kind of scheme member with the right (except in an unfunded scheme) to transfer that pension credit to another pension arrangement. The rules of a scheme can insist that a person awarded a pension credit but who was not otherwise a member of the scheme must transfer that pension credit to another pension arrangement. The costs of the pension sharing to the scheme is recoverable from the divorcing couple.

Disclosure of information and communications

Disclosure of Information Regulations

9.25   Trustees should familiarise themselves with the latest amended version of the *Occupational Pension Schemes (Disclosure of Information) Regulations 1996 (SI 1996/1655)*. Most pension consultants will also have published effective guidance on the Disclosure of Information Regulations. The *Social Security Act 1985* (now revoked) introduced new requirements on trustees to provide members with certain basic information about their schemes automatically, and also rights to receive further information on request. Recognised trade unions also have rights to receive scheme information. Since 6 April 1997, the various disclosure requirements have been extended by regulations made under the *Pensions Act 1995* and cover the requirements relating to the disclosure of the scheme's audited accounts, the information to be given when a member requests to transfer pension rights out of the scheme, and what information must be given to early leavers.

Failure to comply

9.26   Before the coming into force of the *Pensions Act 1995*, if trustees failed to provide the information required by the earlier version of the Disclosure of Information Regulations, aggrieved individuals or a trade union could issue a notice requiring them to do so within 14 days. Alternatively, they could ask the former Occupational Pensions Board (OPB) to act on their behalf. Once the OPB was satisfied that there was evidence of default, it could similarly issue a notice requiring the trustees to comply within 14 days. If the trustees continued to fail to meet the requirements, the aggrieved individuals, the trade union or the OPB on their behalf could apply to the appropriate court for an order. These enforcement procedures were widely criticised as being inadequate, and since 6 April 1997 the *Pensions Act 1995* has made any breach of the new requirements a matter for Opra with explicit penalties on trustees for non-compliance.

Communications

9.27   The principle of voluntary membership was introduced by the *Social Security Act 1986* (by rendering void any clause in an employment contract that has compulsory membership as a condition of employment). Although the December 1998 Green Paper *A New Contract for Welfare: Partnership in Pensions* proposed measures to encourage take-up of scheme membership, including making scheme membership once again a general condition of employment, it explained that it would still be necessary to allow certain employees the ability to opt out of scheme membership provided they could show they met certain conditions. Because of the statutory need to disclose information, the fact of voluntary membership and the rise of personal pensions, it was seen as important for trustees to mount a continuing and effective communication campaign that actively tries to sell membership of the occupational pension scheme to employees.

However, in recent years communication campaigns have tended to be directed at explaining the pension provision, and in particular, at explaining any change in the nature of that provision. For example, a defined benefit final salary scheme may have been closed to new entrants, who are instead offered membership of a defined contribution arrangement, such as a stakeholder pension scheme.

There seems also to be less emphasis on trying to persuade employees to take up membership. In certain quarters, the 'paternalist' approach to the employer/employee relationship seems currently to be out of fashion.

In large organisations, the trustees and the pensions department will need assistance in communicating any pensions message. This may be through local *pension consultative committees*, or though the local personnel function.

Below we list the basic and the optional elements of the trustees' communications package. They constitute good practice but are not themselves a summary of the requirements of the Disclosure of Information Regulations. In many cases, good practice goes beyond these statutory requirements.

All communication materials should use plain English but *not* patronise members. Complex subjects should *not* be avoided on the grounds that they are 'too difficult' for members.

The two most important points about any communication material is that:

(*a*)   it should aim to give as comprehensive an explanation as possible; and

(*b*)   it must be completely accurate.

Any misleading or inaccurate information given in a scheme handbook or benefit statement could constitute scheme maladministration (see **11.4**). If a scheme member relied on such information to his or her financial disadvantage, the Pensions Ombudsman or the courts could direct the trustees to set the matter right – see **CHAPTER 20**.

It is noteworthy that Alan Pickering, in his July 2002 report *A Simpler Way to Better Pensions*, stated that his starting point on communicating pensions was that the rules should be based on the following clear principles:

- Communications should be aimed primarily at influencing behaviour. The information should give individuals the facts that they need to decide whether to join, stay in or leave a scheme.

- Communication should provide members with basic information about their likely pension – including setting out, in broad terms, the risks: for example, in a defined contribution scheme members should receive a reminder that the final pension will depend on investment performance net of fees and annuity rates.

- Individuals should be properly informed of major events that might affect members (for example, relevant changes to scheme design or large numbers of members taking early retirement), and their options on leaving or retiring or what will happen to their pension if they die.

- It is also necessary to provide information to protect members: for example, those in a defined benefit scheme should have access to information about the funding position.

- All communications with members should be tested to see whether they are understandable and will work.

Alan Pickering was sceptical that the current disclosure requirements met these principles and proposed radical simplification to these requirements. In the technical paper accompanying the December 2002 Green Paper, the Government said it would welcome views on:

- what information items that are currently supplied automatically could instead be made available on request;

- what particular pieces of information should continue to have specific time limits attached to them; and

- what other areas of legislative prescription could be removed without having an adverse effect on members and their understanding of their pension arrangements.

There is a danger inherent in Alan Pickering's call for pensions communication to be used first and foremost to influence members' behaviour. Although clearly not his intention, it should be remembered that 'communication designed to influence behaviour' is often also, more simply, known as 'propaganda'. Information regarding one's occupational pension scheme should not be presented on the public relations principle of 'accentuate the positive and omit the negative'!

Also, the emphasis on the 'keep it simple' approach in order that all members should be able to understand inevitably means that important but difficult information – such as the detailed analysis of the pension scheme's accounts – would either be omitted or simplified and so not be available, or not easily available, neither to those members who were willing to put in the effort to come to grips with it, nor to external commentators such as trade unions and journalists.

Basic elements

9.28   Trustees may wish to consider posting some of the following material to the employee's home rather than handing it out at work. There are certain advantages: the material is less likely to be mislaid or lost and the member's family is also more likely to see it. If this option is chosen, it should be designed so that it can be easily pushed through the average size letter box.

Handbook

9.29   A scheme handbook ought to be given to all potential new members. Amendments should be given to all members when they are made. New editions should be produced and given to all members rather than allowing amendment sheets to accumulate. The handbook should describe all the contribution conditions and the benefits offered.

Benefit statements for active members

9.30   Each member should receive an annual benefit statement which is easily understandable. Supporting material such as a newsletter can be included with the benefit statement. The annual benefit statement is the piece of scheme information that is most likely to be read in full by the recipient. The arrival of statutory money purchase illustrations (SMPI) should help members of defined contribution schemes better understand the expected value of the pension income, in today's money. Joint benefit statements incorporating the individuals' entitlement from the state as well as from their current scheme give a broader understanding of the totality of future income, even if they fail to be able to incorporate future income from deferred pension rights in a single statement.

Benefit statements for pensioners

9.31   All pensioners should be sent annual benefit statements and told of the amount of any pension increase. Again, a newsletter could be included in the mailing.

Annual report

9.32   The trustees are required to produce an annual report containing the audited accounts, the actuarial valuation and statement and other information required by the legislation. Some large occupational pension schemes have decided that a popular annual report should be given automatically to all active members and pensioners. Copies of the full annual report are, of course, still provided on request.

However, any popular annual report should not be designed so as to evade the proper provision of information about the scheme. Trustees might like to encourage their communication advisers to try to make the full annual report and accounts more 'popular' instead. The annual report can be used to give the history of the scheme over the previous year and items can be reported which are of interest to the membership at large. Trustees should, nevertheless, be reconciled to the fact that many members will not read the annual report and accounts, whether it is the popular or the formal version.

Trustees are required to prepare, revise and maintain a statement of investment principles (see **16.8**). This can be a separate document available to members on request. However, because of its importance, the trustees often choose to place it within the annual report and accounts. This seems to be a very good idea.

Optional elements

Newsletters

9.33   If the employer issues a company newsletter, it might be useful for trustees to negotiate a regular column on pension scheme news (there is rarely any shortage!). Some very large schemes may issue their own occasional newsletter.

Promotional leaflets and brochures

9.34   Attractive promotional leaflets and brochures can be designed and produced to be given to new employees to point out the advantages of belonging to the company scheme. The Maxwell affair was over a decade ago, but as a cause of distrust among the members it has been replaced by a plethora of reports concerning the closure of underfunded final salary schemes. Such material will need to address issues of security head on. Yet, it must be acknowledged that in recent years some supplies of attractive promotional leaflets were probably junked when the scheme was closed to new entrants.

Videos

9.35   Videos explaining the pension scheme and taking members through any major scheme redesign can be very effective. They are expensive and need to be used very carefully in conjunction with employee meetings and supporting written material. It may be useful to lend the video out for members to take home; this involves the member's family who also have an interest in the message being relayed. It should, nevertheless, be remembered that Robert Maxwell made effective use of video presentations to members of his companies' schemes.

Intranet and internet sites

9.36   Electronic communication and in particular interactive media are being rapidly adopted as an extra means of communication by many pension schemes. Some schemes have set up web sites that are open to all and contain much information about the scheme – for example the contents of the latest annual report. Others put this information on a CD-ROM which is given to any member with a multi-media PC at home. A company-wide intranet is a particularly useful means of communication since it can be designed to allow members to ask 'what if' type questions based on their own personal circumstances. Ensuring the security of personal information is important in such systems.

Professional help

9.37   Most pension consultants offer extensive communication services – see **CHAPTER 12**. Help in preparing the material can also be obtained from the company's public relations department. Effective communication does not need to be expensive, but it does need to be thoughtful.

Giving advice

9.38   Trustees should be aware of the restrictions placed by the *Financial Services and Markets Act 2000* on the giving of financial advice. Only those who are directly authorised under that Act are permitted to give detailed financial advice on investments to others. Most trustees are not authorised to give financial advice.

There is no problem in trustees giving advice to members:

- about the occupational pension scheme since it is not classed as an investment;

- about general principles of why an occupational pension scheme may provide better benefits than a personal pension; and

- about the general advantages of making additional voluntary contributions.

Trustees should be wary of giving specific advice on the merits of the XYZ personal pension scheme or free-standing AVC scheme since both of these products are classed as controlled investments. However, there is a feeling that trustees and pension administrators have been too cautious in giving advice and that in practice they would not be prosecuted under the earlier *Financial*

Services Act 1986 if it was clearly seen that they were not in the business of giving investment advice and received no commercial benefit from so doing. Guidance from the Securities and Investments Board (now the Financial Services Authority (FSA)) in any case should have made it clear that it is not normally best advice to sell a personal pension to an active member, or potential member of an occupational pension scheme. The arrival of the concurrency option introduced in April 2001 (see **2.15**) has greatly reduced the danger of the mis-selling of personal pensions.

The problem may commonly arise where an early leaver approaches the trustees (or a member of the pensions or the personnel department) and asks whether he/she should go for a buy-out policy with the ABC insurance company or a personal pension with the XYZ insurance company. The trustee could point out the general options of preservation in the scheme, transfer to a buy-out policy, a personal pension or to the next employer's scheme and express a general opinion. The trustee should avoid specific advice in this instance. Those selling any transfer plan will have to carry out a detailed transfer value analysis in any case.

The selling of stakeholder pension schemes from April 2001 is also a regulated activity, even if the stakeholder pension is legally established as an occupational pension scheme. The FSA regulates the conduct of stakeholder pensions business which includes the use of a set of draft 'decision trees' – a graphical critical path of decision boxes to guide the individual in deciding whether or not to contribute to a stakeholder pension scheme.

Many in the financial services industry are concerned that the limit on charges placed on all stakeholder pension schemes will leave very little scope for the giving of advice to potential stakeholder customers. However, many on the consumer side point to the distinct lack of quality in the advice given in earlier times in relation to the selling of personal pensions. There is an argument that if the quality of the product meets minimum standards, then the need for costly advice is less. This has been reflected in the FSA's approach.

Where a stakeholder is governed by trustees, they will be responsible for ensuring that those advising potential and actual members of their stakeholder pension scheme comply with the FSA's requirements. Most new stakeholder pension business is likely to be 'non-advised'. The importance of the decision trees devised by the FSA, and which are incorporated into the regulatory process, is that they should enable individuals to make a choice, where they reasonably can, without having to pay for advice, and to help identify instances in which advice or further information is necessary.

Checklist 9

- Trustees have a duty to act fairly between the different classes of members.

- Trustees are directly responsible for ensuring that their scheme's rules and actual practice respect the principle of equal treatment between men and women in matters of access, contributions and benefits.

- Scheme rules and practice must also respect other statutory requirements such as those contained in the *Race Relations Act 1975* and the *Disability Discrimination Act 1995*.

- Trustees must ensure that women on maternity leave are treated at least in accordance with statutory requirements.

- Trustees must pay rigorous attention whenever there are scheme reconstructions involving mergers, demergers and bulk transfers to ensure that the accrued and future pension rights of their own members are not disadvantaged nor diminished.

- If benefit improvements are to be made using a scheme fund surplus, trustees should consider the needs of all groups, although this does not mean that benefit improvements cannot be made which only favour one group of members. Such partial improvements can be made provided the use of the surplus funds in this way does not jeopardise the accrued rights and legitimate future expectations of other groups.

- Trustees should recognise the distinct interests of active members, early leavers including deferred pensioners, pensioners, widows, widowers and other dependants including divorced spouses.

- Trustees must observe the disclosure of information requirements but ought to go further and strive to enthuse members about their scheme by the use of good communications. Communication materials that are thoughtfully put together may be more effective than materials that have simply cost a good deal of money. Giving full explanations in plain English about complicated subjects is preferable to glossy materials written in a 'popular' style that leave out anything that is felt 'too difficult' for the members.

- Trustees of trust-based stakeholder pension schemes will need to ensure that those promoting the stakeholder pension scheme comply with the requirements of the FSA although the use of decision trees alone will not constitute the giving of financial advice.

Chapter 10

Professional advisers

Expert advice

10.1   Whether individual trustees are drawn from senior management or the employees generally, it is not expected that they will bring with them an expert knowledge of trust law, pensions administration, actuarial matters, pensions accountancy and institutional investment. All trustees will need to take expert advice. Even professional trustees will need to take advice from other professionals working in a different field.

When Paul Myners published his report *Institutional Investment in the UK: A Review* in March 2001, there was a widespread view that he was proposing the 'professionalisation' of pension fund trusteeship. During the ensuing debate it has become clearer that this is not his intention.

It is accepted that there are benefits in having trustees drawn from a great variety of backgrounds and with different areas of expertise. It is also accepted that pension fund trustees will need access to good quality advice from paid professional advisers.

What Paul Myners and the Government advocate is that, especially in the area of pension fund investment, the trustees should be *familiar with the issues concerned* so that they can effectively question and challenge the advice they are given. It must be said that it is difficult to quarrel with this view. If the trustees are in reality bamboozled by the complexity of the issues involved in running a pension scheme, they cannot be acting in the best interests of their members. In such a situation the professional advisers will in reality be those making the key decisions. The Government states that it is seeking to ensure that *those responsible for decisions in law are those taking them in fact* – and that surely ought to be the trustees. The issues raised by Paul Myners' review are further explored in **CHAPTER 17**.

It is in fact a trustee's duty to take advice, and trustees who act in important matters without taking expert, independent advice could certainly betray the interest of the beneficiaries. They are also likely to fail to meet the many statutory requirements of the *Pensions Act 1995* and as a result suffer a penalty imposed by Opra. Trustees who fail to take advice could in addition leave themselves open to action for a breach of trust.

Indeed, in many situations statutory law will require that the trustees obtain the expert services of an outside professional. For example, in a defined benefit scheme, an actuary must carry out the required periodic valuations of the scheme's assets and liabilities.

However, just because professional advice has been obtained, it does not follow that trustees have no choice but to follow it. If there is a difficulty, perhaps a second opinion should be sought. Ultimately, the responsibility for a decision will rest with the trustees.

The trust deed and rules will almost certainly give trustees the power to appoint professional advisers and pay them from the fund's resources.

Some advisers, in particular accountants, actuaries and solicitors, will be covered by a professional indemnity insurance. This ought to help trustees recover any losses which the fund sustains as a direct consequence of poor professional advice.

Advisers to employers or to the trustees?

10.2   The *Pensions Act 1995* made important changes on 6 April 1997 as to how professional advisers are appointed, the nature of their role and the nature of their responsibilities. In summary, trustees can be fined or removed if, with certain limited exceptions:

- they rely on auditors, actuaries, lawyers, custodians or fund managers whom they have not appointed (e g the employer has appointed them instead);

- they do not appoint a scheme auditor and, except in the case of money purchase schemes where the pension is secured by annuities rather than being paid from the fund, a scheme actuary.

But in the case of the investment manager or managers, the appointment may be made either by the trustees or by someone authorised to do so on their behalf.

The overall intention of the Government was that scheme advisers should be appointed by, take their instructions from, and report to the trustees, rather than the employer.

It has always been important to understand to whom the advisers owe their primary loyalty: the trustees or the employer. Professional advisers will naturally need to ensure they comply with statutory law and the standards and codes set by their own professional associations. They will, however, owe a duty of confidence to their client. And prior to 6 April 1997 their client may have been the trustees or it may have been the employer. That dilemma has been removed.

The adviser may, however, also separately be an adviser to the employer; for example, the same accountancy firm may audit the company accounts and the pension fund accounts.

Few commentators say that trustees should not accept advice from an adviser in a firm that has also been engaged to provide services to the employer. In many circumstances, this may be appropriate. For example, the same actuary could advise both the sponsoring employer and the trustees and in most cases this will be a sensible use of resources. However, there are areas where there are genuine conflicts of interest, and the duty of trustees will be more than just to take professional advice; it will be to take *independent*, expert advice. Professional advisers should inform the trustees if they think there is a conflict of interest.

The actuary or auditor, with certain narrow exceptions, should not be connected to any of the trustees.

Advisers and beneficiaries

10.3   Professional advisers will not be directly accountable to the beneficiaries of the pension fund. If the fund has paid for the advice, though, under trust law it could be argued that beneficiaries have a right to have sight of that advice. Such a right would go beyond the specific requirements of the Disclosure of Information Regulations.

This is not the case in other jurisdictions – for example in the US, federal legislation insists that professional advisers have fiduciary duties to the members. There are signs that this approach may be adopted in the UK. In its proposals for a replacement for the minimum funding requirement (MFR) (see **13.9**), the Government has suggested that the scheme actuary should have a statutory duty of care to the members. Also, in its consultation paper setting out legislative proposals for an enhanced standard of care by trustees when making investment decisions (see **17.7**) the Government asks:

> 'The ERISA provisions in the US legislation on which the current proposals are based extend to fiduciaries other than pension scheme trustees. This means that fund managers and, for example, custodians also have a fiduciary responsibility to pension scheme beneficiaries. Should a provision similar to this be introduced in the UK?'

Whistle-blowing duties

10.4   One of the criticisms of the system of regulating and supervising occupational pension schemes at the time of the Maxwell scandal was that there was no specific duty on the various scheme advisers to share any misgivings they had about how a pension scheme was being run with a supervisory body. They did of course often have to give certified statements to the various supervisory bodies about the scheme, but the Report of the House of Commons Social Security Committee investigating the Maxwell case levelled some general criticism at professional advisers who adopted a rather 'letter of the law' approach.

The criticism was developed in the Report of the Pensions Law Review Committee under the chairmanship of Professor Goode. Three weaknesses in particular were identified:

- advisers reported any irregularities to those who had appointed them and on whose behalf they acted, i e the employer or trustees;

- there was no regulatory body with general supervisory powers over pension schemes to which such reports could be made;

- reports to a third party such as a regulator were inhibited in any case by the confidentiality that the advisers owed to their clients.

The Government agreed with this analysis and the policy to rectify these shortcomings lies at the heart of the *Pensions Act 1995*.

A new powerful regulator, Opra, with a more wide-ranging remit than its predecessor, the Occupational Pensions Board (OPB), has been created.

Two key advisers, the auditor and the actuary, are given under *section 48* of the *Pensions Act 1995* a statutory duty to 'blow the whistle'. They must, when they have reasonable cause to believe that irregularities have occurred in a scheme, make an immediate written report of the matter to Opra.

Furthermore, if they do so, they cannot be sued for breach of confidence by their client.

The onus is on the scheme auditor and actuary to decide whether a matter must be reported to Opra. In practice, they will need to consider three questions:

- Is there reasonable cause to believe there is an irregularity?

- Is there any duty relevant to the administration of the scheme that is not being complied with?

- Is the failure to comply likely to be of material significance to Opra?

Auditors and actuaries who fail to carry out their duty to blow the whistle could face a fine levied by Opra but the Government has indicated that it would prefer the professional bodies to carry out the role of disciplining their members – this could involve the removal of a professional's practising certificate.

Other professional advisers (other than the scheme auditor and actuary), as well as any trustee or scheme administrator who has reasonable cause to believe that there is some irregularity *may* report the matter to Opra, but is not under any statutory duty to do so. If they do blow the whistle to Opra, they cannot be sued for breach of confidentiality by their client or employer. It is important to understand that the protection afforded under the *Pensions Act 1995* to those who blow the whistle only extends to those involved in the administration of the scheme. For example, an employee who works in the employer's payroll department is not likely to be covered. The key publication in this area is *Opra Note 6 – The Right to Report Problems to Opra*. In fact, many of the reports received by Opra are sent in by the trustees. If the trustees discover a breach of the requirements, Opra encourages them in the first instance to prepare a draft report, show this to their scheme actuary or scheme auditor and then submit it jointly.

An exception from this protection for breach of confidence is made in the case of any legal adviser to the scheme. Solicitors and barristers must observe the principles of legal privilege and the Government acknowledged that employers and trustees must be able to disclose information to, and seek advice from, their legal advisers without fear that their position might be prejudiced or that information would automatically be passed to Opra.

Opra has published detailed guidance for the use of scheme actuaries and auditors. This is *Opra Note 1 – Section 48: Reporting to Opra* which was first issued in March 1997. This is a key document underpinning the new regulatory regime for pension schemes and pension scheme trustees should obtain a copy from Opra (tel. 01273 627600 or visit http://www.opra.gov.uk/publications/notes/on1-01.shtml). The document contains guidance on the following areas:

- the role of the professional bodies;
- *section 48* of the *Pensions Act 1995*;
- Opra's functions and the obligations it is there to enforce;
- Opra's general approach to penalties;
- reaching a judgement about whether to make a report;
- breaches of general law and trust law that are important to Opra;
- wind ups;
- information received in other capacities;
- the timing of reports to Opra and liaison between the scheme actuary and auditor, and with the trustees;
- joint reports by the advisers and the trustees; and
- practical procedures.

The Opra Note explains that, when reasonable cause has been established and a decision is made that an event needs to be reported to Opra, the law states that a written report should be made to Opra immediately, whatever the circumstances of the breach. Opra advises actuaries and auditors, in deciding whether reasonable cause may exist, that they must feel free to ask for explanations from the trustees or others in a position to clarify the position but adds:

> 'Clearly this would not be the right course if some risk to the scheme's security was evident or if there was evidence of dishonesty. Discretion is advised, particularly if there is cause to believe that the matter should be reported and that it is most unlikely that any explanation would change this position. ... If seeking explanations would be likely to lead to concealment of evidence or make it harder to recover assets, then the correct course must be to inform Opra without seeking further explanation. Scheme actuaries and auditors may wish to copy their written report to the trustees and other persons concerned, including other professional advisers to the scheme. However, discretion must be applied particularly where there is a suspicion

of dishonesty or the possibility that such notification will make it harder to uncover evidence or would be likely to make it harder to recover assets.'

Yet it is clear that Opra wants the trustees themselves to take the initiative in reporting any breach of the requirements set out in the *Pensions Act 1995*. As the regulator explains, it wants to see the whistle-blowing duty exercised in a constructive way so that trustees are confident that:

● if they report a breach that does not involve any significant danger to members' benefits; and

● show that they are dealing with the matter so that future breaches will not re-occur;

then Opra will take an understanding view and not impose a penalty.

In October 2002 Opra announced plans for a review of its guidance given in *Opra Note 1* for statutory whistleblowers, i e the auditor and actuary appointed by the trustees of occupational pension schemes. The new guidance is to set out to auditors and actuaries matters they must report and those that Opra does not expect to be reported. It is hoped that this should significantly reduce the high number of reports on minor breaches Opra currently receives, and enable Opra to increase its focus on:

● breaches that can have a significant detrimental impact on members' benefits;

● breaches that carry a criminal penalty;

● matters that can indicate potential dishonesty or mis-use of assets or contributions; and

● matters that demonstrate a poor standard of stewardship by the trustees

The review began after the Government's pension Green Paper was published in December 2002. Until further notice, Opra expects scheme auditors and actuaries to continue to follow the current requirements. This process follows upon Alan Pickering's report which recommended a 'new kind of regulator' or 'NKR', a report from the National Audit Office and Opra's own quinquennial review carried out by an independent agent for the Department for Work and Pensions.

Opra publishes quarterly *Bulletins* which report on trends and casework so that trustees and scheme administrators can understand how the regulator works and how it deals with non-compliance. Trustees can receive their own free Opra Bulletins direct by joining the mailing list (tel. 01273 627204) or visiting http://www.opra.gov.uk/publications/bulletins/index.shtml. During the twelve months ending 31 March 2002, Opra reported that just under 40%of the breaches being reported were in fact being made by the trustees themselves. In most cases the trustees were reporting employers failing to pay over contributions on time, but many trustees also reported their own failings. Opra commented back in 1998 that: ' ... voluntary self-reporting shows the significance attached by many in the occupational pensions sector to developing a constructive and co-operative relationship with their regulator.

Even more importantly, it increases the likelihood of problems being nipped in the bud as early as possible.'

Trustees can contact Opra as follows:

Opra
Invicta House
Trafalgar Place
Brighton
BN1 4DW
Tel: 01273 627600
Fax: 01273 627688
email: helpdesk@opra.gov.uk
Website: www.opra.gov.uk

How to choose – beauty parades

10.5   Current practice in how professional advisers are appointed varies from scheme to scheme. More significantly, it depends on the kind of adviser concerned. If external investment managers are engaged, it will usually be a well-thought-out process involving site visits, and the so-called *beauty parade* whereby a selected shortlist of investment managers make presentations to the trustees. Yet the shortlist may be put together with guidance from a pension consultant. So the question then becomes: 'How is the pension consultant appointed?'.

The appointment of each of the individual advisers is considered in the following chapters. However, there are several general principles:

● A relationship that has grown up over the years will have the important advantage of familiarity and continuity and should not be disturbed simply for the sake of change but trustees should ensure that the services provided are still meeting the required standards.

● New appointments should involve some element of competitive tendering (although fee scales are far from being the only important criterion) and the putting together of a shortlist of likely candidates.

● Trustees should consider whether the status of golfing partner to the company chairman is an objective and satisfactory test in itself for any appointment!

Appointment and removal of professional advisers

10.6   The *Occupational Pension Schemes (Scheme Administration) Regulations 1996 (SI 1996/1715)* made under the *Pension Schemes Act 1995* set out certain conditions for the appointment of professional advisers, and in particular for the appointment of the scheme auditor and scheme actuary. These include the requirement that appointments and terminations of these professional advisers should be given by the trustees in writing and should be acknowledged in writing by the adviser.

The scheme auditor and the scheme actuary may resign at any time by serving the trustees a notice in writing. However, the resignation will not be effective unless the notice contains either:

- a statement specifying any circumstances connected with the proposed resignation which, in the opinion of the auditor or actuary, significantly affect the interests of the members or prospective members or beneficiaries of the scheme; or

- a statement that the auditor or actuary knows of no such circumstances.

If the trustees remove either the scheme auditor or scheme actuary, he or she must, within 14 days, serve on the trustees either:

- a statement specifying any circumstances connected with the removal which, in the opinion of the auditor or actuary, significantly affect the interests of the members or prospective members or beneficiaries of the scheme; or

- a statement that he or she knows of no such circumstances.

If the removed advisor was the scheme actuary, the trustees must then give a copy of this statement to the remaining scheme auditor within 14 days of having received it. Similarly, if the removed advisor was the scheme auditor, the trustees must give a copy of this statement within the same time limit to the remaining scheme actuary (assuming the scheme is not exempt from the requirement to appoint a scheme actuary).

When the scheme auditor or scheme actuary is removed by the trustees, or resigns or dies, the trustees must make a new appointment within three months. The new auditor or actuary must be given a copy of any statement made by the former adviser on or before the day he or she is appointed, or, if later, within 14 days after the trustees receive the statement.

If the trustees fail to comply with these requirements they risk being fined by Opra.

In practice the Auditing Practices Board and the Institute and Faculty of Actuaries, the professional bodies regulating auditors and actuaries respectively, have published approved examples of appointment and engagement letters for the use of auditors and actuaries who are appointed by pension fund trustees.

Trustees may also find it very helpful to read *A Guide to Appointing Professional Advisers*, published in April 2000 by Opra (see http://www.opra.gov.uk/pdf/apa.pdf).

Access to information

10.7 The Scheme Administration Regulations also set out certain requirements regarding the provision of information to advisers that are binding on trustees and on the sponsoring employer and any professional advisers employed by the employer:

- the employer, an auditor retained by the employer, or an actuary retained by the employer must furnish the trustees, the scheme auditor and the scheme actuary with any such information and explanation as may reasonably be required for the performance of the duties of scheme auditor or scheme actuary;

- the trustees must allow the scheme auditor and scheme actuary access at all reasonable times to the scheme's books, accounts and vouchers and furnish the scheme auditor and scheme actuary with such information and explanation as may reasonably be required for the performance of their duties;

- where scheme auditors or scheme actuaries consider that they have failed to obtain all the information and explanation which, to the best of their knowledge and belief, are necessary for the purposes of their audit or actuarial valuations or statements, they must make a statement to that effect and should, so far as they know, give reasons for the failure. The statement must be given to the trustees and Opra must be advised of the failure.

Checklist 10

- The trustees have a duty to take advice.

- Trustees should not abandon decision-making to the advisers by merely rubber-stamping what their advisers say since the trustees remain responsible for the stewardship of the scheme. They should be familiar with the issues with which they are concerned.

- The trustees should appoint all the scheme advisers (although in the case of the fund manager the appointment may be made by someone authorised to do so on their behalf).

- With certain narrow exceptions, the actuary and auditor should not be connected to any of the trustees.

- In some cases the scheme adviser (or another adviser from the same firm) may also be retained by the employer and this may be a sensible use of resources, but all should be aware of the possibility of conflicts of interest.

- Scheme actuaries and auditors have a statutory duty to blow the whistle to Opra if they have reasonable suspicions that there are material irregularities. Other advisers and administrators may blow the whistle. Those who blow the whistle are protected from being

---

sued for breach of confidence if they are involved in the administration of the scheme.

- Trustees should appoint advisers in a professional manner by research and preparation of a shortlist.

- The appointment and removal of advisers, and of the scheme actuary and auditor in particular, are governed by statutory requirements.

- Employers and trustees must supply their advisers with the information they require to carry out their duties.

Chapter 11

Trustees and the pensions manager

Pensions management

11.1   The pensions manager is usually a paid employee of the sponsoring employer (or, in some cases, of the corporate trustee) who has the day-to-day responsibility for the proper running of a self-administered occupational pension scheme.

The Government had originally stated that it did not intend to require the trustees to appoint the person or persons who carry out the day-to-day administration of the scheme. None the less it did wish to encourage the trustees to follow the guidance given by the Pension Law Review Committee that:

> 'As a matter of good practice, trustees who use the administrative services provided by the sponsoring employer in running the scheme should ensure that the services to be provided are clearly defined in the document formalising such an arrangement.'

However, the overwhelming response to the Government consultation paper that had explained that it was not the Government's intention to require trustees to appoint formally the scheme administrator was that this was a matter too important to be left to best practice. Responses highlighted the critical role played by the administrator on behalf of the trustees and pointed out that if trustees were to be held accountable for the proper running of the scheme, then they must be perfectly clear about the terms on which administrative services were provided.

As explained at **8.12**, the *Occupational Pension (Scheme Administration) Regulations 1996 (SI 1996/1715)* require that where it is the employer who makes provision for the administration of the scheme, the employer must disclose to the trustees the terms on which these services are provided.

It should therefore be clear to the employer, to the trustees and to the scheme administrators to whom the scheme administrators owe their contractual duty of confidence.

A large proportion of the larger occupational pension schemes are served by an in-house pensions department which carries out all the day-to-day administration needed to run the scheme. The cost of maintaining the pension administration department may either be borne by the employer or by the pension scheme itself.

Yet many of the larger schemes contract out day-to-day general administration to a third-party, external agency, perhaps a pensions consultancy, an actuarial firm or even another occupational pension scheme: but they will usually still be served by an in-house pensions manager to look after policy areas.

In smaller occupational pension schemes, which tend to be fully insured, the day-to-day administrative tasks are carried out by the insurance company. The company does not employ a pensions manager but rather the company secretary or another senior staff member will liaise on pension matters with the insurance company.

Pension managers often hold a professional qualification from the Pensions Management Institute. The Institute holds examinations each year for those who are employed in the pensions industry and who are following a study programme.

If successful in the ten-part examinations, they qualify to become Associate Members of the Institute (APMI). After further practical qualifying experience, pension managers may become Fellows of the Institute (FPMI). The PMI also has developed an examination leading to the Qualification in Pensions Administration (QPA) designed for general administrative staff working in a pensions department. In addition, the Institute has recently introduced the Retirement Provision Certificate, which is a foundation-level qualification aimed at people whose work requires them to deal with pensions some of the time and at those who are starting out on a career in pensions.

> Pensions Management Institute
> PMI House
> 4/10 Artillery Lane
> London
> E1 7LS
> Tel: 020 7247 1452
> Fax: 020 7375 0603
> email: enquiries@pensions-pmi.org.uk
> Website: http://www.pensions-pmi.org.uk

The PMI has launched a formal system of Continuing Professional Development for those who already hold the APMI and FPMI which stresses the importance of members maintaining high standards and keeping themselves up-to-date with current developments in pensions.

Early in 1996, the PMI announced that it would provide the Secretariat for a new user group specifically for trustees and those involved with or interested in trusteeship issues. The group is known as the *PMI Trustee Group*. Details are available from the above address.

Pensions administration agreement

11.2   It is the responsibility of the pension fund trustees to ensure that their schemes are efficiently run. Before the 1990s, it was probably true to say that pension scheme administration was very much a backroom activity. Yet in the 1990s the office of the Pensions Ombudsman was created and more employers decided to outsource their pensions administration. Service standards and cost effectiveness were put on the trustees' agenda and then steadily proceeded to move up that agenda.

To address the issues that began to emerge from this increasing attention on the quality of pensions administration, in July 2002 various representative organisations published a Model Administration Agreement to offer trustees some help. The organisations involved were:

- the Association of British Insurers (ABI);
- the Association of Pension Lawyers (APL);
- the Law Debenture Trust Corporation;
- the National Association of Pension Funds (NAPF);
- the Pensions Management Institute (PMI); and
- the Pensions Research Accountants Group (PRAG).

The aim in developing the Model Administration Agreement was that it should act as the basis for new agreements between trustees and an administrator, whether that administrator is a third party administrator or is provided by the sponsoring employer. One objective was: 'to give trustees the ability to design their own pre-delivery check, to specify performance levels and to agree the terms of maintenance'.

Yet it was also made clear that it was intended that the Model Administration Agreement could be used to serve as a comprehensive checklist for trustees who already have administration agreements in place and so therefore would, or ought to include all trustee bodies except a small number of corporate trustees who themselves directly employ the administrators running their scheme.

The question raised by this initiative is, therefore, whether trustees should seek to renegotiate their existing agreements along the lines of the model administration agreement. The accompanying press release made it clear that the authors of the agreement hoped that over time it would become the industry standard. The Executive Committee of Pensions Research Accountants Group (PRAG), for example, issued a statement stating that it believes that:

'the model agreement will provide a useful benchmark against which agreements can be considered as they are negotiated and hopes that in due course, the model can be developed to become a standard agreement for pension administration arrangements'.

Much of the impetus for developing the Model Administration Agreement came from a speech made at the Autumn 2000 conference held by the National Association of Pension Funds by Brian Fyfe of the Engineers' and Managers' Association. He set out the experiences of smaller pension schemes by describing how he and his fellow trustees had been 'taken to the cleaners' by their administrators. Clearly, the development of the Model Administration Agreement has been felt by many to have become a pressing need. The Association of Pension Lawyers put the point for strengthening the trustees' hand quite forcefully when it stated:

> 'it is now more important than ever to be clear on what is required from service providers, be they employers or third party administrators. The model agreement ... will also function as a useful checklist for any trustee faced with an external provider's standard form contract'.

The message, therefore, seems clearly to be that trustees would be well advised to ensure that their own agreement follows the Model Administration Agreement and to seek to re-negotiate that agreement if it fails to do so.

The Model Administration Agreement is published with accompanying explanatory notes. This is a helpful format since it provides trustees with an agreement that is appropriately legally drafted, ready to be adapted by the parties' own legal advisers for use in any specific contract between trustees and an administrator (whether provided by the employer or an external provider). But the document also provides trustees with an explanation of why it is worded as it is.

Flexibility is provided by the use of a series of schedules which can be completed or altered by the parties to any particular agreement.

- Schedule 1 sets out general matters, such as contact emails and telephone numbers, those designated by the trustees to give the administrator instructions etc.

- Schedule 2 is a comprehensive list in detail of the services that a pension scheme administrator could provide and, where relevant, leaves space for a time limit to be specified within which the administrator is to complete each task.

- Schedule 3 is blank and is available for the parties to list any variations of the standard terms and conditions set out in the body of the agreement.

- Schedule 4 is blank and is available to list the discretions, if any, that the trustees wish to delegate to the administrator.

- Schedule 5 deals with the payment of services and is blank because the model's standard terms and conditions do not stipulate any particular fee basis. However, Appendix B to the explanatory notes provides a sample of various fee bases so that trustees can see the options and negotiate with the administrator just how the services are to be paid.

We draw attention below to certain key clauses of the Model Administration Agreement.

Clause 13 of the agreement stipulates that the administrator is to submit periodically to the trustees 'a completed and true certificate which is substantially in the form set out in Schedule 6'. Such a certificate is intended to concentrate the administrator's mind on the some of the most important issues for the trustees.

Importantly, clause 2.5 of this compliance certificate asks the administrator to aver that neither it, nor any connected party, has 'become entitled to receive any commission, fee or other similar consideration as a result of our position in relation to the scheme'. This ties in with clause 20 of the model agreement which binds the administrator to account to the trustees for any commission, fee or other consideration that it receives by virtue of acting for the scheme. It is also a welcome sign that the visibility of the costs incurred by the trustees can be an issue in relation to administration as well as investment services.

In practice, an occupational pension scheme can be administered on a day-to-day basis in accordance with established administrative procedures but the administrators may not always have in mind the actual provisions of the scheme's trust deed and rules. A claim for maladministration can easily arise if the administrative procedures fail to implement the provisions of the trust deed and rules. Clause 6.6 of the model agreement specifies that the administrator must provide services in accordance with the trust deed and rules, subject, of course, to the trustees having supplied the administrator with an up-to-date copy of the trust documentation and also ensuring that all properly made amendments are notified to the administrator.

In terms of 'blowing the whistle' (see **10.4**), the Model Administration Agreement, in respect of both in-house and third party administrators, stipulates at clause 11 that if the administrator becomes aware of any matter affecting the scheme that could be expected to lead to a report to Opra under *section 48* of the *Pensions Act 1995*, the administrator must inform the trustees promptly of that matter. This is the case under the Model Administration Agreement notwithstanding the fact that the administrator may not have any duty under the 1995 Act to make such a report. Furthermore, if the administrator reasonably believes that a criminal offence may have been committed in relation to the scheme, it may make a report to Opra without telling the trustees about it first.

One of the difficulties in practice that can arise when the trustees have engaged the services of a third party administrator is to manage properly the transition from that administrator to any eventual successor. The hand-over may be fraught because the dismissed administrator may feel little incentive to put resources into ensuring a smooth transition. Clause 23 of the Model Administration Agreement sets out the actions to be undertaken following the termination of an administration agreement. Specifically, it deals with the question of the hand-over of computerised records. It makes it clear that the administrator must make available to the trustees or the new administrator all the scheme's records without charge, other than the reasonable costs incurred in arranging delivery to the new location. It is also clear, however, that the basis of the provision of the data is to be the standard facility available under the software system in use by the administrator. In the event that an alternative or additional basis is requested by the trustees, the administrator is entitled to make a reasonable charge for any assistance rendered or cost incurred in producing the data in that form.

The full text of the Model Administration Agreement and explanatory notes can be downloaded from the PMI website (http://www.pensions-pmi.org.uk/administration).

Delegation of trustees' powers

11.3   The trust deed and rules must contain a clause which effectively allows the trustees to delegate all or any of their various duties and powers to the pensions manager. In particular, this should cover authorisation to draw cheques on a banking account and to receive money into the pension scheme account. It is sometimes mistakenly thought that trustees cannot delegate their duties and powers. In a modern pension scheme they in practice have to delegate those powers extensively. Two principles remain:

- Trustees can only delegate in accordance with the trust deed and rules.

- Trustees do not abandon their responsibilities by delegating and they should ensure that the tasks are properly carried out.

Trustees cannot delegate their discretionary powers to those who are not trustees but in practice in a large scheme they will usually be advised by their pensions manager as to which is the most suitable action in the majority of straightforward cases. Nevertheless, the formal decision must be made by the trustees.

Maladministration

11.4   Although the trustees delegate the day-to-day administration of the pension scheme to a pensions manager and a pensions administration team, the trustees remain responsible for the proper running of the scheme. Members who feel they have suffered because of maladministration of the pension scheme can raise the issue through the internal disputes resolution procedure, go to the Pensions Advisory Service (OPAS), go to the Pensions Ombudsman, or even go to the court if the maladministration amounts to a breach of trust. See **CHAPTER 20** for more details.

Trustees might well wonder exactly what constitutes 'maladministration'. Failure to apply the trust deed and rules or respect a statutory requirement seem likely candidates but these can give rise to an action in law whereas simple maladministration may not. There is no statutory definition of malaministration but reference is often made to the so-called *Crossman*

Catalogue. When the Parliamentary Commissioner Bill was being taken through Parliament, Mr Crossman, as leader of the House of Commons, gave examples of maladministration (see Hansard HC 18 October 1966, column 51). He mentioned bias, neglect, inattention, delay, incompetence, turpitude, arbitrariness, and so on. More recently the Parliamentary Commissioner suggested other examples, such as rudeness, refusing to answer reasonable questions, knowingly giving advice which is misleading or inadequate and faulty procedures.

However, in the case of *Glossop v Copnall [2001] All ER (D) 92 (Jul), [2001] OPLR 287*, the Vice Chancellor Sir Andrew Morritt upheld an appeal against the Pensions Ombudsman who had held that: 'Mrs Copnall's exclusion from the scheme amounted to indirect discrimination under Article 119. Failure to comply with Article 119 amounts to maladministration as a consequence of which Mrs Copnall suffered injustice ... '. The Vice Chancellor said that this conclusion was wrong because 'there are three decisions of High Court judges which show that *a mere error of law* cannot amount to maladministration' (*our emphasis*). One must bow to the authority of the Vice Chancellor and three High Court judges, indeed the Pensions Ombudsman himself was obliged to do so on this occasion, but perhaps there are others who might wonder that if a '*mere error of law*' does not amount to maladministration, what will?

The debate has now been taken further. In his determination on 25 April 2002 of a complaint brought by Mr Allen (see **18.5** for a discussion of the background), the Pensions Ombudsman stated that:

> 'It would be wrong however to conclude that the absence of a breach of the law means that there is no act of maladministration. Maladministration is in some ways a wider concept than a breach of the law and respondents to complaints may sometimes find themselves judged to have acted with maladministration in circumstances where they would not be regarded as acting unlawfully.'

In order to avoid such failings, trustees might discuss with the pensions manager whether quality certification under the *BS EN ISO 9000* series might be appropriate for the pension scheme. In addition, proper training and motivation for the administrative team undoubtedly has positive effects in terms of service levels and trustees might discuss whether the *Investors In People* programme was also appropriate for the pensions department.

The question of the prevention of maladministration in the running of a pension scheme has, however, recently been discussed in terms of a more systemic failure in the management of UK pension schemes.

In April 2001, the firm Dunnet Shaw published *Raising the Standard of Pension Scheme Administration* as part of a pensions industry initiative to raise the general standard of pensions administration. It commented that certain commonly encountered attitudes acted to undermine good administration standards. They were:

- a systems view that only the highest volume processes justify computerised automation;

- a payroll view that pensions are non-critical and a refusal to take responsibility for the accuracy of data provided to the administrator;

- a management view that outsourced contracts allow the abdication of all responsibility for the administration function to the provider;

- the use of multiple spreadsheets and other applications instead of central and robust administration systems;

- the belief on both sides of an outsourced relationship that the service can be managed on the basis of retrospective quarterly statistics;

- the view of pensions as a low priority when it comes to investment in training and infrastructure; and

- the belief that DC administration is simpler than DB administration.

Following the publication of the April 2001 paper, a steering group was established and held its first meeting in January 2002. The steering group decided that in order to cover all the issues that had been identified, the lifecycle of a pension scheme would be reviewed and a set of high-level guidance notes should be prepared detailing what was expected of a pension administration service. Four working groups were established:

- Group A – Set up of a new scheme.

- Group B – Ongoing administration.

- Group C – Take on/transfer of administration.

- Group D – Wind up of an existing scheme.

The *Raising Standards of Administration Group* involves pension managers working for both in-house occupational pension scheme administration departments and third party administrators, as well as trustee, consultant and insurance company representatives. Details of its work, including the April 2001 paper and the subsequent deliberations, can be found at http://www.raisingadminstandards.com.

In a further initiative, the Society of Pension Consultants (SPC) (see **12.1**) has established a working party comprising SPC members and pensions software designers to look at ways to improve pensions data standards following concerns over the high rates of inaccuracy in much of the data. The SPC has stated that 20% of the UK's largest occupational pension schemes could have 'serious data problems'.

The working party is also looking at ways to improve the manner in which data is passed from one user to another by devising a common standard file format – much as in the banking industry BACS has long served as a single standard for the transmission and receipt of data. One particular aspect of the SPC's work in this area is to devise a common standard for the transmission and receipt of data between the payroll, personnel and pension administrators

– irrespective of whether in any particular case any or all of these administrators are in-house or provided by a third party. Apart from the technical standard itself, which will be written in extensible mark-up language (XML), the working party is examining the possibility of a common set of data validation and reconciliation control totals which will form part of the file format.

Trustee relationship with pensions manager

11.5   The pensions manager relationship with the trustees is a key issue.

He or she will:

* provide the secretariat to support the trustees and organise the taking of minutes for trustee meetings;

* report to the trustees on what is happening in the scheme; and

* carry out the trustees' instructions.

The trustees under the trust deed and rules have overall responsibility for the scheme and they bear a fiduciary duty to the beneficiaries. Unless the pensions manager is also a trustee (which would be very rare), he or she will have no such fiduciary duty but only a contractual duty to his or her employer and a duty to follow any codes of professional conduct.

In most cases, the pensions manager will be a senior officer in the company hierarchy and in certain circumstances could be privy to confidential company information that is not known to the trustees. Therefore, he or she could be placed in a conflict of loyalty. It is for this reason that the *Occupational Pension Schemes (Scheme Administration) Regulations 1996 (SI 1996/1715)* stipulate that, in these circumstances, the employer must specify the terms on which the administration services are provided.

It is recommended that trustees seek a close and professional relationship with the pensions manager and make full use of all his or her acquired skills. However, trustees should never abdicate their responsibility for the stewardship of the pension funds and should ensure that their instructions are carried out.

Data Protection Act 1998

11.6   The trustees are also likely to rely on their pensions manager to ensure that they comply with the requirements of the *Data Protection Act 1998*. The data covered by 1998 Act are any 'personal data' which relate to a living individual who can be identified from the data or from that and other data in the possession of the 'data controller'. In the case of a trust-based occupational pension scheme it is clear that the trustees are the data controller for the purposes of the 1998 Act (although the employer may also be a data controller in respect of the same data).

159

Unlike the old *Data Protection Act 1984*, the data concerned are not restricted to those held on an electronic computer system. The *Data Protection Act 1998* applies to any 'relevant filing system'. This is defined as:

> 'Any set of information relating to individuals to the extent that, although the information is not processed by means of equipment operating automatically in response to instructions for that purpose, the set is structured, either by reference to individuals or by reference to criteria relating to individuals, in such a way that specific information relating to a particular individual is readily accessible.'

Any data controller wishing to process personal data must notify the Data Protection Commissioner and respect the eight data protection principles:

1. Personal data shall be processed fairly and lawfully and, in particular, shall not be processed unless:

    (*a*)   at least one of the conditions in *Schedule 2* is met;* and

    (*b*)   in the case of sensitive personal data, at least one of the conditions in *Schedule 3* is also met.†

2. Personal data shall be obtained only for one or more specified and lawful purposes, and shall not be further processed in any manner incompatible with that purpose or those purposes.

3. Personal data shall be adequate, relevant and not excessive in relation to the purpose or purposes for which they are processed.

4. Personal data shall be accurate and, where necessary, kept up to date.

5. Personal data processed for any purpose or purposes shall not be kept for longer than is necessary for that purpose or those purposes.

6. Personal data shall be processed in accordance with the rights of data subjects under this Act.

7. Appropriate technical and organisational measures shall be taken against unauthorised or unlawful processing of personal data and against accidental loss or destruction of, or damage to, personal data.

8. Personal data shall not be transferred to a country or territory outside the European Economic Area unless that country or territory ensures an adequate level of protection for the rights and freedoms of data subjects in relation to the processing of personal data.

* *Schedule 2* provides that processing of data can only be carried out if one of the following conditions is satisfied:

- the individual has given his or her consent to the processing;
- the processing is necessary for the performance of a contract with the individual;
- the processing is required under a legal obligation;
- the processing is necessary to protect the vital interests of the individual;

- the processing is necessary in order to pursue the legitimate interests of the data controller or certain third parties (unless prejudicial to the interests of the individual).

† *Schedule 3* provides stricter conditions for the processing of sensitive data, and this will include any information relating to a scheme member's health. At least one of the conditions set in *Schedule 3* will have to be met and in the case of occupational pension schemes the condition that is likely to have to be satisfied if sensitive information is to be held is that the member has given his or her *explicit* consent to the processing of the personal data.

Individual members have a right to ask for copies of their data. On payment of a fee (£10), the member must be provided with a description of the data, the purposes for which it is held and the recipients or classes of persons to whom it may be disclosed. The data controller is given 40 days to respond to a request but does not need to respond to repeat requests from the same individual if they are not separated by a reasonable interval.

Checklist 11

- The pensions manager heads up the pensions administration team that carries out the day-to-day running of the pensions scheme.

- The trustees are ultimately responsible for the proper running of the scheme but delegate the day-to-day running of the scheme to the pensions manager and the administration team.

- The introduction of the Model Administration Agreement by representative pension organisations in July 2002 is a very significant step towards an industry standard for pensions administration.

- If the pensions manager and the administration team are employed by the sponsoring employer, the employer must make clear to the trustees the terms on which the administration services are provided.

- Administration services can be provided by external third party providers or in some cases can be provided by an administration team directly employed by the trustees.

- The administration costs can be met by the pension fund or by the sponsoring employer.

- The trustees will be answerable if there is maladministration by the administrators to whom they have delegated responsibility for the day-to-day running of the scheme. Recent initiatives are trying to address some systemic problems in pensions administration that can lead to maladministration. There is a distinction between breaches of the law and acts of maladministration.

- As the data controller, the trustees must ensure compliance with the *Data Protection Act 1998*.

Chapter 12

Trustees and the pensions consultant

Society of Pension Consultants and Association of Consulting Actuaries

12.1   Most large occupational pension schemes engage the services of professional advisers to act as consultants. Firms which offer pension consultancy services are likely to be members of the Society of Pension Consultants or the Association of Consulting Actuaries. Many firms are members of both bodies.

> Society of Pension Consultants
> St Bartholomew House
> 92 Fleet Street
> London
> EC4Y 1DG
> Tel: 020 7353 1688
> Fax: 020 7353 9296
> email: john.mortimer@spc.uk.com
> Website: http://www.spc.uk.com
>
> Association of Consulting Actuaries
> No 1 Wardrobe Place
> London
> EC4V 5AG
> Tel: 020 7248 3163
> Fax: 020 7248 1889
> email: acahelp@aca.org.uk
> Website: http://www.aca.org.uk

Most of the larger pension consultancies will charge on a time basis, with the amount depending on the seniority of the individual consultant. Administration services will more likely be charged on a fixed-fee basis. Some of the smaller consultancies earn most of their money through commission arrangements.

It is generally agreed that the pensions consultancy industry is becoming more competitive; there were a number of mergers of actuarial consultancies during the 1990s.

Services offered by pension consultants

12.2   Most of the larger firms of pension consultants will offer all of the following services to clients. This list is not exhaustive.

Actuarial services

12.3   The role of the actuary is discussed separately in CHAPTER 13.

Administration services

12.4   Pension consultants can advise on how to run an efficient and cost-effective pensions administration system, especially regarding how computer systems and software packages could be used. Some of the larger firms market their own pension administration program software.

Alternatively, the larger firms will either provide an external pensions administration service themselves or advise on hiring the services of a third party pension administration provider.

See also **11.3** for a discussion of pensions administration and in particular of the new Model Administration Agreement.

Benefit design

12.5   Consultants can also advise on what benefit package the occupational pension scheme should offer to its members, bearing in mind company philosophy, competitive practice, relative cost and employee attitudes.

Communications

12.6   Firms of pension consultancies often provide through a subsidiary company the full range of member communication services.

They can design, write and produce benefit statements, scheme booklets, trustee annual reports, pension newsletters and special packages to explain pension changes, such as on the merger of a new scheme.

International benefits

12.7   Most of the larger consultancies are tied into international networks and so can advise companies which operate outside the UK.

Investment of funds

12.8   Pension consultancies will help trustees discuss their overall investment strategy and then draw up a shortlist of external fund managers to form a 'beauty parade' from which the trustees will select those who will manage the pension scheme's assets. This particular aspect of a consultant's work is further discussed below.

Legal and documentation services

12.9   Some of the firms provide pension lawyer services themselves or sub-contract the work to a law firm.

National Insurance Contributions Office and Inland Revenue negotiations

12.10   Pension consultants can liaise between the scheme and the National Insurance Contributions Office and IR SPSS, the business stream of the Inland Revenue that deals with the approval and monitoring of pension schemes. Examples of negotiations might be on the issue of a new contracting-out certificate or a payment from the fund to the employer.

Placing of insurance

12.11   The pension consultant can help either the employer or the trustees to obtain competitive rates for any insured benefits, such as permanent health insurance cover or death-in-service cover.

Retirement counselling

12.12   Seminars and weekends away can be organised by the pension consultant to counsel members on how to prepare for retirement and manage the transition from the world of full-time work.

Trusteeship

12.13   Trustee training services can be provided by the consultant as well as advice to the trustees on any matter. A consultant could advise on the appointment of an independent trustee if this was required.

Trustee relationship with pension consultant

12.14   Pension consultants will maintain a relationship of confidentiality with their client. If the client is the employer, then the consultant may not be in a position to disclose the employer's latest thinking on possible future changes in the benefit structure to employee trustees. Note, however, that as explained in **10.2**, the trustees must be responsible for appointing the scheme actuary.

In cases of a conflict between the trustees and the employer, the pensions consultant, who historically advised both parties without distinguishing between them, might advise that he or she is unable to act for both on this occasion. If so, an independent consultant from another firm might be brought in.

Whereas some schemes have a long-standing relationship with one pension consultancy, others schemes will prefer to use a variety of pension consultancies for different tasks. An experienced in-house pensions management team may also mean that some of the services offered by the pensions consultancies can more effectively be provided in-house.

Myners and investment consultants

12.15   In his review *Institutional investment in the UK*, Paul Myners discussed at length the role of investment consultants. He concluded that the investment consulting industry was highly concentrated in a small number of consulting firms – the four largest firms were found to hold at least 70% of the market share by value of funds in 1999. At the same time, he found that the level of profitability derived from doing this work for the firms involved appeared to be low. He therefore did not have any fears about conventional competition concerns, but thought that the market structure of the pension fund consulting business in the UK was:

> ' ... likely to lead to the provision of advice that is relatively uniform, insufficiently specialised and in particular, poorly equipped currently to deal with alternative asset classes. There appears to be little assessment of the [investment] manager research activities of consultants'.

The reference to 'alternative asset classes' picks up on one of the main themes discussed in **CHAPTER 16**, which discusses the trustees' role in choosing the investment strategy that is appropriate for their scheme – see **16.9**.

Paul Myners went on to recommend that:

- contracts for actuarial services and investment advice should be opened to competition separately. Pension funds should be prepared to pay sufficient fees for each service to attract a broad range of kinds of potential provider;

- trustees should arrange for formal assessment of their adviser's performance and of any decision-making delegated to them;

- trustees should not take investment advice on an asset class from an investment consultant who lacks expertise in that asset class; and

- fees devoted to asset allocation should properly reflect the contribution it can make to the fund's investment performance.

The issue of the appointment of external investment managers, and the role of the consultant, is further discussed at **16.15** below.

Partly in response to these developments, the National Association of Pension Funds (NAPF) issued in 2001 *The Trustee/Asset Consultant Relationship – A Guide to Good Practice*. The framework for good practice between the trustees and their investment consultant, as seen by the NAPF, involves the trustees having to define their expectations of their consultant in relation to the advice and services taken, and then recording these in a contract with the consultant. The trustees would then need to make a regular assessment of whether the consultant had delivered what was expected. This is not always a straightforward process. In considering the evaluation of the advice and service provided by an investment consultant, the NAPF warns that account needs to be taken of the extent to which trustees make final decisions or delegate them to the consultant and the extent, therefore, that the consultant should be held accountable for his or her advice.

Checklist 12

- Trustees or employers may engage the services of a pensions consultant.

- In many cases the consultancy involved will also be the firm that supplies the scheme actuary in which case special considerations apply (see **CHAPTER 13**).

- Pension consultancies can supply a number of useful services on a one-off basis.

- Trustees may feel that the advice and services provided by their own pensions manager and administration team are sufficient in many circumstances.

- Paul Myners raised some concerns about the role of investment consultants in his March 2001 review of UK institutional investment.

Chapter 13

Trustees and the scheme actuary

Introduction

13.1   In the case of any occupational pension scheme which is run on a defined benefit basis, the actuary is the key scheme adviser. The advice of the scheme's actuary will determine what level of contributions now have to be paid into the scheme for it to meet its future liabilities. The *Pensions Act 1995* has if anything increased the importance of the actuary because of the introduction from 6 April 1997 of the Minimum Funding Requirement (MFR).

Institute and Faculty of Actuaries

13.2   Actuaries usually have a background in mathematics and are individually members of one of two professional institutions. In Scotland, actuaries are members of the Faculty of Actuaries. Elsewhere in the UK, they are members of the Institute of Actuaries.

> Faculty of Actuaries
> Maclaurin House
> 18 Dublin Street
> Edinburgh
> EH1 3PP
> Tel: 0131 240 1300
> Fax: 0131 240 1313
>
> Institute of Actuaries
> Staple Inn Hall
> High Holborn
> London
> WC1V 7QJ
> Tel: 020 7632 2100
> Fax: 020 7632 2111
> email: institute@actuaries.org.uk
> Joint Faculty and Institute website: http://www.actuaries.org.uk

Qualified actuaries from elsewhere in the European Union may act as scheme actuaries.

Actuaries are employed directly by insurance companies to advise on the funding level required for insured occupational pension schemes. Actuaries who are engaged to provide advice to self-administered schemes are in practice usually employed by a firm of pension consultants or consulting actuaries – see **12.1**.

A trustee of the scheme must not be appointed as the scheme actuary. The scheme actuary must not be connected with, or an associate of any of the trustees but it is permissible for the same firm to provide the actuary and an independent trustee to the same scheme providing they are different individuals. Special rules concern the appointment and removal of the scheme actuary and the exchange of information between actuary, employer and trustees – see CHAPTER 10.

Principles of how a pension scheme is funded

13.3   Defined contribution (money purchase) schemes are relatively simple and at present require little input from an actuary. If it is thought desirable, though, to fund them to produce targeted benefits for each individual member, this will require at least some actuarial input. Larger money purchase schemes which do not buy out pension liabilities by purchasing annuities from insurance companies, but rather pay pensions directly to pensioners, have to employ the services of an actuary.

Defined benefit (such as final salary) schemes have to be funded on an actuarial basis. An actuarial valuation must be carried out to assess the ability of a pension scheme to meet its liabilities. The object of the exercise is to assess the funding level and derive a recommended contribution rate.

Actuarial methods and assumptions

13.4   In order to carry out actuarial valuations, actuaries make use of various assumptions which are employed in one of various methods.

Assumptions

13.5   The main assumptions that currently enter into an actuary's calculations are:

- the expected return (including capital growth) on investments;
- the expected increase in the income from investments;
- the expected increase in members' earnings;
- the expected increases to pensions-in-payment;
- the expected rate of revaluation of deferred pensions;
- the mortality rate among members and beneficiaries;
- the expected age at which members will retire;
- the balance between pensions and commuted lump sum payments; and
- the ages of members' husbands, wives and dependants.

Often, the assumptions themselves are not critical and what counts is the relationship between them; for example, assumptions about an investment return of 10% and earnings growth of 8% come to much the same as assumptions about an investment return of 7% and earnings growth of 5%. In choosing which assumptions to adopt, the actuary is not necessarily trying to adopt the most accurate forecast. Rather, the intention is to achieve a result that observes two golden rules:

1. The contribution rate should be relatively constant over time.

2. The scheme should always have enough assets to cover the reasonable expectations members have of their benefits earned up to the date of the valuation.

Methods

13.6   However, if two actuaries used identical assumptions in an actuarial valuation, they will produce very different results if they have adopted different valuation methods.

The choice of the valuation method essentially determines when the cost of paying benefits is actually met. Some methods meet the cost as early as possible, some as late as possible. The choice of one method over another will affect the contribution rate and whether the scheme runs a larger or a smaller fund.

There are two broad groups of actuarial valuation methods: the *accrued benefits* valuation methods and the *prospective benefits* valuation methods.

Accrued benefits valuation methods

This is any valuation method in which the actuarial liability at the valuation date relates to:

*   the benefits for pensioners and deferred pensioners and their dependants, allowing for future increases; and

*   the accrued benefits for members in service on the valuation date.

There are four main methods that fall into this group:

–   the projected unit method;

–   the current unit method;

–   the defined accrued benefit method; and

–   the projected accrued benefits method.

Prospective benefits valuation methods

This is any valuation method in which the actuarial liability at the valuation date is the present value of:

*   the benefits for pensioners and deferred pensioners and their dependants, allowing for future increases; and

171

- the benefits which active members will receive in respect of both past and future service, allowing for projected earnings up to their assumed exit date, and for increases thereafter;

less the present value of future contributions payable in respect of current members at the standard contribution rate.

There are three main methods that fall into this group:

- the entry age method;
- the attained age method; and
- the aggregate method.

Each of these methods has different characteristics and the trustees should talk to the scheme actuary about the reasons why he or she has adopted the particular method used for their scheme.

In practice, in most on-going schemes used in the UK the scheme actuary has adopted the *projected unit method* for normal valuation purposes. This is the accrued benefits valuation method in which the actuarial liability makes allowance for projected earnings. The *standard contribution rate* is that rate necessary to cover the cost of all benefits that will accrue in the *control period* following the valuation date by reference to earnings projected to the dates on which the benefits become payable.

Here, *standard contribution rate* is the overall contribution rate (employer's plus employees' contributions) required before taking into account any differences between the actuarial liability and the actuarial value of the assets, i e before taking account of any surplus or deficiency in the fund. *Control period* refers to the period in any accrued benefits valuation method over which the standard contribution rate is calculated to remain constant assuming that at the beginning and end of the period the funding ratio (i e the ratio of the actuarial value of the assets to the actuarial liability) is 100%.

The *projected accrued benefits* valuation method is the method, together with set actuarial assumptions, prescribed by the Inland Revenue for calculating whether a 'statutory surplus' has arisen. If the funding ratio using this method is over 105%, action has to be taken to reduce the surplus – see **19.2**.

Any actuarial valuation using whichever method listed above will need to calculate the value of the scheme's assets less the value of its liabilities. If this is a positive number, the scheme is in surplus, if it is a negative number the scheme is in deficit. When valuing the scheme's assets and liabilities, the actuary may choose, as a starting point, to value the assets at either their current *market value* or at a *discounted value*. The discounted value option has been the traditional approach used by UK actuaries. It involves valuing the assets by calculating the present value of the fund's expected future income stream. However, in recent years, there has been a marked trend away from discounted valuations and over to the market value approach.

However, as we have just stated the actuarial value of the fund is the value of the scheme's assets less the value of its liabilities. When a discounted value is placed on the scheme assets, a consistent discounted value must also be placed on the scheme liabilities. By the same reasoning, if a market value is placed on the scheme's assets, a market value must also be placed on the scheme's liabilities. It is easy to understand what the market value of the scheme's assets means. After all, there is a real market out there for stocks and shares and property etc. But just what is the market for the scheme's liabilities? Trustees whose actuaries use market values should ask their actuary just how he or she has calculated the scheme's liabilities. (We are talking here about the scheme's own normal actuarial valuation, not the specific valuation required by most defined benefit schemes under the minimum funding requirement (MFR) (see below). The MFR is calculated using market values and the market values of liabilities under the MFR are calculated in a very specific way.)

Although the *Pensions Act 1995* has made important changes which affect the task undertaken by the scheme actuary, there are a number of duties that an actuary has long performed and in many cases continues to perform on behalf of the trustees of an occupational pension scheme.

- The Inland Revenue requires an actuarial valuation to be carried out on all large self-administered schemes using a common actuarial method and set of assumptions for the purposes of identifying and controlling pension fund surpluses – see **19.2**. Whenever the actuary carries out any valuation of the pension scheme, a formal report and actuarial certificate must be sent to the Inland Revenue within three months. Valuations must be sent to the Inland Revenue at intervals of not more than $3\frac{1}{2}$ years.

- In the case of a scheme that is or has been contracted out by either the Guaranteed Minimum Pension (GMP) test or the reference scheme test, the scheme actuary has been involved in various certification processes – see **13.12** below.

- The actuary is contracted to provide general advice on the desirable funding level for the scheme and conduct actuarial valuations using different actuarial methods and assumptions from those required for the Inland Revenue. The actuary will complete the investigations and provide the actuarial statement on funding levels that the *Occupational Pension Schemes (Disclosure of Information) Regulations 1996 (SI 1996/1655)* require to be included in the trustees' annual report.

- The actuary must calculate what pension rights in the scheme are bought by an employee who brings a transfer value from a previous pension scheme. Similarly, the actuary calculates the transfer value due to an early leaver from the scheme – see **9.14**.

- The actuary is involved in calculations such as: the commutation rate for a pension to be exchanged for a cash lump sum, reduction rates in cases of early retirement and the cost of augmenting pensions for senior employees.

- In major reorganisations occasioned by takeovers or mergers involving the employing company, the actuary advises on bulk transfer arrangements – see **19.5**. Similarly, an actuary is involved if two or more existing pension schemes sponsored by the same employer are to be merged.

- When a scheme is wound-up the actuary will calculate how the assets are used to meet the current liabilities – see **19.9**.

- The actuary must provide figures for the auditors who prepare the company accounts so that a true and fair pension cost can be calculated – see **CHAPTER 15**.

Changes arising from the Pensions Act 1995

13.7   There were two new functions for the scheme actuary that arose out of the *Pensions Act 1995*. First, defined benefit schemes (and money purchase schemes that pay pensioners directly rather than buying an annuity from a life office) must satisfy the minimum funding requirement (MFR) as assessed by the scheme actuary. The scheme actuary is required to certify that the scheme is being funded at least at 100% of the MFR level, or that contributions are being paid into the scheme at a pace that means that the scheme is likely to meet the 100% target level within a specified time.

Secondly, the GMP test was abolished for contracting out although only for pensionable service after 5 April 1997, and instead the *reference scheme* test was introduced which requires actuarial certification.

Minimum funding requirement (MFR)

13.8   The MFR is simply a requirement that defined benefit schemes should hold sufficient assets to meet their liabilities. The method of calculating the MFR is set out in regulations and in guidance prepared by the Institute and Faculty of Actuaries. The regulations are the *Occupational Pension Schemes (Minimum Funding Requirement and Actuarial Valuations) Regulations 1996 (SI 1996/1536)* and the actuarial guidance is *GN27 Retirement Benefit Schemes – Minimum Funding Requirement.*

Generally, the calculation is intended to provide that a scheme will always be able to continue to provide for pensions already in payment. The calculation is also intended to provide non-pensioner members with a fair transfer value of their accrued rights which, if invested further, should have a reasonable expectation of providing a pension at least as good as the scheme would have provided in respect of those same accrued rights.

For non-pensioner members the calculation is based on the dividend income from UK equities. For pensioners it is based on rates of return from gilt-edged securities. Yet, for non-pensioner members within ten years of normal pension age there is a blending – moving gradually from 100% equities to 100% gilts over the period. (For an explanation of how different kinds of liabilities can be matched to different assets, see **CHAPTER 16**.)

The calculation also includes an expense allowance to take account of the cost of either winding up the scheme or of running off the liabilities in a closed fund. Larger schemes would probably run off their liabilities by becoming closed schemes. (That is, if, say, the employer became insolvent, the scheme would continue to be run except that no new members would join and no new contributions would be paid. The fund would continue to be invested and benefits would be paid when they fall due.) Therefore, the MFR Regulations allow schemes with more than £100m in pensioner liabilities in the twelve-year period from the date of the actuarial valuation to have any liabilities falling due after these twelve years measured by reference to equities rather than gilts.

How the MFR works

13.9   Trustees are required to obtain regular actuarial valuations and funding certificates. The valuations for the purpose of establishing the scheme's ability to meet the MFR are required at intervals of no more than three years. Before 19 March 2002, annual funding certificates were also required in the period between valuations, but since that date such inter-valuation certificates are only required if the scheme was not at least 100% funded against the MFR at the last valuation.

In the normal way, the MFR valuation leads the actuary to recommend a contribution rate. This leads to the *schedule of contributions* that the trustees must enforce and which is described at **8.3**. The 1996 *MFR Regulations* originally stipulated that if the MFR valuation showed that the scheme was less than 100% funded but more than 90% funded, the schedule of contributions should enable 100% funding to be restored within five years or by 6 April 2007 if later. If the funding level was below 90%, employers have to make good the shortfall up to 90% in one year or by 6 April 2002 if later.

Changes were made with effect from 19 March 2002 to extend these deficit correction periods. Actuaries may not now certify a schedule of contributions unless they are of the opinion that contribution rates listed in the schedule are adequate to ensure that the scheme remains, or will become at least 100% funded against the MFR within a ten-year period beginning with the date the schedule is certified. If the valuation shows that the scheme is less than 90% funded against the MFR, the deficit correction period has been extended so that the shortfall below 90% must be corrected within a period of three years from the date the valuation is signed (as well as also becoming 100% funded within the ten-year period beginning with the date the schedule is certified).

The Government estimates that the March 2002 changes will reduce the cash expenditure that employers would otherwise be required to pay into their schemes in the early years by around £750m a year. Yet there will be a somewhat higher ultimate aggregate of payments to be made by the employers to account for the later timing of contributions. They will have to put in £1.25bn a year over ten years rather than £2bn a year over five years.

Note also that contributions paid to correct a MFR deficit cannot be 'backloaded' so that the bulk of the contributions are payable towards the end of the deficit correction period. In order to certify the schedule of contributions, the scheme actuary must be assured that the deficit will be reduced by the making of additional contributions of equal or decreasing amounts, made at not more than twelve-month intervals during the entire life of the schedule. As an alternative, increasing contributions will be acceptable provided that the rate of increase applied to some or all of the contributions remains constant or decreases during the whole period of the schedule.

Where there is 'serious underprovision' – i e the deficit takes the funding ratio to less than 90% of the MFR – the shortfall can be met by contributions being paid in the normal way or, with the trustees' agreement, the employer can secure the shortfall:

- by obtaining letters of credit from a bank;

- by placing assets in a bank account over which the trustees have a charge so that if the employer became insolvent the assets would pass to them; or

- by giving the trustees directly a charge of some of the employer's assets.

Trustee duty to report deficits

13.10   The trustees' duties to police the schedule of contributions have already been set out at **8.5**. In addition, the trustees must make a report to Opra if a valuation shows that their scheme is less than 100% funded against the MFR in any case where the previous valuation showed that it was then at least 100% funded. Furthermore, if the previous valuation had also showed a deficit which the current valuation shows has deteriorated, the trustees must make a report to Opra. The report must be made within three months beginning with the date the trustees received the valuation report. Such reports are termed 'failure reports'.

Where the trustees are required to make a failure report to Opra, they must also make that same report available, on request, to scheme members, prospective scheme members, spouses of members and of prospective members, and any recognised independent trade union.

Abolition of MFR

13.11   The trustees are responsible for ensuring that their scheme is funded at least in line with the MFR. However, it must be made clear that this is only a statutory minimum level of funding. In the future, as in the past, if the employer suddenly went into liquidation and the scheme had to be wound up, it is quite possible that the trustees would find that the available assets were insufficient to meet all the scheme's liabilities. In other words, compliance with the MFR does not ensure that the scheme is solvent. In fact, the MFR has been widely criticised as being a comparatively weak test and in the recent past many defined benefit schemes have been wound up which, at the time, were fully funded against the MFR but which were unable to buy out the full value of non-pensioner members' accrued rights by the purchase of guaranteed, deferred non-profit annuities from insurance companies. Even before the further falls in world stock markets in 2002, such schemes were often found to be only able to buy out, say, 60% or less of the non-pensioners' accrued rights.

The scheme actuary, following an actuarial valuation using his or her preferred valuation method and set of assumptions, must tell trustees what the recommended contribution rate should be. This could be in excess of the contribution rate stemming from the MFR calculation. The trustees should then consult with the employer and ensure that they are happy with the final funding level adopted. In so doing, it is unlikely that trustees could be happy if the funding level is less than that recommended by the scheme actuary. If the employer argues that the cost is simply becoming excessive, a solution might be for the employer to amend the trust deed and rules so benefits build up in future at a more modest rate, or for employees also to pay at a higher rate, or alternatively a combination of both approaches. Such a move may, of course, have serious industrial relations consequences for the employer.

The trustees, however, cannot insist on a level of funding that is in excess of that required to meet the MFR.

Once a schedule of contributions has been agreed, or in default of any agreement, once the schedule of contributions that meets the MFR has been established, the trustees must rigorously ensure that this schedule is respected.

By 1999, the MFR had already begun to meet a tide of mounting criticism in that it had failed to adjust to changes in financial markets and the Government's new policy, implemented in July 1997, on the taxation of dividends paid by UK companies.

The main problem is that the MFR adopts a market value approach (see **13.6** above) to the calculation of the scheme's assets and liabilities and so a market value has to be placed on the scheme's liabilities. The MFR Regulations set out how this must be done (see **13.8** above), which involves matching the liabilities against either the dividend income from UK equities or the yields from UK gilts. Yet, before the recent equity market falls beginning in 2000, dividend yields had fallen in the UK since 1997 as companies preferred to distribute their profits back to shareholders in other ways. UK gilts became more expensive to buy as fewer were issued and so gilt yields also fell. Even if the trustees chose to invest in overseas equities, overseas bonds or other kinds of investments, the MFR Regulations insist that their liabilities are measured against UK dividend and UK gilt yields. This is explored further at **16.27**.

The overall result is that the value of schemes' liabilities were increasing sharply and employer contribution rates had to increase in order to compensate.

The Government responded with a series of initiatives and consultations. The brief history is as follows:

- March 1998 – Government asks the actuarial profession to carry out a review of the MFR.

- September 2000 – Government publishes the actuarial profession's report and issues a further consultation paper looking at alternative ways of providing protection for the pension promise implicit in a defined benefit scheme.

- November 2000 – Paul Myners issues a preliminary report as part of his review of institutional investment arguing that the MFR was distorting trustees' investment decisions by enforcing a shift away from investing in equities and towards investing in bonds.

- March 2001 – The Government accepts that the MFR must be abolished. Consultation begins on how a long-term, scheme-specific funding standard would work.

- September 2001 – Government issues in draft the regulations to extend the deficit correction periods.

- March 2002 – Amending regulations put in place to extend the deficit correction periods and the 'equity MVA' is adjusted (see **16.27**) to ease pressure on employers in the short term.

- July 2002 – Alan Pickering's report recommends abolition of compulsory Limited Price Indexation of pensions in payment and provision of survivors' pensions as a way of reducing the funding pressure on defined benefit schemes,

- September 2002 – The Chairman of the actuaries' Pensions Board writes a letter to all scheme actuaries reminding them of their professional responsibilities, including those in relation to the MFR to ensure that schedules of contributions are adequate, at a time of volatile investment markets.

- December 2002 – The Government publishes its pensions Green Paper and accompanying technical paper which add detail to its March 2001 proposals which include giving trustees new overriding powers.

The key features of the March 2001 consultation paper for a long-term, scheme-specific funding standard are aimed at achieving the twin objectives of providing protection for members while at the same time avoiding damaging consequences for investment.

The Government understands by the term 'long-term scheme-specific funding standard' that the trustees and their advisers would be required to take a view on the proper funding and investment of the scheme in the light of the scheme's own circumstances. And any professional guidance would have to emphasise the duty on all parties to look at the circumstances of the particular scheme and sponsoring employer.

In order to make this work there would have to be put in place a strong regime of transparency and disclosure. The trustees of every defined benefit scheme would have to set out in a clear and straightforward way how they saw the scheme's liabilities growing over time and how, through contributions to the fund and growth in the value of the assets through investment returns, they propose to meet its liabilities. This would constitute a *Funding Statement*, which might form part of a strengthened Statement of Investment Principles (see **16.8**), designed to promote transparency and scrutiny. It would be distributed to members and made publicly available.

There would also have to be a recovery plan for returning the scheme to full funding. Each employer would have to ensure that their scheme was adequately funded and, if it was not, to implement a recovery plan for returning to adequate funding within a relatively short period of time, say, three years.

An important development in these proposals is that the Government has stated that the new funding standard would require that a statutory duty of care towards scheme members would be placed on the scheme actuary. This, says the Government, would mean that there will be a key adviser with a duty of care directly to the scheme members. This would enhance member protection and clarify the actuary's existing whistle-blowing role if something were to go wrong.

In its December 2002 publications, the Government pointed out that it was important for sponsoring employers and scheme trustees to agree on the funding principles for a defined benefit scheme. Yet the Government has addressed the case where there may be failure between these parties to reach agreement by proposing that trustees be given overriding powers to:

- freeze the scheme so that no member accrues any further benefits; and/or

- wind up the scheme.

The technical paper accompanying the December 2002 Green Paper comments that these powers are intended to give a better balance to the options available to the trustees and employer in cases where they disagree. It cites the example where the scheme actuary recommends a higher contribution rate than the employer is prepared to accept, and no satisfactory compromise can be reached. The paper suggests that the trustees might decide in such a situation that insufficient funds would be paid into the scheme to maintain its funding position at a satisfactory level, and that members' interests would be better protected by freezing future accruals and/or winding up the scheme.

The Government's December 2002 publications also include a proposal that the new regulator would be given a new power to fine an employer who fails to pass contributions over to the trustees in accordance with the agreed schedule of contributions. At present, although such a power already exists in relation to a payment schedule for a defined contribution scheme, there is no such power in relation to a schedule of contributions in a defined benefit scheme (see **8.5–8.6**). Also, in such circumstances where the employer refused to observe the schedule of contributions, the trustees would also be able to exercise their overriding power to freeze and/or wind up the scheme.

Reference scheme test

13.12   From 6 April 1997 the reference scheme test replaced for future pensionable service the GMP test as the defined benefit basis for contracting out of the additional pension provided by the state. A scheme satisfies the reference scheme test if the scheme actuary certifies that it provides pensions for members that considered as a whole are broadly equivalent to, or better than, those provided by a reference scheme.

The reference scheme is based on producing a pension at age 65 based on 1/80th for each year of service of 90% of an employee's earnings between the National Insurance lower and upper earnings limits, averaged over the last three tax years, with a contingent spouse's pension set at 50% of the member's pension.

The scheme actuary must re-certify every three years that the scheme will provide a pension at least as good, or better than, that provided by the reference scheme for at least 90% of the scheme members. If the scheme fails the reference scheme test, it will cease to be able to contract out.

The actuary also has to confirm that any pre-6 April 1997 GMP rights that are retained in the scheme are adequately funded during the period up to 6 April 2007.

The method by which employees are contracted out, and whether they are contracted out at all, is chiefly a decision for the employer to take in consultation with employees and recognised trade unions.

The reference scheme test can be adopted if the actuary certifies that at least 90% of the employees to be contracted out will accrue benefits that are better than, or equivalent to, those of the reference scheme. If a considerable proportion of employees' earnings is non-pensionable, e g overtime, it might mean that the scheme could fail the reference scheme test. In other cases, if say, 5% of the employees fall below this threshold, the scheme can still contract them out. This might seem to be invidious, and some employers have decided that they will propose amendments to the scheme rules so that the benefits provided under the reference scheme are introduced as an 'underpin' to the main scheme benefits. That is to say, no member can ever accrue benefits at a rate less favourable than that provided by the reference scheme. There are other solutions – such as making overtime pensionable or contracting out on the money purchase protected rights test or contracting in to S2P.

Following proposals made by Alan Pickering in his simplification review which was published in July 2002, in December 2002 the Government consulted on legislative changes that would weaken the reference scheme test. The accrual rate would be reduced from 1/80th of average qualifying earnings in the last three years to 1/100th of career average earnings as revalued by Limited Price Indexation. Also, instead of qualifying earnings being 90% of earnings between the National Insurance lower and upper earnings limits, they could be based on all earnings. These proposals were part of a package to simplify the contracting-out requirements.

The actuary of a scheme that is contracted out using the reference scheme test was formerly required to submit solvency certificates to the National Insurance Contributions Office once every three years. These are normally submitted with the renewed reference scheme certificate. This requirement to submit solvency certificates (Certificate T) has now been abolished in any case once the first MFR valuation has been completed and the schedule of contributions is in place.

Trustee relationship with scheme actuary

13.13   It is likely that both the trustees and the employer will on occasion need independent advice from an actuary. This is not a problem as the same actuary can advise both the employer and the trustees. Prior to 6 April 1997, in such situations, actuaries had to state clearly whom they were advising so that a conflict of interest could be avoided. If the actuary was advising the employer, the trustees may have judged it prudent in some circumstances to seek advice from another actuary.

As an example, suppose the employer wished to make use of a surplus to provide some benefit improvements. The employer may have asked for a fair estimate of their costs using the same basis as is used for identifying the pension cost in the company accounts, but may also have asked for a separate estimate of the cost using a more conservative funding basis which would be disclosed to members.

If the company wishes to buy or sell a part of the business, it will want the pension terms to work to its advantage; the trustees have to ensure the terms will not damage the interest of any members.

Since 6 April 1997 the problem has been resolved as the scheme actuary has been appointed by the trustees and it is to the trustees that the actuary is answerable. The trustees could face penalties if they were to rely on the advice of an actuary they had not appointed. If the scheme actuary, duly appointed by the trustees, is also to advise the sponsoring employer, the trustees must formally be informed that this will be the case and furthermore the actuary must alert all concerned to any potential conflict of interest. In such circumstances it should always be clear when advice is being given to the trustees and when it is being given to the employer. Actuaries appointed as the scheme actuary should usually communicate directly to the trustees.

The actuarial profession has developed a professional code of practice for scheme actuaries appointed under the *Pensions Act 1995* known as Guidance Note (GN) 29 *Occupational Pension Schemes – Advisers to Trustees or a Participating Employer*. It should be recommended reading for the trustees of all defined benefit schemes, and is available from the website of the Faculty and Institute of Actuaries at: http://www.actuaries.org.uk/files/pdf/map/GN29V5-0.pdf. Trustees should remember that if the actuary has reason to believe there is a material irregularity he or she must report the matter immediately to Opra – see **10.4** above.

Provision of information

13.14   Before 6 April 1997 it was the employer who had to provide the actuary with information which was relevant to a defined benefit scheme's funding position. From 6 April 1997, since the actuary must be appointed by the trustees, it has been the responsibility of the trustees to provide this information. As explained at **8.11** the employer now has an obligation to provide this information to the trustees who in turn are to pass it to their actuary.

Checklist 13

- Trustees of self-administered defined benefit schemes must appoint a suitably qualified scheme actuary. The actuary therefore must regard the trustees as the client to whom he or she owes a duty of confidence.

- The scheme actuary cannot be a trustee, nor connected with or associated with a trustee.

- The scheme actuary can also advise the sponsoring employer but must give notice if there is any conflict of interest. The trustees must be told if the scheme actuary also advises the employer.

- Scheme actuaries appointed under the *Pensions Act 1995* are bound to adhere to a professional code of conduct set out in Guidance Note 29.

- The actuary will carry out periodic actuarial valuations of the scheme to determine the scheme's liabilities, its assets and so the recommended contribution that needs to be made by the employer (net of any employee scheme contributions paid under the scheme rules).

- For the scheme's own purposes, the actuary can choose from a number of actuarial methods and adopt a number of actuarial assumptions – currently many actuaries use the projected unit method.

- The actuary must decide to use either a market value or a discounted value approach in calculating the value of the scheme's assets and liabilities.

- The actuary must use a prescribed method and set of assumptions to apply the Inland Revenue's surplus test.

- The actuary must use a prescribed method and set of assumptions to apply the Minimum Funding Requirement (MFR).

- The MFR is to be abolished and replaced with a long-term, scheme-specific standard which would be the responsibility of the scheme trustees and the actuary to police, and the actuary would be given a statutory duty of care to the members.

- The actuary must certify that a scheme can contract out using the reference scheme test by providing benefits that meet an overall quality test.

- The actuary has a number of other important roles, such as calculating transfer values and transfer credits, commutation rates and the effect of proposed scheme reconstructions.

- The trustees of a defined benefit scheme have a statutory duty to ensure that the schedule of contributions is respected.

- The trustees must supply their scheme actuary with the information he or she reasonably requires.

- The scheme actuary must report to Opra any material non-compliance with the statutory requirements.

Chapter 14

Trustees and the pensions lawyer

Association of Pension Lawyers

14.1   Not all firms of solicitors are able to provide the specialised expertise needed for pensions work. Most of the larger firms will have a number of partners who specialise in acting for pension funds, and trustees of self-administered schemes tend to rely on their legal advice.

Individual solicitors and barristers may be members of the *Association of Pension Lawyers*, a grouping which is recognised by the Law Society.

> Susan Andrews
> Secretary to the Association of Pension Lawyers
> c/o Room 10
> PMI House
> 4–10 Artillery Lane
> London
> E1 7LS
> Website: http://www.apl.org.uk

The Association of Pension Lawyers' website contains a useful set of papers written by lawyers discussing the key, current legal issues facing pension fund trustees.

The Association also produces a quarterly journal *Pensions Lawyer* available on subscription (£40 p a at the time of writing) which contains good, detailed papers, written by pension lawyers but which are accessible to a wider audience. It is a very useful source of in-depth information on pensions legal issues. Those wishing to subscribe should contact the Secretary at the address above.

Services offered by pension lawyers

14.2   Pension lawyers are engaged to provide the following services:

- to prepare documentation for occupational pension schemes, including the trust deed and rules, and to advise on how they should be amended from time to time;

- to negotiate on behalf of the scheme with the Inland Revenue either to gain approval or to ensure that approval is maintained;

- to advise trustees in difficult disputes brought by members or prospective members through the internal disputes resolution procedures or before the Pensions Ombudsman;

- to undertake litigation work through the courts;

- to provide legal advice, especially when changes to pension provision are being proposed, or when the trust deed and rules prove difficult to apply, perhaps because they are defective;

- to provide advice in merger and acquisitions work so that trustees of the scheme belonging to either the purchasing company or the vendor company may agree to the transfer of pension fund assets;

- to provide, in some cases, independent trusteeship services;

- to advise on the distribution of surpluses; and

- to advise on customer agreements between the trustees and investment managers.

Trustee relationship with pension lawyers

14.3   In the past pension lawyers have not been active in marketing their services but this is now changing with an increase in competition. Firms of solicitors now regularly compete for work in beauty parades before trustees. However, Law Society standards and codes may intervene and prevent a solicitor acting in a litigation matter because he or she has previously gained confidential knowledge that could be used unfairly to disadvantage the other side.

The trustees must appoint their own legal advisers. They would face penalties if they relied on the advice of a lawyer appointed by someone else, such as the sponsoring employer. This is not to say that the same lawyer cannot also act for the employer. In accordance with their own professional guidance, lawyers must not disguise any conflict of interest. The general remarks concerning an adviser's primary loyalty to either the employer or the trustees are particularly acute in the case of the pensions lawyer. Obviously, both the employer and the trustees will need independent legal advice in the case of a dispute between them. Even if there is no direct dispute, the trustees should ensure that they have taken independent legal advice. An example would be a payment out of a surplus to the employer: trustees would be foolish in the extreme to accept the legal advice of the lawyer who was acting for the employer. They must obtain advice from another source.

Unlike other advisers, lawyers are specifically excused from any 'whistle-blowing' duty since it is an important principle that lawyers should respect their clients' confidences. Of course, this would not protect a lawyer from prosecution if he or she colluded with any malpractice.

Checklist 14

- Trustees should consult a pensions lawyer whenever they have any serious doubts about how they should carry out their duty under the legislation and in line with the trust deed and rules. This should ensure compliance with the law and that no breach of trust occurs.

- The trustees must not rely on legal advice from a lawyer who has been appointed by the employer or any other party. Any lawyer who is approached for advice must have been appointed by the trustees themselves.

- The services pension lawyers can provide are not limited to drafting scheme documentation and litigation. They can provide a wide variety of services including liaison with the supervisory authorities.

- Pensions law is a specialised area of legal expertise and so trustees will want to ensure that the lawyer they engage has relevant experience in dealing with pension schemes.

Chapter 15

Trustees and the fund accountant

Introduction

15.1   The trustees of almost all occupational pension schemes must appoint a scheme auditor and they may face penalties if they rely on the work of an auditor who has been appointed by the employer or some other third party. Certain kinds of occupational pension schemes, however, are exempt from the general requirement to have an appointed auditor in place. They include unfunded schemes, unapproved schemes, schemes with less than two members and death-benefit-only schemes. Also exempt are small self-administered schemes and executive pension schemes set up on a defined contribution basis, but only provided that certain conditions are met. These conditions include the requirement that all the members of the scheme should also be trustees of the scheme and that all decisions taken by the trustees must be unanimous (or would be unanimous if any trustees who are not members are disregarded).

Special rules apply to the appointment and removal of the scheme auditor and the exchange of information between auditor, employer and trustees – see CHAPTER 10.

Eligibility to be an auditor

15.2   The scheme auditor must be a person who is a member of a recognised supervisory body and is eligible for the appointment under the rules of that body. Furthermore, the auditor must:

● not be a member or trustee of the scheme concerned;

● not be a person employed by the trustees;

● not be the employer of any member of the scheme; and

● neither be an officer nor employee of a company, nor a partner or employee of a partnership, that is the employer of any member of the scheme.

The important principle is that the same individual must not act as both trustee and auditor to the same scheme, and by extension an auditor is ineligible to act for a pension scheme if anyone associated with that auditor is a trustee. This requirement goes further than those applying to the scheme actuary. If a partner or employee of an accountancy firm acts as a scheme trustee, that firm cannot supply the auditors to the pension scheme.

The trustees can appoint either an individual or a firm as the scheme auditor. Qualified auditors from elsewhere in the European Union may act as scheme auditors.

Pension scheme accounts

15.3   The *Occupational Pension Schemes (Requirement to obtain Audited Accounts and a Statement from the Auditor) Regulations 1996 (SI 1996/1975)* came into force on 6 April 1997 and require that:

- the trustees of an occupational pension scheme must obtain, as soon as is reasonably practicable and, in any event, not more than *seven months* after the end of the scheme year, accounts audited by the scheme auditor for that year. This provision has replaced the earlier requirement that the accounts had to be prepared within twelve months;

- the audited accounts must contain the information set out in the schedule to the Requirement to obtain Audited Accounts Regulations; and

- the trustees should include a statement in the annual report that the accounts have been prepared and audited in accordance with the regulations. This replaces an earlier suggestion that at least two of the trustees should authorise the audited accounts since in this way the whole of the trustee board will be responsible for ensuring that the accounts have been prepared and audited in accordance with the statutory requirements.

In July 1996 the Accounting Standards Board (ASB) issued its Statement Of Recommended Practice (SORP) entitled *Financial Reports of Pension Schemes*. A revised version of the SORP was published in November 2002. This sets out the recommendations, intended to represent current best practice, on the form and content of the financial statements issued by pension schemes. Although the SORP is, as its name suggests, not mandatory, the trustees who are responsible for producing an annual report and accounts for their schemes are encouraged to follow it. The Requirement to obtain Audited Accounts Regulations in fact require the trustees to make a statement in the published accounts as to whether they have been prepared in accordance with the SORP. The statement must also indicate any material departures from the guidelines set out in section 2 of the SORP. Because of its importance, it is highly recommended that the trustees take a look at the SORP. It is a very helpful document. Copies are obtainable from:

> Pensions Research Accountants Group
> 145 London Road
> Kingston upon Thames
> KT2 6BR
> Tel: 020 8247 1264

Apart from the specified information covered by the SORP and the 1996 Regulations, the audited accounts must show a true and fair view of the financial transactions of the scheme during the scheme year, the amount and disposition of the assets at the end of the scheme year and any liabilities of the scheme, other than to pay pensions and benefits after the end of the scheme year.

There must be a statement by the auditor as to whether or not contributions have been paid in accordance with the *schedule of contributions* (defined benefit schemes) or with the *payment schedule* (defined contribution schemes) as described at **8.3–8.6**.

After the failure to pay contributions by the statutory deadline, the most common reported act of non-compliance with the regulatory requirements reported to Opra under *section 48* of the *Pensions Act 1995* (see **10.4**) is the failure by trustees to produce their audited accounts within seven months of the end of the scheme year. Non-compliance with this requirement was formerly a criminal offence. The burden of proof needed for Opra to mount a successful prosecution meant that enforcement of the requirement was difficult. On 3 April 2000, however, non-compliance was made subject to a civil penalty in the form of a fine and possible prohibition from acting as a trustee. As a result it should now be easier for Opra to tackle the problem.

In April 2000, to mark the new regime, Opra published a booklet *Getting Your Audited Accounts and the Auditor's Statement on Time – A Guide for Occupational Pension Scheme Trustees*. It is available free of charge from Opra (see **APPENDIX 3**) and can be downloaded from their website at: http://www.opra.gov.uk/pdf/fact5/pdf. In the booklet Opra points out that:

'Preparing pension scheme accounts and making sure they are audited on time isn't just a question of keeping within the law and making us happy. As trustees, you will want to make sure the scheme is run in a businesslike way so that members can have confidence in it'.

In a separate booklet issued in June 2000, Opra issued further guidance on audited scheme accounts entitled *A Guide for People Involved with Insured Salary-Related Pension Schemes* because this was a type of scheme that was experiencing particular problems. The booklet contains a pro-forma timetable for scheme accounts preparation and audit running from twelve weeks before the scheme year end, when the trustees ought to have agreed with the auditor the provisional audit commencement date, until 26 weeks after the scheme year end when the trustees and auditor should both have signed off the accounts.

Scheme financial records and procedures

15.4 The *Occupational Pension Schemes (Scheme Administration) Regulations 1996 (SI 1996/1715)* specify receipts, payments and records that the pension scheme trustees must keep. As mentioned in **CHAPTER 11**, the trustees will inevitably have to rely on their pensions manager and the pensions administration department to carry out all the complex tasks involved in running the financial affairs of an occupational pension scheme. Nevertheless, it should be remembered as always that it is the trustees who are responsible for ensuring that the scheme is administered correctly and efficiently. For more details in this area, 'Part 6 – Financial Management' of *Tolley's Pensions Administration* is recommended reading.

Bank account

15.5   Under the *Pensions Act 1995* there are specific requirements on the trustees to keep any money they receive in a separate bank account held in their name. Similarly, if an employer is responsible for a pension payroll service and therefore makes payments to members, it must deposit any payments which it cannot pay over to members in a separate bank account.

Fraud prevention

15.6   Auditors are not present in the offices of the pension scheme administrators on a day-to-day basis supervising what is going on. They cannot themselves, therefore, prevent fraud. Rather it is up to the trustees themselves to be responsible for ensuring that the accounts are accurately prepared and that there are adequate controls, reporting systems and accounting records in place. Separate sections of the pension administration team should be used to: (*a*) calculate; (*b*) authorise; and (*c*) pay benefits, with different people involved at each of the three stages. Since the audit is carried out some time after the end of the accounting period, the main responsibility for the continuing prevention of fraud or any other malpractice rests with the trustees. However, a good auditor will inform the trustees of any administrative and accounting control weaknesses that are discovered during an audit.

The possibility of fraud should never be dismissed. It can take many forms including:

- the removal of monies from the pension scheme to defraud the beneficiaries;
- the removal of monies from the pension scheme to help a sponsoring employer in financial difficulties but which simply defrauds the scheme beneficiaries;
- employee or employer contributions not properly passed over to the scheme;
- the use of the scheme as a conduit for the removal of employer assets properly due to the employer's creditors;
- cheque frauds;
- unreported deaths;
- phantom pensioners (i e fictional beneficiaries of the scheme to whom benefits are fraudulently being paid from the scheme);
- simple theft;

- diversion or overpayment of transfer payments from the scheme and underpayment of transfer payments received by the scheme; and

- fraud connected with the scheme's investments including their use as unauthorised collateral.

This list is far from comprehensive. Again, detailed discussion of these topics is given in *Tolley's Pensions Administration*. It should be stressed, however, that failure to pay the correct level of benefits as a result of maladministration (see **11.4**) could jeopardise scheme resources to the same extent as fraud.

In November 1997 the Auditing Practices Board (APB) issued Practice Note No 15, *The Audit of Occupational Pension Schemes in the United Kingdom*. For the contact details of the APB see **APPENDIX 3**. The Practice Note is available on the Internet at: http://www.accountancyfoundation.com/ uploaded_documents/PN_15.pdf.

The general purpose of the Practice Notes issued by the APB is to assist auditors in applying the mandatory Statements of Auditing Standards in particular circumstances and industries. Practice Note 15 therefore gives guidance to auditors on how to apply the general Auditing Standards when they are auditing an occupational pension scheme. The Practice Note is very clearly written and pension fund trustees might find it very useful as a standard reference work. In particular, the section of the Practice Note dealing with the treatment of Standard Auditing Statement 300 (accounting and internal control systems and audit risk assessments) makes valuable reading for pension fund trustees. The Practice Note states:

' ... the responsibilities of trustees for ensuring that the scheme is properly administered and its assets properly safeguarded apply irrespective of a scheme's size or administrative arrangements, and the attitude, role and involvement of each scheme's trustees are likely to be fundamental in determining the effectiveness of its control environment'.

The Practice Note advises auditors to take the following factors into account when they are to consider the attitude, role and involvement of a scheme's trustees for the purpose of carrying out their duties under SAS 300:

- the amount of time committed by individual trustees;

- the skills and qualifications of individual trustees;

- development of a Statement of Investment Principles;

- arrangements to monitor adherence to the scheme's Statement of Investment Principles;

- the independence of trustees from each other;

- the dominance of an individual trustee (or employer) over the investment and administration policies;

- the frequency and regularity of trustee meetings;

- the form and content of trustee meetings;

- adequacy of minutes of trustee meetings;

- the division of duties between trustees;

- the involvement of trustees in supervision and control procedures, including matters such as cheque-signing arrangements;

- the adequacy of the accounting records and access of the trustees thereto;

- trustees' attitude towards third parties to whom they delegate the conduct of scheme activities; and

- arrangements for the trustees to monitor scheme income and expenditure.

In May 2000 the Auditing Practices Board issued Bulletin 2000/2 entitled *Supplementary Guidance for Auditors of Occupational Pension Schemes in the United Kingdom.* The Bulletin was issued in the light of a number of developments in the regulation and audit of pension schemes since Practice Note 15 was issued, including the fact that a number of accountancy firms had been subject to disciplinary action by their professional bodies concerning failures to report late scheme accounts to Opra on a timely basis. The Bulletin is of particular note in a number of areas: it is available on the Internet at: http://www.accountancyfoundation.com/uploaded_documents/Bull_00-02.pdf.

The trustees do not have to report to Opra any failure by the employer to pay over contributions by the due date (or, in the case of contributions which have been deducted from employees' pay, the 19th of the calendar month following the month they were deducted) provided that this failure is only the first or second such default in the twelve months ending on the date the contributions became due (see **8.3–8.6**). This easement in the duty to report to Opra has, however, not been granted to auditors. Bulletin 2000/2, therefore, states that it is the view of the Auditing Practices Board that auditors should continue to report to Opra all instances of late payment that come to their attention. It also elsewhere points out that, although the responsibility for obtaining the scheme's accounts is the responsibility of the trustees (who usually appoint an administrator to carry out this task), auditors who are aware of a failure by trustees to obtain audited accounts within seven months of the end of the scheme year, but who fail to report this to Opra on a timely basis, risk being reported by Opra to their professional bodies and that this could result in fines and adverse publicity for the audit firm concerned. For further discussion of the scheme auditor's whistle-blowing duties, see **10.4**.

Trustee relationship with accountant

Which accountancy firm?

15.7   Trustees and employers may wish to employ different accountancy firms for the pension fund accounts and the company accounts so that there is no possibility of a conflict of interest. This was a firm recommendation of the House of Commons Social Security Committee investigating the Maxwell affair. One example of a possible conflict of interest is whether the accountants auditing the employer accounts should immediately report the matter to the trustees if they spotted that employer contributions were not being regularly paid to the pension fund. (This was before the requirement on the trustees to enforce a schedule of contributions/payment schedule – see **8.5**–**8.6**.)

However, the Pension Law Review Committee disagreed with the House of Commons Social Security Committee stating that trustees should be free to appoint an auditor acting for the employer provided that the terms of engagement are clearly set out, the roles and responsibilities of employer, trustees and auditor are clearly defined and that the areas of conflict are known.

Guidelines from the Chartered Accountants' Joint Ethics Committee ban accountancy firms from being appointed as independent trustees to the pension scheme of any company for which they are also acting as an insolvency practitioner.

Trustee responsibilities to auditors

15.8   The trustees' responsibilities are set out in the *engagement letter* sent by the auditor to the trustees, which is normally repeated every three years. The trustees will acknowledge their understanding of these responsibilities in a letter of representation on the accounts which they send to the auditors each year prior to the auditors signing their opinion. The Practice Note 15 (see **15.6** above) gives detailed guidance, with examples of appointment and engagement letters.

Whistle blowing

15.9   As discussed at **10.4** the auditor must blow the whistle to Opra if he or she finds any material irregularity.

Company accounts: SSAP 24 and FRS17

15.10   Accountants engaged by the company will need to account for pension costs in the company's profit and loss account. It used to be normal practice for pension costs to be based solely on the contributions actually paid by the company into the pension fund. So a company taking a contribution holiday would receive an immediate fillip in its figures. Such a system fails to match revenue and costs as they are earned and incurred, which can be seriously misleading.

As a result, the Statement of Standard Accounting Practice No 24 (SSAP 24) was developed. It was first applied in July 1988. The overall aim of SSAP 24 was to give a *true and fair* figure for the cost to the company of providing pension benefits, and works by trying to spread any variations from the regular cost over longer periods.

From the point of view of the trustees of the occupational pension scheme, SSAP 24 has had few direct implications. How pension costs are accounted for in the company's accounts, however, may influence the employer's willingness to sponsor variable-cost defined benefit schemes over fixed-cost money purchase schemes. It should be noted that the disclosure requirements associated with SSAP 24 meant that company accounts were obliged to begin to give more detail of the associated pension scheme.

In 1999, the Accounting Standards Board (ASB) issued Financial Reporting Exposure Draft 20 (known as FRED 20) which set out the proposals for a new accounting standard on the treatment of pensions and other retirement benefits in the company accounts. FRED 20 immediately began to cause considerable consternation because the proposed methodology to be applied to accounting for the costs of defined benefit schemes was bound to generate greater volatility in company accounts.

Despite the consternation caused, the ASB proceeded with the development of the new standard and, in November 2000, it published *Financial Reporting Standard 17 'Retirement Benefits'* or FRS17 as it is universally now known. Upon its publication, Sir David Tweedie, the then Chairman of the ASB commented:

> 'Pension cost accounting has for a long time been an impenetrable black box to users of accounts. This new standard will help all interested parties to understand the implications for a company of running a defined benefit pension scheme. It may not be popular with some who would like the present obscurity to remain but transparency of information must be preferable. It should mean that decisions about pension provision are made on a better informed basis. In my view, the UK now has the best standard in the world for accounting for pensions and I would expect it to trigger similar reviews in other countries.'

The key feature of FRS17 is that the market value of a defined benefit pension scheme's surplus or deficiency will appear as an entry in the balance sheet of the sponsoring employer's company accounts. Under the existing standard SSAP 24, the company's balance sheet showed the accrual of the difference between the contributions paid and the amount charged to profit.

Under FRS17, the company's profit and loss account shows the relatively stable ongoing service cost, interest cost and expected return of assets measured on a basis consistent with international standards. The effects of fluctuations in market values of the pension fund's assets and liabilities are not seen as being part of the operating results of the business and are treated in the same way as revaluations of fixed assets, i e they are recognised immediately in the second performance statement, known as the Statement of Recognised Gains and Losses (STRGL). The ASB argues that this use of the STRGL copes with problems of volatility.

However, in practice, many finance directors have not been convinced and fear that the volatility caused by market changes in the pension fund's assets and liabilities will damage the financial credibility of the sponsoring company. In particular, large negative numbers in the STRGL stemming from a defined benefit scheme deficiency tend to be seen by financial analysts and, importantly, the company credit-rating agencies as a debt to the employer. If a company's credit rating is lowered as a result, it will make it much more expensive for the company to borrow money.

Part of the difficulty is that, unless further qualifications are made in the company's accounts, a pension fund surplus is assumed to be akin to an asset of the company and a deficiency is, as mentioned above, seen as a debt. Yet a surplus cannot simply be paid over to the employer – see **19.3**. Similarly, an employer normally has the right at any stage to end any further accrual of pensions, which will change the FRS17 numbers, or to wind up the scheme. Any deficiency arising in the scheme's fund on winding up currently only becomes a debt on the employer to the extent defined in the legislation as explained at **19.10–19.11**.

While all these difficulties exist, it should be borne in mind that FRS17 itself has not increased the cost of running a defined benefit scheme. It merely changes the way that the cost of providing a defined benefit scheme is accounted for in the company accounts of the sponsoring employer.

FRS17 did not have to come into force in relation to company accounts immediately, although companies have been able voluntarily to operate it for accounting periods ending on or after 22 June 2001. On 2 July 2002, however, the ASB proposed to extend the transitional arrangements for the adoption of FRS 17 and so defer the mandatory requirement for its full adoption. In the meantime, UK financial statements would continue to have to include disclosure of information prepared in accordance with FRS 17 either in the footnotes or, where the standard is voluntarily adopted early, in the main financial statements. This proposal to defer full implementation of FRS17 was put into effect on 25 November 2002.

The ASB's decision to defer full implementation was a direct result of the announcement by the International Accounting Standards Board (IASB) that it had added to its agenda a project to reconsider the provisions of the corresponding international standard IAS 19 *Employee Benefits*. Under European requirements, IASB accounting standards are to become mandatory throughout the Union.

Because it will take the IASB some time before it issues proposals, the ASB decided it should act immediately. Without the proposed amendment, companies with accounting periods ending after 22 June 2002 would have been required to adopt FRS 17 in full for their interim statements at December 2002, and would then face the risk of having to change their accounting a second time when they were required to use IASB standards for their group accounts from 1 January 2005.

The ASB is now proposing that mandatory full adoption of FRS 17 should be deferred during the period of international discussions on IAS 19, and that it will then consult on the early adoption in the UK of a standard based on whatever the IASB puts forward.

Whatever revisions are eventually agreed by the IASB to IAS 19, it is clear that they will not involve any return to a standard such as SSAP24. As the ASB comments:

'The Board has confirmed that it considers the requirements of FRS 17 to be superior to those of the present international standard. We continue to encourage companies to consider voluntarily adopting its requirements in full. The Board is also aware that SSAP 24 has serious deficiencies.'

Checklist 15

- Trustees must appoint a suitably qualified scheme auditor.

- The scheme auditor cannot be a trustee nor connected with or associated with a trustee.

- The same auditors can provide audit services to the scheme trustees and the sponsoring employer subject to rules governing professional conduct.

- Trustees must supply their scheme auditor with the information he or she reasonably requires.

- Scheme accounts are governed by a Statement of Recommended Practice (SORP) and the *Occupational Pension Schemes (Requirement to obtain Audited Accounts and a Statement from the Auditor) Regulations 1996*, and must be received by the trustees not more than seven months from the end of the scheme year.

- Auditors can advise the trustees on ways to improve internal controls to ensure risks of maladministration and fraud are minimised, but the responsibility for the proper financial management of the scheme rests with the trustees, while the day-to-day financial management is carried out by the scheme administrators.

- Until now accountants working for the sponsoring employer have accounted for the pension cost in line with professional guidance given in Statement of Standing Accounting Practice No 24 (SSAP 24). SSAP 24 is now in the process of being replaced by a new financial reporting standard, FRS17, although full mandatory implementation of FRS17 is being deferred prior to the introduction of a new mandatory international standard.

Chapter 16

Investing pension fund assets

Introduction

Insured schemes

16.1   Around one quarter of all employees who are active members of occupational pension schemes belong to schemes in which all the benefits are guaranteed by one insurance company. The employer has simply entered into an *insurance contract*, not specifically an investment management contract. Employer- or employee-nominated trustees of insured schemes have no direct input in determining their scheme's investment policy.

If the number of employees working in a company, or the size of the pension fund, ever reaches a critical threshold, economies of scale would suggest that the scheme stops being a wholly insured scheme and instead becomes a *self-administered scheme*, i e a scheme where the trustees take control of their scheme's overall investment strategy.

Self-administered schemes

Managed funds

16.2   The term *managed fund* describes an arrangement where the trustees of a self-administered scheme have entered into an investment management contract with an insurance company, and the scheme's funds are invested in a pooled arrangement along with many other managed pension funds. The trustees do not have a direct input into the investment policy but they can decide to switch to another managed fund or decide that the pension fund is large enough to become a segregated fund. Pooled funds are also operated by unit trust groups.

Segregated funds

16.3   The term *segregated fund* describes the situation where the trustees of an occupational pension fund have entered into a contract with one or more investment managers who manage the assets of that pension fund independently of any other pension funds. The trustees are responsible for formulating the overall investment policy to be followed by their investment manager or managers.

The largest UK occupational funds are self-administered schemes run as segregated funds, although the trustees will in many cases have decided to keep part of the scheme's assets in managed or pooled funds run by an investment manager, a unit trust or an insurance company.

Trustee investment powers

16.4   The trust deed and rules governing the occupational pension scheme should give the trustees very wide powers of investment. In the past, if they had not done so, the trustees would have been bound by quite severe limitations on the permitted range of investments, which were imposed by default by the *Trustee Investments Act 1961*. The coming into force of the *Trustee Act 2000* gives trustees in general much more modern investment powers, but in practice the investment powers of pension fund trustees are in any case governed by the terms of their trust deed and rules which in general have long given the trustees the power to invest in a wide range of investment assets.

There are a number of general principles that trustees must observe in exercising their investment powers.

The most important principle is that trustees must take the same amount of care in exercising any investment power as ordinary prudent men or women would take 'if they were making an investment for the benefit of other people for whom they felt morally bound to provide'.

The general duty to take advice is especially relevant. Trustees who have not taken investment advice cannot be said to have acted in a prudent and reasonable way; even if they acted sincerely and in good faith. Trustees should ensure that the investment advice they receive is objective and of high quality.

Trustees can, of course, reject the advice, since responsibility for the pension fund lies ultimately with them. However, it is clear that they should not reject advice arbitrarily simply because they disagree with it. They would need to be convinced that to follow the advice was imprudent and unreasonable. In practice, they would have taken further advice from another reputable source.

Under the *Trustee Act 2000* trustees have had a general duty to consider the need for diversification of the investments and the suitability of the kind of investments made. In addition, since 6 April 1997 the *Pensions Act 1995* had already added considerably to the statutory duties placed on occupational scheme trustees in matters concerning investment.

The Government is currently consulting on legislation that would require an enhanced standard of care whereby the trustees must be 'familiar with the issues concerned'. This is discussed in more detail at **17.7**.

Financial services legislation

16.5   The *Financial Services Act 1986* made it a criminal offence to carry on an investment business without proper authorisation. The *Financial*

Services and Markets Act 2000 maintains this position. Since, in general, the trustees of an occupational pension scheme are not authorised, it follows that all the activities that define the carrying on of regulated activities under the 2000 Act must be undertaken by another, authorised, party.

In cases of doubt, trustees should check the *bona fides* of an investment manager directly with the FSA.

Financial Services Authority
25 The North Colonnade
Canary Wharf
London
E14 5HS
Tel: 020 7676 1000
Fax: 020 7676 1099
Website: http://www.fsa.gov.uk

Trustees do not need to be authorised themselves if all day-to-day decisions relating to the scheme's management are taken by an authorised investment manager. This does not mean that effective control over investment policy is no longer in the hands of the trustees: but it does mean that it is very dubious that unauthorised trustees can be involved in individual decisions to buy or sell particular assets.

Pensions Act 1995

16.6   The *Pensions Act 1995* makes it clear that from 6 April 1997, subject to the trust deed and rules, the trustees have the same power to make an investment of any kind as if they were absolutely entitled to the assets of the scheme. The Act therefore has rendered probably void any requirement that the sponsoring employer must approve how the trustees exercise their powers. Any restriction imposed by the trust deed and rules probably will relate to the types of investment in which the trustees are permitted to invest. For example, the trust deed and rules may ban the trustees completely from making any investments in the business of the sponsoring employer.

If the trustees delegate their powers of investment to a fund manager who is authorised under the *Financial Services and Markets Act 2000*, the trustees cannot be held responsible for that fund manager's acts or defaults provided that they have taken all steps to satisfy themselves that the fund manager has the '*appropriate knowledge and experience*' for managing the investments of the scheme, that it is carrying out its work competently, and is complying with all the requirements made under the *Pensions Act 1995* relating to pension fund investments.

The trustees can also delegate their powers of investment under the same conditions, and without liability to a fund manger who is not authorised under the *Financial Services and Markets Act 2000*, if it concerns investment business not covered by the scope of that Act, e g cash or property.

As mentioned above, the Government has proposed introducing a new standard of care which involves a requirement for trustees to be familiar with the investment issues with which they are concerned. The relevant consultation paper setting out these proposals states that, where a decision has been properly delegated, the trustees will, as now, continue not to be liable for the acts or defaults of the person to whom the powers were delegated, provided that they have also fulfilled the new standard of care in relation to the selection, appointment and monitoring of that person. This familiarity principle is discussed at **17.7**.

Investment committees

16.7   Subject to any restriction imposed by the trust deed and rules, the trustees can delegate their investment powers to a sub-committee of two or more trustees, but if they do they will still all remain responsible for the acts and default of this investment committee. Note in this context also that, if member-nominated trustees have been appointed under the trustees' *appropriate rules*, they must not be allocated functions that differ from other employer-nominated trustees, but that this may not be the case with member-nominated trustee directors in the case of a corporate trustee – see **4.12**. The Government's proposals regarding the new standard of care regarding familiarity with investment issues (see **17.7**) include questions for consultation on whether the standard should apply to all individual trustees, or only the trustees of an investment sub-committee or to the trustee board collectively. However, more generally, pension fund trustees as a whole will continue to retain the ultimate responsibility and legal liability for the decisions of the investment sub-committee unless the sub-committee in turn has properly delegated those decisions to a properly appointed person.

Paul Myners held as a key investment principle that it was 'good practice for trustee boards to have an investment sub-committee to provide appropriate focus'.

Statement of Investment Principles

16.8   The trustees must prepare and maintain from time to time a written statement setting out the principles governing decisions about scheme investments. The trustees of wholly insured schemes are exempted from this requirement provided the trustees have no discretion over the investment policy. In order to prepare or revise such a statement, the trustees must obtain and consider written advice from a professionally qualified adviser. The trustees must also consult with the employer who sponsors the pension scheme.

The statement must cover policy on the following matters:

- the kinds of investments to be held;
- the balance between different kinds of investments;
- risk;

- the expected return on investments;

- the realisation of investments; and

- the trustees' policy on using the voting rights attached to the shares held by the fund in companies and on socially responsible investment issues (see **16.25** below).

In addition, the statement must cover the trustees' policy for securing compliance with the following specific requirements:

- the need for diversification of investments in so far as is appropriate to the circumstances of the scheme;

- establishing the suitability of the proposed investments and the suitability of the proposed categories of investments;

- the need to obtain and consider proper advice in writing from a suitably qualified person on the suitability of the scheme's investments, apart from those listed in the *Trustee Investments Act 1961* as 'narrower range investments not requiring advice';

- the need to determine how often investment advice should be updated; and

- the need, if applicable, to meet the Minimum Funding Requirement (see **13.8**).

Trustees who do not comply with the requirements of the *Pensions Act 1995* regarding their investment duties risk being removed as trustees, or being fined, by Opra.

The trustees' Statement of Investment Principles should be a key document governing the scheme, changing as the scheme changes. For example, the investment principles governing a small scheme with no pensioner members and a young workforce will be very different from those governing a large scheme with a higher proportion of pensioners and deferred pensioners than active members. The importance of the requirement for a Statement of Investment Principles lies in the fact that the trustees must set out their own investment standards in the document and then are bound to comply with those self-same standards.

Asset management

16.9   The fund that financially underpins an occupational pension scheme is not static. It is a dynamic system with money constantly moving. Except when there is a complete, but temporary, *contribution holiday* for employers and employees (or perhaps it is a non-contributory scheme as far as employees are concerned), there is a regular flow of contributions into the scheme. New members may also bring transfer credits into the scheme from other pension schemes.

Similarly, the investments or assets already in the fund will also generate income. For example, shares in companies will give rise to income from dividends, property let to businesses will bring in rental income and interest will accrue from cash deposits.

Some or all of this income can be used to meet the cost of paying benefits and the scheme's expenses such as paying the scheme's advisers their fees, and meeting any day-to-day administrative costs for which the scheme rather than the employer is responsible.

However, any excess income can be used to make fresh investments. Likewise, existing financial assets can be sold and the money re-invested to buy other assets.

It may be that in a very mature scheme, the inflow of money from contributions and investments is no longer enough to meet the scheme's expenses and the cost of paying benefits. In this event, a carefully controlled sale of assets will need to be managed to release the required money.

If assets are bought and sold at random it is likely that the fund will perform very badly. If a fund is to meet its desired objectives, all financial advisers are agreed that it must be properly managed according to a thought-out plan: the process of asset management. Asset management, however, does not mean that the plan that is adopted need be inflexible and that investment opportunities should be ignored if they do not immediately fit in with that plan.

Conventionally, asset management is thought of as taking place at three levels; each of which requires a differing level of involvement from the trustees.

Level	*Trustee involvement*
Strategic asset management	High involvement
Tactical asset management	Medium involvement
Stock and individual asset selection	Low involvement

Strategic asset management

16.10   This is the level of the overall and long-term investment policy. It involves primarily the process known as *asset allocation* (i e how the fund's investments are divided between the various asset classes). When trustees, following the advice of their actuary or other financial advisers, decide how the pension fund's assets should be divided up into the various asset classes, they are said to be following a *top-down approach*.

The major asset classes are:

- *UK equities* – Ordinary shares in companies traded on the UK stock exchange.

- *Overseas equities* – Ordinary shares traded on foreign stock exchanges.

- *Junior market equities* – Ordinary shares in companies that do not fulfil the requirements for a listing on the main Stock Market.

- *Private equity (including venture capital)* – investment in private companies not listed on a stock market.

- *Property* – Either direct ownership of buildings that are let commercially or for residential accommodation or pooled investments in a property fund.

- *Fixed-interest bonds* – Investments in securities issued by companies, local authorities and governments which give a fixed rate of interest for a predetermined length of time. The fixed-interest securities issued by the UK Government are called gilts.

- *Index-linked bonds* – Securities, usually issued by the Government, where the interest and capital repayments are linked to the movements in the Retail Prices Index.

- *Cash/short-term deposits* – Cash that is invested at high short-term rates.

- *Other assets* – Can include works of art, yachts, rare coins etc.

Financial instruments

16.11   These include the following:

- *Financial futures* – Contracts binding two parties in a sale or purchase at a specified date at a price which is fixed at the time the contract is made.

- *Traded options* – A contract under which the payment of a sum of money gives a right, but not an obligation, to buy or sell something at an agreed price on or before a specified date.

- *Convertibles* – Fixed-interest securities that can be converted into equities on predetermined terms.

- *Warrants* – A stockmarket security with its own market price which can be converted into a specific share at a predetermined price.

Each of these asset classes has particular characteristics. For example, looking at long periods of time during the 20th century, equities have outperformed fixed-interest securities. However, they seem to be inherently more risky. In bad trading conditions, companies reduce the dividend paid to their shareholders or even pay no dividend at all. Similarly, share prices rise and fall, and, of course, if a company fails, the shares may become worthless.

In the case of a defined benefit scheme, after taking advice from the scheme's actuary, trustees will know the future pattern of liabilities that the scheme must meet. This can guide them in deciding how the fund should be divided up between the various asset classes.

For example, a defined benefit scheme which is long established in an industry that is contracting in size may have many more pensioners and deferred pensioners than active members. Employee contributions will tend to fall and its trustees will need to realise its assets in the near future in order to pay pensions. Such a scheme may hold a high proportion of fixed-interest stock which will mature in the near future.

Another defined benefit scheme may be recently established in a growth industry with a very young workforce. The scheme will need to build up its fund but will have a comparatively low level of liabilities in the near future. Such a fund could invest in assets which are more difficult to turn into liquid cash at short notice. Examples are property and equities which are asset classes thought to be more likely to register high growth over long periods.

It was the view of Paul Myners, and one that is embodied in his investment principles (see **17.4** and **17.5**), that the mandate given by the trustees to the investment manager or managers, and the scheme's trust deed and rules 'should not exclude the use of any set of financial instruments, without clear justification in the light of the specific circumstances of the fund'.

A new strand of thinking, however, has developed in recent years in relation to the kind of investments that should be held by a defined benefit scheme. The key ideas were set out by Jon Exley, Shyam Mehta and Andrew Smith in 1997 in a paper published by the Institute of Actuaries entitled *The Financial Theory of Defined Benefit Pension Schemes*. The position taken is that fixed-interest and index-linked bonds provide a better match than equities for defined benefit liabilities. Nevertheless, although bonds provide a better match for their liabilities, the majority of pension schemes continue to hold a significant proportion of their assets in equities. This is because it is commonly held that equities are expected to give rise to higher long-term investment returns than bonds. The downside of this extra expected return is that it comes with risks attached. After adjusting for the risks, it is argued that equities do not reduce the cost of providing defined benefit pensions. Furthermore, there is no guarantee that equities will always outperform bonds.

In 2001, the trustee of the Boots Pension Scheme announced that, over the 15 months ending in July that year, it had authorised the selling of all the scheme's equities and short-term bonds and had moved all its assets into high-credit-rated long-term bonds. John Ralfe, then a member of the Trustee Investment Committee of the Boots Pension Scheme, saw three main arguments in favour of this move, which had caused a sensation in the pensions world:

(*a*)   it increased members' security by matching assets to liabilities with the result that the value of the assets should always be enough to pay all pensions;

(*b*)   it reduced investment management charges and dealing costs in the case of the Boots Pension Scheme from £10m p a down to £250,000 p a; and

(*c*)   it reduced the company's risk by removing the possibility that, by holding equities, a deficit could be created that would have increased employer contributions.

The views put forward by Exley, Mehta and Smith, and famously put into practice at Boots are ground in corporate finance theory. They are, however, not accepted by many actuaries who believe that equities are an appropriate investment for pension funds to hold when matched against the liability to pay a pension that will not fall until several years into the future. Opinions are sharply divided and exchanges of view have on occasion been heated. The eventual outcome of this debate is not yet known but, at the time of writing, it is taking place against the background of three years' negative returns in the world's major equity markets and the emergence of substantial deficits in many, if not most, defined benefit schemes.

Tactical asset management

16.12   The overall strategic decisions are not implemented in an inflexible way. For example, the trustees may have put down a *benchmark* stipulating that the fund is to retain 40% of its total value in overseas equities. That is a long-term average. It could be that during a world-wide recession with generally falling stock markets, the trustees may be advised that it is temporarily better to hold a smaller percentage in the form of equities generally and a higher percentage in cash on short-term deposit. Such decisions will involve the trustees but will be recommended by financial advisers such as the pension consultant as well as the investment managers themselves.

In practice, one might find that the scheme's Statement of Investment Principles will set out the trustees' benchmarked asset allocation policy as in the following table.

Asset class	Benchmark	Allowable range
UK equities	40%	30% to 50%
Overseas equities	20%	10% to 30%
UK fixed-interest bonds	12.5%	7.5% to 17.5%
UK corporate bonds	10%	5% to 15%
Index-linked bonds	7.5%	5% to 10%
All overseas bonds	5%	0% to 10%
Property	2.5%	0% to 5%
Cash	2.5%	0% to 5%

In other words, although the benchmark, for example, for UK equities is that they should represent 40% of the pension fund, the investment manager is free to decrease or increase that weighting anywhere in the range from 30% to 50% of the fund.

In any case, market movements in asset prices will mean that the weighting will change without the investment manager being involved in buying one asset class and selling another. For example, suppose during a year UK equities fell in market value and UK fixed-interest bonds (gilts) rose in market value. In this instance, therefore, assuming at the start of that year the scheme held each of the assets at its exact benchmark proportion, the scheme's UK equities portfolio would drop below its 40% benchmark and the UK gilts portfolio would rise above its 12.5% benchmark simply because of the overall market movements.

If the overall market movements were sufficiently large, the UK equities portfolio would drop through the 30% bottom end of its permitted range, and the UK gilts portfolio would break through its 17.5% ceiling. At this point, the fund managers would seek to rebalance the fund and would begin buying UK equities to bring the scheme's UK equities portfolio back up over 30% of the fund, and begin selling UK gilts to bring the UK gilts portfolio back down below 17.5% of the fund.

Of course, the result of the trustees' policy is that the investment manager buys assets which are currently falling in value and sells assets which are currently rising in value. This may seem to some to be a strange thing to want to do at that time.

On the other hand, trustees who decide to adopt an asset allocation policy are not seeking to maximise the scheme's investment performance over the short term but rather to pursue a long-term investment strategy which usually involves a degree of matching different kinds of assets against different kinds of liabilities.

Stock and individual asset selection

16.13 An investment policy that concentrates on individual stock selection is called a *bottom-up approach*. But even if, as in most cases, a *top-down approach* has been adopted, the decision to buy, say, Glaxo in December 1987 but not to buy, say, Polly Peck is obviously of vital importance since Glaxo soared and Polly Peck went bust.

The trustees will not usually be involved in decisions about which particular shares to buy and sell. As explained above, the *Financial Services and Markets Act 2000* prohibits trustees who are not authorised from being involved in day-to-day decisions – and individual stock selection is perilously close to a day-to-day decision. In the main, these decisions will be left to the investment managers.

There are certain exceptions. Trustees might want to be involved in the discussions of whether to invest in the latest privatisation issue. Particularly large purchases and sales in a directly-managed property portfolio might also mean closer discussion with the trustees.

Trustees will want to ensure that stock selection is properly diversified and that shares in any particular company do not represent too large a percentage of the overall fund. Shares in a large, blue-chip, UK company will rarely form more than 6% or 7% of the total value of any fund.

Similarly, trustees may lay down certain guidelines that set specific restrictions on stock selection. For example, the trustees of a pension fund in a particular industry may prefer to see the pension fund invest in that industry and it is rare that trustees will object to shares being held in a competitor company. Trustees may also wish to invest in a Venture Capital Fund which invests in small businesses in the specific geographical area of the country where most of the pension fund members are located. Such restrictions should not be allowed to jeopardise the overall financial return of the pension fund. See also the discussion of socially responsible investment at **16.26** below.

The law now restricts pension fund investment in the sponsoring employer – see **16.21**.

Appointing investment managers

16.14   The trustees must appoint the investment manager or managers. They must not rely on the advice of an investment manager who has been appointed by a third party unless that appointment was made on behalf of the trustees.

In-house investment managers

16.15   Where the employer is a bank, insurance company or another financial institution, the associated occupational pension scheme is usually provided by the employer's in-house investment managers. However, some of the UK's larger occupational pension schemes outside the financial sector also employ their own in-house investment management teams. In some cases these in-house investment management teams also compete to take on business from other, unconnected, occupational pension schemes.

Very large schemes can achieve cost savings by using in-house investment teams and there is an obvious advantage in having the expertise at hand, uniquely dedicated to the needs of just one pension fund. Internal communication between trustees and investment managers should ensure a very intimate involvement in the investment process for the scheme's trustees. One possible disadvantage lies in the great difficulty trustees would have in changing in-house managers if they were to lose confidence in them. Some schemes use a combination of in-house and external investment managers.

In the case of the pension funds in the Maxwell Group of companies, the investments were managed by a financial institution that also formed part of the same group of companies. Nevertheless, there have been few calls to ban in-house investment management, but there are implications for custodial services – see **16.23** below.

External investment managers

16.16 Most occupational pension schemes use external investment managers since the benefits of scale of employing an in-house team only begin to emerge when the total assets managed are very large, perhaps well in excess of £1bn.

Trustees may engage just one investment management firm to look after all the fund's assets, or two or more may be appointed either with the same or differing investment briefs.

Trustees have a completely different relationship with external investment managers compared to any of the other professional advisers they may hire. The trustees are likely to build up a long-term and intimate relationship with their actuary or pension consultant. The relationship with the investment manager will usually depend on the investment manager attaining performance targets over relatively short periods of three to five years. Research conducted by Russell/Mellon CAPS, the investment information services provider, shows that on average trustees stay with an investment manager for just over seven years.

The trustees do not usually have a completely direct relationship with the investment managers although trustees and investment manager will usually meet together at least quarterly to review progress. The relationship is often mediated by the pension consultant or actuary.

Appointment of investment managers

16.17 The appointment of the investment manager will be governed by the trust deed and rules: it may be the responsibility of the trustees as a whole, or a sub-group of trustees who form an investment committee.

Generally, the overall investment policy will have been developed by the trustees and the scheme's pension consultant/actuary. Once developed, the policy may indicate what kind of investment managers are needed.

The pension consultant/actuary is then usually asked to draw up a shortlist of potential investment managers for the scheme. Some trustees responsible for the appointment make visits to the premises of the investment management and spend time discussing the requirements.

The shortlisted investment managers will come to meet the trustees and make presentations. Those who are responsible for the appointment will usually put some emphasis on the investment manager's past performance. Eventually a decision will be made and the investment manager or managers are appointed.

Some criticism is now being made of the role of the actuary/pension consultant in drawing up the shortlist. It has been alleged that the consultants need to play safe and only tend to nominate the larger well-known firms of investment managers. If the consultants recommended a smaller player who turned out to perform badly, the consultant could be blamed by the trustees and employer for having gone out on a limb. If they recommend the large firms and they perform badly, it is less likely that the consultant will be blamed for having taken the consensus view.

In the recent past, however, the largest investment managers have not dominated the market to the same extent as previously. In part this has been because some of the investment managers have lost clients through lower investment performance. In part it has been as a result of greater use of smaller specialist investment managers. In June 2002 the *Financial Times* published research showing that in 2001 the 25 largest investment managers collectively managed £397.9bn of assets belonging to 3,078 individual segregated funds. Some 46% of this amount was managed by the five largest investment managers. This is still a high concentration of assets in the biggest five investment funds but it represents a considerably smaller proportion than in the recent past. The comparable percentage for 2000 was 53%.

Types of investment managers

Balanced/specialist managers

16.18 A balanced fund manager will manage assets across a range of asset classes. The breakdown between the classes will reflect any asset allocation policy worked out by the trustees unless the trustees have given the fund manager discretion to determine the asset allocation policy itself.

A specialist fund manager will manage assets only in one asset class. This is usually, and has long been, the case with property because of the specialised nature of the market. However, specialist managers may now offer expertise in other niche markets, such as Far East Equity Markets or Government Bonds.

Many occupational pension schemes hire a mix of balanced and specialist investment managers.

Active/passive managers

16.19 An active investment manager will try to achieve an overall return from the investments which is superior to an agreed performance benchmark.

A passive manager will try to achieve through stock selection the same weighting in the investment portfolio as makes up some standard index of investments. For example, if managing a portfolio of UK shares, that portfolio of UK shares could be made up of shares in the same weighted proportions as in the FTSE–100 index. The aim is to achieve the same performance as the chosen index.

Again, a mix of active and passive fund managers may be hired by the trustees of an occupational pension scheme.

Customer agreements

16.20   Since the coming into force of the *Financial Services Act 1986*, investment managers and the pension fund trustees have had to enter into a signed customer agreement. This is a lengthy document and should establish all the contractual terms governing the relationship.

It is highly recommended that the trustee's legal adviser should check the contract to ensure that it is satisfactory. The customer agreement should settle the question of fees. In the UK, investment managers usually levy their charges for the provision of investment services to pension fund trustees by means of what is known as an *ad valorem fee*. This is a fee that varies as an annual percentage of the funds being managed according to the absolute amount of these managed funds. The following is a purely hypothetical example of such a scale adopted by the balanced, active investment manager of a £50m pension fund.

Slice of fund	Fee as a percentage	Amount
On the first £12m	0.6% p a	£72,000
On next £30m	0.3% p a	£90,000
On £8m balance	0.15% p a	£12,000
Total £50m	0.348% p a	£174,000

The table is given simply to explain how the *ad valorem* fee system works, but since it is hypothetical it should not used a benchmark. (Note that the fees are expressed in this table as a *percentage* of the value of the fund because that is how most of us tend to express one number as a proportion of another. But investment managers tend to express fees not as percentages but as *basis points*. A basis point is 1/100th of a percentage point, i e rather than say that the fee was 0.4% of the fund managed, the investment manager would say that it was set at 40 basis points.)

Such direct fees will also vary according to the portfolio of assets being managed. An investment manager looking after only equities is likely to charge double the rate of an investment manager looking after only bonds. Similarly, an active manager will probably charge more than double the rate of a passive manager. In both cases, the differences in the rates of charges can be justified by the differences in the complexity of the task that the investment manager is being asked to perform. Such a charging structure, although it can be criticised on some grounds, has at least the virtue of being clear and easily visible.

The customer agreement should also deal with one issue that has long been a concern in the industry. This is the visibility of certain transaction charges that might be met by the pension fund. In particular, the concern relates to soft commission or *softing* and *bundling*.

Softing refers to the practice whereby services or products (such as computers and information services) are provided by the broker to the investment manager, in part exchange for a predetermined minimum level of the commission-bearing business of carrying out the transactions relating to the investment manager's clients, such as pension funds.

Bundling refers to the practice whereby the investment manager's payment to the broker includes not only a payment to meet the cost of the broker's intermediation services but also the cost of the 'soft' products or services provided by the broker to the investment manager.

The concern is that, under such practices, trust funds can be used in deals whose prime purpose is to gain commission for the investment manager. This expenditure is in practice incurred on the trustees' behalf by the investment manager. This is because the commissions are added to the cost of the purchase, or deducted from the proceeds of the sale, of the asset involved in the transaction and settled against the pension fund's account with the custodian. As Paul Myners said in his March 2001 review of institutional investment: 'In other words, they are paid directly by the pension fund'.

Soft commission is not illegal and the current practice and regulatory framework make it difficult for trustees to opt out of such arrangements, but one of the leading pension consultancies has described soft commission as a 'murky practice' and back in the early 1990s called for it to be made unlawful.

Paul Myners in his review of institutional investment proposed that investment mandates should always incorporate a management fee inclusive of the cost of any external research, information or transaction services acquired or used by the investment manager, rather than having these costs passed on to the pension fund.

On 27 July 2001, the Treasury announced how it proposed to carry forward this aspect of Paul Myners' recommendations, an aspect to which the Treasury obviously accorded a high degree of importance, since it commented that responses to the consultation exercise it had carried out after the publication of Paul Myners' review had to led it to believe that the problem was 'if anything, greater than Mr Myners originally suggested'. The Treasury's chief concerns was that the issue suggested that:

- there were insufficient competitive pressures in investment broking and market-making activities; and

- the present obligation under the financial services legislation for 'best execution' (i e getting the best deal possible for your client) was not working properly to protect pension funds.

The Government acted to amend the two sets of investment principles devised by Paul Myners (see **17.3**). The relevant principles now state that:

> 'Trustees, or those to whom they have delegated the task, should have a full understanding of the transaction-related costs they incur, including commissions. They should understand all the options open to them in respect of these costs, and should have an active strategy – whether through direct financial incentives or otherwise – for ensuring that these costs are properly controlled without jeopardising the fund's other objectives. Trustees should not without good reason permit soft commissions to be paid in respect of their fund's transactions.'

The Treasury also asked Paul Myners to develop a set of indicative questions that would help pension fund trustees require better disclosure of the investment costs their fund incurs, and obtain clearer incentives for their managers and brokers. In response, in October 2001, Paul Myners suggested the following ten questions that should be addressed by the trustees to their investment managers:

'1. What is your best view of the level of transaction costs – including not only commission but also market impact and opportunity cost – borne by our fund during the reporting period?

2. What action have you taken to minimise transaction costs while still dealing effectively?

3. Please explain any major differences between the level of costs incurred by you on our behalf and those incurred by other managers as reported in reputable surveys.

4. Were commission rates uniform across all transactions, and if not, what determines the commission rate on a transaction? Explain trend rates on these.

5. Which dealing venues and methods did you choose for our portfolio, why, and how did your choices affect our dealing costs?

6. Which brokers did you deal through and how did you select them?

7. Where you are not using an execution-only broking service, please list other services that you buy or benefits that you receive from the broker concerned – such as research and access to Initial Public Offers (IPOs). Please explain how you evaluate the benefit these generate for us relative to the cost.

8. If you make use of both external research and in-house research, explain what distinguishes the former, for which we pay an additional charge, from the latter, which is covered by your management fee, and how you decide which to use.

9. Explain your rules on entertainment of your staff by brokers and those with whom you transact on our behalf where we bear the cost. Make available the records you keep, your policy guidelines and the approximate number, type and overall value of the events attended.

10. If you wish to make a case for soft commission arrangements, explain how our interests are better served by the broker providing you with services rather than securing lower commission costs for us.'

The Treasury advises trustees to compare the answers given by different investment managers with a view to understanding the extent to which:

- the fund is incurring a higher or lower level of transaction costs through the trustees' investment manager than would be normal for similar mandates with this or other managers;

- the investment manager satisfactorily addresses any conflicts of interest between its own commercial interests, those of its associated and other clients and of the trustees' pension fund; and

- the investment manager is proactively seeking to increase the efficiency of execution of transactions to buy and sell assets though innovation, including the use of new dealing venues, new technologies, the terms of customer agreements and financial instruments.

The Treasury also states:

'Trustees should be clear that their responsibility is not simply limited to asking the initial question. Where appropriate they must challenge the resulting answers if they are incomplete or unsatisfactory. In line with the principles of investment, they should ensure that they have the appropriate skills and information to address these issues. In particular, they should ensure that those providing advice on these issues have expertise in transaction issues. Trustees should consider the full range of transaction costs, including custody, foreign exchange and deposit arrangements.'

One problem, of course, is that investment managers will necessarily prepare stock answers to the questions which Paul Myners has devised.

Although the Treasury states that its preference is for these issues to be tackled through market mechanisms and commercial negotiations, it recognises that this represents a 'significant challenge, especially for pension fund trustees'. The Treasury had already asked the Financial Services Authority (FSA) to explore how investment managers comply with the 'best execution' rule and this has now been widened to take in the issues presented by the use of soft commissions and the bundling of services. In February 2002, the Treasury announced that the FSA was intending to publish its research and policy proposals in the near future.

As a long-stop, if after two years the aim of these non-statutory measures fails to deal with the problems, the Treasury will ask the Office of Fair Trading to examine the whole area.

Performance measurement

16.21   Trustees of occupational pension funds are urged by the National Association of Pension Funds (NAPF) to subscribe to one of the professional performance measurement services. Performance measurement will allow trustees to judge in an objective manner how their investment managers are performing by obtaining the figure for their fund's annual investment return and allow them to compare that performance either with other pension funds over the same period or with the relevant benchmark.

Calculating investment performance is not a totally straightforward exercise. Looking at the market value at the beginning and end of the scheme year will take no account of the flow of money into the scheme from contributions and transfer credits and the flow of money out of the scheme to pay for benefits, transfer payments and administration costs. The performance measurer will need to use *money-weighted* or *time-weighted* techniques to establish the investment performance, allowing for this flow of money into and out of the fund. In brief, a money-weighted technique measures the actual investment return of a particular fund while a time-weighted technique measures what the performance would have been assuming new money had been invested evenly during the period under consideration.

In making comparisons, trustees will also have to consider the degree of *discretion* that they have given the investment manager. If UK equities have performed badly over the period, but the trustees' *asset allocation* policy limits the percentage of the fund that should be held in UK equities, the effect may have been to raise the investment return in comparison to other funds where the investment managers have had complete discretion to decide the scheme's asset allocation policy.

Trustees will want to use performance figures achieved by their investment managers in deciding whether they should be retained or replaced. However, they should give any investment manager a reasonable period over which to gauge performance: a three-year minimum is often recommended. Indeed it forms part of Paul Myners' investment principles (see **17.3–17.5**) that clear timescale(s) of measurement and evaluation should be agreed before the appointment of an investment manager, such that the trustees agree not to terminate that appointment before the expiry of the evaluation timescale by reason of underperformance alone.

It should also be remembered that changing investment managers always involves some cost and investment risks. Trustees are now being advised to appoint a specialist *transition manager* when a change of investment managers is proposed. The aim is to ensure that the transition is effected in the most efficient way so that risks are controlled and costs minimised. The NAPF issued a guide *Transition Management Made Simple – What a Trustee Needs to Know* in November 2001 which gives useful advice in this area.

Because an investment manager knows that the investment performance of the funds it manages will be measured (and also that its mandate will be retained, increased, reduced or removed altogether as a result of that eventual measurement), just *how* the investment performance is measured is bound to influence the investment manager's behaviour.

For example, if a balanced, discretionary fund manager is going to be judged against the median performance of other balanced, discretionary fund managers, then it is very likely that this investment manager will seek to maintain an asset allocation policy that does not differ substantially from the typical asset allocation policy adopted by most balanced, discretionary managers (the so-called 'herd instinct'). To do otherwise is to risk producing an investment performance that differs substantially from the median result.

One problem in such a strategy is that the asset allocation assumed by such a manager trying to achieve the default median performance may be unsuitable for the needs of the pension fund in question, because the assets are not likely to match its liabilities (e g a mature fund with a high proportion of pensioners might be thought to require a high proportion of its fund in bonds, but setting a performance target of beating the median fund's performance might be thought to entail having a much higher proportion of the fund in equities).

In fact, many trustees have moved away from the practice of comparing their fund's performance against the median achieved by other pension funds. Instead, with the advice of their investment consultant, often associated with the firm of the scheme's actuary, trustees often set customised performance benchmarks for their investment manager or managers. Russell Mellon CAPS, the investment information services company, reported that 77% of the 1,527 pension funds in its universe had adopted a scheme-specific benchmark compared to just 12% ten years earlier.

These benchmarks rely on the trustees having made an asset allocation policy decision, again with the help of an investment consultant, such that it is decided, for example, that 20% of the fund should be invested in European equities. That fund's investment manager charged with looking after the fund's European equities might then be given the annual performance target of beating by a certain specified margin the year-on-year change in one of the relevant indices measuring the investment return on European equities.

But just as one can criticise the shortcomings of measuring the investment performance of a pension fund against the median achieved by a large number of other, often dissimilar funds, the customised benchmark approach is also not without its difficulties.

One particular difficulty is the choice of the relevant index for the asset class chosen (for example, the portfolio of shares in European companies held by the investment manager may differ from the shares making up the Index). The choice of an index, and how closely the investment manager is expected to track that index, will affect whether the investment manager feels able to buy or sell any particular share. This could be a 'sub-optimal investment strategy'.

As Paul Myners notes in his review of institutional investment:

'The customised benchmark approach relies on asset allocation being carried out in a system with limited resources and suboptimal systems of performance measurement. As many of the ultimate customers (that is, trustees) lack expertise to interpret critically the issues and difficulties inherent in the advice they are given, they have little choice but to follow it. Yet they – and not those providing the advice – retain full legal responsibility for their decisions.'

When going through the process of selecting an investment manager, the trustees are usually also interested in that manager's previous track record. In May 1999 a new UK Investment Performance Standard (UKIPS) was introduced via the former Pension Fund Investment Performance Code Monitoring Group, now known as the UK Investment Performance Committee. The code sets out how investment managers must present their own investment performance figures. Although the code is voluntary and is being introduced over a transitional period, in practice it is unlikely that pension fund trustees would want to continue to employ investment managers who did not comply with the UKIPS requirements. The code is internationally recognised and the UK version requires the investment manager to have its performance figures independently verified.

Self-investment

16.22   Self-investment (known more correctly as *employer-related investment*) can take the form of the pension fund owning shares held in the sponsoring company, making loans made to the sponsoring company or the occupational pension scheme owning and leasing back the employer's business premises.

In fact, the trust deed and rules of many schemes have always specifically prohibited any level of self-investment.

During the 1990s there were many instances of the sponsoring company running into financial difficulties. The trustees, who were often senior executives of the company, had borrowed money from the pension fund to help with company cash-flow problems. The company, none the less, went into liquidation and the beneficiaries were left not only jobless but with pension promises that were underfunded or completely worthless.

It was always commonly held that the assets of the occupational pension scheme were at arm's length from those of the company. Where, however, there was self-investment, this could not be true.

As a result of these problems, the *Occupational Pension Schemes (Investment of Scheme's Resources) Regulations 1992 (SI 1992/246)* came into force on 9 March 1992. They restricted to 5% the proportion of the resources which most kinds of occupational pension schemes may invest in the sponsoring company, or any other company associated or connected with it. The legislation is now contained in the *Occupational Pension Schemes (Investment) Regulations 1996 (SI 1996/3127)*.

The regulations include transitional provisions that give schemes time to reduce any existing self-investment to within the permitted limit.

The Investment Regulations 1996 have prohibited most kinds of pension scheme from making any loan to the sponsoring employer (regardless of whether or not the loan exceeds the 5% limit).

Any breach by trustees of the self-investment rules is a serious offence which would result in severe fines and in serious cases Opra will instigate criminal proceedings where the breach of the self-investment rules is deliberate or fraudulent.

The employer-related investment restrictions do not, however, apply to small self-administered schemes and executive pension schemes, provided certain conditions are met, including having all the members as trustees and requiring all decisions to be taken unanimously.

Custodial and administrative arrangements

16.23   Custody and administration refers to:

- the safekeeping of all investment securities;

- the process of settlement ensuring that money is paid out for securities that are purchased and that money is received for securities that are sold;

- the transfer of all documentation resulting from the purchase and sale of the securities;

- the collection of dividends resulting from shareholdings;

- carrying out other corporate actions, in particular exercising the voting rights attaching to shares owned by the pension fund;

- the reclaiming of tax;

- the necessary action where discretionary decisions arise in cases of corporate actions or capital changes, such as a new rights issue of shares etc; and

- the full accounting of all transactions and the production of regular financial reports.

The custodian's role in essence is to make the investment decision an actual reality; it comprises all the backroom activities necessary in the investment process.

Given that it is a very different kind of activity from the actual investment decision itself, many investment managers contract out this role to a custodian, often a bank, while other investment managers will work with an associated company acting as the custodian.

The term *global custodian* has emerged to describe the services offered by a custodian skilled in working with several separate investment managers. In such cases, the trustees appoint the global custodian completely independently of whom they choose as their investment managers.

Trustees should pay particular attention to the custodial and administrative arrangements set out in the customer agreement that they sign with their investment managers. It is important, especially post Maxwell, that trustees take reasonable steps to ensure that money cannot be removed fraudulently from the pension fund assets held by the custodian.

The investment manager and custodian should make up any fraudulent loss that they were in a position to prevent.

Procedures which may help include:

- reviewing the authorisation procedures for the transfer of any assets out of the pension fund account;

- specifying the accounts to which money can be transferred; and

- ensuring advance notification for any transfer of money above a stated amount.

The major hazards associated with custody are as follows:

- misappropriation through fraud (including computer/electronic systems fraud), and the use of, or failure to detect, forged documents of title or transfer documents, wilful or accidental destruction of records or documents, theft and other loss of documents, including while in transit;

- delivery otherwise than in accordance with authorised instructions;

- the improper use of one customer's investments to settle or secure another's obligations;

- failure to:

    - maintain adequate records identifying an individual customer's entitlement to, and status of, investments;

    - account for entitlements to benefits and tax recoveries; and

    - respond to corporate events (such as preferential share issues to existing shareholders);

- unauthorised use of customers' investments for the custodian's own purposes or commingling of customers' investments with the custodian's own investments in such a way as to place customer's investments at risk in the event of the custodian's insolvency;

- custodians defaulting, in particular when customers' investments are held in an overseas jurisdiction where laws and market practice restrict the recovery and separate identification of investments; and

- deficiencies in documentation such that the division of responsibilities in the event of loss as between customer, an authorised firm and any third parties is unclear.

The 1995 collapse of Barings Bank heightened concerns about the soundness of the custody function. Since 6 April 1997 the *Occupational Pension Schemes (Disclosure of Information) Regulations 1996 (SI 1996/1655)* have required trustees to give the name of their custodian in their annual report to members.

In the wake of the recommendations made in March 2001 by Paul Myners, the Government issued in February 2002 a consultation paper discussing his proposal that there should be a statutory requirement for pension fund trustees to appoint a custodian who is completely independent of the employers who sponsor the pension scheme (see **17.6**). The Government's view was that there was no clear-cut evidence that the existence of an independent custodian within the chain of pension scheme management would do much to prevent fraud. Indeed the Government expressed the view that such a legislative requirement could merely succeed in giving scheme members a sense of security that would not be matched in practice.

The February 2002 paper asked for opinions on whether the appointment of independent custodians should be governed by legislation or by a code of good practice, but also went on to explore other ways of improving pension fund security against fraud. Most of these alternative avenues for promoting security involved tightening up on the customer agreement between the trustees and the investment manager (see **16.19** above).

Stock lending

16.24   The customer agreement should, in particular, be clear about whether and under what conditions *stock lending* is permitted.

Stock is lent by the custodian to institutions involved in the trading of shares for short periods of time in return for a fee. The fee may be passed on to the pension fund, or simply used to reduce the level of fees charged by the custodian.

In normal circumstances, there is no particular risk to the pension fund but the trustees need to ensure that the trust deed and rules of the scheme actually permit stock lending. Trustees would also need to ensure that their fund was reasonably indemnified in case of any default.

Corporate governance issues for trustees

16.25   The trustees of UK self-administered occupational pension schemes now own around 18% of all the shares of UK companies listed on the stock exchange. In other words, these trustees are the shareholders owning nearly one-fifth of British industry. UBS Global Asset Management reports, however, that this represents a decline in the UK pension fund share of the UK equity market from a peak of just over 30% in 1989.

Corporate governance is the term used to describe the relationship between the owners of the shares, those who control those shares and the directors of the companies in which the shares are invested. In the case of occupational pension schemes, therefore, it refers to the relationship between trustees, the investment managers of pension funds and the management boards of companies in which the pension funds have invested.

Until the late 1980s institutional investors were not overtly involved in the management decisions of the companies in which they invested. If performance was poor, the investors would pull out and invest elsewhere. Such a policy is not tenable indefinitely, and institutional investors as shareholders have begun to be more involved in pressing for change.

The key issue for the trustees of occupational pension schemes is how the voting rights that go along with share ownership are exercised. The National Association of Pension Funds (NAPF) urges all its members to exercise their shareholder votes whenever possible. Trustees wishing to ensure that this happens must first check that the customer agreement they sign with their investment managers and custodian services makes the relevant provisions, and secondly see that these provisions are observed in practice. Trustees should also consider if they should engage the services of one of the voting services agencies who prepare profiles of companies and alert investors to upcoming issues to be discussed at annual general meetings. There has also in the past been concern that voting instructions issued by pension funds have not always been executed.

The development of corporate governance should strengthen the links between companies and those who invest in them. The *Institutional Shareholders Committee* issued way back in December 1991 a Statement of Best Practice on Corporate Governance whose main points include the following:

(*a*)   Institutional investors should encourage regular, systematic contact at senior executive level to exchange views and information on strategy, performance, board membership and quality of information.

(*b*)   Institutional investors will not wish to receive price-sensitive information as a result of such dialogue but may agree to accept it on an exceptional basis as the price of a long-term relationship, although this would require that they suspend their ability to deal in the shares.

(*c*)   Institutional investors are opposed to the creation of equity shares that do not carry full voting rights.

(*d*)   Institutional investors should support boards by a positive use of voting rights, unless they have good reasons for doing otherwise. Reasons for voting against a motion should be made known to the board beforehand.

(*e*)   Institutional investors should take positive interest in the composition of boards of directors, with particular reference to:

(i)   concentrations of decision-making power not formally constrained by checks and balances appropriate to the particular company; and

(ii)   the appointment of a core of non-executives of appropriate calibre, experience and independence.

(*f*)   Institutional investors support the appointment of compensation and audit committees.

(*g*)   Institutional investors encourage disclosure of the principles upon which directors' emoluments are determined.

(*h*)   In takeover situations institutional investors will consider all offers on their merits and will not commit themselves to a particular course of action until they have reviewed the best and most up-to-date information available.

(*i*)   In all investment decision-making institutional investors have a fiduciary responsibility to those on whose behalf they are investing, which must override other considerations.

The last point is crucial. Consider an institutional investor which has 30% of the share capital of Company A. This 30% represents the funds of ten occupational pension schemes, each of whom own 3% of Company A's shares. In each pension fund, shares in Company A represent 5% of the total pension fund. Company A makes a hostile takeover bid for Company B. Company B has an occupational pension scheme which is one of the ten schemes with a 3% holding in Company A. The institutional investor will owe a fiduciary duty to the trustees of the pension fund of Company B who might be expected to oppose the takeover.

The hostile bid fails, then Company B makes a counter hostile bid for Company A. As a result, the shares of Company A rapidly rise in the market. The institutional investor will consider the offer on its merits and the trustees of the ten occupational pension funds may urge the institutional investor to accept the bid. If the takeover were to fail, the share price of Company A would fall again and an opportunity for the beneficiaries of the pension funds to have profited from the high bid price would have been lost. The institutional investor would not have acted in the interest of the pension fund beneficiaries.

The issue that trustees should consider is that although they own the pension fund assets on behalf of the scheme's beneficiaries, effective control of the fund lies with the institutional investor, the investment manager, who is none the less bound by the customer agreement with the trustees.

During the 1990s recommendations by a number of committees were made concerning the proper relationship between institutional investors and the boards of directors of the companies in which those institutions invested. The recommendations of the Cadbury Committee, the Greenbury Committee and the Hampel Committee have had a crucial impact on the development of corporate governance in the UK, especially on sensitive issues such as levels of company directors' pay and contract conditions. Furthermore, pension funds, as one of the largest institutional shareholders of UK companies, have a key role to play in the current major review of company law.

In July 1999 the report of the committee of inquiry into UK Vote Execution, known as the Newbold Committee, was published. It examined the problems that pension funds were actually having in executing the voting rights that attached to their shareholdings. The report recommended that regular, considered voting should be regarded as a fiduciary responsibility by pension fund trustees to the membership. It also encouraged trustees to develop written voting policies which included setting down procedures to ensure that, where voting was delegated to the custodian or investment manager, the votes had indeed actually been lodged. In fact, the *Occupational Pension Schemes (Investment) Regulations 1996 (SI 1996/3127)* were amended with effect from 3 July 2000 so that trustees are required to publish in their statement of investment policy (see **16.8**): 'their policy (if any) in relation to the exercise of the rights (including voting rights) attaching to investments'.

The review of institutional investment in the UK conducted by Paul Myners and published in March 2001 (see **CHAPTER 17**) considered the corporate governance issue in depth. The review found that there was a lack of active intervention by institutional investors (i e mainly self-administered pension funds and insurance companies) in the companies in which they invest. This was so even where there was a reasonable expectation that this would enhance the value of investments.

As a result, Paul Myners recommended that UK law should incorporate a duty on those responsible for the investment of pension scheme assets actively to monitor and communicate with the management of the companies in which they invest, and that they exercise their right to vote as shareholders, where, after taking into account the costs of any action, there was a reasonable expectation that such activities were likely to enhance the value of the investment.

In particular, Paul Myners suggested that UK law should adopt a similar requirement to that already in place in the USA (in particular he cited a US Department of Labor Interpretative Bulletin which is reproduced as **APPENDIX 6**). This recommendation was generally supported by the Confederation of British Industry and the Trades Union Congress.

In its official response to Paul Myners' review, the Government indicated that it would propose legislation in this area (see **17.6**), and in February 2002 it published a consultation paper setting out its proposals. Subject to views expressed in response to the consultation paper, the Government proposes to frame a general requirement to the effect that:

> '[those who are] responsible for the investment of the assets of a retirement benefits scheme must, in respect of any company or undertaking (wheresoever resident or incorporated) in which they invest such assets, use such rights and powers as arise by virtue of such investment in the best interests of the members and beneficiaries of such scheme'.

The important point is that this proposed *activism duty* would apply to the pension fund trustees as well as the investment managers. The duty would be applied to the trustees and investment managers of both defined benefit and defined contribution occupational pension schemes, regardless in the latter case of whether or not the members had any discretion as to how monies are invested.

The duty would also generally apply irrespective of the size of the occupational pension scheme, although the costs of actively engaging with companies and exercising shareholder votes for small schemes might well mean that in practice no action was normally taken. This is because to do so would simply not be in the members' best financial interests because the cost would be disproportionate. (The requirement would not be applied to a small self-administered scheme (SSAS) where all the members are trustees of the scheme and those trustees invest the scheme's assets directly.)

The proposed new duty would override any contrary provision in a scheme's trust deed and rules but the trustees could vary the wording of the requirement in the customer agreement with their investment manager in so far as the investment manager is instructed to comply with a specific trustee voting policy.

It is likely that the trustees would have to disclose to their members their approach to the activism duty, including details of how they would ensure that this statutory duty would be met, possibly through the existing statement of investment principles (see **16.8**) or through the scheme's annual report and accounts (see **9.32**).

In the event, however, in response to the Government's February 2002 consultation on proposed legislation on shareholder activism, the Institutional Shareholders Committee (see above) issued a guidance note on the role of institutional shareholders in shareholder activism on 21 October 2002. The proposals set out in the new statement of principles include strengthened responsibilities for institutional shareholders and their agents, as well as the proposal that the new principles should be included in industry fund management contracts. The Committee proposed to review the effects of this guidance after two years, at which point the Government has said it will examine whether this alternative, non-legislative approach has been successful in delivering change.

Socially responsible investment

16.26   In the famous case between the National Coal Board Trustees of the Mineworkers' Pension Scheme and the National Union of Mineworkers heard before the then Vice Chancellor Sir Robert Megarry in 1984 (*Cowan v Scargill [1984] 2 All ER 750, [1990] PLR 169*), the Vice Chancellor said:

'In considering what investments to make the trustees must put on one side their own personal interests and views. Trustees may have strongly held social or political views. They may be firmly opposed to any investment in South Africa or other countries, or they may object to any form of investment in companies concerned with alcohol, tobacco, armaments or many other things. In the conduct of their own affairs of course they are free to abstain from making such investments. Yet if under a trust investments of this type would be more beneficial to the beneficiaries than other investments, the trustees must not refrain from making the investments by reason of the views that they hold.'

Nevertheless, since that judgment the whole issue of socially responsible investment has gained ground. SRI covers a range of areas including the following:

- *Economic issues*, for example whether to invest in local venture capital funds to support the local economy where members and beneficiaries live.

- *Political issues*, for example whether to invest in countries with considerable human rights abuses or even to exercise corporate-governance-type pressures on companies who make donations to political parties.

- *Environmental issues*, such as the adoption of a policy of favouring green investments and pressurising companies who are perceived to damage the environment.

- *Ethical issues*, for example whether to invest in companies making armaments.

Since 1984, some evidence has begun to accrue to suggest that purely on financial grounds it may be imprudent to invest in, say, polluting industries since they will become less profitable on a *polluter pays* principle while heightened public awareness will make companies producing environmentally acceptable products more competitive. The result is that socially responsible investment policies are held to be permissible, even desirable, *provided all other things are equal*. The December 1998 Consultation Paper issued by the then DSS reports that the Government believes that pension scheme trustees should consider in a positive way how their funds are invested. It states: 'We believe that trustees should be free to consider moral and social issues in relation to their investments, provided trustees adhere to the obligations placed on them by trust law and always put the beneficiaries' interests first'.

From 3 July 2000, the trustees have been required to state in their policy 'the extent (if at all) to which social, environmental or ethical considerations are taken into account in the selection, retention and realisation of investments'. This policy statement must be included in their overall Statement of Investment Principles as explained at **16.8** above.

Additional voluntary contributions

16.27 All occupational pension schemes must offer their active members an opportunity to make additional voluntary contributions (AVCs). In a money purchase scheme, this may often be an opportunity simply to pay more than the minimum employee contribution required under the scheme rules. In some defined benefit schemes, there will be an opportunity to purchase 'added years' pensionable service via an AVC arrangement. In most defined benefit schemes, however, AVC vehicles are money purchase vehicles offered by an external third party provider.

In many cases a choice of providers is offered. For example, a scheme may offer a deposit-based investment provided by a building society and a with-profits type investment provided by an insurance company.

What is often forgotten is that the trustees of the occupational pension scheme have a duty to ensure that the AVC investments being offered to active members are well managed and represent good value. Trustees should be as concerned with the investment performance of the AVC vehicles as they are with the performance of the pension fund itself. The reality of this duty became apparent at the time of the recent difficulties of Equitable Life, which was the UK's largest provider of AVC policies, although in practice it is not reasonable to have expected trustees to have foreseen the particular difficulties that Equitable Life was to experience.

Trustees should consider what the effect of any charges that are borne by the members will mean for those members who are able only to contribute comparatively modest amounts – any fixed charges will disproportionately penalise this group. Similarly, many active members who pay AVCs have an eye on early retirement possibilities. In certain insured AVC arrangements there are quite severe early surrender penalties for those who do not continue to pay contributions for the full-term of the policy. This may not be made clear to the members by the AVC provider at the time they start out on the policy, and in certain instances the capital sum they have accumulated when they want to draw their pension turns out to be less than the total AVCs that they have paid in. This is unacceptable and trustees should act to protect the interests of their members who entrust their savings to an AVC arrangement provided by the scheme. As an aside, this is one reason that Equitable Life had such a good reputation prior to its troubles: its charges were among the lowest in the market and its administration procedures were very efficient.

The decision to allow all members of occupational pension schemes earning no more than £30,000 to contribute up to £3,600 (including tax relief at the basic rate) to any scheme subject to the new DC tax regime, and in particular to stakeholder pension schemes (see **2.15**), is likely over time to have a huge impact on the AVC and FSAVC markets. It could well be that this group of members will prefer to use stakeholder pensions rather than AVCs as the preferred method of topping up pension benefits. This is not only because of the control over charges ensured by the stakeholder pension scheme regime; but also because stakeholder pensions can be taken in part as a tax-free lump sum as this is not open to members of FSAVC schemes or any AVC contract entered into since 8 April 1987.

The valuation of bonds and equities

16.28   UK pension funds hold most of their assets in bonds (chiefly those bonds issued by governments and in particular those issued by the UK government) and in the ordinary shares (equities) issued by companies listed on the world's major stock markets. Both bonds and equities normally give rise to an income stream. Both kinds of assets also normally give rise to a capital gain or loss if and when the pension fund comes to sell them in the market.

If you divide the income generated by a bond or an equity by the price of that bond or equity, you find out the 'yield' of that investment. It follows therefore that when the price of a bond or share rises, the yield will fall and when its price falls, the yield will rise.

It should be remembered that under the requirements of the minimum funding requirement (MFR), because scheme's assets are taken at their market value, the scheme's liabilities must also be measured at a market value (see **13.6** for a full discussion of this topic). The MFR uses a 'market value adjustment' (MVA) as part of the prescribed method for calculating the value of the scheme liabilities. The equity MVA makes an assumption for a 'par' value of the net yield obtained by equities. From 15 June 1998 to 6 March 2002 the assumed par value for the net yield from equities had been 3.25%. Since 7 March 2002 this has been set at 3.00%.

The equity MVA is:

$$\frac{3.00\%}{\text{actual yield on the FTSE Actuaries All Share Index}}$$

If the yield on the FTSE Actuaries All Share Index is lower than that assumed par value, as it generally has been in recent years, then the market adjusted value of the scheme's liabilities measured against equities is increased.

For example, the actual yield on the FTSE Actuaries All Share Index on 8 February 2002 was 2.68%. This means that the equity MVA on that day was 3.25%/2.68% or around 1.21. An MVA at 1.21, therefore, increased the value of the scheme's equity liabilities by more than a fifth as much again. A similar story can be told concerning the bond MVA.

But since 8 February 2002, two events have occurred. First, the par value assumed for the net yield from equities has been weakened by the reduction from 3.25% to 3.00%. Second, the market value of the FTSE Actuaries All Share Index has fallen dramatically with the result that the actual yield has risen to reach 4.03% on 11 March 2003.

The equity MVA on 11 March 2003 was therefore 3.00%/4.03% or around 0.74. An MVA at 0.74 as a result decreased the value of the scheme's equity liabilities by nearly one quarter.

In other words, the yield obtained from equities and bonds for most of the history of the MFR had been lower than was expected when the MFR was first established. This had remained the case even after the significant global falls in share prices during 2001. The yield had fallen since the MFR was put in place because, in the main, share and bond prices first increased dramatically and then fell back but, from the evidence of the par values chosen by actuaries, shares and bonds were still overvalued as at 8 February 2002. The Government responded by weakening the par value assumed for the net yield from equities. This would have changed the equity MVA from 1.21 on 8 February 2002 to 1.12 if it had been introduced one month earlier. In other words, it would have increased the scheme's liabilities by a little over one-eighth as much again, rather than a little more than one-fifth as much again.

Yet in 2002 the world's equity markets tumbled with the result that by 11 March 2003 the yield being obtained from equities was by then much higher than had been expected. Of course, the higher yield had come, not from the fact that companies were paying higher dividends, but from the fact that their share prices had fallen. So although the equity MVA acted to decrease a defined benefit scheme's liabilities for the purpose of the MFR, it results from a serious reduction in the scheme's equity assets.

It should also be noted that under the actuaries' guidance GN27, a defined benefit scheme's liabilities for active and deferred members are valued assuming long-term investment returns from equities of 9.0% p a before the equity MVA is applied. Writing in the March 2003 issue of *The Actuary* magazine, the Chairman of the Pensions Board of the Institute and Faculty of Actuaries wrote that if the MFR was being designed now rather than back in 1997, the long-term investment return might be 5.6% p a. Such a 'new MFR' would produce liabilities about 5% higher than under the current MFR at the older ages and around *three times* higher at younger ages.

But how are bonds and equities valued? There are a number of traditional measures.

Equities

16.29 The *dividend yield* is the value of the dividends paid out per share during a year by a company, divided by that company's current share price and the result is expressed as a percentage. As explained above, the higher the company's share price, the lower the dividend yield and vice versa. Dividend yields either reflect actual past dividends (*historic yields*) or best-guess forthcoming dividends (*prospective yields*). The amount of dividends paid out by a company essentially reflects its level of profits. However, companies can distribute profits by buying back shares instead of distributing dividends. Also, some companies that have made no profits and so have paid out no dividends can still have high share prices because investors guess that they will be profitable in future.

For example, last year the ABC Company paid out a total net dividend of 50 pence per share. Its current share price is 339.5 pence. The historic dividend yield is 14.7%.

The *earnings per share* figure is the company's earnings after corporation tax divided by the number of shares in issue. It tells you the total amount earned for each share during the year. It should be noted that not all of these earnings are distributed to the shareholders. Some will be kept to reinvest in the company.

For example, last year the ABC Company had post-tax profits of £1.276bn and had issued to date 1,446,155,227 shares. The earnings per share figure is therefore 88.2 pence.

The price/earnings ratio (p/e ratio) is the ratio of the share price divided by the earnings per share. One way of looking at this is to say that it tells you how many years of profits are needed to equal the current market value of the company. The higher the price/earnings ratio, the greater is the expectation among investors that the company's profits will grow. Price/earnings can also be based on past data (*historic ratios*) or the estimated profits over the coming year (*prospective ratios*). The price/earnings ratio always moves in the opposite way to the dividend yield.

For example, the ABC Company's share price was 339.5 pence. Its earnings per share was 88.2 pence. Its historic price/earnings ratio was therefore 3.8.

Bonds

16.30   UK pension funds mostly buy long-dated gilts, that is to say bonds issued by the UK Government which will pay a fixed amount of interest each year until their redemption date, which is more than 15 years from the date they were first issued. After the 15-year period the Government will buy them back at their issue price.

The *coupon* is the fixed amount of interest payable each year by the gilt. It is expressed as a percentage of the issue price. So a *Treasury 8pc '15* is a gilt which will pay each year a coupon of 8% of its issue price until the last payment made in 2015 when the original amount borrowed by the Government will be repaid. This amount is known as the *redemption price*.

UK bonds are actively traded and their market price will normally be different from their *redemption price*.

The *current yield* (also known as the *running yield* or the *interest yield*) of the bond is calculated by dividing the bond's coupon by the bond's current market price and expressing the result as a percentage. Therefore as the price of a bond rises, its current yield will fall, and vice versa.

For example, on 11 March 2003, the Treasury 8pc '15 had a market price of £137.70. The current yield was therefore 5.81%.

The *redemption yield* takes account of the fact that the Government will pay the investor holding the bond the bond's redemption price when it matures. This gives rise to a capital gain or loss depending on whether the current market price is higher or lower than the redemption price. (Note that immediately before the bond's redemption date, the market price of the bond will equal its redemption price.) This capital gain or loss is in addition to the guaranteed future stream of income from the bond. Professional investors will therefore take into account the current value of the capital gain or loss implied by the current market price as well as the future flow of coupons. The formula for calculating the redemption yield is a little complicated but the redemption yield is printed in each day's *Financial Times*. For example, on 11 March 2003, the Tr 8pc '15 had a redemption yield of 4.16%.

Checklist 16

- Trustees of self-administered schemes have a duty to invest under the 'prudent men and women' principle and have a duty to take advice. They will in future have a higher standard of care expected of them – of being familiar with the issues concerned.

- The *Financial Services and Markets Act 2000* precludes trustees who are not authorised from taking the day-to-day investment decisions – these must be delegated to an authorised investment manager.

- Trustees have the power to make investments as if they were absolutely entitled to them.

- The trustees' use of their investment powers cannot be made subject to the employer's consent.

- The trustees must prepare, maintain and then comply with a *Statement of Investment Principles* which should be a key scheme document.

- The trustees must, with advice, decide on the relative allocation of scheme's resources among the various asset classes and in many ways this will be affected by the nature of the scheme's emerging liabilities and, where applicable, of the minimum funding requirement.

- The trustees of a self-administered scheme must appoint the scheme's investment manager or managers and must not rely on the investment advice of a manager appointed by a third party unless that appointment was made on behalf of the trustees.

- Trustees should be happy about the content of the customer agreement between themselves and the investment manager and ensure that it has been checked by their lawyer. The agreement

---

should be completely transparent regarding the investment manager's fees.

- Trustees ought to subscribe to one of the performance measurement services. Trustees should also agree with their investment managers at the time of their appointment over what period of time their performance will be assessed, and not dismiss them before the end of that period on the ground of poor investment performance.

- Self-investment (employer-related investment) is subject to strict statutory limits and may be banned altogether by the trust deed and rules.

- Trustees should be vigilant about custody arrangements to ensure that they are efficient and contain safeguards to prevent fraud.

- Trustees should not seek to avoid their corporate governance responsibilities and should employ the voting power of shares that are held by the fund. In future there may be a legislative requirement on trustees to become active shareholders of the companies in which they invest, where this is in the best interests of their members, but currently there exists a voluntary approach to strengthening the role of institutional investors in the governance of the companies of which they are part owners.

- Trustees are not prevented from taking ethical and other socially responsible investment issues into consideration but this must not displace their duty to invest the funds for the financial benefit of their members.

- Trustees also have a duty to ensure that in-house AVC arrangements represent good value and offer satisfactory investment performance.

Chapter 17

Investment issues after Myners

Introduction

17.1   In his budget speech of 21 March 2000, the Chancellor of the Exchequer announced that he had asked Paul Myners, then Chairman of Gartmore Investment Management, to look at whether there were 'factors discouraging institutional investors from investing in smaller firms' and to report back with recommendations by the next Budget. Paul Myners subsequently issued in May 2000 a wide-ranging consultation paper in which he stated:

> 'Pension fund trustees do not in general seem to be drawn from the ranks of those experienced in investment. Anecdotal evidence suggests that while some pension funds do have high quality training programmes for trustees, many trustees receive little training. Moreover, most are employed, and in practice appear to have limited time to devote to their duties, which of course extend beyond simply investment decision making.

> Given this, and given also pension funds' objectives as set out above, it seems reasonable that trustees' major concern is likely to be to avoid what they perceive as underperformance. With limited time and expertise available to meet this goal, one would expect them to rely heavily on professional advice and to feel most comfortable replicating the practices and decisions of others.'

He then asked those considering the consultation paper whether this was a valid description of the approach of a significant number of pension fund trustees and whether trust law provided an appropriate basis for pension scheme governance, particularly investment decisions.

Paul Myners made a interim report to the Chancellor of the Exchequer and also to the Secretary of State for Social Security (now Secretary of State for Work and Pensions) in November 2000. This was so that he could himself respond to the separate Government consultation exercise on the minimum funding requirement (MFR) by recommending that it should be abolished because, among other things, he saw it as seriously distorting pension fund investment decisions.

His overall response was made in his final report *Institutional Investment in the UK: A Review* which was published on 6 March 2001, the day before the Chancellor's Budget speech. This is an important document and should be required reading for all pension fund trustees. It is available on the Treasury website at: http://www.hm-treasury.gov.uk/media//843F0/31.pdf. The recommendations made in that report, which were accepted in principle by the

Chancellor the day following its publication, form the substance of this chapter.

Following the publication of Paul Myners' review, the Government launched a two-month further consultation period ending on 15 May 2001. On 27 July 2001, the Treasury announced how it proposed to carry forward one particular recommendation that Paul Myners had made. This concerned how a pension fund's investment transaction costs, such as brokers' services, should be met (see **16.19**). Later, on 2 October 2001, the Treasury published its overall, detailed response to *Institutional Investment in the UK: A Review*.

Voluntary code for pension fund investment

17.2   A key component of Paul Myners' review was the drawing up of two sets of investment principles for pension funds, one for defined benefit schemes and one for defined contribution schemes. The Treasury made some minor revisions to these sets of principles and issued the revised sets of principles as part of its detailed response to Paul Myners' review.

The Government's policy is that pension fund trustees should adopt these principles as best practice, and expects them to disclose publicly their compliance with them on a voluntary basis. However, as recommended by Paul Myners himself, there was to be a public assessment carried out by the Government of the effectiveness of the principles in bringing about the desired changes two years after the publication of the review. The Government assessment began in March 2003.

The Government has proposed that the principles, as revised, should not apply to insured occupational pension schemes, where in effect the trustees have delegated responsibility for all investment decisions except for the choice of the fund manager. It should also be noted that insured occupational pension schemes are subject to the separate review that was undertaken by Ron Sandler, as commissioned by the Treasury following a recommendation by Paul Myners for such a review. The Sandler review embraced all retail savings products, not only insured pension schemes, and was published in July 2002.

The Government has not exempted other small schemes from the new requirements set out by Paul Myners but has stated that it recognises that it is more difficult for small schemes to implement certain elements of the revised principles. The Government's view is that the appropriate course of action is for the trustees of a scheme in this position to explain why they have not implemented the element in question.

Revised text of principles

17.3   We reproduce below the text of the principles devised by Paul Myners in *Institutional Investment in the UK: A Review* as revised by the Government and released on 2 October 2001. As explained above, there are two sets of principles: the first relates to defined benefit schemes and the second to defined contribution schemes.

Defined benefit pension schemes

DB Principle 1. Effective decision-making

17.4   Decisions should be taken only by persons or organisations with the skills, information and resources necessary to take them effectively. Where trustees elect to take investment decisions, they must have sufficient expertise and appropriate training to be able to evaluate critically any advice they take.

Trustees should ensure that they have sufficient in-house staff to support them in their investment responsibilities. Trustees should also be paid, unless there are specific reasons to the contrary.

It is good practice for trustee boards to have an investment sub-committee to provide the appropriate focus.

Trustees should assess whether they have the right set of skills, both individually and collectively, and the right structures and processes to carry out their role effectively. They should draw up a forward-looking business plan.

DB Principle 2. Clear objectives

Trustees should set out an overall investment objective for the fund that:

- represents their best judgement of what is necessary to meet the fund's liabilities given their understanding of the contributions likely to be received from employer(s) and employees; and

- takes account of their attitude to risk, specifically their willingness to accept underperformance due to market conditions.

Objectives for the overall fund should not be expressed in terms which have no relationship to the fund's liabilities, such as performance relative to other pension funds, or to a market index.

DB Principle 3. Focus on asset allocation

Strategic asset allocation decisions should receive a level of attention (and, where relevant, advisory or management fees) that fully reflect the contribution they can make towards achieving the fund's investment objective. Decision-makers should consider a full range of investment opportunities, not excluding from consideration any major asset class, including private equity. Asset allocation should reflect the fund's own characteristics, not the average allocation of other funds.

DB Principle 4. Expert advice

Contracts for actuarial services and investment advice should be opened to separate competition. The fund should be prepared to pay sufficient fees for each service to attract a broad range of kinds of potential providers.

DB Principle 5. Explicit mandates

Trustees should agree with both internal and external investment managers an explicit written mandate covering agreement between trustees and managers on:

- an objective, benchmark(s) and risk parameters that, together with all the other mandates, are coherent with the fund's aggregate objective and risk tolerances;

- the manager's approach in attempting to achieve the objective; and

- clear timescale(s) of measurement and evaluation, such that the mandate will not be terminated before the expiry of the evaluation timescale for underperformance alone.

The mandate and trust deed and rules should not exclude the use of any set of financial instruments, without clear justification in the light of the specific circumstances of the fund. Trustees, or those to whom they have delegated the task, should have a full understanding of the transaction-related costs they incur, including commissions. They should understand all the options open to them in respect of these costs, and should have an active strategy – whether through direct financial incentives or otherwise – for ensuring that these costs are properly controlled without jeopardising the fund's other objectives. Trustees should not without good reason permit soft commissions to be paid in respect of their fund's transactions.

DB Principle 6. Activism

The mandate and trust deed should incorporate the principle of the US Department of Labor Interpretative Bulletin on activism [see **16.25** and **APPENDIX 6**]. Trustees should also ensure that managers have an explicit strategy, elucidating the circumstances in which they will intervene in a company; the approach they will use in doing so; and how they measure the effectiveness of this strategy.

DB Principle 7. Appropriate benchmarks

Trustees should:

- explicitly consider, in consultation with their investment manager(s), whether the index benchmarks they have selected are appropriate; in particular, whether the construction of the index creates incentives to follow sub-optimal investment strategies;

- if setting limits on divergence from an index, ensure that they reflect the approximations involved in index construction and selection;

- consider explicitly for each asset class invested, whether active or passive management would be more appropriate given the efficiency, liquidity and level of transaction costs in the market concerned; and

- where they believe active management has the potential to achieve higher returns, set both targets and risk controls that reflect this, giving the managers the freedom to pursue genuinely active strategies.

DB Principle 8. Performance measurement

Trustees should arrange for measurement of the performance of the fund and make formal assessment of their own procedures and decisions as trustees. They should also arrange for a formal assessment of performance and decision-making delegated to advisers and managers.

DB Principle 9. Transparency

A strengthened Statement of Investment Principles should set out:

- who is taking which decisions and why this structure has been selected;

- the fund's investment objective;

- the fund's planned asset allocation strategy, including projected investment returns on each asset class, and how the strategy has been arrived at;

- the mandates given to all advisers and managers; and

- the nature of the fee structures in place for all advisers and managers, and why this set of structures has been selected.

DB Principle 10. Regular reporting

Trustees should publish their Statement of Investment Principles and the results of their monitoring of advisers and managers. They should send key information from these annually to members of these funds, including an explanation of why the fund has chosen to depart from any of these principles.

Defined contribution pension schemes

DC Principle 1. Effective decision-making

17.5   Decisions should only be taken by persons or organisations with the skills, information and resources necessary to take them effectively. Where trustees elect to take investment decisions, they must have sufficient expertise and appropriate training to be able to evaluate critically any advice they take.

Where scheme members are given a choice regarding investment issues, sufficient information should be given to them to allow an appropriate choice to be made.

Trustees should ensure that they have sufficient in-house staff to support them in their investment responsibilities. Trustees should also be paid, unless there are specific reasons to the contrary.

It is good practice for trustee boards to have an investment sub-committee to provide appropriate focus.

Trustees should assess whether they have the right set of skills, both individually and collectively, and the right structures and processes to carry out their role effectively. They should draw up a forward-looking business plan.

DC Principle 2. Clear objectives

In selecting funds to offer as options to scheme members, trustees should:

●   consider the investment objectives, expected returns, risks and other relevant characteristics of each fund, so that they can publish their assessments of these characteristics for each selected fund; and

●   satisfy themselves that they have taken their members' circumstances into account, and that they are offering a wide enough range of options to satisfy the reasonable return and risk combinations appropriate for most members.

DC Principle 3. Focus on asset allocation

Strategic asset allocation (for example for default and lifestyle options) should receive a level of attention (and, where relevant, advisory or management fees) that fully reflects the contribution they can make to achieving investment objectives. Decision-makers should consider a full range of investment opportunities, not excluding from consideration any major asset class, including private equity.

DC Principle 4. Choice of default fund

Where a fund is offering a default option to members through a customised combination of funds, trustees should make sure that an investment objective is set for the option, including expected returns and risks.

DC Principle 5. Expert advice

Contracts for investment advice should be open to competition, and fee rather than commission based. The scheme should be prepared to pay sufficient fees to attract a broad range of kinds of potential providers.

DC Principle 6. Explicit mandates

Trustees should communicate to members, for each fund offered by the scheme:

- the investment objective for the fund, its benchmark(s) and risk parameters; and

- the manager's approach in attempting to achieve the objective.

These should also be discussed with the fund manager concerned, as should a clear timescale(s) of measurement and evaluation, with the understanding that the fund mandate will not be terminated before the expiry of the evaluation timescale for underperformance alone.

Trustees, or those to whom they have delegated the task, should have a full understanding of the transaction-related costs they incur, including commissions. They should understand all the options open to them in respect of these costs, and should have an active strategy – whether through direct financial incentives or otherwise – for ensuring that these costs are properly controlled without jeopardising the fund's other objectives. Trustees should not without good reason permit soft commissions to be paid in respect of their fund's transactions.

DC Principle 7. Activism

The mandate and trust deed should incorporate the principle of the US Department of Labor Interpretative Bulletin on activism [see **16.25** and **APPENDIX 6**]. Managers should have an explicit strategy, elucidating the circumstances in which they will intervene in a company; the approach they will use in doing so; and how they measure the effectiveness of this strategy.

DC Principle 8. Appropriate benchmarks

Trustees should:

- explicitly consider, in consultation with their investment manager(s), whether the index benchmarks they have selected are appropriate; in particular, whether the construction of the index creates incentives to follow sub-optimal investment strategies;

- if setting limits on divergence from an index; ensure that they reflect the approximations involved in index construction and selection;

- consider explicitly for each asset class invested, whether active or passive management would be more appropriate given the efficiency, liquidity and level of transaction costs in the market concerned; and

- where they believe active management has the potential to achieve higher returns, set both targets and risk controls that reflect this, giving managers the freedom to pursue genuinely active strategies.

DC Principle 9. Performance measurement

Trustees should arrange for measurement of the performance of the funds and make formal assessment of their own procedures and decisions as trustees.

They should also arrange for a formal assessment of performance and decision-making delegated to advisers and managers.

DC Principle 10. Transparency

A strengthened Statement of Investment Principles should set out:

- who is taking which decisions and why this structure has been selected;

- each fund option's investment characteristics;

- the default option's investment characteristics, and why it has been selected;

- the agreements with all advisers and managers; and

- the nature of the fee structures in place for all advisers and managers, and why this set of structures has been selected.

DC Principle 11. Regular reporting

Trustees should publish their Statement of Investment Principles and the results of their monitoring of advisers and managers. They should send key information from these annually to members of these funds, including an explanation of why the fund has chosen to depart from any of these principles.

Legislative proposals

17.6   Although the Government's formal response to Paul Myners' review issued on 2 October 2001 stressed that it wanted pension fund trustees to adopt the investment principles voluntarily as best practice, with the caveat the they should disclose publicly their compliance with them, the response also listed two areas where the Government was considering whether to introduce legislation in the near future. These two areas of proposed legislation were as follows:

- where pension fund trustees are taking an investment decision, they should be able to take it with the skill and care of someone familiar with the issues concerned;

- UK law should incorporate an activist duty (similar to the one imposed under US legislation) on those responsible for the investment of pension scheme assets so that pension fund trustees or their investment managers intervene when necessary in the governance of the companies in which the pension fund holds shares.

On 4 February 2002 the Government issued further consultation papers outlining its proposals for legislation in these two areas, plus a further paper asking whether legislation would be necessary in a third area, custody, where Paul Myners had suggested that legislation was needed. The issues regarding custody and corporate governance are discussed in **CHAPTER 16** (see **16.22** and **16.24** respectively), but in both cases the Government has since confirmed that the results of the consultation have led, at least in the immediate term, to a decision not to go down the legislative route but instead to rely on the existing requirements and voluntary codes.

The Government's proposals for a legislative requirement that pension fund trustees be familiar with the investment decisions with which they are concerned are set out below.

The familiarity requirement

17.7 The February 2002 consultation paper, concerning a legislative proposal that pension fund trustees should be familiar with the investment issues with which they are concerned, stresses that the overarching trust law requirement that pension fund trustees should act in the main interests of the fund's beneficiaries will remain in place. In changing the legal duty of pension fund trustees, the Government states that it is seeking to ensure that:

- the investment decisions made about pension fund assets are taken by those with sufficient skill and information to make them effectively; and

- those responsible for decisions in law are those taking them in fact.

When Paul Myners first issued his review in March 2001, many of those working in pensions surmised that what the Government was seeking to achieve was the professionalisation of pension fund trusteeship. The fear was that the Government believed that lay trustees, drawn from the management of the employer and from the membership generally, could not be expected to carry out their stewardship role of running a pension fund adequately.

The Government denies that this is the case. The February 2002 consultation paper states:

'The Government does **not** wish to require pension scheme trustees to become experts in investment who do not need to take advice. Nor does it consider it desirable that pension scheme trustees should be drawn solely from the ranks of investment professionals. Pension scheme trustees should not be required to become investment experts and should be entitled to make use of the expertise of others. At the same time, they should have sufficient expertise to be able to evaluate whether advice is complete, up to date and based on appropriate assumptions and should exercise their own judgment when considering and acting upon advice – irrespective of the source of that advice (the fund manager, scheme administrator or any other adviser).'

As stated, the Government's policy very much reflects the long-standing tenet of *Tolley's Pension Fund Trustee Handbook*, which is that pension fund trustees should not be expected to be experts. They must rely on a host of advisers whom they appoint. What is important is that they must understand the nature of their relationship with those advisers and be prepared to question them critically and if, necessary, seek alternative advice.

What the Government proposes is to amend the legislation to introduce an enhanced standard of care for pension fund trustees who undertake investment functions. The proposed new standard as stated in the February 2002 consultation paper is as follows:

(a) Pension scheme trustees should act with the care, skill, prudence and diligence under the circumstances then prevailing that a prudent person acting in a like capacity and familiar with such matters would use in the conduct of an enterprise of like character and with like aims.

(b) In addition, where a pension scheme trustee has, or holds himself out as having, any special knowledge or experience, he must exercise such care and skill as is reasonable in the circumstances.

(c) Where a pension scheme trustee acts in the course of a business or profession, he must exercise such care and skill as is reasonable in the circumstances, having regard to any special knowledge or experience that it is reasonable to expect a person acting in the course of that kind of business or profession.

For lay trustees, therefore, point (a) is the most important since it expressly requires them to be familiar with the issues in respect of which they are responsible. This requirement is almost a straight lift from the *Employment Retirement Income Security Act* (ERISA), which contains the relevant US legislation governing the standard of care needed by fiduciaries running pension schemes. In the UK context, this new standard of care, known in short-hand as the 'familiarity requirement', does indeed go beyond the general 'prudent man or woman' principle (see **16.4**) that so far has underpinned all forms of trusteeship. Something extra will now be expected of pension fund trustees, although it may not be unreasonable, given the importance of the job, to expect such an enhanced standard of care.

The Government does not believe that it is necessary or desirable to set out in the legislation itself any further detail as to what being 'familiar with the issues' involves, or what a lay trustee must do in order to comply with the new standard of care. However, the February 2002 consultation paper asks whether it would be useful to have extra guidance to supplement the legislation, giving examples of the types of investment-related decisions to which the new standard of care is likely to apply and the level of skill and care that will be needed by trustees to comply with that new standard.

The February 2002 consultation paper also sought views on a further key issue: should this new standard of care apply to all the individual trustees, or only to any trustee sub-committee that may exist, or to the trustee board collectively? The question raises issues concerning the dynamics amongst the individual trustees of a trustee board (or among the individual directors of a corporate trustee). Obviously it would normally be expected that the familiarity with investment issues of a newly-elected member-nominated trustee is going to be less than that of an experienced company finance director who is a long-serving member of the trustee board. It is to be hoped that all of the trustees will receive adequate training so that they can carry out their functions properly (see **CHAPTER 24**) but naturally there will always be differences among the level of skills and competencies possessed by the individuals who make up the trustee body.

As discussed above (see **16.7**), it would seem important to hold on to the requirement that the trustee body works on the principle of collective responsibility, even if in practice the required level of familiarity with investment issues resides principally among the members of an investment sub-committee.

Enforcement of the familiarity requirement

17.8   At present the general prudent man or woman principle required of a pension fund trustee (see **16.4**) is enforceable from the courts. The February 2002 consultation paper envisages that such civil proceedings will continue to apply as the means to enforce the new standard of care represented by the familiarity requirement. Yet the consultation paper also asks for comments on whether it would be more appropriate for enforcement to be delivered other than through the courts – for example by Opra or the Pensions Ombudsman (see **CHAPTER 20**).

Latest developments

17.9   On 13 March 2003 the Government confirmed that the review of voluntary compliance with Paul Myners' investment principles had begun. The review will run until the end of 2003 but an initial qualitative stage of research will end earlier during the summer of 2003. The results of this qualitative research, which will be published, will inform a second stage of quantitative survey research. The final results are to be published around the end of 2003 or the beginning of 2004. Paul Myners will himself contribute to the review in an advisory capacity.

The Minister of State at the DWP stated that: 'This review will give us the evidence we need to determine if the non-legislative approach to the Myners' principles is working. We are determined to ensure that this sea change will take place.'

The Financial Secretary to the Treasury likewise commented that:

> 'This review will be the acid test of whether the industry has taken the Myners' investment principles on-board sufficiently. I am delighted that Paul Myners will contribute to the review in an advisory capacity and it underlines the commitment the Government has to making his proposals work.'

As regards the 'familiarity principle', the December 2002 Green Paper *Simplicity, Security Choice: Working and Saving for Retirement* announced that the Government would be consulting further on how to implement this proposal. The Green Paper states that:

'The Government consulted earlier this year on a proposal to legislate to require trustees to be "familiar with the issues" when they are taking investment decisions. The Government is committed to legislating. The role of trustee is of the highest importance: trustees need to have appropriate expertise to look after the investment of other people's pensions.

However, the consultation process delivered some important messages about the approach the Government had proposed to take to legislation. Respondents felt that it would be necessary to define further what was meant by 'familiar with the issues'. They thought that leaving this to the courts to decide would be cumbersome and expensive for schemes and their trustees.

The Government agrees that it would be helpful to give schemes as much certainty as possible, by better defining what expertise would be required. A strong element of practitioner input will be necessary to arrive at this definition, and decide how it would be given legal force. It will also be important for legislation to maintain flexibility to meet changing circumstances. The Government will also want to take account of the two-year review of the Myners' principles, and any possible changes to wider pensions legislation, before finalising legislative proposals.

Before finalising legislation, the Government wants to work with practitioners – in the light of the two-year review – to define what expertise trustees need to carry out their investment duties.'

Checklist 17

- Trustees of an occupational pension scheme are strongly advised to read *Institutional Investment in the UK – A Review*.

- Trustees should be familiar with the set of investment principles applying to their scheme and should adopt these principles as best practice.

- Trustees should disclose publicly their compliance with these investment principles, explaining why in any particular case they have departed from any of those principles.

- The Government began to assess the level of voluntary compliance with the investment principles in March 2003 and might introduce a legislative requirement if levels of compliance are found to be disappointing.

- A key investment principle set by Paul Myners is that where trustees elect to take investment decisions, they must have sufficient expertise and appropriate training to be able to evaluate critically any advice they take.

- The Government at first indicated that it intended to legislate during 2002 in order to introduce a new standard of care for trustees to the effect that investment decisions made about pension fund assets must

---

taken by those with sufficient skill and information to make them effectively. After further consultation, the still-intended legislation is being deferred so that it will not left to the courts to define what being 'familiar with the issues' might mean.

- Pension scheme trustees are not required to become investment experts but they should have sufficient expertise to be able to evaluate whether the advice they receive is complete, up to date and based on appropriate assumptions, and should exercise their own judgement when considering and acting upon advice.

Chapter 18

Conduct of trustee meetings

Introduction

18.1   The following description of how Robert Maxwell chaired a trustee meeting was given by a former trustee of Mirror Group Pension Fund to the House of Commons Social Security Committee:

> 'The style of the meetings was that you would be kept waiting around for hours, including senior Directors and Editors of newspapers, and suddenly he would whirl in in his shirt sleeves and conduct two hours of business in five or six minutes. You just could not raise matters, they were steamrollered through. The helicopter would arrive, and out he would go in a puff of smoke, and you were left asking, "what was that?".
>
> At one stage we asked for verbatim minutes to be taken, because we were so unhappy that minutes as recorded did not agree with all our understandings of what happened at the meeting. Often minority viewpoints frequently expressed by myself and other trustees were just simply not recorded and there was no comeback. We could protest, but still we were not able to get meetings scheduled, we could not raise agenda items and we could not get the minutes published. There was also quite a lot of manipulation in the way the meetings were held. They could be held at two days' notice, with no access to the previous minutes, no agenda, and the reports and valuations were placed before you at the meetings. It is very difficult to wade through all that detailed information at one minute's notice.'

Clearly, in such a meeting, trustees are unable to carry out their duty of care towards the scheme's beneficiaries and a breach of trust is almost certain.

The trust deed and rules may specify how trustee meetings are to be conducted or it may give the trustees power to make their own regulations on how they should operate. What is important is that there should be formal rules of conduct which are observed. That is not to say that the meeting itself should be unduly formal in tone.

Who chairs the trustee meeting?

18.2   The trust deed and rules may specify who should chair the trustee meetings or alternatively simply state that the trustees should make their own rules on how a chairman is appointed. In practice, the appointment is usually in the gift of the employer.

Setting the agenda

18.3 An occupational pension scheme has its own regular annual calendar marked by the need to issue trustee reports, consider auditor's reports, listen to reports from the investment manager, decide on the level of discretionary increase to pensions and the like. Other items, such as the need to exercise a discretionary power as to who is to receive a death-in-service lump sum, can arise at any time in the year. Actuarial reports may be on a three-yearly cycle. Important items such as a merger with another scheme, or a major change in benefit design will require detailed discussion. Trustees will also want to consider wider issues that may arise from time to time. For example, the trustees may need to discuss the effect on the scheme of any new legislation.

Much of the agenda will necessarily be set by the needs of the scheme. It will be usual, therefore, for the scheme's pensions manager, who ordinarily acts as the secretary at the trustees' meeting, to prepare an agenda to include all the matters of business that must be considered. This will then be agreed with the chairman.

However, matters raised by trustees at the last meeting and which it was agreed would appear on the next meeting's agenda must not be forgotten.

It may be best practice for the secretary to the meeting to send to each trustee a reminder notice of the approaching trustee meeting and ask if he or she has items that should be placed on the agenda.

Reaching decisions

18.4 Probably most trustee meetings reach most of their decisions purely by resolution. A piece of paper is circulated, discussed and nodded through. No formal vote is taken.

Yet to be valid any decision must be passed by a quorum at a meeting and to this end the trust deed and rules or the trustees' own formal regulations should specify how many trustees have to be present to form that quorum. In the case of a corporate trustee, the quorum may be specified in the Articles of Association. In practice either two-thirds or a majority of the trustees is usually specified as the quorum. In cases where 'member trustees' and 'management trustees' are separately distinguished, the rules may specify that a minimum number from each trustee category must be present for the meeting to be quorate.

The trust deed and rules or the trustees' own regulations should also specify whether the trustees are to act by unanimous or majority decision. (If they do not, then under the *Pensions Act 1995* decisions must be by majority, whereas the previous default under trust law required unanimity. This provision technically only applies to meetings of trustees rather than the trustee directors in the case of a corporate trustee.) If a vote is evenly split, it should similarly be specified if the chairman is to have the casting vote.

The *Occupational Pension Schemes (Scheme Administration) Regulations 1996 (SI 1996/1715)* also set out rules governing the proper notice that must be given to each trustee of trustee meetings. Normally, notice should be sent not less than ten working days before the meeting. Meetings can be held at shorter notice where this is necessary as a matter of urgency to make a decision. The notice must specify the time, date and place of the meeting. If an individual trustee finds that he or she has not been invited to a meeting, or meetings at short notice were held without his or her consent, the trustee can complain to Opra. The trustee responsible for convening meetings, i e the chairman of the trustees, could be fined or removed by Opra if he or she fails to take reasonable steps to ensure the proper conduct of meetings. Again, technically these regulations only apply to meetings of trustees, not of trustee directors in the case of a corporate trustee.

It is important to remember that each individual trustee bears a collective responsibility for any action or inaction of the trustee body. If a trustee knows that a decision will constitute a breach of trust, he or she is not absolved simply by voting against it.

Recording decisions

18.5   The *Pensions Act 1995* requires trustees to ensure that there are written records of all their meetings, including meetings of any trustee sub-groups.

The *Occupational Pension Schemes (Scheme Administration) Regulations 1996 (SI 1996/1715)* require that these records should at least contain the following details:

- the date, time and place of the meeting;
- the names of all the trustees invited to the meeting;
- the names of the trustees who attended the meetings and those who did not attend;
- the names of any professional advisers or any other person who attended the meeting;
- any decision made at the meeting; and
- whether, since the previous meeting, there has been any occasion where a decision has been made by the trustees and if so, the time, place and date of such a decision; and the names of the trustees who participated in that occasion at which a decision was made.

Although the wording of the Act does not apply to meetings of trustee directors, it would seem to be a good idea that trustee directors should adopt a comparable standard of record keeping.

It is not intended under the Act that records of trustee meetings should necessarily be disclosed to scheme members. Rather, the intention is that all trustees, including any who may not have been involved when any decision was taken, should have access to these records. The minutes of trustees' meetings may be automatically copied to the scheme's auditors and also made available where relevant to the scheme's other advisers, in particular the scheme actuary and scheme lawyer.

In a court case known as *Re Londonderry's Settlement [1964] 3 All ER 855, [1965] Ch 918*, the Court of Appeal held that minutes of trustee meetings containing the reasons the trustees had exercised their discretionary powers in a particular way do not have to be disclosed to the beneficiaries of the trust. This principle stands even though the minutes are considered to be the property of the trust. The confidentiality of the minutes is a long-standing principle and based on the view that individuals could not be called upon to serve as trustees and to exercise the discretionary powers given to them by the trust deed if, in the absence of bad faith, they were to have their reasons called into question either by the beneficiaries or by the court. It should be noted, however, that if the trustees do give their reasons, those reasons are then open to question.

The Scheme Administration Regulations require a record to be kept of trustees' decisions taken at a meeting but do not specify the amount of detail that needs to be recorded on how the trustees came to make that decision in that particular way. It might be thought that the trustees should not record the reasons they arrived at a particular decision, but in view of the *Wednesbury Principles* (see **5.4**) it might be useful if the minutes could demonstrate that the trustees did consider all the relevant facts, and just as importantly, did not take into consideration any irrelevant facts, in arriving at their decision. If the trustees can be shown to have:

- asked themselves the correct questions;

- directed themselves correctly in law; in particular they must adopt a correct construction of the trust deed and rules; and

- not arrived at a perverse decision, i e a decision to which no reasonable body of trustees could arrive;

then neither the Pensions Ombudsman nor the courts are likely to overturn a decision made by trustees properly using their discretionary powers. It should be noted that in the case of *Wilson v The Law Debenture Trust Corporation [1995] 2 All ER 337, [1995] OPLR 103* the judge held that, in the absence of evidence to the contrary, the presumption is that the trustees have exercised their discretion properly.

Furthermore, in the *Wilson* case the judge held that, in the absence of any evidence of impropriety, the court will not compel the trustees of a pension scheme to disclose the reasons they exercised their discretion in any particular way. However, this needs to be set against the statutory powers given to the Pensions Ombudsman to force discovery of scheme documents. These statutory powers are set out at *sections 149* and *150* of the *Pension Schemes Act 1993*. The Pensions Ombudsman in investigating a complaint may require any person responsible for the management of the scheme to which the complaint relates to furnish information or produce documents relevant to the investigation.

On 25 April 2002 the Pensions Ombudsman issued a determination involving a complaint brought by Mr Allen against the corporate trustee of the TKM Group Pension Scheme. The determination is reported as *C Allen Determination by the Pensions Ombudsman [2002] PLR 333*. The main issue was that the trustee had refused to disclose minutes of a meeting during which Mr Allen's application for an unreduced early retirement pension had been refused. The determination is of interest because of the remarks made by the Pensions Ombudsman to the effect that an absence of a breach of law does not mean there is no act of maladministration – see **11.4**, where this part of the Pensions Ombudsman's determination is quoted.

In other words, just because there is no legal duty on trustees to make a copy of their minutes available to a complainant, this does not imply that in actually refusing to do so, the trustee could not be committing an act of maladministration. The Pensions Ombudsman went on to state:

'As a matter of good administrative practice trustees should provide reasons for their decision to those with a legitimate interest in the matter and, subject to the need to preserve rights to privacy of individual members, should also make the minutes of their meeting available to scheme members. I can see no good reason for the trustee not to have done so in this case and the failure of the trustee to do this for Mr Allen was also maladministration. Not knowing the basis on which an adverse decision is taken is itself an injustice.'

The Editor of the Pensions Law Reports series commented that this determination sat uncomfortably with the *Wilson* case cited above, but that comments made in the case of *Edge v Pensions Ombudsman [1998] 2 All ER 547, [1998] OPLR 51* when it was before the High Court (see **9.1**) tended to support the idea that reasons must sometimes be given. He hoped that a suitable case would come before the courts so that the matter might be clarified.

Frequency of meetings

18.6   How many trustee meetings are needed in a year will depend on the kind of scheme. Trustees of a small insured scheme may meet only once a year. Most large occupational pension schemes will meet at least quarterly. The trust deed and rules or the trustees' own formal regulations will usually specify that a special meeting may be called by any one of the trustees. Sometimes a special resolution can be passed without physically calling a meeting if all the trustees are willing to sign a copy of the resolution. There is no particular reason why video-conferencing technology could not be used if this would facilitate full attendance of all the trustees. However, it is more practicable to schedule the next four or so meetings on a rolling basis well in advance. Trustees should ensure that attendance at a trustee meeting takes priority over other work commitments and that they prepare adequately for the meeting by reading thoroughly any relevant papers sent in advance of the meeting, as well as considering seriously whether there might be any unintended implications of the decisions that are to be taken at the meeting. For example, if one particular clause of the trust deed and rules is to be amended, it is sometimes the case that there is a cross-reference to that clause elsewhere in the trust documentation and that by making the intended change, the cross-reference means that an unintended change is also made.

Checklist 18

- In practice, the decision on who chairs the trustees is usually made by the employer.

- In practice, the agenda of the trustees' meeting will be set by the chairman working with the pensions manager (secretary of the trustees), but any trustee can table an agenda item.

- The trust deed and rules or the articles of association of a corporate trustee should specify the quorum necessary for any decision to be valid and whether decisions are to be unanimous or by majority.

- Proper notice of at least ten working days should normally be given to each trustee and the notice should also specify the time, date and place of the meeting, although the requirement can be overridden when as a matter of urgency it is necessary to make a decision.

- Proper minutes of each meeting must be kept.

- Although the law does not require the trustees to let a complainant see minutes of the meeting at which his or her complaint was considered, it may amount to maladministration if the trustees decide not to do so.

- Trustees should not meet too infrequently.

- Trustees should prepare themselves adequately for the meeting.

Chapter 19

Special situations

Pension fund surpluses

19.1   In practice, the question of pension fund surpluses and fund deficiencies (see **19.10** below) only arises in defined benefit schemes, although theoretically they could also arise in defined contribution schemes.

It should be remembered that a surplus that arises in an on-going scheme is a very notional sum of money. If the scheme actuary had varied the assumptions and narrowed the estimated gap between investment return and earnings growth, or if the actuary had chosen another valuation method, the surplus might have been increased, reduced or even turned into a deficit. Surpluses, in most circumstances, only arise in self-administered defined benefit schemes.

The employer should want to ensure that the pension fund runs a surplus, otherwise higher contributions will be necessary if the scheme is to continue. Running a moderate surplus will also allow the scheme trustees to follow an investment strategy that does not fully match the scheme's liabilities under the minimum funding requirement (MFR). This will allow the trustees to hold a higher proportion of the scheme's assets in equities with the possibility (but not certainty!) of a higher investment return than would be the case in a fully-matched investment strategy where a proportion of the equities would be replaced by bonds, traditionally producing a lower investment return. However, if a very large surplus begins to emerge, the employer will want to reduce it because:

- if employer contributions are not needed by the scheme, they might be better used in helping to increase company profitability; and

- a large surplus in the pension fund could make the employer a target for hostile takeover bids.

The Inland Revenue also wishes to see pension fund surpluses reduced. It argues that full tax relief is being given unnecessarily since more assets are being held than are needed to provide the benefits and are being used to depress the employer's taxable profits.

In *Pension Trust Principles*, the guide produced by the former Occupational Pensions Board, the authors comment that trustees must ensure that, in cases where any surplus is to be used at least in part in order to provide benefit improvements or reductions in members' contributions, they have regard to fairness between different classes of beneficiary. However, this may mean that the trustees should do no more than carefully consider the interests of each class of member – see **9.1** for a fuller discussion.

It should be said that the need to control the growth of surpluses became a major issue during the 1980s and 1990s. At the beginning of the 21st century, however, the overall situation has changed quite dramatically and many, and perhaps at the time of writing a substantial majority of all trustees of defined benefit schemes are facing the opposite problem of how to deal with a scheme deficiency.

The Finance Act 1986

19.2   The *Finance Act 1986* introduced new requirements on pension fund surpluses and clarified the existing law.

On using the projected accrued benefit method and assuming that the margin of investment returns over earnings growth is 1.5%, as well as making various other assumptions, if a self-administered defined benefit scheme runs a surplus of over 5%, action must be taken to reduce it to not more than 5% within, in most cases, the following five years.

If no action is taken, the scheme will lose part of its tax exemption.

The trustees can decide to reduce the surplus using any combination of the following:

- suspension or reduction of employer contributions for up to five years;

- suspension or reduction of employee contributions for up to five years;

- improvement of scheme benefits (in particular past service benefits) up to Inland Revenue limits; and/or

- payment of some or all of the surplus to the employer, taxed at 35%.

If a payment from the fund is given to the employer, the actuarial value of the surplus cannot be reduced to less than 5%.

Valuations must be sent to the Inland Revenue at intervals of, currently, not more than $3\frac{1}{2}$ years.

Payment of surplus to the employer

19.3   One legislative provision is that no payment out of the fund can be made to the employer until at least Limited Price Indexation (LPI) (that is, annual increases in line with the retail prices index limited to 5% in any one year) has been guaranteed on all pensions in payment and all future pensions when they come into payment.

The *Pensions Act 1995* has provided since 6 April 1997 that where the trust deed and rules permit a payment out of surplus to be made to the employer, that power can only be exercised by the trustees. Furthermore, the trustees can only exercise that power if:

- it results from a statutory surplus as defined in the *Finance Act 1986*;

- the trustees are satisfied that it is in the members' interests;

- Limited Price Indexation is in place for all pension rights; and

- notice has been given to the members (including pensioners).

Members have two months from this first notice to respond to the trustees. The trustees must then send a second notice informing members of the trustees' decision and the members will have a further three months from the second notice to take any complaint to Opra. No payment to the employer can be made if a complaint is still outstanding.

Practice on surpluses

19.4   Among the larger schemes, pension fund surpluses have typically been reduced by a combination of benefit improvements and employer contribution holidays. Figures released by the Inland Revenue show that cumulatively since the measures set out in the *Finance Act 1986* came into effect, statutory surpluses have been reduced as in the following table:

Method of reduction	No. of schemes	Amount of reduction (£ million)
Contributions holiday (employer)	2,881	13,184
Contributions holiday (employee)	174	262
Contributions reduction (employer)	1,566	4,745
Contributions reduction (employee)	256	851
Payment to employer*	293	1,217
Increase in benefits	1,835	9,029
New benefits	215	175
TOTAL		29,463

Figures relate to the period 1987/88–2000/01 and represent the total amount to be eliminated by each of the methods indicated. Some of the reductions would be made in years after 2000/01. (Note that the total number of schemes cannot be deduced as some scheme surpluses are reduced using more than method.)

* The figure for payments to employers excludes the amount paid over by schemes reported to be wound up in each year.

Source: Inland Revenue

In an on-going scheme, it seems that surpluses can be dealt with, if not always amicably, at least practically in the context of the normal industrial relations life of the company. Nevertheless, several major court cases during recent years have centred on the question of *who owns a surplus?*

The Court of Appeal, giving its judgment in the case of *National Grid Co plc v Mayes & others [1999] All ER (D) 126, [1999] OPLR 95* set out some basic principles which have become fairly well established. These are as follows:

- A court will always try to ensure that the rules of the pension scheme, as set out in the trust deed and rules, are followed (provided they are not overridden by legislation) and the court's approach should be 'practical and purposive, rather than detached and literal', i e to try to follow what was actually intended and to construe the wording in a reasonable and practical way – this principle was famously set out in the case of *Mettoy Pension Trustees v Evans [1991] 2 All ER 513, [1990] PLR 9*.

- When an employer exercises a power given to it by the trust deed and rules, the employer will not necessarily be treated as a fiduciary (i e the employer can look to its own interests) but nevertheless the employer must not, without reasonable and proper cause, take action which is 'calculated or likely to destroy or seriously damage the relationship of confidence and trust between employer and employee'. This is the 'implied duty of good faith' set out in the case of *Imperial Group Pension Trust v Imperial Tobacco Ltd [1991] 2 All ER 597, [1990] PLR 263* (see **8.2** above).

- Employees have no automatic right to a surplus revealed by an actuarial valuation but they have 'a reasonable expectation that any dealings with that surplus, whether by the employers or the trustees of the scheme acting within the powers of the scheme, will pay a fair regard to their interests, since the express purpose of the scheme is to provide benefits for their retirement'. This principle was set out in the case of *Re Courage Group's Pension Schemes [1987] 1 All ER 528, [1989A] PLR 67* (see **7.1**).

- To the extent that an employer is under an obligation to make contributions, it is fair for some purposes to regard those as part of the employees' overall remuneration package, just as much as contributions made by the employees from their salaries and wages, a comment made by the judge in the case of *Thrells Ltd (1974) Pension Scheme in Liquidation v Lomas [1993] 2 All ER 546, [1992] OPLR 21*.

- It is not the case that members of a contributory pension scheme have interests in the application of a surplus equivalent to rights of property – a point affirmed by the Court of Appeal in *National Grid Co plc v Mayes & others*.

However thought-provoking these general principles may be, members, employers and trustees should not be misled into thinking that they are the starting point in deciding whether or not any particular course of action is permitted when it comes to considering how an actuarial surplus will be used in any particular case. When it came to setting out its judgment in the *National Grid* case, the Court of Appeal said that: 'The solution to the present problem lies within the terms of the scheme itself, and not within a world populated by competing philosophies as to the true nature and ownership of an actuarial surplus'.

In the event, the Court of Appeal's own judgment in the *National Grid* case was overturned by the Law Lords (*[2001] UKHL 20, [2001] 2 All ER 417, [2001] OPLR 15*). This latter judgment centred on the specific interpretation of the scheme's trust documentation and so does not invalidate any of the general principles set out above. The House of Lords' eventual decision in the case, however, has been seen as evidence that the courts should also take a practical and commercial view of the way in which pension schemes operate.

In the decision of the Court of Appeal in July 1999 in the case of *Edge v Pensions Ombudsman [1999] 4 All ER 546, [1999] OPLR 179*, Lord Justice Chadwick dealt with the duty of trustees to consider the interests of all the classes of beneficiaries who could benefit from a pension fund surplus. The trustees would want to consider the circumstances in which the surplus had arisen but he added that, having done so, the trustees would not be bound to take any particular course as a result of that consideration, provided it was a matter of the use of trustee discretion. He said: 'The essential requirement is that the trustees address themselves to the question of what is fair and equitable in all the circumstances. The weight to be given to one factor as against another is for them'. See **9.1** above for further discussion on this point about the use of the trustees' discretionary power in agreeing to how a surplus should be used.

Mergers and takeovers

19.5   If one company (the vendor company) runs an occupational pension scheme, and sells a business or subsidiary company to another company (the purchasing company) which also runs an occupational pension scheme, then part of the vendor's pension scheme is likely to be transferred to the purchaser's pension scheme.

The two companies will negotiate a deal in the normal way. The normal way means that the vendor will want to sell at the highest price possible and the purchaser will want to buy at the lowest price possible. The sale will be clinched by a purchase and sale agreement.

The Occupational Pensions Board gave trustees the following advice in *Pension Trust Principles*:

'You will need to be particularly clear about your duty to act in accordance with the trust deed and rules if the employer is engaged in the sale and purchase of an undertaking which involves a bulk transfer of members and assets out of or into the scheme. The two employers involved will have entered into a sale agreement which will cover the pension terms of the transferring employees and the associated financial arrangements. You and your fellow trustees will not normally be parties to the agreement, and indeed the trustees of the two schemes may not have been consulted fully, if at all. You must ensure that you act strictly in accordance with the trust deed and rules, even if the terms of the sale agreement differ from these. The employers will have to solve any difficulties that arise.'

The trustees of the vendor company's scheme must not transfer too great a proportion of their fund to the new fund as this would not be in the interests of beneficiaries who remain.

The trustees of the purchasing company must not accept an influx of new members without ensuring that adequate new funding is also transferred into the fund as this will not be in the interests of either the existing or the transferring beneficiaries.

The members who are being asked to transfer will want to ensure that their existing expectations will be realised in the new scheme.

Under the *Occupational Pension Schemes (Preservation of Benefit) Regulations 1991 (SI 1991/167)*, bulk transfers of members from one scheme to another scheme may be permitted without the consent of the members involved. However, the actuary to the transferring scheme must certify that the past service rights and expectations to be provided to the transferring members in the new scheme are equivalent on an overall basis to their past service rights and expectations in the original scheme. Even if the actuary gives such a certificate, it does not absolve the trustees of the transferring scheme from their fiduciary duty to the members involved.

If an entire company is taken over by another, the latter will become the principal employer of the former company's pension scheme. If then the scheme of the company that has been taken over is to be merged with another scheme sponsored by the company that has now become the principal employer, the situation from the point of view of the two sets of trustees is the same as just described, i e they must act in the interests of their own members – see also the discussion of issues concerning bulk transfers at **9.8**.

In cases of a group of companies, the principal employer may want to have admitted into membership of a pension scheme employees who work for other employers in the group. Those employees may be members of another pension scheme which is to be wound up or they may not currently be members of any pension scheme. The usual approach would be to adhere those other employers in the group as participating employers to the scheme's trust deed. In such cases, the trustees of the pension scheme concerned must ensure that adequate bulk transfer payments are made to cover any past service rights that are in future to be provided by their scheme. The future contribution rates made by these employers must also be in line with actuarial recommendations. If the existing scheme is running a surplus it might not be acceptable for the new employers to benefit immediately from a contribution holiday. Rather they would be expected to contribute at the recommended rate for a minimum period of time. This issue was the subject of court action in the case of *Hillsdown Holdings v Pensions Ombudsman [1997] 1 All ER 862, [1996] OPLR 291* (see **7.1**) where the judge distinguished between an employer who takes a contribution holiday in respect of a category of existing members and an employer who introduces a large class of new members and takes a contribution holiday in relation to them so as to accelerate the effect of the contributions holiday in relation to the existing members.

Sometimes in the past when a well-funded scheme was merged with a less well-funded scheme, the trustees agreed to ring-fence some of the assets for the members of one of the schemes, so that these members were protected if the scheme was subsequently wound up. However, changes made by the *Pensions Act 1995* in the priority order for paying liabilities on winding up mean that such ring-fencing agreements made on or after 6 April 1997 may not be effective in this event.

All of the above discussion is based on the premise that the employer with a pension scheme is selling a business to another employer who also runs a pension scheme. Of course, that is not always the case. At present, the *Transfer of Undertakings (Protection of Employment) Regulations 1981 (SI 1981/1794)* (TUPE) specifically single out future rights under an occupational pension scheme as an employee benefit that does not automatically transfer from one employer to another when a business changes hands. The regulations embody in domestic legislation the requirements of the European Acquired Rights Directive, and these also originally excluded future occupational pension scheme rights from the scope of the protection afforded to employees on transfers of businesses. Yet the Directive was amended in 1998 so that each member state could decide whether this exclusion should continue.

At the time of writing the UK Government is considering whether or not to amend the TUPE Regulations so that in future an employer taking over a business of another employer, where the employees are eligible to join an occupational pension scheme, will have to offer those transferring employees membership of at least some kind of occupational pension scheme from the date of the transfer.

However, for the present, if active members of an occupational pension scheme are transferred as part of a business sale by the sponsoring employer to another employer who does not sponsor an occupational pension scheme, it seems that those employees will simply become early leavers of the scheme. This conclusion must, nevertheless, be qualified by the effect of the European Court of Justice in the case of *Beckmann v Dynamco Whicheloe Macfarlane Ltd [2002] All ER (D) 05 (Jun), [2002] PLR 287.* In that case, the ECJ held that the exception granted under the Acquired Rights Directive that allows occupational pension schemes to be excluded from the overall protection offered by the TUPE Regulations, must be applied narrowly and strictly interpreted. As a result, the ECJ held that the exception granted applied, as in the wording of the Directive, only to 'old-age, invalidity and survivors' benefits', and so would not be applied to a benefit where it is paid not on the ground that the employee had reached the relevant retirement age, but on the ground that he or she had become entitled to early payment of a pension and a retirement lump sum by reason of dismissal for redundancy.

Scheme reconstructions

19.6   In some circumstances, following reorganisations such as a merger or a change in the benefit design policy by the employer, employees who joined a scheme before a certain date may continue to be active members building up rights to further benefits but no new members are admitted into membership.

Instead, new employees are possibly offered membership of another occupational pension scheme, a group personal pension arrangement or a designated stakeholder pension scheme. In such cases, the responsibility of the trustees of the scheme that is closed to new members remains solely the members of that scheme. They must ensure that those members receive their due benefits when they fall due in the normal way. The funds held by the closed scheme can only be used in accordance with the trust deed and rules and the trustees cannot transfer those assets gratuitously to the other pension scheme for the benefit of the new employees.

In other cases, new members are admitted into the existing scheme but into a new section where differing rules apply, while those who remain in the original section of the scheme enjoy *grandfathered* rights. An example might be a defined benefit section which is closed to new members but where existing members are given grandfathered rights. New employees are offered membership of a newly created money purchase section within the same scheme. In this case the scheme trustees owe a fiduciary duty to the members of both sections.

In such a situation as just described where, say, there is a significant surplus in the pension scheme, there might be no particular reason in principle why the trustees could not agree to some of that surplus being run off to provide the employer contributions to the money purchase pensions of the new members, provided always that this did not disadvantage the reasonable pension expectations of the members of the final salary section. If effect, it would be equivalent to a continuing contribution holiday for the employer. However, for this to happen it is very important for the pension scheme's trust deed and rules to make it clear that the surplus accrued in the final salary section of the scheme can be applied for the benefit of the new members in the money purchase section of the scheme, even if it is already clear that the two sections form part of one overall pension scheme.

This problem arose in the High Court case *Kemble v Hicks [1999] Ch 53, [1999] OPLR 1* where the scheme's governing documentation failed to make this point explicit. Subject to the particular facts of that case, Justice Rimer observed:

> 'But it does appear to me that the establishment of the money purchase scheme involved what was, within that overall scheme, a scheme quite separate from the final salary scheme and to which different considerations applied ... It seems to me to follow that, to the extent that the surplus in [the final salary scheme] was thereafter used to fund the employer contributions to the money purchase scheme, the money purchase scheme members were thereby improperly and unfairly subsidised by the final salary scheme members, because the surplus remained held on the trusts of the final salary scheme.'

The facts of *Kemble v Hicks* are very specific to that case, but in March 2000 the Pensions Ombudsman upheld a complaint against Barclays Bank which has closed its final salary scheme to new members and opened instead a new money purchase scheme, but again within one overall pension scheme with a common set of trustees. The Pensions Ombudsman agreed that the new money purchase scheme was part of one overall scheme incorporating the final salary scheme, but he did not consider that the new money purchase scheme was part of the pre-existing final salary scheme. If there was no provision in the documentation for a cross-subsidy, there could be no legal basis for the employer's contributions to the money purchase scheme to be paid out of the surplus in the final salary scheme. The Pensions Ombudsman directed the employer to repay contributions with interest to the pension fund.

This determination by the Ombudsman was, however, rejected on appeal to the High Court by Justice Neuberger in the case of *Barclays Bank plc v Holmes [2000] PLR 339*. He decided that the correct interpretation of the scheme's trust documentation was that it constituted a single trust fund subject to two separate schemes, with the result that the bank was not obliged to pay contributions into the fund while the fund was in surplus. Justice Neuberger also made it clear that *section 67* of the *Pensions Act 1995*, which acts to prevent any scheme amendment being made which would worsen the 'accrued rights' of members without their consent (see **6.3**), did not mean that having a pension fund surplus preserved for the benefit of the members could count as an 'accrued right' that had to be protected under that section of the Act. He said that: '[I]t cannot sensibly be contended that a member of a pension scheme has any 'right', let alone an 'accrued right' to or in relation to a surplus.'

It must be said that life becomes more difficult for trustees where a common pension fund guarantees the benefits of several different classes of active members, with different scales of benefit rights, as well as those of deferred pensioners and pensioners. Trustees must act equitably towards all classes of the membership.

Prompted by the emergence of funding deficits (see **19.10**) especially since 2001, the sponsoring employers of a high proportion of the UK's final salary schemes have taken action to cut future pension costs by making changes to these schemes. In many cases, the employer has invoked its power under the trustee deed and rules and begun to wind up the scheme (see **19.9–19.13** below). In other cases, alternative action has been taken including:

- closing the final salary scheme to new entrants but allowing existing members to continue to build up further rights as described above;

- requiring employees to pay higher contributions or offering them a choice of paying higher contributions in order to maintain the same accrual rate (e g 1/60th) or continuing at the same employee contribution rate while moving to a lower rate of accrual (e g 1/80th) for future service;

- redesigning certain aspects of the pension scheme (e g removing or reducing enhanced terms for early retirement); and

- closing the final salary scheme not only to new entrants but also to further accrual of benefits for the existing members: this can be done in two ways:

  - existing members accrue no further pensionable service (e g a member with 15 years' pensionable service will build up no more years of service even if he or she remains an employee for another 15 years) but their benefits will still be calculated on their final pensionable earnings as at the time the benefits become due (e g on the date they retire); or

  - existing members accrue no further pensionable service and are treated in the same way as a deferred pensioner with their benefits being calculated using their final pensionable earnings as at the date further pensionable service ended, subject to statutory revaluation thereafter (see **9.16**).

None of the options listed above falls foul of the legal principle that amendments to schemes must not reduce the pension rights that have already been accrued (see **6.3**) since they all relate only to pension rights built up, or the lack of them, from the date of the change.

There are potential legal problems for the employer in taking up any of these options if the employees can show that there are either express or implied terms in their contracts of employment that indicate that they have a contractual right to continue to build up final salary benefits. Closing a final salary scheme to further accrual is highly likely to give rise to difficult industrial relations for the employer. See also the discussion at **7.5**.

Speaking at the spring 2003 conference of the Pensions Management Institute, Chris Mullen, National Head of Pensions at law firm Pinsent Curtis Biddle, described the issues that the trustees needed to consider during such changes, especially the option of closing the scheme for future accrual.

First, it is highly probable that the trustee body will contain members of senior staff of the sponsoring employer who have received advice from external sources and who are implementing the change. The trustee body itself must also take independent legal advice as to how to proceed. This legal advice must be kept confidential to the trustees who are bound to carry out their duties under the trust deed and rules and to act in the interests of all members (not just the active members). There is therefore a conflict since it would not be proper for senior employees of the employer who are charged with putting this new policy into effect to be privy to the details of the legal advice received by the trustees. It is true that the trustees can also take into account any duty they may have to have a care for the employer's interests, but in such circumstances where the change is being proposed by the employer, usually with external legal advice that is confidential to the employer, the trustees would seem also to have duty to seek their own confidential and independent legal advice. It is suggested that those trustees who are also senior staff of the employer might absent themselves from the meeting between the other trustees and their legal advisor. Alternatively, the trustees may appoint an independent trustee to take legal advice and act in their name on this issue.

Second, as already noted at **7.1**, the High Court in the case of *Hillsdown Holdings v Pensions Ombudsman [1997] 1 All ER 862, [1996] OPLR 291* has made it clear that in certain circumstances it is correct for the trustees to negotiate with the sponsoring employer. It is perfectly proper, therefore, to bargain with the employer in the circumstances where the employer has proposed to close the scheme to future accrual. For genuine bargaining to take place, it is therefore all the more important that the legal advice that the trustees receive is kept confidential from the employer. The main options open to the trustees are:

- to agree to the proposal or to suggest alternatives (e g a lower accrual rate going forward; moving to a career average design; asking the employees to agree to pay higher contributions);

- to bargain for better protection for member's accrued rights (e g retaining a link to final pensionable earnings at the date the member ceases to be an employee; buying out members' rights using deferred or immediate non-profit annuities); and

- to refuse agreement to the closure of the further accrual. Although this may prompt the employer to wind up the scheme immediately, it is also possible that the employer may not wish to do this since it would also immediately crystallise any debt to the employer under the *Occupational Pension Schemes (Deficiency on Winding Up etc.) Regulations 1996 (SI 1996/3128)* – see **19.10** and **19.11** below.

If, having taken independent legal advice, the trustees of the scheme are of the opinion that the employer is asking them to agree to a proposal that is in conflict with their duties under the trust deed and rules of the scheme or of statutory provisions, the trustees should consider going to the court for directions.

Employer ceases to trade

Independent trustee

19.7   Any insolvency practitioner (or the Official Receiver), who has been appointed because the employer is insolvent, must ensure that an independent trustee is appointed to the trustees of any defined benefit occupational pension scheme sponsored by that employer.

An independent trustee:

- can have no interest in the assets of the employer or of the scheme, other than as a trustee of the scheme;

- cannot be connected or associated with the employer or the insolvency practitioner (or the Official Receiver);

- cannot have provided services to the trustees or managers of the scheme, or the employer, in relation to the scheme within the previous three years;

- cannot be connected or associated with a person who has an interest in the assets of the employer or of the scheme, other than as a trustee of the scheme; and

- cannot be connected or associated with a person who, within the previous three years, has provided services to the trustees or managers of the scheme, or to the employer in relation to the scheme.

If the employer was sole trustee, the independent trustee replaces the employer as trustee.

In all cases, the independent trustee will have sole exercise of any discretionary powers given by the scheme's trust deed and rules. The insolvency practitioner must provide the trustees with any information that is reasonably requested.

Payment for the independent trustee's services must be met from the scheme's resources. *Section 25(6)* of the *Pensions Act 1995* stipulates that a trustee, who has been appointed as an independent trustee of a defined benefit scheme by an insolvency practitioner, is:

> 'entitled to be paid out of the scheme's resources his reasonable fees for acting in that capacity and any expenses reasonably incurred by him in doing so, and to be so paid in priority to all other claims falling to be met out of the scheme's resources'.

As signalled at **3.5**, there is increasing disquiet about the apparent lack of accountability in respect of the fees of independent trustees who are appointed to wind up the defined benefit scheme of an insolvent employer. As has been observed, an independent trustee in such circumstances can decide its fee, agree that it is reasonable and sign the cheque to draw the payment from the pension fund.

In 2003, after three years of negative returns, there is a high probability that a pension fund will have a large deficit on the discontinuance basis used to calculate members' benefits on a winding up (see **19.9** below). In many cases, a high proportion of scheme members will lose the bulk of their pension rights. The prospect of the fund being diminished even further by what inevitably to the ordinary members will seem exorbitant fees will cause great resentment.

What happens

19.8 Unless a new principal employer takes over in place of the former employer and is substituted in the trust deed and rules, the scheme will normally be wound up and all the scheme's assets, after meeting the expenses of winding up, are liquidated to buy annuities from insurance companies or to provide transfer values in respect of all its members. However, the trustees of very large schemes may continue to run the scheme with all its members as deferred pensioners or pensioners. Such a *closed scheme* would continue in operation until all its liabilities had been secured. The *Pensions Act 1995* gives trustees the power to defer winding up a defined benefit scheme in this way, even if the scheme's trust deed and rules state otherwise. Running on as a closed scheme can often be advantageous since the scheme assets do not have to be liquidated all at the same time. This is especially relevant where the pension scheme's asset values are severely depressed.

Winding up a pension scheme

19.9   An occupational pension scheme may be wound up due to a number of reasons, not all of them detrimental for the members concerned. A large employer with several schemes may wish to harmonise them into one scheme with superior benefits. A larger employer may have bought out a smaller employer and wish to move its members into its own scheme. However, in other cases, it may be that the employer may no longer choose to include an occupational pension scheme among the benefits offered to its employees or the employer may have become insolvent.

In all cases the trust deed and rules of a defined benefit scheme should specify how the scheme is to be wound up, the priority rule defining the relative importance of the benefits and the order in which the assets are to be used to purchase these benefits. However, since 6 April 1997 there is a new, overriding priority rule set by statute (see **19.11** below). If the trust deed and rules are deficient, Opra can make an order for the scheme to be wound up.

The actuary of a defined benefit scheme will have to make a special kind of valuation (a discontinuance valuation) which is based on the actual market value of the assets and the precise benefits due to each individual. The surplus or deficiency that arises on a discontinuance valuation is very different from the notional surplus or deficiency identified at a normal valuation. The surplus or deficiency that is identified at a discontinuance valuation is a measure of whether or not the pension fund has enough money to pay the members their accrued benefits.

On a winding up, the trustees will have to ensure that a comprehensive list of the scheme's beneficiaries is available. If any beneficiaries are accidentally omitted and receive no benefit (for example, some deferred pensioners), they will be able to pursue the trustees for breach of trust even after several years. Trustees are often advised to ensure that they take out indemnity insurance to protect them in such circumstances – see **CHAPTER 22**.

A scheme that is subject to a winding up will cease to be able to be contracted out. When a contracted-out scheme ceases to be contracted out, the trustees must make arrangements to secure all contracted-out rights that have been accrued by members of the scheme. Detailed guidance is given in the National Insurance Contributions Office manual CA15.

The responsibility for paying the benefits can either be:

- transferred to another scheme (as in the case of a harmonisation or absorption into another employer's scheme after a takeover); or

- bought out by purchasing annuities from an insurance company;

or alternatively individual members and deferred pensioners may take transfer values to another pension arrangement.

Trustees during this entire process will need to take advice to ensure that the interests of the beneficiaries are safeguarded. If for some reason there are no remaining trustees to carry out the winding up, Opra has the power to appoint an independent trustee.

Deficiency in the scheme

19.10   In recent years, the attention of the trustees of many defined benefit schemes has not so much been directed to any problems associated with a large fund surplus: on the contrary, the serious problem being addressed by many trustees is the revelation of a scheme deficiency. A scheme deficiency will not result in a disaster for the membership if there is an employer who is ready and able to fund the scheme so that the deficiency is removed over time. However, if this is not the case, the mettle of the trustees is likely to be severely tested. It is not going to be an easy time.

When a scheme is wound up, the value of the scheme's liabilities and assets must be calculated for the purposes of the discontinuance valuation in a manner approved by the trustees' actuary. The calculation will be carried out in line with two professional guidance notes (GN19 and GN27), and most importantly in line with *section 74* of the *Pensions Act 1995*, the *Occupational Pension Schemes (Minimum Funding Requirement and Actuarial Valuations) Regulations 1996 (SI 1996/1536)* and the *Occupational Pension Schemes (Deficiency on Winding Up etc.) Regulations 1996 (SI 1996/3128)*.

New priority order from 6 April 1997

19.11   *Section 73* of the *Pensions Act 1995* sets out how, when a scheme begins to wind up from 6 April 1997, the assets of any pension scheme subject to the minimum funding requirement (MFR) (see **13.8**) must be used towards meeting its liabilities. The measure overrides whatever scheme rules may state to the contrary.

After meeting any external liabilities such as winding-up expenses and debts, the trustees must use the assets to satisfy liabilities in the following priority order:

(1)   benefits secured by members' AVCs;

(2)   pensions in payment (including contingent payments to survivors) but not future increases to pensions in payment;

(3)   any liability for accrued rights to GMPs excluding increases (but only where winding up starts before 6 April 2007);

(4)   future pension increases on pensions in payment;

(5)   future increases on GMPs;

(6)   accrued pension rights and repayments of contributions.

After April 2007 the priority order is due to change to the following:

(1)   benefits secured by members' AVCs;

(2)   pensions in payment (including contingent payments to survivors) but not future increases to pensions in payment;

(3)   accrued pension rights and repayments of contributions;

(4)   future pension increases on pensions in payment and accrued benefits.

All the liabilities must be calculated in the same way as for the purposes of the MFR so that a scheme that was 100% funded on the MFR basis will, on winding up, attribute to each member the actuarial value of his or her accrued rights, including their rights to indexation. If a scheme has satisfied the liabilities set out in the statutory priority order and there are assets remaining, the scheme rules will operate for the distribution of the remaining funds.

Section 73(5) of the *Pensions Act 1995* places the responsibility for applying the priority order firmly on the trustees, whatever the trust deed and rules might say to the contrary. Opra can remove and fine trustees who fail to take reasonable steps to comply.

The problem in practice is that even 100% funding on the MFR basis does not amount to an assurance of solvency. In practice, the cost of buying out the members' accrued rights and pensioners' entitlements by means of the purchase of deferred and immediate annuities from an insurance company is likely to cost more than the value of a fund valued at 100% on this basis (see **13.11**).

This fact, coupled to the effects of the statutory priority order, means that the value of the fund first goes towards meeting the costs of winding up, then is used to buy out the entitlements of the existing pensioners. Having allotted the pension fund to meet these costs, the trustees often then find that there is too little remaining money to buy out the full accrued rights of the non-pensioner members (on a winding up the active members cease to build up further benefits and so automatically become deferred pensioners). There have been many instances where the trustees of a scheme that was 100% funded on the MFR basis can only meet a fraction of the cost of buying out the accrued rights of these members.

Furthermore, if the employer is insolvent, the fact that the trustees are not granted the status of being a preferential creditor means that the debt on the employer provisions may not in practice result in any new funds being obtained to meet the scheme's liabilities.

On the other hand, even if the employer is still trading and perfectly solvent, under the current requirements set out in the *Occupational Pension Schemes (Deficiency on Winding Up etc.) Regulations 1996 (SI 1996/3128)*, the trustees can only pursue the employer for any shortfall in the funding level of the scheme that is being wound up if that shortfall has been measured on the MFR basis. If the fund was at least 100% funded on the MFR basis, there is no statutory debt on the employer that the trustees can enforce, even if in practice the deferred pensioners are receiving only a fraction of their accrued rights. This ability of solvent employers 'to walk away' and ignore the plight of their pension scheme members after having put the scheme voluntarily into wind up has understandably caused a good deal of anger – and not just from trade unionists and others representing the interests of the membership!

In September 2001, the Department for Work and Pensions (DWP) proposed interim changes to the Deficiency on Winding Up Regulations, prior to the eventual replacement of the MFR (see **13.12**) to improve the situation for members in such cases of 'voluntary wind up'. The DWP proposed to strengthen the debt on the employer as in the first two elements above, while continuing to calculate transfer values for non-pensioner members on the MFR basis. On 19 March 2002, the appropriate amendments were made broadly as proposed, therefore the method of calculating the debt on a sponsoring employer who decides to wind the scheme up now must include:

(*a*)   the actual costs of winding up the scheme;

(*b*)   the actual costs of annuities for pensioner members; and

(*c*)   minimum 'cash-equivalent' transfer values on the MFR basis for non-pensioner members.

The change has improved the situation but, in the case of the non-pensioner members, minimum cash equivalent transfer values rather than deferred annuities still in effect represent the conversion of a defined benefit 'promise' into a money purchase benefit.

One of the most difficult problems that trustees can encounter comes in the period prior to the scheme going into a wind up, where there is going to be a deficiency in the funds available. This is because anyone who successfully moves from being an active member or deferred pensioner to become a pensioner of the scheme before wind-up begins has changed his or her status from a lower to a higher priority in terms of having an earlier call on the available funds. It is a sad comment that those who succeed in so doing are usually senior employees or executives of the company who have prior knowledge of the decision to wind up the scheme.

Trustees must observe the rules of the scheme, but in using their discretionary powers to grant early retirement pensions they should take wider issues into consideration. Are some senior managers and directors who have knowledge of the likely impending insolvency of the employer trying to secure their own accrued pension rights at the expense of others? It should be noted that where a scheme has begun to be wound up, transferred values that have been requested but not yet paid can be reduced or not paid in order to comply with the winding-up requirements set by *s 73* of the *Pensions Act 1995* and the Deficiency on Winding Up Regulations.

The short answer to all these problems is that trustees of an on-going defined benefit scheme should do everything in their power to avoid scheme deficiencies arising, not so much as required under the MFR but more importantly under the long-term basis using the methodology and assumptions of the scheme actuary. Yet this in itself does not mean that the scheme could meet all its liabilities should it be discontinued. Ideally, the trustees might want to improve the funding position beyond any statutory minimum so that, were the scheme to be discontinued, the fund would still be able to meet the cost of all the members' accrued rights. Such a policy, however, may not be readily attainable.

In September 2001, in its consultation paper setting out its interim proposals to modify the MFR, the Government explained that it had considered, but rejected, the call to impose a debt on the employer in scheme wind-ups of the full amount needed to buy out (through annuities and guaranteed deferred annuities) the pension liabilities for all members. The Government stated:

'While the Government is keen to strengthen protection for members when their schemes wind up, moving to such a stringent requirement would lead to high and uncertain costs hanging over ongoing schemes. This could be unsustainable for many UK companies and could have damaging consequences, including scheme closures in some cases. This would be in no-one's interests. It should also be realised that guaranteed deferred annuities are not necessarily the most appropriate vehicle for younger scheme members, who might do better over the long period before retirement by investing the value of their existing pension rights in a stakeholder pension or other arrangements. Finally, the very large size of some schemes is such that movement to an annuity buy-out basis for wind-ups might simply be impractical: there are doubts as to whether the insurance industry could deal with what might be required. Under current conditions and based on the estimated number of schemes which would normally wind-up each year, based on past experience, the cost of moving to a full annuity buy-out basis could amount to around £1 billion a year, as against a broad estimate of £100 million a year under the current rules (both figures net of Corporation Tax).'

The December 2002 technical paper issued with the pensions Green Paper, however, discusses the options for going further in cases where a still solvent employer winds up a pension scheme. One such option would be to ensure that the employer is prepared to provide sufficient additional funds to the scheme so that all scheme members can be bought either immediate or deferred non-profit annuities which could guarantee their full pension. Another option would be to require the employer to provide sufficient additional funds to provide full protection for pensioners and those nearing retirement while younger non-pensioners would receive, as now, fair value transfer values. The paper nevertheless states that the Government will be guided by: 'the aim of not increasing the overall burden on employers providing pensions'.

19.12   *Special situations*

New ways of discharging liabilities

19.12   The *Pensions Act 1995* also provides trustees with more flexibility as to how, since 6 April 1997, they can discharge pension liabilities on a scheme winding up.

Most trust deeds and rules formerly only gave the trustees the option of discharging liabilities by buying annuities from an insurance company, and once a winding up had started any requests from individual scheme members for a transfer value were usually frozen.

Such rules have become more difficult to observe in recent years because annuities bought from insurance companies have become much more expensive than the minimum transfer value that would be payable to active members and deferred pensioners. As discussed above, this is why so often schemes that have been solvent on an on-going basis have been found to be insolvent on a winding up.

The *Pensions Act 1995* overrides what the trust deed and rules might say to the contrary and gives trustees the opportunity of offering active members and deferred pensioners transfer payments rather than buying them out with annuities.

Under the *Occupational Pension Schemes (Winding Up) Regulations 1996 (SI 1996/3126)* the trustees are granted a statutory discharge of their liability to pay benefits provided they comply with the statutory requirement by providing each member and beneficiary of the scheme with a discharge notice. Each discharge notice must specify the sum available to be used to discharge the liability of the scheme to the member or beneficiary. If there is a shortfall between the amount available and the full amount of the liability, the notice must specify the amount of the shortfall and the reason for the difference. These amounts must be calculated using a modified form of the method used to calculate the minimum funding requirement (MFR) – see **13.8**.

The discharge notice must also specify the way or ways in which the trustees propose to discharge the liability and indicate whether or not the consent of the member or beneficiary is needed. If each member's or beneficiary's consent is required, the discharge notice given to each member or beneficiary must also inform the member:

- how long the member has to consider the available options (the period must not be less than three months from the date the notice is given);

- that it would be advisable for the member to obtain independent financial advice before proceeding; and

- how the trustees will proceed if the member chooses not to give the required consent.

In all cases the discharge notice must give the details of any relevant insurance company or occupational pension scheme through whom the trustees propose to discharge their liability.

If the member or beneficiary is offered options, the discharge notice must specify what these options are and inform the member or beneficiary that he or she must give the trustees a written notice to that effect specifying the way or ways in which the liability is to be discharged and the name of the relevant provider to be used. This written notice must be received by the trustees within three months from the date the member or beneficiary received the discharge notice. The discharge notice should tell the member or beneficiary that it would be advisable to seek independent financial advice before deciding what alternative option to request.

However, since the coming into force of the *Pensions Act 1995*, it is still the case that trustees normally discharge their liabilities by selling the assets of the scheme in order to buy immediate and deferred non-profit annuities from an insurance company.

It is possible that once the liabilities have been discharged, there will be some excess assets remaining in the scheme fund. In some cases these excess assets can be paid by the trustees to the employer (or, if the employer is insolvent, to the insolvency practitioner). However, before this can be done the trustees must ensure that:

- all pension rights under the scheme will increase in payment at a minimum in line with the Limited Price Indexation formula (annual rise in the retail prices index or 5% if lower); and

- they have either exercised any discretionary power given to them under the trust deed and rules to distribute some or all of the excess assets to the members, or have decided not to exercise that power.

A payment of excess assets on wind up can normally only be made to the employer/insolvency practitioner if the trust deed and rules confer such a power on the trustees. If the trust deed and rules do not confer this power, a modification order would have to be obtained from Opra.

As with a payment to the employer made from a surplus in an on-going scheme, a payment out of excess assets on a winding up can only be made to the employer/insolvency practitioner if a two-stage consultation exercise is first carried out with the membership. On a winding up this consultation exercise can be carried out either by the trustees or the employer. The members have the right to make written representations and to appeal to Opra if they feel that the statutory requirements have not been met.

In exceptional circumstances where the trust deed prohibits the distribution of any excess assets to the employer/insolvency practitioner, it is possible, nevertheless, to make such a payment provided all the members' benefits have first been increased up to the Inland Revenue maxima. This avoids a situation of *bona vacantia* whereby excess assets remaining in a trust that has been wound up fall to the Crown in default.

The *Child Support, Pensions and Social Security Act 2000* has introduced a package of new measures with the aim of speeding up the process of winding up pension schemes. At present, it is not unusual to find that schemes can take ten or more years to wind up in cases where the employer has become insolvent. This is not a satisfactory state of affairs. The new measures are based on the twin concepts of introducing greater accountability and giving Opra a more active role in monitoring the winding-up process, with the power to issue directions.

The carrying out of the winding up of a scheme falls on the trustees, but this can raise difficulties when all the trustees have been employees of a now insolvent employer. If the scheme is of the defined benefit type, the insolvency practitioner has to appoint an independent trustee (see **19.7** above) but this does not apply to defined contribution schemes. Particular difficulties therefore arise in defined contribution schemes if the employer has been the sole trustee. One of the principle aims of the new measures is, therefore, to ensure that Opra is kept informed so that it can take action to appoint a trustee if necessary.

Once the winding up is underway, Opra will need to be kept informed of what progress is being made if winding up has not been completed within the first three years. Opra's powers are being extended so that the regulator will, if necessary, be able to direct that the trustees or scheme administration take specific action to further the winding-up process.

Latest developments

19.13   The technical paper accompanying the December 2002 Pensions Green Paper sets out a number of possible measures that the Government may be able to introduce to increase the protection afforded to members when their scheme is left with insufficient assets on winding up.

The Government wishes to retain a priority order within legislation but proposes possible changes to the existing priority order so that either the priority given to people who are approaching retirement age could be increased, or the priority could depend on the number of years the individual has contributed to the scheme, irrespective of age.

The paper invites views on options to achieve a fairer sharing of assets between those with larger and smaller pensions after making adjustments to take account of each individual's scheme membership, for example through a capping mechanism for early retirees. If there were insufficient assets to meet all liabilities, pensions of early retirees, for instance, could be fully protected up to a certain level, but amounts above this cap would be returned to the pension fund to be shared out among the non-pensioner members who might otherwise see their pensions reduced. Such a system might not be limited to early retirees but could be applied to all existing pensioners at the time of the wind up so that, for example, only the first £30,000 of any pension in payment would be safeguarded and any excess would only continue to be paid once the full accrued rights of the non-pensioner members had been secured.

It is also suggested that a new category of creditor could be created, so that pension schemes could be given a higher priority than other unsecured creditors but still have lower priority than preferential and secured creditors. The Government argues that this would reduce the potentially adverse economic effects on members but at the expense of other unsecured creditors.

The Government is interested in considering the establishment of a centralised 'clearing house' fund into which members could choose to pay the funds that they receive on wind up. This central fund could then negotiate the purchase of deferred annuities with providers. As the paper comments:

> 'Members facing wind-up might expect to get a better deal because it would become more attractive to provide deferred annuities: administrative costs would be more widely shared and risk would be more widely pooled. In addition, trustees' negotiating position would be strengthened by their coming together in a single fund.'

Alternatively, an insurance scheme or a central discontinuance fund could be introduced to provide pensioners and non-pensioners with greater protection if their scheme wound up on the insolvency of the employer. Different models would offer differing degrees of benefit replacement and guarantee. This additional protection could be funded, suggests the technical paper, by a reduction in pension benefits or increased contribution rates. It is clear that it is not the Government's policy that any such pooled discontinuance fund would enjoy any government guarantee of last resort. The paper adds: 'The cost would need to be balanced against the greater overall level of security offered.'

Checklist 19

- Surpluses only ordinarily arise in defined benefit schemes and, in an on-going scheme, are simply any positive balance of the actuarial value of the scheme's assets less the actuarial value of the scheme's liabilities.

- A modest surplus provides a cushion against adverse market conditions but a large surplus is not desirable from the employer's viewpoint since the assets might be better used to invest in the employer's business.

- The Inland Revenue requires surpluses to be reduced once they have reached a specified size.

- In the past surpluses have been reduced by payments from the fund to the employer, subject to a tax deduction, but this is becoming more difficult.

- Surpluses are usually reduced by a combination of benefit improvements and discretionary pension increases combined with an employer contribution holiday.

- Trustees must be vigilant in ensuring that, as a result of any bulk transfer of members into the scheme, the scheme receives a payment

---

that meets the extra pension liabilities taken on and that, on a bulk transfer out of the scheme, the departing members will have their reasonable expectations met but that the payment is not excessive.

- When new classes of active members are created in the same scheme following a scheme reconstruction, the scheme trustees must act equitably to all the classes of members, including the existing deferred pensioners and pensioners.

- Many final salary schemes are now closed to new members and sponsoring employers are seeking other ways to contain future costs including closing schemes to further accrual for existing members. Trustees should ensure that in such circumstances they obtain independent and confidential legal advice and should consider negotiating with the employer.

- If the employer ceases to trade because of insolvency, the insolvency practitioner will appoint, in the case of a defined benefit scheme, an independent trustee who will have sole power to exercise any discretionary powers contained in the trust deed and rules. The scheme, if very large, may run on as a closed scheme but most schemes will usually be wound up.

- Opra has the power to appoint an independent trustee if, for example, on a winding up there are no remaining trustees left in post.

- The *Pensions Act 1995* defines a new priority order for the payment of benefits in the case of schemes that wind up after 6 April 1997. Any deficit will be a debt on the employer but this is unlikely to help the membership if the discontinuance valuation reveals a deficit.

- The trustees will face severe difficulties if there is a funding deficiency and there is no solvent employer able to make up any funding shortfall upon a winding up: such difficulties can also arise even in the case of solvent employers.

Chapter 20

Resolution of individual disputes

Introduction

20.1   It is possible that from time to time the industrial relations life of a company will witness a collective dispute which has arisen simply because the occupational pension scheme is inevitably considered as an element of the employees' terms and conditions of employment. In such a case, the trustees should not normally be involved directly because the matter is part of the industrial relations life of the company as a whole. Resolution of any dispute may be the responsibility of a special pensions negotiating forum or other negotiating committee as discussed in CHAPTER 7.

In contrast, when a dispute arises not as part of the industrial relations of the employer, the trustees may well become involved. In an occupational pension scheme of any size, individual disputes are bound to occur – sadly, in some cases as a result of maladministration. In too many cases, the dispute arises over inaccurate data, a subject discussed at **11.4**. Yet many disputes arise because of poor communications. Poor communications frequently result in a mis-match between the realities of a member's pension entitlement and what he or she may have held as a genuine expectation. The communications issues addressed in CHAPTER 9 are, therefore, directly relevant in a consideration of disputes.

Ultimately, any dispute involving a member will usually involve the trustees because they are the party with overall responsibility, but more particularly because the legislation now gives them a specific role in resolving such disputes.

Internal dispute mechanisms

20.2   The *Pensions Act 1995* requires the trustees of an occupational pension scheme to establish a disputes resolution scheme that will deal with complaints from:

● the active, deferred and pensioner members of the scheme;

● a widow, widower or surviving dependant of a deceased member of the scheme;

● a prospective member of the scheme – that is anyone who under his or her contract of employment or the scheme rules:

  – is able voluntarily to become a member of the scheme; or

  – will become able voluntarily to join after the end of a waiting period; or

- will be admitted automatically to the scheme unless he or she chooses not to do so; or

- may be admitted to the scheme at the employer's invitation with the employer's consent;

• anyone who has been one of the above within the previous six months of making the complaint; and

• any person who claims to be in one of the above four categories, even if the scheme's administrators dispute that this is the case.

A complainant can ask a representative to pursue a complaint on his or her behalf.

First stage

20.3   Dispute resolution involves a two-stage process. The individual makes a complaint that is considered by, say, a pension administrator who must make a reply which should include an explanation for the decision, referring to any part of the scheme rules, trust deed, or legislation that has formed the basis for the decision. The reply should also refer to the complainant's right, if dissatisfied, to ask the trustees or managers of the scheme to consider the dispute. The reply should contain a reminder that the services of the Pensions Advisory Service (OPAS) (see **20.7**) are available to assist members and beneficiaries of the scheme in connection with any difficulty which remains unresolved. OPAS's address must be given.

The reply from the scheme should be sent within two months of the date of the application for a decision, except in exceptional circumstances. If a scheme is unable to reply within that time because, for example, they are seeking information that may take longer, they should send an interim reply explaining the reason for the delay and an expected date for a substantive reply.

Once the reply has been sent, the complainant has a right of appeal to the trustees. The complainant has a maximum of six months in which to exercise this right of appeal.

Second stage

20.4   Under the second-stage arrangements the trustees' response to the appeal should, again, contain an explanation for their own decision, referring to any part of the scheme rules, trust deed, or legislation that has formed the basis for the decision. If the trustees have exercised discretion in arriving at the decision under dispute it is not a requirement that they make the reasons for their decision public, although they may do so if they wish (see **18.5**). Trust law does not require trustees to give reasons since to do so could fetter their decisions in future. However, the decision of the trustees should refer to the relevant part of the scheme rules or trust deed that gives them the right to exercise their discretion in a given case.

The second-stage reply from the trustees should also contain information about the services of OPAS (see **20.7**) and the Pensions Ombudsman (see **20.8**), so that should the complainant remain dissatisfied with the explanations given, he or she may refer his complaint, ideally first to OPAS and then, if still unresolved, to the Pensions Ombudsman for consideration and possible investigation.

The reply from the trustees should be sent within two months from the receipt of the application from the complainant. If this is not possible, an interim reply must be sent within this time saying when the matter will be considered by the trustees. It will be open to a complainant to refer his or her complaint to OPAS or the Pensions Ombudsman if the handling of the complaint is unduly protracted.

Disputes which can be excluded

20.5   Certain disputes are excluded from the scope of an internal dispute procedure. These are disputes that have been accepted for investigation by an outside agency such as OPAS, the Pensions Ombudsman, an employment tribunal or the courts.

Proposals for reform

20.6   The technical paper accompanying the December 2002 pensions Green Paper explains that, while the concept of some form of complaints procedure had not been questioned during earlier consultations, views had been expressed that the current internal disputes resolution procedure was too restrictive, complicated and failed to allow the trustees to adapt the process set down by the legislation so that it was more manageable for their particular scheme. The Government was broadly in agreement with these criticisms and was considering replacing the current requirements with one of the approaches suggested by Alan Pickering in his July 2002 report. The framework would be such that:

- all schemes must have a published formal disputes procedure, but the trustees can choose whether it is formed of one or two stages;

- complainants must have access to the trustees as part of that process;

- there is a prescribed time limit for the decision in the case to be reached (six months is suggested), and if no decision is given within that time the complainant can take the matter to the Pensions Ombudsman; and

- the complainant must be told that OPAS can help when the complaint is received, and about the role of the Pensions Ombudsman if the scheme's disputes procedure cannot settle the dispute.

The Pensions Advisory Service (OPAS)

20.7   If the internal dispute resolution mechanism fails to satisfy the individual who has made the complaint or if the individual has difficulties in making his complaint via the internal dispute mechanism, he or she can approach the Pensions Advisory Service (OPAS). OPAS maintains a network of volunteers, who are experts in the field of occupational pensions, who can take up most problems directly with the scheme administrators or trustees on behalf of any beneficiary of that scheme. OPAS has traditionally worked in close liaison with the Citizen's Advice Bureaux. Formerly supported by voluntary donations, OPAS now receives a government grant.

In general, OPAS works by a process of negotiation and conciliation, relying very much on good will. It cannot undertake formal arbitration services nor can it initiate legal action.

OPAS offers its services free of charge.

Local OPAS volunteers can be approached via the local Citizens' Advice Bureaux or the London headquarters:

> OPAS
> 11 Belgrave Road
> London
> SW1V 1RB
> Pensions helpline: 0845 6012923
> General office tel: 020 7630 2250
> Fax: 020 7233 8016
> email: enquiries@opas.org.uk
> Website: http://www.opas.org.uk

Under the *Occupational Pension Schemes (Disclosure of Information) Regulations 1996 (SI 1996/1655)*, trustees must notify members of the role and the address of OPAS. This may usually be included in the Pension Handbook.

In its latest report, OPAS reported that the problems brought to it by members of occupational pension schemes were broken down as follows:

Type of enquiry	2001/02 percentage
Entitlement and membership conditions	21%
Leaving service benefits and transfers	15%
Ill-health and early retirement	14%
Tracing	10%
Sex equality/part-timers	8%
Winding-up, merger and use of surplus	8%
Delays and non-response	6%
AVCs	5%
Other	13%

One area where there has been an increase in complaints received is that of incorrect early retirement quotations. OPAS has commented that all too often serious mistakes occur in the calculation of benefits on which members are expected to base fundamental, financial decisions. Yet trustees and administrators sometimes seek to avoid the consequences of this mis-information by hiding behind the fact that when the quotation was given it was described as being an estimate. OPAS takes the view that the word 'estimate' cannot be used to excuse a mistake that results in figures significantly lower than those first given.

Pensions Ombudsman

20.8   If OPAS is unable to resolve a difficult dispute to its own satisfaction and feels that the complainant has a good case, it may, with the individual complainant's consent, pass the case to the Pensions Ombudsman. Similarly, if the individual is dissatisfied with the action taken by OPAS, he or she can direct the complaint to the Pensions Ombudsman. (A complainant has a right to approach the Pensions Ombudsman directly, bypassing OPAS, once he or she had tried the internal disputes resolution procedure. The Pensions Ombudsman and OPAS, however, both prefer the complainant to try OPAS first.) The Pensions Ombudsman may be contacted as follows:

> The Pensions Ombudsman
> 11 Belgrave Road
> London
> SW1V 1RB
> Tel: 020 7834 9144
> Fax: 020 7821 0065
> email: enquiries@pensions-ombudsman.org.uk
> Website: http://www.pensions-ombudsman.org.uk

Jurisdiction

20.9   The Pensions Ombudsman can investigate:

- complaints made by, or on behalf of, actual or potential beneficiaries of an occupational or personal pension scheme who allege that they have 'sustained injustice in consequence of maladministration in connection with any act or omission of a person responsible for the management of the scheme';

- complaints made by, or on behalf of, a person responsible for the management of an occupational pension scheme who 'in connection with any act or omission of another person responsible for the management of the scheme' alleges maladministration of the scheme;

- complaints made by, or on behalf of, the trustees or managers of an occupational pension scheme who 'in connection with any act or omission of any trustee or manager of another such scheme' allege mal-administration of the other scheme;

- disputes of fact or law that arise in relation to an occupational or personal pension scheme between a person responsible for the management of the scheme and an actual or potential beneficiary who is a party to the dispute and which has been referred to the Pensions Ombudsman by, or on behalf of, that actual or potential beneficiary; and

- disputes of fact or law that arise between the trustees or managers of an occupational pension scheme and another person responsible for the management of the scheme or any trustee or manager of another occupational pension scheme and which has been referred to the Pensions Ombudsman by any of the parties to the dispute.

In the above, the term 'managers of the scheme' is defined as the trustees or managers themselves and the employer. Under separate regulations (the *Personal and Occupational Pension Schemes (Pensions Ombudsman) Regulations 1996 (SI 1996/2475)*) the Pensions Ombudsman is also given jurisdiction to investigate and determine complaints made against the scheme 'administrator'. Here 'administrator' means generally any person concerned with the administration of the scheme other than a manager of the scheme and so can cover the scheme actuaries and other advisors.

In the case of *R (on the application of Britannic Asset Management Ltd) v Pensions Ombudsman [2002] EWCA Civ 1405, [2002] 4 All ER 860, [2002] PLR 527*, the Court of Appeal held that, although *section 146(4)* of the *Pension Schemes Act 1993* gave power to Parliament to pass regulations that would give the Ombudsman jurisdiction to issue determinations affecting those 'concerned with the financing or administration of, or the provision of benefits under, the scheme', in the event the regulations mentioned above did so only in relation to 'those concerned with the administration of the scheme' and that, as a consequence, the Pensions Ombudsman does not have jurisdiction over 'those concerned with the financing of a scheme' nor with 'the provision of benefits under the scheme' unless they are also concerned with the administration of the scheme.

Following the Court of Appeal's judgment, the Pensions Ombudsman stated that:

> 'The people who need the law's protection are not those in charge of the funds but those from whom money has allegedly been filched. A legal system which concentrates on preventing alleged maladministration from being called to account is failing the people.'

The term 'actual or potential' beneficiaries refers to:

- a member of the scheme, i e someone who is or has been an active member of the scheme;

- the widow, widower, or any surviving dependant of a deceased member of the scheme;

- from 1 December 2000, a person entitled to a pension credit as against the trustees under the pension sharing on divorce provisions;

- a person claiming to be a member or the widow, widower or surviving dependant of the member; and

–   a person who is or has been entitled to the payment of benefits under the scheme.

Following the enactment of the *Child Support, Pensions and Social Security Act 2000*, the Pensions Ombudsman may now under the changes made by *s 53* of that Act also deal with:

- complaints made by, or on behalf of, an independent trustee who alleges maladministration of the scheme in connection with an act or omission committed by the other trustees or former trustees of the scheme (but not by another independent trustee);

- any dispute between different trustees of the same occupational pension scheme provided that the dispute has been referred to the Pensions Ombudsman by at least half of the trustees to the scheme. (This includes any dispute in schemes where an independent trustee is to be appointed because of the insolvency of the employer and which arises between an independent trustee of the scheme and the other trustees or former trustees, but not with another independent trustee, and which has been referred to the Pensions Ombudsman by, or on behalf of, the independent trustee who is party to the dispute);

- any question relating, in the case of an occupational pension scheme with a sole trustee, to the carrying out of the functions of that trustee and which has been referred to the Pensions Ombudsman by, or on behalf of, the sole trustee.

The second point listed immediately above is important because it allows the trustees to ask the Pensions Ombudsman to clarify for their benefit any scheme rule that is unclear. This may be attractive as a cheaper option for the pension fund than taking the matter to the courts.

Other extensions of the Pensions Ombudsman's jurisdiction include being able to accept complaints made against the employer in connection with personal pension schemes (including therefore stakeholder pension schemes legally established as personal pensions).

Since the regulations governing internal dispute resolution came into force, the Pensions Ombudsman regulations have been amended to exclude from his jurisdiction cases that have not been subject to the internal dispute resolution procedures, although the Ombudsman has the discretion to take on such cases where it seems reasonable to him that he should do so – for example when it seems there is no real prospect of the trustees issuing a response to the claimant. The Pensions Ombudsman has discretion to accept a case if he is satisfied that a complaint has been made to the scheme and the trustees have replied even if the internal dispute resolution procedure was not correctly followed.

The Pensions Ombudsman cannot act in a case where court proceedings have already started or when a court has already given a final decision. However, an amendment made by the *Child Support, Pensions and Social Security Act 2000* allows the Pensions Ombudsman to accept a case if it has been previously referred to a court or employment tribunal but has subsequently been discontinued other than on the basis of a binding settlement. On the other hand if, after the Pensions Ombudsman has already taken up a case, one of the parties to the dispute starts legal action in a court, then any party to the legal proceedings can apply to the court to have those legal proceedings halted. The court will usually agree to halt the proceedings if the matter is seen to fall within the scope of the Pensions Ombudsman.

In normal circumstances, there is a three-year time limit for making a complaint or referring the dispute. The period runs from the date of the act, or failure to act, that gave rise to the dispute or from the date the complainant first learned of the problem.

Procedure

20.10   Legislation prevents unnecessary overlap between the remits of Opra and the Pensions Ombudsman. Broadly, the role of Opra is one of *enforcement* and that of the Pensions Ombudsman is *adjudication*.

If the Pensions Ombudsman feels there is prima facie evidence of maladministration (see also **11.4**), the Pensions Ombudsman will write to the trustees, managers, scheme administrators (such as an insurance company) or employers and ask for their observations. This in itself may prompt a settlement of the dispute, or the Ombudsman may decide that the complainant does not have a case. Further correspondence may follow and the Pensions Ombudsman has extensive powers to insist on the production of relevant documents or relevant information. An oral hearing may be set up. At the end of the process the Pensions Ombudsman gives a determination, with reasons and in writing, to the complainant and to the trustees/managers/administrators/employers.

Directions

20.11   Where the Pensions Ombudsman finds that a party has been guilty of maladministration, he can issue a direction to remedy the effect of that maladministration. The remedy will be to put the complainant in the position he or she would have been in if the maladministration had not occurred. So, if a benefit was promised that was too high, there may be maladministration, but the Pensions Ombudsman will not uphold the incorrect benefits promise. Restitution can be made, however, if there was injustice resulting in financial loss, for example, if the complainant can show that he or she relied on an incorrect benefit promise of too high a benefit to enter into financial commitments. Similarly, the maladministration may have given rise to an overpayment which the trustees are bound to try and recover. Since the overpayment resulted from a mistake, there is no general provision in law that allows the beneficiary to retain the overpayment. However, if the beneficiary can show that the overpayment has been spent as a result of a financial transaction that he or she would not otherwise have entered into then the Pensions Ombudsman may issue directions to prevent any injustice resulting from the original maladministration. The Pensions Ombudsman can also direct that sums of up to £1,000 can be paid to a complainant as compensation for distress and disappointment suffered in consequence of maladministration.

Under the *Occupational Pension Schemes (Disclosure of Information) Regulations 1996 (SI 1996/1655)*, trustees must notify members of the function and the address of the Pensions Ombudsman.

Appeals

20.12   The Pensions Ombudsman can make a direction which is enforceable by a court. The decision is final and binding. The only recourse from a determination of the Pensions Ombudsman is an appeal to the High Court, or in Scotland to the Court of Session, purely on a point of law.

Despite this restriction, many trustees and employers have appealed to the courts against a determination issued by the Pensions Ombudsman after he has upheld a complaint or dispute brought by a scheme member. In many cases the court has accepted that the appeal is truly on a point of law rather than a finding of fact and has gone on to reverse the Ombudsman's determination.

The appeal procedure, however, raises a difficult problem. The Pensions Ombudsman is a law tribunal available at no cost to the complainant. Yet in the case of an appeal from a determination of the Pensions Ombudsman, the losing party at the High Court, if represented, has to meet the costs of the winning party. In practice, therefore, if a complainant succeeds with the Pensions Ombudsman but the trustees/employer appeal to the High Court, the complainant faces a serious financial risk of having to meet the costs if he or she is represented in the Court to oppose the appeal. The net result is that the individual complainant is likely to choose not be represented in the appeal.

In the early 1990s, the practice developed with the first Pensions Ombudsman of offering to appear in an appeal if the court felt that this would be of assistance. The second Pensions Ombudsman originally found this approach odd since elsewhere in the judicial system it does not happen that a lower tribunal appears to assist a court to make a judgment on appeal. Instead, the practice developed of the Pensions Ombudsman writing a letter to the judge setting out the arguments. However, criticism from judges in the High Court led the second Ombudsman to revert to the earlier practice of being represented in the appeal. If the appeal reversed the earlier determination, the Ombudsman at first had to bear the cost of both parties. This was later held not to be correct because if the Ombudsman had not been represented, no costs would have been recoverable from him and the appellant would still have been faced with the costs of the action. It was therefore decided that if the appeal was successful in the High Court, the Pensions Ombudsman would have to bear the cost only of the additional expenditure incurred by the successful appellant resulting from the Pensions Ombudsman's being represented. Later, however, this practice was again reversed and the full cost once again fell on the Ombudsman's office. The third Pensions Ombudsman has now decided that he will not be represented on appeals unless they raise a question of the legal jurisdiction of the Pensions Ombudsman.

The overall result is that if the trustees/employer appeal against a determination issued by the Pensions Ombudsman, it is quite probable that they will be the only party heard by the judge in the High Court. Such a situation is rather unsatisfactory.

The Edge case

20.13   In July 1999, in the case of *Edge v Pensions Ombudsman [1999] 4 All ER 546, [1999] OPLR 179*, the Court of Appeal ruled that the Pensions Ombudsman could not carry out any investigation where no effective remedy could be given, because any directions issued by the Pensions Ombudsman would be unenforceable because they would also necessarily affect the interests of those who had not been represented during the investigation. In short, it seemed that the Court of Appeal had seriously curtailed the role of the Pensions Ombudsman. Suppose, for example, a death benefit had been paid to one person by the trustees and not to another. Would the Court of Appeal's judgment mean that the Pensions Ombudsman could not accept a complaint from the legal spouse as it would affect the interests of the person who had instead been granted the death benefit, since that person under the current rules could not be a party in the carrying out of the Pensions Ombudsman's determination? It would also seem to make any form of 'class action' impossible.

In what was a clear statement of support for the Office of the Pensions Ombudsman, and indeed for the Pensions Ombudsman himself, the then Government Minister of State with responsibility for pensions explained that measures would be introduced into the Child Support, Pensions and Social Security Bill, then before Parliament, to ensure that the Pensions Ombudsman could continue to carry out his role.

Essentially the new measures would have allowed the Pensions Ombudsman to join to a case under investigation those whose interests may be affected by the outcome of the case. The Pensions Ombudsman would therefore have been permitted to appoint a person to represent a group of members or potential members who had the same interest in the complaint or dispute. He would also have had the power to order that the costs of legal expenses in a particular case should be met from the pension fund. This new extension would not have applied to any cases that have not been referred to the Pensions Ombudsman before the date the measure brought in by *section 54* of the *Child Support, Pensions and Social Security Act 2000* had actually been brought into force. In December 2001 the Department for Work and Pensions circulated draft amending regulations which had to be made before the new measures could come into force. After a long period, on 18 March 2003, the Government announced that it would not be introducing the new regulations, and that *section 54* of the Act would not be brought into force. The Minister of State stated:

'We have considered very carefully the comments received as a result of consultation on the draft amendment rules. We are concerned that the changes made by *section 54* would not be as beneficial as originally envisaged and that they would also add a further layer of complexity to an area of legislation which needs to be simplified and not complicated further. This would not be in line with Government policy which is to simplify the rules governing disputes and complaints about personal and occupational pensions whenever possible. The principles underlying the changes are sound but we want to explore how they can be made to work as effectively as possible. We do not want to bring into effect legislation which is complex and moreover does not fully achieve what is needed. We will consider how best to resolve this in the light of the Pensions Green Paper and its key messages of simplification and protection.'

Inevitably, the Government's turn around will be seen by some as a victory for the judges in a long-running turf war they have waged against the office of the Pensions Ombudsman; for the lawyers, many of whom did not favour *class actions* being determined by the Pensions Ombudsman; and possibly also for trustees and employers on the ground that any weakening of the office of the Pensions Ombudsman strengthens their hand against members bringing a complaint.

It will be interesting to see how the Government can now achieve its aim of making the principles that *section 54* was drafted to address work in practice.

The courts and tribunals

20.14 A civil court case is usually a prohibitively expensive route for an individual member or beneficiary to follow in trying to resolve a dispute. However, in an extreme case the court has jurisdiction to grant an order that representative beneficiaries of a pension fund are entitled to pursue claims with their costs being met from the pension fund itself. This is only likely to occur in a group action. However, it is common to find pensions issues appearing as an employment law case in an employment tribunal, often in unfair dismissal cases where, for example, loss of future pension rights might need to be quantified. The High Court of Chancery is also regularly involved in hearing appeals on a point of law against a determination made by the Pensions Ombudsman.

Checklist 20

- Trustees must ensure that there is in place a two-tier internal disputes resolution procedure which gives the complainant a right of appeal to the trustees themselves.

- If the complainant is unhappy with the trustees' decision, he or she can call on OPAS to mediate in the dispute.

- If the complainant is dissatisfied with the result of mediation by OPAS, he or she can take the matter to the Pensions Ombudsman, or

---

OPAS may refer the case to the Pensions Ombudsman if it feels the trustees are being unreasonable. Trustees must comply with the determinations of the Pensions Ombudsman, with an appeal to the High Court being permissible only on a point of law.

- The issue of how costs are met in an appeal from a determination of the Pensions Ombudsman to the High Court may be thought to be rather unsatisfactory.

- Members can bring legal action through the courts or, in employment-related matters, an employment tribunal.

Chapter 21

Breaches of trust

Introduction

21.1   The trustees are collectively responsible for any breach of trust that might be committed. If a trustee believes that a breach of trust is being committed but fails to convince the majority of the trustees to take preventative action, he or she should seek professional advice.

Trustees owe a duty of care to each and every beneficiary of the occupational pension scheme. Any trustee who fails to carry out his or her *fiduciary* duty as set out under the trust deed and rules could be found by the courts or the Pensions Ombudsman to have committed a breach of trust. All the trustees are likely to be held individually and collectively liable for this breach. Even if a trustee was not directly responsible for a breach of trust, he or she could be sued. If it is found that the trustees have committed a breach of trust which results in a loss of scheme assets, they could be personally liable to restore the loss.

A breach of trust is also likely to be of material significance to the regulator, Opra. Under the *Pensions Act 1995* Opra has power to seek an injunction from the courts in order to prevent any misuse or misappropriation of the assets of an occupational pension scheme. Details of how to contact Opra are given at **10.4** above.

Trustees, therefore, bear an important level of responsibility. In practice, it is recognised that trustees who carry out their duties honestly and prudently should not be exposed to unlimited liability. In **CHAPTER 22** various forms of protection for trustees are examined. However, the protection will depend on the severity of the breach of trust committed.

One pragmatic form of protection for trustees against being taken to court for an alleged breach of trust is the sheer expense of mounting such an action. The cost is too prohibitive for all but the richest individuals. However, the Pensions Ombudsman could also rectify a breach of trust by issuing a determination that might also order that restitution should be made personally by the trustees themselves. The services of the Pensions Ombudsman are provided at no cost to the complainant. As an alternative, a trade union or other group using representative beneficiaries could help to bring an action for breach of trust through the courts and in some exceptional cases the court might agree that the cost of bringing the action could be met from the pension fund itself.

Breaches of trust can be categorised in various ways.

Unintentional and innocent

21.2   It is likely that many unintentional and innocent technical breaches of trust occur every day. A member may have taken voluntary retirement and the pension should have been reduced because it was going to be paid early. An administrative error occurred and the member received an unreduced pension, part of which was taken as a lump sum. The error comes to light a few years later. The trustees may feel it inappropriate to reduce the pensioner's income at that point and the lump sum is probably long spent. The error occurred in the pensions administration department but the trustees are responsible. The pension fund has suffered loss as a benefit was paid out but not in accordance with the trust deed and rules.

Negligent and culpable

21.3   In a negligent and culpable breach of trust the trustees will have acted carelessly but still in good faith. They may have used fund assets to buy a new computer system from a persuasive salesman from a small software house without commissioning a proper study and without taking independent advice. Once bought, the software package proves totally inadequate, and when the trustees seek compensation they find that the software house has gone into liquidation.

Culpable and fraudulent

21.4   In a culpable and fraudulent breach of trust one or more of the trustees will have attempted to misappropriate, or succeeded in misappropriating, the scheme's assets. This could include a case of a director who is also a trustee taking an unauthorised loan from the pension fund to stem a disastrous cash-flow problem in the company. There is *wilful misconduct*.

Breaches of statutory law

21.5   Trustees might also act in breach of some statutory requirement. Examples could include the *Equal Pay Act 1970*, the *Race Relations Act 1975*, the *Sex Discrimination Act 1975*, the *Pension Schemes Act 1993*, the *Pensions Act 1995*, the *Disability Discrimination Act 1995*, the *Data Protection Act 1998*, the *Welfare Reform and Pensions Act 1999* and the *Financial Services and Markets Act 2000*.

A summary of the penalties that can be imposed on trustees by Opra under the *Pensions Act 1995* and *Welfare Reform and Pensions Act 1999* is given in APPENDIX 1.

Under the Act Opra has the power:

- to apply to the courts for an injunction if it is likely that a trustee (or anyone else) is about to misappropriate scheme assets; and

- to apply to the courts for a restitution order if the trustees have wrongly exercised any power to make a payment to the employer or contravened the self-investment rules.

Checklist 21

- Trustees who commit a breach of trust that results in a loss of scheme assets can be personally liable to restore that loss.

- All the trustees could be found to be individually and collectively liable for a breach of trust committed by just one trustee.

- It is important that those undertaking the responsibility of acting as trustees should take their duties seriously and be satisfied that there are in place adequate measures to give them protection from the results of unintentional or negligent breaches of trust.

- Trustees may also face penalties if they are found to have acted in breach of a statutory requirement.

Chapter 22

Protection for trustees

Introduction

22.1   Any trustee who commits a *culpable and fraudulent* breach of trust may have to face prosecution for a criminal offence. The only protection, as such, is that the individual may qualify for legal aid.

Trustee Act 1925

22.2   In certain circumstances, trustees may be excused breaches of trust through *section 61* of the *Trustee Act 1925*. Three conditions set out in the Act have to be satisfied.

The trustees:

● must have acted honestly;

● must have acted reasonably; and

● 'ought fairly to be excused'.

It is probable therefore that trustees are protected in cases of *unintentional and innocent* breaches of trust. But if the trustees were *negligent and culpable* it is more difficult to see how they can be excused under this measure.

It is likely that the court would consider it important whether the trustees sought legal or other professional advice in relation to the action which led to the breach of trust. If the trustees were following legal advice, the court is likely to hold that they were acting reasonably.

Employment Rights Act 1996 and Pensions Act 1995

22.3   The *Employment Rights Act 1996* offers comfort to trustees (including directors of a corporate trustee) in as much as it:

● offers protection to employee trustees against unfair dismissal by the employer if the dismissal was related to the carrying out of their trustee duties (see **8.9**); and

● offers protection to employee trustees who are subjected to any detriment by their employer because of decisions they have taken as trustees – an example might be that an employee is deliberately passed over for promotion by the employer because he or she argued against a rule change favoured by the employer (see **8.9**).

The *Pensions Act 1995*, which introduced the above two measures before they were re-enacted in the *Employment Rights Act 1996*, also:

- offers protection to trustees who *blow the whistle* to Opra by preventing them from being sued for breach of confidence (see **10.4**); and

- makes clear that trustees are not normally responsible for any act or default of any properly appointed and authorised fund manager (see **16.6**).

Indemnity and exoneration clauses

22.4   The trust deed and rules should contain an indemnity clause which excuses trustees from liability arising from a breach of trust except in cases of *wilful negligence* or *wilful misconduct*. The trust deed and rules may specify that the indemnity is given by the pension fund or by the employer.

In short, the trustees' acknowledged liability for the loss brought about by the breach of trust is financially covered in such circumstances by the fund or the employer.

Instead of, or in addition to, an indemnity clause, the trust deed and rules may contain an exoneration clause. The trustees are simply exonerated from responsibility for any action or lack of action on their part which led to a financial loss for the pension fund – always provided that there was no *wilful negligence* or *wilful misconduct*.

The trustees would bear no personal liability to meet the amount of the shortfall.

If the fund simply meets the cost of the trustee's indemnity, no beneficiary is financially more secure as a result of the court's or Pensions Ombudsman's decision that a breach of trust has taken place. Provision that any shortfall in the fund will be met by the employer is either of very limited or no value at all if the employer has gone into liquidation.

The position is not so clear if some trustees were kept unaware of the wilful misconduct being carried out by others. All action or inaction by trustees is legally held to result from a unanimous decision. The innocent trustees might then have to bring a legal action against the guilty trustees: a course with particular difficulties if the other trustees have disappeared or are already bankrupt. A partial solution may be found with special types of indemnity insurance.

It must be said that the possible scope of the various forms of exoneration clause found in trust deeds is not always very clear. In some cases, the courts have held that a widely drawn clause could exonerate even deliberate breaches of trust. There is actually little legal authority for the idea that it is contrary to public policy to exclude liability for gross negligence by an appropriate exoneration clause clearly worded to have that effect. Lord Justice Millet of the Court of Appeal has acknowledged that there is now a widespread view that these clauses 'have gone too far'. In his opinion, if such clauses are to exclude exemption for wilful misconduct or gross negligence, this should be done by Parliament enacting new legislation. Certainly there is a strong feeling that such clauses should not be available to excuse a professional independent trustee in such cases.

The lead case in this area is that of *Armitage v Nurse [1998] Ch 241, [1997] PLR 51* where the Court of Appeal held that an exemption clause could exclude the trustee from liability for loss to the trust fund: 'no matter how indolent, imprudent, lacking in diligence, negligent or wilful he may have been, so long as he has not acted dishonestly'. As may be seen, the Court of Appeal held that even 'wilful' action by the trustee could be exempted by such a clause as long as the trustee was not actually fraudulent.

In December 2002, the Law Commission published a consultation paper, *Trustee Exemption Clauses (Consultation Paper 171)*. The paper examines the current law and practice relating to trustee exemption clauses, considers the economic implications of regulation of such clauses, sets out the options for reform and makes provisional proposals for change on which views were invited.

The tenor of the dilemma the Law Commission experienced in dealing with this issue is best summed up in the following two paragraphs taken from its consultation paper.

'The Law Commission does not believe that an absolute prohibition on all trustee exemption clauses is justifiable at present. One of the advantages of the trust is its flexibility and its adaptability to different factual circumstances and to different kinds of relationship. To deny settlors all power to modify or to restrict the extent of the obligations and liabilities of the trustee would have a very significant impact on the nature of the trust relationship. The trust would inevitably become more inflexible. We are particularly concerned that excessive regulation of trustee exemption clauses may deter lay trustees from assuming the responsibility of trusteeship in the first place.'

'At the same time, the Law Commission does believe that there is a very strong case for some regulation of trustee exemption clauses. Their increased use in recent years has without doubt reduced the protection afforded to beneficiaries in the event of breach of trust. While there is a need to maintain a balance between the respective interests of settlor, trustee and beneficiary, we believe that the current law is too deferential to trustees, in particular professional trustees who hold themselves out as having special knowledge skills and experience, charge for the services they provide and insure themselves against the risk of liability for breach of trust.'

In an interesting determination (J00273) issued in April 2000, the Pensions Ombudsman formulated a set of principles for guidance derived from a number of key court cases to determine whether the trustees' legal costs, where not met by the other party, can be met from the pension fund. He held that if there is an express indemnity clause allowing costs to be recovered from the fund even if there has been misconduct then those costs can be taken from the fund, provided that the trustees have not been guilty of wilful default. However, if there is an exoneration clause but no indemnity clause, any liability for legal costs is undertaken personally by the trustees and the exoneration clause cannot defeat that liability.

Liability and negligence insurance

22.5   Insurance companies have made negligence insurance available, which may be most important if any indemnity provision cannot be made because the employer has gone into liquidation. If negligence insurance is provided, it should be in the name of the trustees (even if the employer meets the cost of the premiums).

It is to be expected that any negligence insurance will exclude claims arising out of *wilful negligence* or *wilful misconduct*. Because the non-fraudulent trustee can suffer claims as a result of breaches of trust carried out by his or her fraudulent colleagues, some negligence insurance will now cover cases of fraud where trustees other than those who acted fraudulently have claims made on them. The insurance company will require extensive and precise details on the trustees and their advisers. The cost of such insurance is high, and generally relates to the size of the pension fund's assets.

Limitations on indemnity and exoneration clauses and liability and negligence insurance

22.6   *Section 33* of the *Pensions Act 1995* specifically provides that, with certain exceptions, liability for any breach of an obligation placed on trustees by law to take reasonable care, or exercise skill in the carrying out of their investment duties, cannot be excluded or restricted by any prior agreement such as an exoneration clause in a trust deed. *Section 33*, however, does not mean, according to the Department for Work and Pensions, that trustees need to be held personally liable. If there is an indemnity clause, the trustees can still have recourse to its protection, although under the terms of that clause cases of *wilful negligence* or *wilful misconduct* are likely to be excluded as explained above.

We noted in **CHAPTER 17** that in February 2002 the Government proposed to introduce a new standard of care involving a requirement for trustees to be familiar with the investment issues with which they are concerned. To ensure that this new standard of care is effective, the Government has proposed to extend the existing prohibition in *section 33* to cover all matters to which the new standard of care will apply.

More specifically, however, the trustees cannot be indemnified out of the scheme assets for any fines or penalties for offences for which they have been convicted or which have been imposed by Opra for breach of the requirements of the Act. Furthermore, the scheme assets cannot be used to pay insurance premiums for any liability insurance that would cover such fines or penalties. If trustees accept reimbursement out of the assets of the scheme to cover any fine or penalty, they are guilty of an offence and are liable on summary conviction to a fine and on conviction on indictment to imprisonment or a fine or both.

Employer reimbursement policies

22.7 Reimbursement policies are sometimes provided by insurance companies to cover the employer against costs arising out of a breach of trust committed by the trustees. They do not therefore offer protection to the trustees themselves but are a means for the employer to insure against additional costs stemming from the need to honour an indemnity clause or from simply having to pay higher contributions into the pension scheme.

Legal costs

22.8 Trustees might need to initiate court action in some circumstances, perhaps to clarify the nature of their powers to deal with a situation not envisaged in the trust deed and rules (although in some circumstances the Pensions Ombudsman may also be able to determine the issue – see **20.7** above). In other cases, the trustees may need to go to court to pursue litigation against another party, or indeed to defend the fund against hostile litigation. It is important that the trustees are not personally liable to meet the legal costs involved. Trustees are therefore able to approach the court for a preliminary ruling that their costs can be met from the pension fund before embarking on the litigation itself. This preliminary action is called a *Beddoe Judgment*.

Some lawyers now advise trustees to ensure that they are insured for any costs incurred in defending themselves in a criminal action. They argue that a trustee could be prosecuted for a criminal offence such as some kind of illegal share-dealing or tax evasion.

Liability of a corporate trustee

22.9 At **3.3** above, we discussed how it was very common for there to be a corporate trustee responsible for a pension scheme rather than a group of individual trustees. The corporate trustee will normally be set up as a limited company. If the members of a pension scheme run by a corporate trustee needed to sue their trustee for breach of trust they would be suing a limited company rather than individuals. In practice this is not likely to result in much recompense since the corporate trustee will usually have very few assets. The corporate trustee could then become insolvent. (Independent corporate trustees, if set up as a trust corporation, must in contrast have more significant assets.)

The directors of the corporate trustee (known generally as 'trustee directors') owe fiduciary duties to that company. However, in the case of *HR v JAPT*

[1997] OPLR 123, which was heard in the High Court in 1997, it was held that there is no direct fiduciary relationship between the directors of a corporate trustee and the beneficiaries of the pension scheme. The only fiduciary relationship to which the beneficiaries of the pension scheme could be a party would be with the corporate trustee company itself.

Generally speaking, the directors of a corporate trustee are not automatically liable for breaches of trust committed by the corporate trustee, even if the director or directors concerned were involved in the breach.

A court can impose liability upon a director of a company in cases where, on the evidence, the wrongdoer was the company, but only where the actions of that director involve an assumption of personal liability. Therefore, a director of a corporate trustee could be personally liable to the beneficiaries of the pension scheme if that director had taken a risk that was 'commercially unacceptable' because it might jeopardise the position of others.

Otherwise, in such cases involving a corporate trustee it may be possible for redress to be obtained by indirect means. For example, some members might sue the corporate trustee and on the basis of the judgment in that case succeed in having that corporate trustee wound up. The members could then require the liquidator of that company to sue the former directors so that anything that was recovered could then be distributed to them.

Protection after winding up

22.10   If the trustees complete a winding up of a pension scheme, it is sensible for them to obtain insurance cover to protect them from the possibility of future claims from scheme beneficiaries of whom they were unaware at the time of the winding up. Of course, there may have been a indemnity clause in the scheme's trust deed and rules, and in theory this may continue. However, if the indemnity was backed by the employer and the reason for the winding up was the employer's insolvency, this indemnity will now be of little value.

It is also possible that *s 61* of the *Trustee Act 1925* could be of help (see **22.2** above) but the trustees may not wish to rely on a court finding in their favour, especially if it can be shown that the failure to pay the correct benefits was due to maladministration or an act of negligence.

There are also statutory discharge provisions contained in *s 19* of the *Pension Schemes Act 1993* and *ss 74* and *81* of the *Pensions Act 1995*. For defined benefit schemes starting to wind up on or after 6 April 1997, *s 74* of the *Pensions Act 1995* is the most important of these provisions, but it does not protect trustees if scheme members or beneficiaries have in fact not received their correct benefit during the winding up.

All these considerations make continuing cover after the completion of the winding up by means of a suitable insurance contract an important issue for the trustees.

Checklist 22

- A court might excuse trustees who have committed a breach of trust if they have actually acted honestly and reasonably.

- The *Pensions Act 1995* offers protection to trustees against unfair dismissal or from being subjected to any detriment by the employer, from being sued for breach of confidence if they 'blow the whistle' and from being pursued for breach of trust because of losses caused by a properly appointed and authorised fund manager.

- The trust deed should contain adequate indemnity and/or exoneration clauses protecting the trustees except in cases of wilful misconduct.

- In certain circumstances the *Pensions Act 1995* removes the power of a trust deed to exclude or restrict the liability of trustees if they fail to take care or exercise skill in the carrying out of their investment duties.

- The trustees cannot be indemnified out of the pension fund for any fines or penalties that they have been ordered to pay by Opra, nor can the fund be used to meet insurance premiums that would cover such fines or penalties.

- Liability and negligence insurance is available, except where wilful misconduct has been demonstrated, to protect trustees who have been ordered to make restitution – such insurance may be operative where the employer is insolvent and not able to indemnify the trustees.

- Trustees who need to approach the court to decide a question or otherwise make a ruling may be granted by a preliminary ruling made by that court the right to have the legal costs met from the pension fund.

- The Pensions Ombudsman may also be able to help where there is dispute among the trustees.

- Trustees who complete a winding up of their schemes are advised to ensure that they remain protected against future claims from members or beneficiaries who failed to receive their due benefits.

Chapter 23

Compensation schemes

Introduction

23.1   In the past, if an occupational pension scheme defaulted, and its beneficiaries did not receive the pension entitlement which had already accrued to them (without considering the loss of any future expectations of pension benefits), some mechanisms existed to mitigate their loss. Yet for members of many schemes the compensation available might be absolutely minimal or completely non-existent. Following the Maxwell debacle, there were calls for a comprehensive compensation scheme. The Government responded via the *Pensions Act 1995* which established a Pensions Compensation Board (PCB) and Pensions Compensation Scheme.

Pensions Compensation Scheme

23.2   The Compensation Scheme came into effect on 6 April 1997 and is designed to protect the members of occupational pension schemes that are set up as trusts if:

- the sponsoring employer is insolvent;

- the value of the assets of the scheme has been reduced and there are reasonable grounds for believing that the reduction was caused by mis-appropriation, fraud or some other prescribed offence;

- the amount of the shortfall means that for defined benefit schemes the value of a scheme's assets is less than the specified *protection level*; and

- it is reasonable in all the circumstances for the Pensions Compensation Board (PCB) to assist the scheme members.

Originally compensation was limited to 90% of the value of the missing assets, or, if less, the amount required to restore, where appropriate, the scheme's assets to 90% of the minimum funding requirement (MFR) (see **13.8**).

The *Welfare Reform and Pensions Act 1999* changed the conditions that must be met for compensation to be made available and the maximum level of compensation that can be paid. Instead of having to fall below 90% of its total liabilities, a scheme is eligible for compensation if its assets fall below the 'protection level'. This protection level is the combined value of 100% of its most urgent liabilities and 90% of its other liabilities. The most urgent liabilities include those to its members already receiving a pension, and those to its members within ten years of retirement – a group already identified separately for the minimum funding requirement (MFR) valuation.

The technical paper issued by the DWP alongside the December 2002 pensions Green Paper explains that the Government is proposing to remove the existing restrictions so that, in future, schemes with an insolvent employer can be compensated for the full amount lost as a result of acts of dishonesty.

The Compensation Scheme is financed by a levy on occupational pension schemes and is run by the PCB which has power to borrow money, determine whether compensation is payable, make advance compensation payments to maintain pensions in payment and to authorise final payment of compensation. Payments can be fully or partially recovered if the PCB later decides that they were excessive.

In its March 2001 proposals for the replacement of the MFR with a long-term, scheme-specific funding standard (see **13.12**), the Government pointed out that there would need to be an extension of the Pensions Compensation Scheme. The level of compensation for fraud would have to be increased to cover not simply what are the MFR liabilities as at present, but also the cost of securing members' accrued benefits (or the amount of the loss from fraud, if less). As mentioned above, the December 2002 technical paper has now reiterated the Government's intention to the extend the cover provided by the Compensation Scheme.

If trustees need help from the Compensation Scheme, they should contact:

> Pensions Compensation Board
> 11 Belgrave Road
> London
> SW1V 1RB
> Tel: 020 7828 9794
> Fax: 020 7931 7239

Financial Services Compensation Scheme

23.3   Following the collapse of a UK insurance company, the Government of the day brought in the *Policyholders Protection Act 1975*. This guaranteed that all members and beneficiaries of an occupational pension scheme that was fully insured would receive at least 90% of their accrued pension benefit in the event of the insurance company becoming insolvent. There was no cash ceiling on the amount of compensation stipulated in the Act and the fund to cover such claims was financed by a levy on insurance companies. The security of the members and beneficiaries depended on the employer having paid over all the due contributions to the insurer, on the scheme trustees not undertaking any assignment or pledge on the insurance contract, and on the trustees ensuring that all payments out of the scheme were to genuine beneficiaries of that scheme.

This provision has now been revoked and replaced by the Financial Services Compensation Scheme.

In the case of the collapse of a financial services company regulated under the requirements of the *Financial Services Act 1986*, or its successor legislation, the *Financial Services and Markets Act 2000*, there has been only very limited compensation to mitigate any loss suffered by an occupational pension scheme which had invested scheme assets with the failed company. Under the rules of the former Investors Compensation Scheme (ICS), pension funds were classed as multiple investors and received the same compensation as a single individual investor. The scheme paid out 100% of the first £30,000 invested, and 90% of the next £20,000 invested. This gave a maximum £48,000 compensation. In the case of the failure of a Bank (such as BCCI) or a Building Society, compensation offered by the Deposit Protection Board was limited to 90% of the first £20,000, i e £18,000.

The recent reforms taking place in the world of financial services provided an opportunity to review the former compensation and default protection schemes covering those activities which now all fall under the scope of the Financial Services Authority (FSA).

As a result there is now a single compensation scheme – the Financial Services Compensation Scheme (FSCS). The FSCS is a company, independent of the FSA, whose function it is to administer arrangements for assessing and making compensation payments in accordance with rules made by the FSA. These arrangements apply where regulated firms are in liquidation or are otherwise unable to meet their obligations to consumers.

However, as a matter of policy, it was concluded that the FSCS should focus on those consumers who are least able to sustain financial loss. The new compensation limits follow closely those existing under the former schemes. They are as follows:

Asset type	Compensation calculation	Maximum
Deposits	100% of first £2,000 and 90% of up to £33,000 of any remaining loss	£31,700
Investments	100% of first £30,000 and 90% of up to £20,000 of any remaining loss	£48,000
Long-term insurance	At least 90% of the value of the policyholder's guaranteed fund at the date of default	No maximum

The situation for pension fund trustees is set out in the FSA's Compensation Sourcebook rules and can be summarised as follows:

(a)   If the claim is in respect of lost deposits, pension fund trustees *are unable* to claim compensation from the FSCS *unless* the claimant is a trustee of a small self-administered scheme, or the trustee of an occupational pension scheme of an employer that is neither a 'large company', nor a 'large partnership', nor a 'large mutual association'.

(*b*)   If the claim is in respect of designated investment business, pension fund trustees *are unable* to claim compensation from the FSCS *unless* the claimant is a trustee of a small self-administered scheme or the trustee of an occupational pension scheme of an employer that is neither a 'large company', nor a 'large partnership', nor a 'large mutual association'.

(*c*)   If the claim is in respect of a contract of long-term insurance arising from the failure of an insurance company or friendly society, pension scheme trustees *are able* to claim compensation from the FSCS.

Under the FSA's Compensation Sourcebook the following definitions are applied:

- A 'large company' is a *body corporate* that does *not* qualify as a 'small company' under *s 247* of the *Companies Act 1985*. Under *s 247* a company is regarded as a 'small company' essentially if it is a company that satisfies at least two of the following criteria:

  – it does not have more than 50 employees;

  – its turnover is not more than £2.8m;

  – its balance sheet total is not more than £1.4m.

- A 'large partnership' is a partnership or unincorporated association with net assets of more than £1.4m.

- A 'large mutual association' or unincorporated association is one with net assets of more than £1.4m.

Unpaid contributions

23.4   *Section 124* of the *Pension Schemes Act 1993* allows certain unpaid pension contributions to be paid into the occupational pension scheme by the Government in circumstances where the employer has become insolvent. The unpaid contributions can be employer contributions or employee contributions. The employee contributions must have actually been deducted from employees' pay. However, provided the contributions had actually been deducted from the employee's pay but not paid to the scheme, the Government could pay an equivalent amount to the scheme. As regards unpaid employer contributions, compensation paid by the Government is limited to the lower of the following:

- employer contributions due in respect of the twelve months before the employer became insolvent;

- an amount equal to 10% of the total paybill over the twelve months before the employer became insolvent;

- in the case of a defined benefit scheme, the amount certified by an actuary as necessary to meet the scheme's liability.

The schedules of contributions (defined benefit schemes) and payment schedules (defined contribution schemes) required by the *Pensions Act 1995* (see **8.3**) should ensure that non-payment of contributions is restricted to relatively short periods before an employer insolvency occurs.

Schemes contracted out before 6 April 1997

23.5   Prior to 6 April 1997 members of contracted-out schemes also built up rights, albeit reduced rights, in SERPS. In the event that a scheme, that retains liability for either pre-6 April 1997 contracted-out GMPs, or protected rights, is wound up and the scheme's resources have been so depleted that they are unable to secure the GMPs or protected rights perhaps by using insured, non-profit annuities , the DWP will treat the state scheme premiums as having been paid.

The relevant legislation is contained in *sub-paras (3A)* to *(3E)* of *para 5* of *Schedule 2* to the *Pension Schemes Act 1993* and *regulations 49* and *50* of the *Occupational Pension Schemes (Contracting-out) Regulations 1996 (SI 1996/1172)*.

In effect this means that any deduction from the individual's entitlement to SERPS which would have been made because that individual had been contracted out while a member of the scheme will not in the event actually be made. The SERPS pension payable is the same as if the individual had never been contracted out. With the abolition of future rights to GMPs on 6 April 1997, the compensation has only affected contracted-out rights built up from 1978 to 1997.

EU Insolvency Directive and the Francovich case

23.6   On 20 October 1980, the European Community adopted Council Directive (EEC) 80/987 which deals with the approximation of the laws of the European Community member states relating to the protection of employees in the event of the insolvency of their employer.

The preamble of the Directive states that it has been adopted because: ' … it is necessary to provide for the protection of employees in the event of the insolvency of their employer, in particular to guarantee payment of outstanding claims … '

Article 8 of the Directive says:

'Member states shall ensure that the necessary measures are taken to protect the interests of employees and of persons having already left the employer's undertaking or business at the date of the onset of the employer's insolvency in respect of rights conferring on them immediate or prospective entitlement to old-age benefits, including survivors' benefits, under supplementary company or inter-company pension schemes outside the national statutory social security schemes.'

The Directive is binding on all member states who were required to bring in national legislation to enforce the Directive within 36 months of its notification (i e by October 1983).

303

23.6   *Compensation schemes*

In 1992, the European Court of Justice decided the case of *Francovich v Italy [1992] ECR I–5357, [1992] IRLR 84*. Italy was judged to have failed to implement the Employer's Insolvency Directive and, as a result, the plaintiff, Signor Francovich, could claim damages from the Italian Government to compensate him for the loss he had suffered.

The UK Government's view is that it has complied with the requirements of Directive by implementing the requirements of *s 124* of the *Pension Schemes Act 1993* which deal with unpaid contributions (see **23.4** above). However, there is a body of legal opinion that believes that the Directive acts more broadly to protect employees' pension rights upon the insolvency of their employer.

As discussed at **19.10**, there is a requirement for the trustees of defined benefit schemes that are found to be underfunded on a winding up to pursue the employer for the required deficiency payment. However, because the deficiency payment is currently calculated on the MFR basis, it may not actually be sufficient to secure each member's accrued rights in full in the situation where the scheme is winding up. Furthermore, if the employer is insolvent, the unsecured status of the employer's debt to the trustees means that in practice the debt may not be recoverable. It is argued, therefore, that these legislative measures, made under *s 75* of the *Pensions Act 1995*, cannot be said to implement the Directive either. Employees whose pension rights held in a defined benefit scheme are not fully bought out during the winding up of a scheme, in a case where the employer has become insolvent, may therefore be advised to pursue a claim against the UK Government for failure to implement the Directive, along the lines of the *Francovich* case.

It is of note that in January 2003 the Iron and Steel Trades Confederation trade union announced that it was considering taking legal action against the Government on these grounds. The announcement was made after 800 workers had lost their jobs when Allied Steel and Wire went into receivership in July 2002. The company had sponsored two final salary pension schemes that are being wound up but which are unlikely to have sufficient assets to secure more than two-thirds, and possibly less, of the non-pensioners' accrued pension rights.

Checklist 23

- The *Pensions Act 1995* set up a new compensation scheme for members of trust-based occupational pension schemes – compensation is only payable if the employer is insolvent and the loss occurred through misappropriation.

- The operation of the Financial Services Compensation Scheme provides little comfort to the trustees of an occupational pension scheme except in relation to a contract of long-term insurance arising from the failure of an insurance company or friendly society.

- If an employer becomes insolvent not having paid contributions due to a pension scheme, the state can make up for the missing contributions up to a specified limit.

- GMPs and notional GMPs from protected rights built up until 6 April 1997 are guaranteed by the state.

- The EU Insolvency Directive instructs member states to protect employees' pension entitlement on the insolvency of the employer.

Chapter 24

Training opportunities for trustees

Introduction

24.1   Greater emphasis has been placed on the proper training of trustees since the revelations of the Maxwell scandal. Stress must be placed on the quality of training offered, always bearing in mind that trustees drawn from company management or the employees generally are not expected to become professional pension experts. Indeed, as has so often been mentioned in this book, one of the duties of all trustees is to take professional advice. Training courses offered to trustees should therefore not be geared so much towards improving their technical understanding of pensions but rather emphasising the need for trustees to understand that:

- they, the trustees, are in control;

- they, the trustees, bear the responsibility for the safekeeping of the trust funds;

- they, the trustees, must question keenly their advisers, including the pensions manager, who are all answerable to them; and

- they must never become complacent.

It is notable that there is no requirement in the *Pensions Act 1995* for trustees to receive any training at all, although as noted at **8.8** trustees are entitled to paid time off work to perform trustee duties and undergo training. However, the first of Paul Myners' principles for the trustees of both defined benefit and defined contribution schemes (see **17.4** and **17.5**) is that:

> 'Decisions should be taken only by persons or organisations with the skills, information and resources necessary to take them effectively. Where trustees elect to take investment decisions, they must have sufficient expertise and appropriate training to be able to evaluate critically any advice they take.'

The Pensions Management Institute (PMI) (see **11.1**) launched in 1993 the *Trustee Certificate of Basic Pensions Knowledge* which gives formal recognition of an individual trustee's basic knowledge of what is involved in undertaking pension trustee work.

The certificate is awarded to those who successfully complete a short examination. The examination is available, on a totally voluntary basis, to all pension fund trustees as well as to any other interested individual.

The examination lasts about one hour and takes the form of answering multiple-choice questions designed to test basic knowledge across the syllabus. Each item either poses a question or makes a statement which requires completion. This is followed by four possible responses, one of which is the correct response. Candidates' answers to each item will therefore be (*a*), (*b*), (*c*) or (*d*). The examination does not involve writing essays.

The 26 topics listed below form the basis of the syllabus:

- pension arrangements and membership;
- regulatory framework;
- Inland Revenue requirements;
- basic concepts of a trust;
- relationship between trustees and others;
- different forms of trusteeship;
- main duties of trustees;
- powers of trustees;
- discretions of trustees;
- trustees' liabilities and protections;
- winding up and/or merging schemes;
- trustee meetings;
- powers of delegation and responsibilities of trustees;
- collection and investment of contributions;
- keeping of records and calculations of benefits;
- disclosure of information;
- annual report;
- individual and bulk transfers;
- typical investment objectives of trustees;
- different classes of investments;
- characteristics of the different classes of investments;
- different investment management structures;
- investment performance and monitoring and investment manager meetings;
- custody of scheme assets;
- role of the actuary; and
- frequency and main features of an actuarial valuation.

The examination should be taken after a short period of experience of being a trustee, and some background reading and attendance at a trustee training course run by a consultancy, training provider, trade union or other body. The PMI itself does not run trustee training courses nor does it recommend or endorse any particular training courses. It has assembled a list of providers of trustee training courses which is available on request from the address below or from the PMI's website.

Further information can be obtained from:

Education Secretary
The Pensions Management Institute
PMI House
4–10 Artillery Lane
London
E1 7LS
Tel: 020 72471452
Fax: 020 73750603
Website: http://www.pensions-pmi.org.uk

Checklist 24

- Trustees do not have to be pension experts – they have professional advisers for that purpose.

- Trustees should, however, understand that they are responsible for the safe keeping of the pension fund and that it is vital that they take their duties seriously – training should be directed to this end.

- Trustees must be given paid time off work to undertake their trustee duties and to undergo training. The principles put forward by Paul Myners state that trustees should receive training in relation to investment matters.

- Trustees should consider taking the PMI's *Trustee Certificate of Basic Pensions Knowledge* which is not biased towards those who are good at writing essays.

- There are many training providers in the marketplace – regularly updated lists are available from the PMI.

Penalties that can be imposed on trustees

The following table groups the various duties placed on pension fund trustees under the penalty that can be imposed for non-compliance. Note that only the penalties that can be imposed on trustees have been listed – not those that can only be applied in the case of employers or scheme advisers. The reference to the relevant legislation is also given.

Key

PSA 93 – Pension Schemes Act 1993

PA 95 – Pensions Act 1995

WRPA 99 – Welfare Reform and Pensions Act 1999

CSPSSA 2000 – Child Support, Pensions and Social Security Act 2000

Penalty: prohibition order only

Serious or persistent breach of a duty concerning scheme registration, transfer values, disclosure of information and the levy on occupational pension schemes. [*PA 95, s 3(2)*.]

Leaving excess assets on a winding up by failing to take reasonable steps to distribute the assets in accordance with the Act. [*PA 95, s 77(5)*.]

Failing to take reasonable steps to recover any assets of value to the extent possible without disproportionate cost when an application is made to the Pension Compensation Scheme. [*PA 95, s 81(6)*.]

Penalty: fine only

Failing to take reasonable steps to secure compliance with the requirement to provide a member of a defined benefit scheme with a statement of entitlement of his or her guaranteed transfer value within the prescribed time limit. [*PSA 93, s 93A(4)* as inserted by *PA 95, s 153*.]

Failing to take reasonable steps to carry out a member's legitimate right to proceed with a transfer of rights out of the scheme within six months of either the guarantee date (defined benefit scheme) or receipt of the application (defined contribution scheme). [*PSA 93, s 99(7)(b)* as inserted by *PA 95, Sch 6, para 6(e)*.]

Failing to take reasonable steps to inform a member of a defined benefit scheme of the amount of the transfer value of pension credit under the pension sharing on divorce legislation. [*PSA, s 101H(4)* as inserted by *WRPA 99, s 37.*]

Failing to take reasonable steps to comply with a transfer notice from a member wishing to transfer a pension credit under the pension sharing on divorce legislation. [*PSA, s 101J(4)(b)* as inserted by *WRPA 99, s 37.*]

Failing to take reasonable steps to ensure that their failure to comply with a transfer notice from a member wishing to transfer a pension credit under the pension sharing on divorce legislation is reported to Opra within the stated deadline. [*PSA, s 101J(5)* as inserted by *WRPA 99, s 37.*]

Failing to comply with the duty to report to Opra that no independent trustee has been appointed to a defined benefit scheme with an insolvent employer. [*PA 95, s 26A(7)* as inserted by *CSPSSA 2000, s 47.*]

Failing to take reasonable steps to secure a dispute resolution procedure. [*PA 95, s 50(6).*]

Failing to take reasonable steps to supply a statement of guaranteed entitlement to a transfer value to a member of the scheme within the prescribed time. [*PA 95, s 153(4).*]

Failing, without reasonable excuse, to comply with the requirements of the *Occupational Pension Schemes (Disclosure of Information) Regulations 1996 (SI 1996/1046). [PA 95, s 10(3)* and *regulation 11* of the Regulations.]

Failing to take all reasonable steps to comply with requirements to supply within the time limits a statement of entitlement to a transfer value. [*PA 95, s 10(3); PSA 93, s 93A;* and *regulation 20* of the *Occupational Pension Schemes (Transfer Values) Regulations 1996 (SI 1996/1847).*]

Failing, without reasonable excuse, to provide information regarding transfers of accrued pension rights made without the consent of the members involved. [*Regulation 27B* of the *Occupational Pension Schemes (Preservation of Benefit) Regulations 1991 (SI 1991/167).*]

Failing to comply with the requirement to obtain an actuary's certificate or the member's individual consents to a scheme modification as required by *PA 95, s 67.* [*PA 95, s 10(3)* and *regulation 8* of the *Occupational Pension Schemes (Modification of Schemes) Regulations 1996 (SI 1996/2517).*]

Failing, without reasonable excuse, to comply with any requirement of the *Occupational Pension Schemes (Independent Trustee) Regulations 1997 (SI 1997/252). [PA 95, s 10 (3)* and *regulation 7(6)* of the Regulations.]

Failing, without reasonable cause, to comply with any duty to inform the Registrar within three months that their scheme has become registrable or to notify the Registrar of any change in the information that must be provided; or failing without reasonable cause to prevent the use of information supplied by the Registrar for the purposes of marketing a product or service. [*PA 1995, s 10* and *regulation 7(2)* of the *Register of Occupational and Personal Pension Schemes Regulations 1997 (SI 1997/371)* as amended by *regulation 3(2)* of the *Occupational and Personal Pension Schemes (Penalties) Regulations 2000 (SI 2000/833)*.]

Failing, without reasonable cause, to comply with the requirement to pay a levy to the Registrar. [*Regulation 12* of the *Occupational and Personal Pension Schemes (Levy) Regulations 1997 (SI 1997/666)*.]

Failing to take reasonable steps to discharge their liability in respect of a pension credit under the pension sharing on divorce legislation within the deadline. [*WRPA 99, s 33(2)(b)*.]

Failing to notify Opra that they have failed to do what is required to discharge their liability in respect of a pension credit under the pension sharing on divorce legislation within the deadline. [*WRPA 99, s 33(3)*.]

Penalty: prohibition order and fine

Failing without reasonable excuse to obtain accounts audited by the scheme auditor or the auditor's statement about contributions within seven months of the end of the scheme year. [*PA 95, s 10(3)* and *regulation 2(3),(4)* of the *Occupational Pension Schemes (Requirement to obtain Audited Accounts and a Statement from the Auditor) Regulations 1996 (SI 1996/1975)* as substituted by *regulation 2* of the *Occupational and Personal Pension Schemes (Penalties) Regulations 2000 (SI 2000/833)*.]

Failing to take reasonable steps to comply with a Direction from Opra following a failure by the employer to pay benefits; or to publish a statement drafted by Opra in the annual report; or to send members a copy of a statement prepared by Opra. [*PA 95, s 15(4)*.]

Failing to take reasonable steps to comply with the duty to implement arrangements for the selection of member-nominated trustees. [*PA 95, s 21(1),(2)*.]

Failing to take reasonable steps to ensure that the scheme assets are not used to indemnify trustees for fines or civil penalties. [*PA 95, s 31(3)*.]

Failing to take reasonable steps to give proper notice of a trustee meeting where a decision is to be taken by majority voting. [*PA 95, s 32(5)*.]

Failing to take reasonable steps to prepare a written statement of investment principles or to have taken or considered professional advice before preparing such a statement of investment principles. [*PA 95, s 35(6)*.]

Failing to take reasonable steps to obtain professional advice in choosing the scheme's investments. [*PA 95, s 36(8).*]

Making a payment out of surplus to the employer without take reasonable steps to comply with the requirements of the Act. [*PA 95, s 37(8).*]

Failing to take reasonable steps to observe the restrictions on self-investment (employer-related investments). [*PA 95, s 40(4).*]

Placing reliance on an adviser who has not been appointed by the trustees. [*PA 95, s 47(3).*]

Failing to take reasonable steps to appoint a scheme auditor, a scheme actuary or a scheme fund manager, when required to do so by the Act, or failing to appoint in compliance with the requirements of the Act. [*PA 95, s 47(8).*]

Failing to take reasonable steps to disclose information to the scheme's professional advisers. [*PA 95, s 47(11).*]

Failing to take reasonable steps to comply with the requirement to have a separate bank account, keep records of their meetings or to keep specified books and records. [*PA 95, s 49(6).*]

Failing to take reasonable steps to ensure that the failure by the employer to pay over contributions that have been deducted from an employee's earnings to the occupational pension scheme is reported by the relevant deadline to Opra and the employee. [*PA 95, s 49(10)* as substituted by *WRPA 99, s 10(1).*]

Failing to take all reasonable steps to comply with the requirement to keep written records of their decisions relating to the winding up of an occupational pension scheme. [*PA 95, s 49A(4)(5),* as inserted by *CSPSSA 2000, s 49.*]

Failing to take reasonable steps to comply with the duties under the minimum funding requirement. [*PA 95, s 57(7).*]

Failing to take reasonable steps to comply with the duty to prepare, maintain and revise the schedule of contributions underpinning the minimum funding requirement. [*PA 95, s 58(8).*]

Failing to take reasonable steps to inform Opra and the members of the scheme that contributions required under the schedule of contributions have not been paid by the due date or that the minimum funding requirement has not been met. [*PA 95, s 59(4).*]

Failing to take reasonable steps to inform Opra and the members of the scheme that the employer has not restored the scheme's funding to at least 90% of the MFR within the required period. [*PA 95, s 60(8).*]

Failing to take all reasonable steps to comply in making a required report to Opra relating to the supervision of a scheme which is being wound up. [*PA 95, s 72A(9)*, as inserted by *CSPSSA 2000, s 49.*]

Failing to comply with a direction from Opra concerning the winding up of an occupational pension scheme. [*PA 95, s 72C(3)*, as inserted by *CSPSSA 2000, s 50.*]

Failing to take reasonable steps to comply with the requirements of the Act relating to the winding up of the scheme and order of priorities for satisfying liabilities. [*PA 95, s 73(6).*]

Distributing assets to the employer on a winding up without take reasonable steps to comply with the requirements of the Act. [*PA 95, s 76(6).*]

Failing to take reasonable steps to comply with the requirement to prepare, maintain and revise a payment schedule for a money purchase scheme. [*PA 95, s 87(5).*]

Failing to take reasonable steps to inform Opra and the members when any contributions listed on the payment schedule for a money purchase scheme have not been paid by the due date. [*PA 95, s 88(4).*]

Failing to take reasonable steps to ensure that a scheme registered as a stakeholder pension scheme fulfils the required conditions for a scheme to be so registered. [*WRPA 99, s 2(4).*]

Failing to take reasonable steps to ensure that the failure by an employer, who has entered into a direct payment arrangement to pay a contribution to a registered stakeholder pension, is reported by the relevant deadline to Opra and to the employee concerned; or failing to send the member concerned a statement setting out the amounts and dates of the payments made under the direct payment arrangement. [*WRPA 99, s 9(9),(10).*]

Penalty: criminal prosecution

Refusing or wilfully neglecting to provide the Inland Revenue with information or produce any document relevant to non-payment of pension contributions by an employer and which may become payable by the state; or to knowingly or recklessly make a false statement in purporting to comply with this requirement [*PSA 93, s 157(3),(4).*]

Knowingly or recklessly providing the Registrar with information that is false or misleading in a material particular. [*PSA 93, s 168A* as inserted by *PA 95, s 155(1).*]

Purporting to act as a trustee while being prohibited or suspended from doing so. [*PA 95, s 6(1).*]

Acting as auditor or actuary when serving as a trustee or being connected with a trustee. [*PA 95, s 28(1)*]. Such a person may also be prohibited from acting as trustee. [*PA 95, s 28(4)*.]

Acting as a trustee while an actuary or auditor. [*PA 95, s 28(1)*]. Such a trustee can also be prohibited from acting as a trustee by Opra. [*PA 95, s 28(4)*.]

Acting as a trustee when disqualified from doing so. [*PA 95, s 30(3)*.]

Being reimbursed out of the pension fund because of suffering fines or civil penalties. [*PA 95, s 31(5)*.]

Being knowingly concerned in the fraudulent evasion of the obligation on the employer to pass over contributions that have been deducted from an employee's earnings to an occupational pension scheme by the prescribed deadline. [*PA 95, s 49(11),(12)* as inserted by *WRPA 99, s 10(1)*.]

Intentionally delaying an Opra inspector, neglecting or refusing to produce a document required by Opra or neglecting or refusing to answer questions or provide information when so required. [*PA 95, s 101(3)*.]

Knowingly or recklessly providing Opra with false or misleading information. [*PA 95, s 101(5)*.]

Intentionally altering, suppressing, concealing or destroying a document required by Opra. [*PA 95, s 101(6)*.]

Disclosing restricted information obtained by Opra in the course of its functions that relates to another person. [*PA 95, s 104(3)*.]

Neglecting or refusing to produce a document required by the Pensions Compensation Board. [*PA 95, s 111(1)*.]

Knowingly or recklessly providing the Pensions Compensation Board with false or misleading information. [*PA 95, s 111(4)*.]

Intentionally altering, suppressing, concealing or destroying a document required by the Pensions Compensation Board. [*PA 95, s 111(5)*.]

Breaching regulations made under the *Pension Schemes Act 1993* or knowingly or recklessly supplying the Occupational Pensions Registrar with false or misleading information. [*PA 95, s 155*.]

Failing, without reasonable cause, to comply with the requirement that where a scheme became registrable before 1 April 1997 the specified information should be provided to the Registrar before 30 June 1997. [*PA 1995, s 116(1)* and *regulation 7(1)* of the *Register of Occupational and Personal Pension Schemes Regulations 1997 (SI 1997/371)* as amended by *regulation 3(1)* of the

Occupational and Personal Pension Schemes (Penalties) Regulations 2000 (SI 2000/833).]

Applying to register a scheme as a stakeholder pension scheme and knowingly or recklessly providing Opra with information which is false or misleading in a material particular. [*WRPA 99, s 2(5),(6).*]

Being knowingly concerned in the fraudulent evasion of a direct payment arrangement for the payment to a personal pension (including a stakeholder pension established legally as a personal pension) in respect of any contribution which has been deducted from an employee's earnings. [*WRPA 99, s 9(12),(13).*]

Exempt-approved occupational pension schemes – maximum and typical contributions and benefits

Defined benefit scheme

Note

Remuneration *does not include share or share option gains or 'golden handshakes' on retirement. For all members joining existing schemes since 1 June 1989 remuneration is limited by a cash ceiling set by the pensionable earnings cap.*

Eligibility

Maximum: All employees.

Typical: An upper-entry age set shortly before normal pension age. A lower-entry age set at age 16, 18, 20 or 21. A minimum period of qualifying service occasionally set but usually less than one year. Eligibility currently often restricted to employees on permanent contracts.

Employer contributions

Maximum: No maximum if actuarially certified.

Typical: For contributory schemes normally around 10% of pensionable earnings. For non-contributory schemes normally around 16% of pensionable earnings. (Temporary effects of contribution holidays had until recently reduced typical employer contribution rates very markedly).

Employee contributions

Maximum: 15% of remuneration.

Typical: For contributory schemes normally around 5% of pensionable earnings. Around one-fifth of the larger schemes are non-contributory.

Additional voluntary contributions by employee

Maximum: Balance of 15% of remuneration after normal contribution.

Typical: Usually 15% of members make AVC payments – no data on typical amount.

Appendix 2

[Note that the *Finance Act 2000* permits members of approved defined benefit schemes, provided that they earn no more than £30,000 p a, also to contribute a maximum of £3,600 (including tax relief at the basic rate) to a scheme approved under the new DC tax regime, such as a personal or stakeholder pension scheme, in addition to the maximum contribution (15%) described above. See **2.15**.]

Definition of pensionable earnings

Maximum: All remuneration.

Typical: Pensionable earnings often limited to basic earnings or basic plus three-year average of bonuses. Pay below National Insurance Lower Earnings Limit or level of basic state pension often ignored (a process known as integration).

Definition of final pensionable pay

Maximum: Highest remuneration in any of last five years where remuneration is aggregate of basic pay and previous three-year average of bonuses. Alternatively, yearly average total remuneration for any three consecutive years in last ten years may be taken. Some further restrictions exist.

Typical: Actual pensionable earnings over last twelve months or average pensionable earnings over best three consecutive years in last ten years.

Accrual rate

Maximum: $\frac{1}{30}$ths up to maximum of 20 years (or, if a member before 17 March 1987, $\frac{2}{3}$rds of final remuneration after ten years).

Typical: $\frac{1}{60}$th.

Normal pensionable age

Maximum: 75.

Typical: 65, but 60 also popular. Many schemes allow retirement on full accrued pension from age 60.

Retirement lump sum

(Usually obtained by commuting part of the pension into the tax-free cash lump sum. Value of lump sum and pension cannot exceed maximum approvable pension. Equivalent pension value for benefit limit purposes of lump sum obtained by dividing lump sum by 12).

Maximum: $\frac{3}{80}$ths of final remuneration up to 40 years or, if higher, 2.25 times initial annual rate of actual pension (including that bought by voluntary contributions). Limited to 1.5 times pensionable earnings cap for members joining after 1 June 1989.

If a member joins before 17 March 1987, 1.5 times final remuneration at normal pension age and maximum lump sum available after 20 years. Limited, in most cases, to £150,000 for members joining between 17 March and 31 May 1989 inclusive.

Typical: Usually up to Inland Revenue maximum. Unisex commutation rate for those aged 65 would often be in range £9 to £9.80 for each £1 of pension commuted.

Pension increases

Maximum: In line with the rise in the Retail Prices Index after augmenting pension to Inland Revenue maximum.

Typical: In line with rise in the Retail Prices Index up to a 5% increase in any one year but very often with discretionary increases in addition.

Ill-health pension

Maximum: Benefit that would be payable at normal pension age based on current value of final pensionable earnings.

Typical: Benefit in line with Inland Revenue maximum is common but the accrued pension, or the accrued pension and half due from future potential service, is also used. The level of the benefit may depend on the seriousness of the incapacity. In practice, ill-health pensions are sometimes avoided by use of permanent health insurance policies.

Early retirement

Maximum: In most cases available from age 50. If the member joined before 17 March 1987, a proportion of the maximum permitted pension at normal pension age is calculated by multiplying by the ratio of completed service to total potential service. A $\frac{1}{60}$th accrual rate is always permitted. For members subject to the pensionable earnings cap, pensions may accrue at an accrual rate of up to $\frac{1}{30}$th for up to 20 years.

Typical: In cases of voluntary early retirement, the accrued pension based on current value of final pensionable pay is reduced either actuarially or on a specially devised scale. Reductions usually in range of 4% to 6% for each year taken early. In cases of compulsory early retirement it is more likely that no reduction is made to the accrued pension.

Death-in-service lump sum

Maximum: Four times remuneration at date of death plus return of member's contributions with reasonable interest. Limited to four times pensionable earnings cap for members joining after 1 June 1989 if this is less.

Typical: Three or four times remuneration now most common.

Survivors' pension (death-in-service)

Maximum: ⅔rds maximum potential pension that would have been payable to the member at normal pension age based on current value of final remuneration.

Typical: Usually ½ of maximum potential pension that would have been payable to the member at normal pension age based on current value of final remuneration plus children's benefits.

Survivors' pension (death-after-retirement)

Maximum: ⅔rds of maximum pension which could have been provided at normal pension age (ie before pension was commuted) as increased in line with Retail Prices Index until date of death. Member's pension can be guaranteed for five years: the balance paid as lump sum or as pension.

Typical: Usually ½ of member's pension at date of death ignoring effect of commutation and plus any children's benefits. Five-year guarantee also common.

Defined contribution scheme

Inland Revenue approved defined contribution occupational pension schemes are subject in essence to the same maximum contribution and benefit limits as apply to approved defined benefit occupational pension schemes. Note, however, that from 6 April 2001 it is possible for defined occupational pension schemes to convert to become subject to the new DC tax regime instead (see **2.15** above).

Proposals for a new unified tax regime

The paper *Simplifying the Taxation of Pensions: Increasing Choice and Flexibility for All* jointly issued by the Inland Revenue and the Treasury on 17 December 2002 sets out detailed proposals for changes that are widely regarded as adopting a radical approach, setting out a unified tax regime governing all private pension provision. The consultation period ran from 18 December 2002 until 11 April 2003.

The main characteristics of the proposed new tax regime, which could come into effect from as soon as 6 April 2004, are as follows:

(*a*)   The tax regime would cover all funded private pension schemes.

(*b*)   Full concurrency would be permitted so that an individual could be an active member of several personal pension schemes, stakeholder pension schemes and occupational pension schemes.

(*c*)   Contributions made by any individual would be permitted in any one tax year up to the higher of:

  (i)   £3,600; and

  (ii)   100% of annual remuneration.

(*d*)   Total contributions made by or on behalf of an individual in any one tax year, plus the additional value of accrued pension built up by that individual in a defined benefit scheme in the same tax year, would be subject to an income tax charge on the individual concerned at the individual's marginal rate once the combined value of the contributions plus additional accrued defined benefit exceeds £200,000; the tax charge being applied to the excess over £200,000 (see Box 1).

(*e*)   Investment income and capital gains would be largely subject to the present rules applying to approved schemes.

(*f*)   A lifetime limit will be applied to the total value of the aggregate pension rights that come into payment to an individual, which will be initially set at £1.4m, with this figure to be uprated annually in line with prices. If the value of the individual's pension rights, once they have been drawn, on an cumulative approach, exceeds 100% of the lifetime limit applying in that tax year, a free-standing tax charge (known as the recovery charge) set at 33% will be applied to the value of the excess over £1.4m. After deduction of this tax charge, the excess benefits will be taxable at the individual's marginal rate (equating therefore to a combined charge of 59.8% in the case of a 40% taxpayer).

(*g*)   Whenever an individual brings a pension into payment, the pension provider will state what percentage the value of those rights represents of the lifetime limit in that tax year. This information will be given by the pension provider both to the member and to the Inland Revenue. Provided that the aggregate of those percentages is less than 100%, the individual can use all the assets to provide pension benefits without the recovery charge being applied (see Box 2).

(*h*)   A tax-free lump sum can be taken on drawing pension rights, of up to 25% of the value of those rights up to the lifetime limit (ie initially a maximum tax-free lump sum of £350,000). Where the recovery charge operates on the value of benefits in excess of 100% of the lifetime limit, up to the 25% of the value of the excess benefits, after deduction of the recovery charge, can be taken in lump sum form but subject to tax at the individual's marginal rate.

(*i*)   From 2010 the minimum age for drawing a private pension (other than in cases of ill-health) will be raised from 50 to 55.

(*j*)   There will be greater flexibility in the way that retirement income can be taken.

(*k*)   Tax relief on an individual's contributions can be either on the basis of the net pay arrangement currently operated by occupational pension schemes or the deduction-at-source basis currently operated by personal and stakeholder pension schemes, provided that in the case of any one pension scheme the same system of giving tax relief is applied to all members.

(*l*)   Transitional arrangements will protect the pension rights already built up at the date of the introduction of the new regime (see Box 3).

Box 1

Value inflows in any one tax year will comprise:

(*a*)   the total amount of contributions paid into a defined contribution scheme during the tax year, irrespective of who makes them;

(*b*)   the whole annual increase over the tax year in the value of the increase of the pension rights held by an active member in a defined benefit occupational pension scheme;

(*c*)   the increase in value of any deferred defined benefit pension rights that are in excess of any greater statutory revaluation and the increase in national average earnings; and

(*d*)   any discretionary increases in a pension already in payment that exceed price indexation.

Value inflow (*a*) is relatively straightforward, although the calculation must take into account whether the individual's own contributions are paid under a net pay arrangement or by deduction at source (see below). National Insurance age rebates derived from contracting out would, however, not count as a value inflow towards the annual limit.

Value inflow (*b*) would be calculated by standardised actuarial tables. Suppose Martha is aged 50 and earns £60,000 a year and that her final salary pension accrues at the rate of $\frac{1}{60}$th. In the last year her pension rights would have risen by £1,000. The valuation table might give a value of a rise in the pension rights of a woman aged 50 at £11 per £1 of income, so Martha's value inflow is £11,000.

Value inflows (*c*) and (*d*) are likely to be comparatively rare, (*d*) being the equivalent of an augmentation of the individual's pension rights at retirement.

Box 2

The Inland Revenue gives the following two examples of the operation of the lifetime limit.

Example 1: Robert decides to draw benefits of £700,000 from his pension fund. This is well below the lifetime limit. His pension provider sends him a certificate to verify that he has used up 50% of the £1.4m lifetime limit and the Inland Revenue registers this. Some years later, Robert decides to make use of the remainder of his pension fund, amounting to £150,000. The lifetime limit is now £1.5m so the second drawing of pension benefits is 10% of the limit at that time. The two slices of the pension fund have provided benefits together worth 60% of the lifetime limit (50% plus 10%) so Robert has no additional charge to pay.

Example 2: Barbara decides to use £1.12m of her pension rights, using up 80% of the lifetime limit of £1.4m. When she comes to take the remainder of her pension benefits some years later, she has £750,000 – 50% of the then lifetime limit of £1.5m. She can take £300,000 of this (20% of the current lifetime limit, namely the limit less the 80% she has already used) subject to the standard rules for drawing pension benefits. But Barbara must bear a recovery charge of 33% on the remaining £450,000. After the recovery charge there is a residual fund of £300,000. This can be paid as a lump sum of up to £75,000 plus a pension from the remaining £225,000. Both the lump sum and pension will be taxed at Barbara's marginal rate.

Source: *Inland Revenue & HM Treasury*

Box 3

A one-off valuation of all member's pension rights will need to be undertaken when the new pension tax regime is introduced in order to protect the pension rights of the minority of individuals whose existing pension rights, though within existing occupational pension scheme benefit limits or having been built up from contributions that have respected the contribution limits currently imposed on personal and stakeholder pension schemes, nevertheless exceed the new £1.4m lifetime limit.

If existing pension rights do exceed the lifetime limit, they will be protected. So, if the existing pension rights of an individual were valued at, say, £2.8m, or 200% of the lifetime limit when first introduced, when those pension rights become payable no recovery charge would be applied if they were then valued at less than 200% of the then value of the lifetime limit.

Pensions legislation and guidance

The aim of this appendix is to list the major pieces of legislation that govern occupational pension schemes as well as official guidance issued by government agencies and professional bodies. It does not cover the legislation dealing with personal or stakeholder pensions unless the legislation also has direct relevance to occupational pension schemes.

There are many who say that reading the legislation itself is too difficult for ordinary lay trustees and that this should be left to the trustees' professional advisers. Trustees, they say, would do well just to read good guides on the subject areas (such as this book!). The view of the author of this book is that, certainly, reading the legislation is not easy but that it should be recognised that any guide does not fully explain all the legislation. Trustees who wish to get to grips with the legislative requirements should at least know where to look. This appendix aims simply to list for the benefit of trustees the legislation dealing with specific topics.

There are two levels to legislation:

- *Acts of Parliament (primary legislation)*

  Acts are divided up into *sections* **of** the Act, and often also *Schedules* **to** the Act. Each section and schedule in any Act is given a number. Schedules are divided into paragraphs. Each Act is known by its title and the year in which it received Royal Assent, e g the *Pensions Act 1995*.

- *Statutory Instruments (secondary legislation)*

  Statutory Instruments take the form either of sets of *Regulations* or *Orders*. Regulations on a specific subject can only be made by Parliament if there is a specific power to do so set out in an Act of Parliament. Each set of Regulations is divided up into individual *regulations* and sometimes also *schedules*. Each regulation and schedule in a set of regulations is given a number.

Each set of regulations is known by its title and two numbers – the year in which the regulations were made and a second number indicating the chronological order in which the regulations were made by Parliament in that year, e g the *Occupational Pension Schemes (Scheme Administration) Regulations 1996 (SI 1996/1715)*.

Orders are like regulations except that each set of orders is divided into individually numbered *articles* rather than regulations.

Official guidance

Government agencies and recognised professional bodies can issue guidance that can be given official standing. If so, this guidance is virtually mandatory in its effect.

Below we set out in list form:

- the primary social security legislation relating to occupational pension schemes;

- the secondary social security legislation relating to contracting out by means of an occupational pension scheme;

- the secondary social security legislation relating to occupational pension schemes;

- the primary Inland Revenue legislation relating to retirement benefit schemes;

- the secondary Inland Revenue legislation relating to retirement benefit schemes;

- guidance from the Occupational Pensions Regulatory Authority (Opra);

- guidance from the Inland Revenue's Savings, Pensions, Share Schemes business stream;

- guidance from the National Insurance Contributions Office;

- guidance from the actuarial professional bodies; and

- guidance from the accountancy professional bodies.

The list is not comprehensive but the aim is to have included all of the most important pieces of legislation that were in force as at March 2003.

When consulting the legislation covering occupational pension schemes, readers should make sure that they use a consolidated version of the relevant Act or Regulations/Orders. A consolidated version is one which takes in all the changes made to the Act or Regulations by later legislation.

In our list of statutory instruments, only the *substantive* or *principal* statutory instrument is given. In many cases this substantive statutory instrument will have been changed by subsequent *amending* statutory instruments, making it important that the latest consolidated version is used in order to try and find out what the current legislation says.

The *NAPF Pensions Legislation Service* published by Butterworths contains all these pieces of legislation in their consolidated versions.

In this appendix we use the following abbreviations:

328

s = section of the Act
Sch = Schedule to the Act
ss = sections of the Act
SI = Statutory Instrument

Primary social security legislation

Social Security Act 1989

s 23 & Sch 5 — Establishes the law for dealing with pension rights during periods of paid maternity leave and family leave.

Pension Schemes Act 1993

s 1 — Defines 'occupational pension scheme'.

s 6 — Establishes the law that details of occupational pension schemes must be lodged in an official registry.

ss 7–34 & Sch 2 — Establishes the law on how occupational pension schemes may contract employment out of SERPS/S2P.

ss 41–49 — Deals with effect on National Insurance contributions and SERPS/S2P benefits for members of contracted-out occupational pension schemes. See also *s 31 & Sch 4* of the *Child Support, Pensions and Social Security Act 2000*.

ss 50–68 — Deals with the termination of contracted-out employment and the payment of state scheme premiums.

ss 69–82 — Establishes the law dealing with the preservation of the pension benefits of early leavers from occupational pension schemes.

ss 83–86 & Sch 3 — Establishes the law on how the preserved pensions of early leavers must be revalued during the period of deferment before they become payable.

ss 87–92 — Deals with the protection of increases in GMPs from being franked to pay for the revaluation of other benefits. Prospectively replaced by *Part II* of *Schedule 5* to the *Child Support, Pensions and Social Security Act 2000*.

ss 93–101 — Establishes the law on transfer values.

ss 109–110 — Deals with increases to GMPs.

s 111 — Deals with AVCs.

ss 111A–111B — See *Welfare Reform and Pensions Act 1995, s 9*.

ss 113–117 — Establishes the law that occupational pension schemes must disclose information to their members. See also *Pensions Act 1995, s 41*.

Appendix 3

ss 123–127	Deals with duty of DWP to pay unpaid contributions to schemes.
s 128 & Sch 4	Deals with the priority in bankruptcy of unpaid statutory pension contributions.
ss 129–132	Establishes how legislation may override trust deed and rules.
ss 145–152	Establishes the office of the Pensions Ombudsman and defines its powers. See also *ss 53–54* of the *Child Support, Pensions and Social Security Act 2000*.
ss 153–193	General, miscellaneous and supplementary provisions. See *Pensions Act 1995, s 165*.

Pensions Act 1995

ss 1–15	Establishes Opra and defines its powers.
ss 16–21	Establishes the law governing member-nominated trustees. Prospectively substantially modified by *ss 43–46* of the *Child Support, Pensions and Social Security Act 2000*.
ss 22–26C	Re-enacts *ss 119–122* of the *Pension Schemes Act 1993* and stipulates that independent trustees must be appointed when an employer becomes insolvent. Now substantially modified by *s 47* of the *Child Support, Pensions and Social Security Act 2000*.
ss 27–30A	Establishes who is disqualified from acting as a trustee.
s 31	Stipulates that trustees cannot be indemnified for fines or civil penalties out of the resources of the fund.
s 32	Allows trustees to take decisions by majority unless the trust deed specifies otherwise.
ss 33–36	Deals with trustees' investment duties.
s 37	Deals with a payment out of surplus to the employer.
s 38	Deals with the trustees' power to defer the winding up of a scheme.
s 39	Allows trustees who are also members of the scheme to exercise a power that benefits themselves simply because they are members of the scheme.
s 40	Re-enacts *s 112* of the *Pension Schemes Act 1993* and establishes the law limiting pension fund investment in the sponsoring employer.
s 41	Re-enacts *s 114* of the *Pension Schemes Act 1993* and establishes the law that occupational pension schemes must disclose information to their members.

ss 42–45	Establishes the right of employee trustees to paid time off to complete trustee duties and undertake training. *Sections 42–45 are re-enacted as ss 58–60 of the Employment Rights Act 1996.*
s 46	Extends employment protection measures against detriment and unfair dismissal to employees acting in their capacity as trustees. *s 46 is re-enacted as s 102 of the Employment Rights Act 1996.*
ss 47–48	Establishes the law governing the duties of professional advisers to trustees and in particular their duty to blow the whistle to Opra.
s 49	Deals with trustees' responsibilities to open a separate bank account, keep records and for the employer to put unpaid benefits into a separate bank account and pay over contributions deducted from employees' earnings.
s 50	Establishes the law that trustees must set up internal dispute resolution procedures.
ss 51–55	Replaces *ss 102–108* of the *Pension Schemes Act 1993* and establishes the rules for pension increases. See also *s 51* of the *Child Support, Pensions and Social Security Act 2000.*
ss 56–61	Establishes the minimum funding requirement binding on all defined benefit schemes.
ss 62–66A	Establishes in UK legislation the law on equal treatment and its impact on occupational pension schemes.
ss 67–72C	Modifies some of *ss 136–143* of the *Pension Schemes Act 1993* and establishes the power of trustees or Opra to modify occupational pension schemes. See also *s 50* of the *Child Support, Pensions and Social Security Act 2000.*
ss 73–77	Establishes the law governing the winding up of occupational pension schemes.
ss 78–86	Establishes the Pensions Compensation Board and how the Pensions Compensation Scheme is to operate and be funded.
ss 87–90	Establishes the law relating to contribution payment schedules for money purchase schemes.
ss 91–95	Establishes the law on the assignment and forfeiture of pension rights.
ss 96–114	Deals with reviewing decisions of Opra and its powers to gather and disclose information as well as the information gathering powers of the Pensions Compensation Board.
ss 115–125	Deals with general matters.

ss 135–151	Establishes the law governing the new system for contracting out of SERPS and S2P. See also *s 31 & Sch 4* of the *Child Support, Pensions and Social Security Act 2000*.
ss 152–154	Extends the legislation governing transfer values – see *ss 93–101* of the *Pensions Act 1993* – and related disclosure requirements.
s 155	Sets out new penalties for breach of regulations made under the *Pension Schemes Act 1993*.
ss 156–160	Modifies the law governing the office of the Pensions Ombudsman – see *ss 145–152* of the *Pension Schemes Act 1993*.
s 161	Repeals *ss 136–143* of the *Pension Schemes Act 1993*.
s 165	Modifies *s 175* of the *Pension Schemes Act 1993* which deals with the levy on occupational pension schemes.
ss 166–167	Establishes the law regarding the treatment of pensions in divorce settlements.

Welfare Reform and Pensions Act 1999

ss 1–8 & Sch 1	Sets out the primary legislation governing stakeholder pension schemes.
s 9	Inserts *ss 111A* and *111B* into the *Pension Schemes Act 1993* which introduce the requirement for employers' payments to personal pension schemes (including stakeholder pension schemes legally established as personal pensions) to be monitored.
s 10	Substitutes a new *s 49(8)* into the *Pensions Act 1995* making non-fraudulent delays by the employer in paying over contributions deducted from employees' earnings subject to a new civil penalty.
ss 11–16	Establishes new legislation dealing with the treatment of the pension rights and pension entitlements of individuals who become bankrupt.
s 17	Modifies *ss 81* and *83* of the *Pensions Act 1995* by modifying how the Pensions Compensation Scheme operates.
s 18 & Sch 2	Makes various miscellaneous amendments to the pensions legislation
ss 19–51 &	Introduces the social security legislation dealing with pensions
Sch 3–6	Deals with sharing on divorce including new sections *15A, 68A–68D* and *101A–101Q* inserted to the *Pension Schemes Act 1993*.

Child Support, Pensions and Social Security Act 2000

s 31 & Sch 4	Introduces the method of calculating S2P entitlement for those who have been contracted out.
ss 43–46	Prospectively amends *ss 16–21* of the *Pensions Act 1995* to introduce a modified system of member-nominated trustees.
ss 47–50	Amends various sections of the *Pensions Act 1995* and inserts *s 26A–26C* and *ss 71A & ss 72A–72C* into that Act in order to make provision for the speeding up of the winding-up process.
s 51	Inserts *s 51A* into the *Pensions Act 1995* restricting the limited price indexation requirement in cases when an investment-linked annuity is bought.
s 52	Amends *s 113* of the *Pension Schemes Act 1993* to allow for the requirement that members of defined contribution schemes must be given an illustration of their future pension entitlement.
ss 53–54	Modifies *ss 145–152* of the *Pensions Schemes Act 1993* to extend the jurisdiction of the Pensions Ombudsman to allow a greater range of people to refer complaints, and to allow the Pensions Ombudsman to investigate cases where others will be affected by the eventual determination by giving him the power to appoint representative members.
s 55	Inserts *s 66A* into the *Pensions Act 1995* to comply with a EU Directive safeguarding occupational pension scheme rights of those moving within the EU.
s 56 & Sch 5	Prospectively replaces *ss 87–92* of the *Pension Schemes Act 1993* to introduce an alternative to the anti-franking provisions, and make amendments to the contracting-out provisions of the *Pension Schemes Act 1993*; to amend *s 98* of that Act to allow members to take transfer values even if part of their pension rights under the scheme has already come into payment; and inserts *s 30A* into the *Pensions Act 1995* concerning the register of disqualified trustees maintained by Opra.

Secondary social security legislation

This list is in alphabetical order by keywords.

Only the substantive or principal regulations in force as at March 2003 are listed below.

This list is divided into those regulations or orders which deal with the contracting-out legislation and those which cover occupational pension

Appendix 3

schemes generally. The list does not include regulations dealing with issues concerning pension rights on divorce.

Contracting-out legislation

*Personal and Occupational Pension Schemes (**Abatement of Benefit**) Regulations 1987 (SI 1987/1113)* deal with the notional Guaranteed Minimum Pension (GMP) bought by protected rights in a Contracted-out Money Purchase (COMP) scheme from 1988 to 1997.

*Occupational Pension Schemes (**Age-related Payments**) Regulations 1997 (SI 1997/946)* prevent age-related top-up payments being paid to a scheme contracted out by the protected rights test if members are transferred into that scheme at some specified age.

*Occupational Pension Schemes (Contracting-out) (**Amount Required for Restoring State Scheme Rights and Miscellaneous Amendment**) Regulations 1998 (SI 1998/1397)* deal with the restoration of members' rights under SERPS in cases where an occupational pension scheme winds up insolvent.

*Occupational Pension Schemes (**Contracting-out**) Regulations 1996 (SI 1996/1172)* are the main regulations dealing with the contracting-out requirements including the issue of contracting-out certificates and the detailed requirements of both the reference scheme test and the protected rights test.

*Occupational and Personal Pension Schemes (**Contracting-out etc.: Review of Determinations**) (SI 1997/358)* set out the procedure to be followed if there is to be a review of the National Insurance Contributions Office's decision on the issue, cancellation or variation of a contracting-out certificate.

*Occupational Pension Schemes (**Discharge of Liability**) Regulations 1997 (SI 1997/784)* set out how schemes contracted out by the reference scheme test can discharge their liability to pay contracted-out pension rights.

*Occupational Pension Schemes (**Discharge of Protected Rights on Winding Up**) Regulations 1996 (SI 1996/775)* set out how protected rights must be secured if a scheme contracted out by the protected rights test is being wound up.

*Occupational Pension Schemes (**Mixed Benefit Contracted-out Schemes**) Regulations 1996 (SI 1996/1977)* set out the details of how schemes may contract out some employments using the reference scheme test and other employments using the protected rights test.

*Personal and Occupational Pension Schemes (**Protected Rights**) Regulations 1996 (SI 1996/1537)* set out what pension rights must be designated protected rights, the way that protected rights must be calculated and how the rights must be secured in pension form.

*Contracting-out (**Protection of Pensions**) Regulations 1991 (SI 1991/166)* amplify the anti-franking legislation set out in ss 87–92 of the *Pension Schemes Act 1993.*

*Social Security (**Reduced Rates of Class 1 Contributions and Rebates**) (**Money Purchase Contracted-out Schemes**) Order 2001 (SI 2001/1355)* sets out the total amount of age-related payments made by the National Insurance Contributions Office and the employer/employee to the trustees of occupational pension schemes that are contracted out by the protected rights test. Also sets out by how much the employer's and employees' National Insurance Contributions are reduced if the employee is a member of such a scheme.

*Social Security (**Reduced Rates of Class 1 Contributions**) (**Salary Related Contracted-out Schemes**) Order 2001 (SI 2001/1356)* sets out by how the employer's and employees National Insurance Contributions are reduced if the employee is contracted out by the reference scheme test.

*Contracting-out (**Transfer and Transfer Payment**) Regulations 1996 (SI 1996/1462)* deal with the conditions for transfers of Guaranteed Minimum Pensions and rights under a scheme contracted out by the reference scheme test.

*Protected Rights (**Transfer Payment**) Regulations 1996 (SI 1996/1461)* deal with the conditions for transfers of protected rights.

In addition, each year the Department of Social Security will issue:

- ***Guaranteed Minimum Pension Increase*** *Orders* which specify the percentage by which any Guaranteed Minimum Pension (GMP) accrued between 6 April 1988 and 5 April 1997 must be increased when in payment.

- ***Revaluation of Earnings Factors*** *Orders* which specify the *section 148 Orders* that determine the percentage by which past earnings used to calculate additional pension from SERPS/S2P and Guaranteed Minimum Pensions are revalued.

Occupational pension scheme legislation

*Occupational Pension Schemes (**Assignment, Forfeiture, Bankruptcy etc.**) Regulations 1997 (SI 1997/785)* amplify the requirements set out in *ss 91–95* of the Pensions Act 1995.

*Occupational Pension Schemes (Requirement to obtain **Audited Accounts** and a Statement from the Auditor) Regulations 1996 (SI 1996/1975)* require the trustees to obtain audited accounts within seven months of the scheme year end, set out what the accounts must contain and specify the content of the auditor's statement that must appear in the annual report.

*Occupational and Personal Pension Schemes (**Bankruptcy**) Regulations 2002 (SI 2002/427)* amplify the provisions originally introduced in the *Welfare Reform and Pensions Act 1999* dealing with the treatment of the pension rights of a bankrupt.

*Occupational Pension Schemes (**Deficiency on Winding Up** etc.) Regulations 1996 (SI 1996/3128)* concern the treatment under *s 75* of the *Pensions Act 1995* of a deficit in the assets of an occupational pension scheme as a debt owed by the employer to the trustees.

*Occupational Pensions Regulatory Authority (**Determinations and Review Procedure**) Regulations 1997 (SI 1997/794)* set out the procedures to be followed in the review of any determination made by Opra, and the time limits for paying civil fines imposed by Opra.

*Occupational Pension Schemes (**Disclosure of Information**) Regulations 1996 (SI 1996/1655)* set out in detail what items of information must be disclosed to members, potential members, beneficiaries and recognised trade unions by the trustees of occupational pension schemes. The regulations cover basic information about the scheme, information that must be made available to individuals, the information that must be included in the annual report and the availability of actuarial valuation reports, schedules of contributions, payment schedules and statements of investment principles.

*Occupational Pension Schemes (**Equal Treatment**) Regulations 1995 (SI 1995/3183)* amplify the equal treatment requirements set out in *ss 62–66* of the *Pensions Act 1995*.

*Occupational Pension Schemes (**Independent Trustee**) Regulations 1997 (SI 1997/252)* amplify and modify the requirements set out in *ss 22–26* of the *Pensions Act 1995* concerning the statutory appointment of an independent trustee when the employer sponsoring a defined benefit scheme becomes insolvent.

*Occupational Pension Schemes (**Indexation**) Regulations 1996 (SI 1996/1679)* amplify *s 51* of the *Pensions Act 1995* dealing with Limited Price Indexation once in payment of pension rights earned after 5 April 1997.

*Occupational Pension Schemes (**Internal Dispute Resolution Procedures**) Regulations 1996 (SI 1996/1270)* set out the detailed procedures that the trustees must ensure are in place to carry out the requirement of *s 51* of the *Pensions Act 1995* to put in place a mechanism for resolving complaints brought by members and beneficiaries and potential members and beneficiaries of the scheme.

*Occupational Pension Schemes (**Investment**) Regulations 1996 (SI 1996/3127)* give detail on the requirements put in place by *s 40* of the Pensions Act 1995 dealing with avoiding self-investment or employer-related investments and set out some exemptions from the need to prepare a statement of investment principles under *s 35* of that Act.

Occupational and Personal Pension Schemes (**Levy**) Regulations 1997 (SI 1997/666) *set out the rules governing the payment by occupational pension schemes of two levies to pay for Opra, the Pensions Registry, OPAS, the Pensions Ombudsman and the Pensions Compensation Scheme.*

*Occupational Pension Schemes (**Member-nominated Trustees and Directors**) Regulations 1996 (SI 1996/1216)* set out the detailed requirements made under *ss 16–21* of the *Pensions Act 1995* for a statutory consultation exercise to be carried out at least every six years to test the existing arrangements for the nomination and selection of trustees. The regulations also set out the detailed requirements to be met when either the trustees propose appropriate rules or use the prescribed rules to govern the nomination and appointment of member-nominated trustees.

*Occupational Pension Schemes (**Minimum Funding Requirement** and Actuarial Valuations) Regulations 1996 (SI 1996/1536)* amplify the requirements of *ss 56–61* of the *Pensions Act 1995* dealing with the detail of how the minimum funding requirement operates on defined benefit schemes.

*Occupational Pension Schemes (**Modification of Schemes**) Regulations 1996 (SI 1996/2517)* amplify *ss 67–68* of the *Pensions Act 1995* which set out what conditions have to be met before changes can be made by trustees or employers to the trust deed and rules of any occupational pension scheme.

*Occupational Pension Schemes (**Payments to Employers**) Regulations 1996 (SI 1996/2156)* amplify *ss 37 & 76* of the *Pensions Act 1995* which set conditions that must be met before any payment can be made to the employer out of a pension fund that is either continuing in operation or being wound up.

***Pensions Compensation Board (Determinations and Review Procedure)** Regulations 1997 (SI 1997/724)* set out the procedures to be followed by the Pensions Compensation Board when determining whether or not to pay compensation to trustees following a loss of pension fund assets as a result of dishonesty and the insolvency of the employer.

*Occupational Pension Schemes (**Pensions Compensation Provisions**) Regulations 1997 (SI 1997/665)* relate to the payment of compensation to the trustees of occupational pension schemes by the Pensions Compensation Board as provided for under *ss 81–85* of the *Pensions Act 1995*.

*Personal and Occupational Pensions Schemes (**Pensions Ombudsman**) Regulations 1996 (SI 1996/2475)* expand upon the legislation contained in *ss 145–152* of the *Pension Schemes Act 1993*.

*County Court (**Pensions Ombudsman**) (**Enforcement of Directions and Determinations**) Rules 1993 (SI 1993/1978)* provide for the enforcement of the Directions issued by the Pensions Ombudsman by the county courts.

*Personal and Occupational Pension Schemes (**Pensions Ombudsman**) (**Procedure**) Rules 1995 (SI 1995/1053)* set out the procedure to be followed where a complaint or dispute is referred to the Pensions Ombudsman.

*Personal and Occupational Pension Schemes (**Perpetuities**) Regulations 1990 (SI 1990/1143)* relate to *s 163* of the *Pension Schemes Act 1993* which exempts approved occupational pension schemes that are set up as trusts from a general rule of trust law that states that benefits can only be held under a trust for a limited period of time.

*Occupational Pension Schemes (**Preservation of Benefit**) Regulations 1991 (SI 1991/167)* amplify the requirements of *ss 69–82* of the *Pension Schemes Act 1993* dealing with the rights of early leavers to have their pension rights vested in the pension scheme. The regulations also deal with some of the alternatives to preservation, notably buying out benefits and early retirement. The regulations set out the conditions to be met if bulk transfers without members' consent are to be permitted.

*Occupational Pension Schemes (**Prohibition of Trustees**) Regulations 1997 (SI 1997/663)* add to the circumstances, set out in *s 3* of the *Pensions Act 1995, in which Opra may prohibit a person from being a trustee.*

Register of Occupational and Personal Pension Schemes Regulations 1997 (SI 1997/371) establish that there shall continue to be a Registrar of Occupational Pension Schemes and that it will be operated by Opra. The regulations set out the information that is required from schemes.

*Occupational Pension Schemes (**Revaluation**) Regulations 1991 (SI 1991/168)* amplify the requirements set out in *ss 83–86* of, and in *Sch 3* to, the *Pensions Schemes Act 1993* that pension rights of early leavers must be revalued during the period of deferment.

*Occupational Pension Schemes (**Scheme Administration**) Regulations 1996 (SI 1996/1715)* add to the list of advisers that must be appointed by the trustees; set out what kind of schemes are exempt from the need to appoint auditors or actuaries; specify the qualifications needed for appointment as scheme auditor or actuary and the manner and the terms of appointment and removal of scheme advisers; require the employer and the trustees to disclose information to the scheme advisers; specify that the actuary does not become ineligible to act just because someone else in the same actuarial firm is a trustee of the scheme; specify that an actuary or auditor is not ineligible to act just because he or she is connected to a pensioner trustee; amplify the requirements for giving notice of a trustee meeting; set out the exceptions to the requirement that the trustees set up an independent bank account; specify the books and records that the trustees must keep and how long those books and records should be kept; specify the details that must be recorded in the minutes of trustee meetings and how long the minutes must be kept; specify how quickly contributions deducted from employees' earnings must be passed to the trustees; and amplify the requirements relating to payment schedules in money purchase schemes.

Occupational Pension Schemes **(Transfer Values)** *Regulations 1996 (SI 1996/1847)* deal with transfers of pension rights and amplify *ss 93–101* of the *Pension Schemes Act 1993*.

Pension Schemes **(Voluntary Contributions Requirements and Voluntary and Compulsory Membership)** *Regulations 1987 (SI 1987/1108)* set out exceptions to the general requirement on schemes to provide AVC facilities made by *s 111* of the *Pension Schemes Act 1993*, and exceptions to the general requirement preventing employers making membership of occupational pension schemes compulsory made by *s 160* of the *Pension Schemes Act 1993*.

Occupational Pension Schemes **(Winding Up)** *Regulations 1996 (SI 1996/31260* amplify *ss 73–77* of the *Pensions Act 1995* (winding up) and *s 38* of the *Pensions Act 1995* (power to defer winding up).

Occupational Pension Schemes **(Winding Up Notices and Reports etc.)** *Regulations 2002 (SI 2002/459)* implement the detailed provisions originally introduced by the *Child Support, Pensions and Social Security Act 2000* designed to speed up the winding up of occupational pension schemes.

In addition, each year the Department for Work and Pensions will issue:

Occupational Pension **(Revaluation)** *Orders* which specify the percentage by which all the preserved pensions of early leavers in excess of any Guaranteed Minimum Pension must be increased over the time until the pension becomes payable. They do not apply to money purchase schemes.

Primary Inland Revenue legislation

Income and Corporation Taxes Act (ICTA) 1988

ICTA 1988 is the principal tax Act containing all the main tax measures concerning occupational pension schemes (called retirement benefit schemes by the Inland Revenue). It also contains the tax legislation governing personal pensions and stakeholder pensions.

Part XIV

ss 590–591D	Conditions for the approval of retirement benefit schemes.
ss 592–594	Tax reliefs.
ss 595–603	Charges to tax in certain cases.

ss 604–612   Supplementary provisions.

ss 630–655   Personal pensions

Finance Act 1989

Contains some legislation not consolidated into *ICTA 1988* that concerns principally the pensionable earnings cap and the associated 1989 tax regime. It also deals with overfunding of additional voluntary contribution schemes.

s 75 & Sch 6   Approved schemes: general – approved schemes: AVCs.

s 76   Non-approved retirement benefits schemes.

Secondary Inland Revenue legislation

*Occupational Pension Schemes (**Additional Voluntary Contributions**) Regulations 1987 (SI 1987/1749)* govern the tax treatment of free-standing AVCs.

*Personal Pension Schemes (**Concurrent Membership**) Order (SI 2000/2318)* governs how the remuneration of an active member of an occupational pension scheme is calculated for the purpose of establishing whether or not it exceeds £30,000 for the purposes of concurrent contributions to a personal or stakeholder pension scheme.

*Personal Pension Schemes (**Conversion of Retirement Benefits Schemes**) Regulations 2001 (SI 2001/118)* amplify provisions of *Sch 23ZA* to the *Income and Corporation Taxes Act 1988* allowing defined contribution occupational pension schemes to convert to the tax regime governing personal pension schemes.

*Retirement Benefits Schemes (**Continuation of Rights of Members of Approved Schemes**) Regulations 1990 (SI 1990/2101)* govern transitional and special arrangements that define those who have continued rights under the tax regimes existing before the measures introduced by the *Finance Act 1989*.

*Retirement Benefits Schemes (Tax Relief on Contributions) (**Disapplication of the Earnings Cap**) Regulations 1990 (SI 1990/586)* govern transitional and special arrangements that define those who have continued rights to pensionable earnings not limited by the pensionable earnings cap introduced by the *Finance Act 1989*.

*Retirement Benefits Schemes (**Information Powers**) Regulations 1995 (SI 1995/3103)* extend and modernise the Inland Revenue's power to gain access to pension scheme information within specified time limits and require trustees to keep records of certain events and transactions available for a period of at least six years. There are new penalties for failure to comply.

*Occupational Pension Schemes (**Maximum Rate Lump Sum**) Regulations 1987 (SI 1987/1513)* detail the maximum lump sum that is payable to a member who joined an occupational pension scheme before 17 March 1987 and has less than 20 years pensionable service when he or she becomes entitled to the pension.

*Retirement Benefits Schemes **(Restriction on Discretion to Approve)** (Additional Voluntary Contributions) Regulations 1993 (SI 1993/3016)* deal with the treatment of surplus funds that arise from AVC payments.

*Retirement Benefits Schemes **(Restriction on Discretion to Approve)** (Excepted Schemes) Regulations 1996 (SI 1996/1582)* allow schemes approved before 27 December 1993 to continue to remain approved if they have not made rate amendments concerning the repayment of surplus AVCs, provided they comply with *SI 1993/3016* and the code of practice on repayment of surplus AVCs.

*Retirement Benefits Schemes **(Restriction on Discretion to Approve)** (Small Self-administered schemes) Regulations 1991 (SI 1991/1614)* govern small self-administered schemes, in particular controlling the situations, and setting conditions, for any loanbacks to the sponsoring employer.

*Pension Scheme **Surpluses** **(Administration)** Regulations 1987 (SI 1987/352)* set out how the scheme administrator will make a 35% tax deduction on any authorised payment to the employer from the pension fund.

*Pension Scheme **Surpluses** **(Valuation)** Regulations 1987 (SI 1987/412)* deal with how the assets and liabilities of occupational pension schemes are to be actuarially valued and how surpluses of assets over liabilities valued at over 5% of the fund must either be reduced or a tax charge levied on the amount of the surplus.

*Personal Pension Schemes **(Transfer Payments)** Regulations 2001 (SI 2001/119)* deal with restrictions placed on transfers from occupational to personal pension schemes.

*Occupational Pension Schemes **(Transitional Provisions)** Regulations 1988 (SI 1988/1436)* govern transitional and special arrangements that define those who have continued rights under the tax regime existing before 17 March 1987.

In addition, each year the Inland Revenue will issue:

*Retirement Benefits Schemes **(Indexation of Earnings Cap)** Orders* which set the annual level of the pensionable earnings cap.

Guidance from the Occupational Pensions Regulatory Authority

The Occupational Pensions Regulatory Authority (Opra) publishes a series of *Notes* and *Updates*.

As at March 2003 the *Notes* that have been published are:

Note 1 (March 1997, revised July 1999) Pensions Act 1995, Section 48 – Reporting to Opra

Note 2 (August 1997) Pensions Act 1995 Transfer Values – Current Issues

Note 3 (June 1998) Pensions Act 1995 Payment of Surplus – Opra's Role

Note 4 (January 1999) Pensions Act 1995 Determinations and Their Review – Opra's Procedures

Note 5 (April 1999) Appointment of Trustees by Opra

Note 6 (February 2000) Pensions Act 1995 The Right to Report Problems to Opra

Note 7 (September 2000) Disclosure of Information to Members and Others

Note 8 (February 2001) Direct Payment Arrangements by Employers to Personal Pension and Stakeholder Pension Schemes

Note 9 (April 2001) Minimum Funding Requirement – Making Extension Applications to Opra

Note 10 (October 2002) Winding Up

Note 11 (October 2002) Stakeholder Pension Scheme Charges

In addition, the following *Update* has been published:

Update 1 (February 2003) Calculation and Payment of Cash Equivalent Transfer Values

Opra has also published important detailed guidance:

A Guide for Pension Scheme Trustees (July 1997, revised June 2001)

Guidance to Trustees Appointed by Opra from its Panel of Trustees (May 1998)

Guidance to Lay Trustees Appointed by Opra from its Trustee Panel (April 1999)

A Guide to the Minimum Funding Requirement (May 1999)

Paying Pension Contributions on Time. A Guide for Employers with Occupational Pension Schemes (March 1999, revised April 2000 and February 2002)

Getting Your Audited Accounts and the Auditor's Statement on Time. A Guide for Occupational Pension Scheme Trustees (April 2000)

A Guide to Audited Scheme Accounts. A Guide to Help Those Involved with Insured Salary-Related Pension Schemes (June 2000)

A Guide to Solving Disputes (August 2000)

A Guide to Appointing Professional Advisers (October 2000)

Opra and Pension Scheme Auditors (June 2002)

Opra publishes a quarterly *Bulletin* which contains any important general messages that the Regulator wishes to give, key facts and figures summarising its regulatory work and general explanatory articles.

For more details on Opra publications contact:

Helpdesk
Opra
Invicta House
Trafalgar Place
Brighton
BN1 4DW
Tel: 01273 627600
Fax: 01273 627688
email: helpdesk@opra.gov.uk
Website: http://www.opra.gov.uk

Guidance from the Inland Revenue

Practice Notes on Approval of Occupational Pension Schemes IR12 (2001) is the principal publication of the Pension Schemes Technical Advice team within the Inland Revenue Savings, Pensions, Share Schemes business stream. It gives detailed instructions on how an occupational pension scheme can gain exempt-approved tax status under the discretionary approval provisions of *section 591* of the *Income and Corporation Taxes Act 1988.*

The Inland Revenue also issues a series of *Updates* which detail changes in how it exercises its discretionary approval over occupational pension schemes.

These publications are available from the Inland Revenue's website.

Paper copies of the Pensions Updates and paper amendments to IR12 will cease to be published with effect from 30 November 2003.

The IR Savings, Pensions, Share Scheme office can be contacted at:

IR SPSS
Yorke House
PO Box 62
Castle Meadow Road
Nottingham
NG2 1BG
Tel: 0115 974 1600
Fax: 0115 974 1480
Website: http://www.inlandrevenue.gov.uk/pensionschemes/index.htm

Guidance from the National Insurance Contributions Office

The National Insurance Contributions Office is an executive agency of the Inland Revenue and is responsible for operating the National Insurance scheme. Within the National Insurance Contributions Office is *National Insurance Services to Pensions Industry* (NISPI) (formerly the Contracted-out Employments Group (COEG)) which has a number of tasks relating to contracted-out occupational pension schemes. For example, NISPI considers elections from employers who wish to contract out of SERPS and is responsible for supervising contracted-out schemes to ensure that their resources meet their contracted-out liabilities and that they continue to satisfy the conditions for contracting out. NISPI also processes the forms that are completed when a contracted-out employee becomes an early leaver.

The National Insurance Contributions Office publishes the following guidance which explains the requirements of the contracting-out legislation and sets out the required administrative procedures:

CA14   Termination of Contracted-out Employment – Manual for Salary-Related Pension Schemes and Salary Related parts of Mixed Benefit Schemes

CA14A   Termination of Contracted-out Employment – Manual for Money Purchase Pension Schemes and Money Purchase Parts of Mixed Benefit Schemes

CA14B   Contracted-out Guidance on Re-elections for Salary Related Pension Schemes and Salary Related Overseas Schemes (transitional guidance for the period up to 31 January 1998)

CA14C   Contracted-out Guidance for Salary Related Pension Schemes and Salary Related Overseas Schemes

CA14D   Contracted-out Guidance for Money Purchase Pension Schemes and Money Purchase Overseas Schemes

CA14E   Contracted-out Guidance for Mixed Benefit Pension Schemes and Mixed Benefit Overseas Schemes

CA14F   Technical Guidance on Review of Determinations

CA15   Cessation of Contracted-out Pension Schemes

Enquiries should be made to:

National Insurance Contributions Office
National Insurance Services to Pensions Industry
Chillingham House
Benton Park View
Benton Park Road
Longbenton
Newcastle upon Tyne
NE98 1ZZ
Tel: 0191 213 5000

Note, however, that the operational aspects of determining new elections to contract out and maintaining information on current contracted-out schemes will transfer to the Nottingham office of IR SPSS (see above) from May 2003.

Guidance from the actuarial professional bodies

The joint Pensions Board of the Institute of Actuaries and Faculty of Actuaries has issued a series of Guidance Notes (GN) which for the most part set out the mandatory practice to be followed by actuaries acting for pension schemes.

GN3   Certain Certificates for Contracting-Out

GN9   Retirement Benefit Schemes – Actuarial Reports

GN11   Retirement Benefit Schemes – Transfer Values

GN16   Retirement Benefit Schemes – Bulk Transfers

GN17   Accounting for Pension Costs under Statement of Standard Accounting Practice No 24

GN19   Retirement Benefit Schemes – Winding-up and Scheme Asset Deficiency

GN24   Illustration of Defined Contribution Pension Benefits

GN26   Pension Fund Terminology

GN27   Retirement Benefit Schemes – Minimum Funding Requirement

GN28   Retirement Benefit Schemes – Adequacy of Benefits for Contracting-out on or after 6 April 1997

GN29   Occupational Pension Schemes – Actuaries Advising the Trustees or a Participating Employer

Contact:

> Institute of Actuaries
> Staple Inn Hall
> High Holborn
> London
> WC1V 7QJ
> Tel: 020 7632 2100
>
> Faculty of Actuaries
> 18 Dublin Street
> Edinburgh
> EH1 3PP
> Tel: 0131 240 1300

The Guidance Notes may also be accessed from the actuaries' website (http://www.actuaries.org.uk)

Guidance from the accountancy professional bodies

Practice Note 15 – The Audit of Occupational Pension Schemes in the United Kingdom, plus *Supplement 2000/02*, issued by the Auditing Practices Board. It is available on the Internet at http://www.accountancyfoundation.com/ uploaded_documents/PN_15.pdf.

Financial Reports of Pension Schemes – A Statement of Recommended Practice (SORP), issued by the Pensions Research Accountants Group and approved by the Accounting Standards Board.

Financial Reporting Standard (FRS) 17 Retirement Benefits, issued by the Accounting Standards Board.

This guidance is all available from:

> Croner CCH Group Limited
> 145 London Road
> Kingston upon Thames
> Surrey
> KT2 6SR
> Tel. 0870 777 2906

Guidance to professional trustees

The following guidance was published by the Occupational Pensions Regulatory Authority (Opra) in *Opra Bulletin Issue 3*, issued in May 1998. The guidance is intended for use by independent, professional trustees appointed to occupational pension schemes by Opra. The professional trustees involved will be drawn a from trustee panel chosen by Opra.

'Opra wants professional trustees to ensure no money or time is spent unnecessarily. The people most likely to suffer from any such unnecessary work are the scheme members themselves.

1   Opra expects trustees to have access to Opra publications.

Any trustee who is not already on the Opra mailing list can complete the 'publications mailing list' form to ensure they get copies of all future Opra publications automatically. Opra publications are also available free of charge from the helpdesk (see 'how to contact us').

2   Opra expects trustees to keep themselves up-to-date on relevant legislation.

3   Opra requires that appropriate indemnity cover is in place at all times.

Opra should be notified immediately if this is not the case.

4   Opra expects trustees to keep the scheme members regularly informed.

Updates at least every six months would seem reasonable – more frequently if the scheme's resources allow and events are moving rapidly.

5   Opra expects trustees to use appropriate advisers where required, taking into consideration the size, nature and complexity of the scheme to which they have been appointed.

For example, where a straightforward, money-purchase, insured, contracted-in type arrangement is being wound up, Opra would not expect the trustees to require the use of the services of a large or expensive City law firm.

6   Trustees must always keep the interests of the members paramount.

Trustees should seek to avoid incurring costs which would produce no benefit to the members. Trustees should also avoid taking actions which would cause unreasonable abatement of benefit (for example, complex or expensive investigations, where the cost outweighs any possible recovery of assets).

7   Opra expects trustees to make it a first priority to check the scheme's compliance with the requirements of the Pensions Act 1995.

It is, of course, understood that the reason for the appointment by Opra may well be the fact that the scheme has not been compliant with requirements of the relevant legislation. Steps should be taken to regularise the situation as soon as reasonably practicable (probably within two months of appointment) or to report to Opra where this is not possible. An action plan should be drawn up to assist trustees to establish compliance priorities.

8   Opra expects to be provided with the hourly charge-out rates of the trustee, together with the hourly rates of grades of staff that they employ.

9   Opra requires that trustees will undertake to notify Opra of any changes to the charge-out rates.

10   Opra requires trustees to agree to keep detailed and accurate records of the hours and work which they, their staff and their advisers carry out for schemes to which they have been appointed.

Trustees are required to provide Opra, at such times as Opra may reasonably require, with a detailed account of the work carried out, the number of hours spent and fees charged. This means that they should also ask for, and keep, a detailed breakdown of the work their advisers have carried out. As a matter of good practice, all files relating to the pension scheme should be kept in good order. This will help effective administration and reduce costs in the long term.

11   Opra requires that trustees agree to their fees (and the fees of any advisers they have appointed) being subject, at Opra's discretion, to review by an independent assessor appointed and paid for by Opra.

This would not preclude Opra itself from considering in the first instance any complaint about the level of fees charged by a trustee appointed by Opra. Where, having considered such a complaint, Opra considers the level of fees to be reasonable, Opra may still ask the independent assessor to investigate the complaint. But in such a case, the complainant would be expected to pay the fees of the independent assessor.

12   Opra expects to be notified immediately if trustees consider that they have a conflict of interest in relation to the scheme (or schemes) to which they have been appointed.

This guidance does not replace any of the duties or powers which the law gives to trustees. It is NOT intended for use by lay trustees (such as ordinary scheme members) who have been appointed by Opra but who are not members of Opra's trustee panel.'

Appendix 5

State pension provision

In this appendix we set out a basic description of the following state benefits:

- incapacity benefit;
- bereavement payment;
- widowed parent's allowance;
- bereavement allowance;
- basic state pension;
- additional pension from SERPS;
- additional pension from S2P; and
- minimum income guarantee.

These benefits have been chosen because they correspond to the ill-health, death and retirement benefits provided by pension schemes.

Please note that in this appendix:

- *lower earnings limit* (LEL) is the earnings threshold at which, and above which, entitlement to contributory state benefits begin to accrue. In 2003/04 the lower earnings limit is set at £77 p w or £334 per month.

- *upper earnings limit* (UEL) is an earnings threshold such that an employee who earns above this limit in any pay period pays no National Insurance contributions on the slice of earnings above this limit. In 2003/04 the upper earnings limit is set at £595 p w or £2,579 per month.

For the purposes of the SERPS/S2P calculations, since 6 April 2000 the claimant's entitlement is based on the slice of earnings in any one pay period lying between the lower earnings limit applying to that pay period and the upper earnings limit applying to that pay period. For any entitlement to S2P to accrue, however, the employee's annual earnings in the tax year must exceed the *qualifying earnings factor* (QEF) which is 52 times the weekly LEL or £4,004 in 2003/04.

State pension age (SPA) currently means age 60 in the case of a woman and 65 in the case of a man. However, for women born on or after 6 April 1950 state pension age is being raised. Women born on or after 6 April 1955 will reach state pension age when they are 65. Women born on or after 6 April 1950 but before 6 April 1955 will reach state pension age at an intermediate age between 60 and 65 during the period running 6 May 2010 to 6 March 2020 as given in the following table.

Appendix 5

Period within which woman was born	*Date state pension age attained*
6 April 1950 to 5 May 1950	6 May 2010
6 May 1950 to 5 June 1950	6 July 2010
6 June 1950 to 5 July 1950	6 September 2010
6 July 1950 to 5 August 1950	6 November 2010
6 August 1950 to 5 September 1950	6 January 2011
6 September 1950 to 5 October 1950	6 March 2011
6 October 1950 to 5 November 1950	6 May 2011
6 November 1950 to 5 December 1950	6 July 2011
6 December 1950 to 5 January 1951	6 September 2011
6 January 1951 to 5 February 1951	6 November 2011
6 February 1951 to 5 March 1951	6 January 2012
6 March 1951 to 5 April 1951	6 March 2012
6 April 1951 to 5 May 1951	6 May 2012
6 May 1951 to 5 June 1951	6 July 2012
6 June 1951 to 5 July 1951	6 September 2012
6 July 1951 to 5 August 1951	6 November 2012
6 August 1951 to 5 September 1951	6 January 2013
6 September 1951 to 5 October 1951	6 March 2013
6 October 1951 to 5 November 1951	6 May 2013
6 November 1951 to 5 December 1951	6 July 2013
6 December 1951 to 5 January 1952	6 September 2013
6 January 1952 to 5 February 1952	6 November 2013
6 February 1952 to 5 March 1952	6 January 2014
6 March 1952 to 5 April 1952	6 March 2014
6 April 1952 to 5 May 1952	6 May 2014
6 May 1952 to 5 June 1952	6 July 2014
6 June 1952 to 5 July 1952	6 September 2014
6 July 1952 to 5 August 1952	6 November 2014
6 August 1952 to 5 September 1952	6 January 2015
6 September 1952 to 5 October 1952	6 March 2015
6 October 1952 to 5 November 1952	6 May 2015
6 November 1952 to 5 December 1952	6 July 2015
6 December 1952 to 5 January 1953	6 September 2015
6 January 1953 to 5 February 1953	6 November 2015
6 February 1953 to 5 March 1953	6 January 2016
6 March 1953 to 5 April 1953	6 March 2016
6 April 1953 to 5 May 1953	6 May 2016
6 May 1953 to 5 June 1953	6 July 2016
6 June 1953 to 5 July 1953	6 September 2016
6 July 1953 to 5 August 1953	6 November 2016
6 August 1953 to 5 September 1953	6 January 2017
6 September 1953 to 5 October 1953	6 March 2017
6 October 1953 to 5 November 1953	6 May 2017
6 November 1953 to 5 December 1953	6 July 2017
6 December 1953 to 5 January 1954	6 September 2017
6 January 1954 to 5 February 1954	6 November 2017
6 February 1954 to 5 March 1954	6 January 2018

6 March 1954 to 5 April 1954
6 April 1954 to 5 May 1954
6 May 1954 to 5 June 1954
6 June 1954 to 5 July 1954
6 July 1954 to 5 August 1954
6 August 1954 to 5 September 1954
6 September 1954 to 5 October 1954
6 October 1954 to 5 November 1954
6 November 1954 to 5 December 1954
6 December 1954 to 5 January 1955
6 January 1955 to 5 February 1955
6 February 1955 to 5 March 1955
6 March 1955 to 5 April 1955

6 March 2018
6 May 2018
6 July 2018
6 September 2018
6 November 2018
6 January 2019
6 March 2019
6 May 2019
6 July 2019
6 September 2019
6 November 2019
6 January 2020
6 March 2020

Incapacity benefit

Employees who become ill for a *period of incapacity for work* (PIW) lasting up to 28 weeks will normally be entitled to receive statutory sick pay (SSP) paid by the employer through the payroll. Often this is part of the employees' contractual entitlement to occupational sick pay from the employer. If employees are suffering from a long-term illness that prevents them from working beyond 28 weeks, they may become entitled to state incapacity benefit.

From day 197 of the PIW, employees may claim short-term incapacity benefit at the higher rate. From day 365 of the PIW they may claim long-term incapacity benefit. Both these benefits are payable directly by the state to the individual concerned.

As a result of the *Welfare Reform and Pensions Act 1999*, new entitlement conditions for incapacity benefit came into force in April 2001. Incapacity benefit is now payable only if the claimants have actually paid National Insurance contributions on earnings at least equal to 25 times the weekly lower earnings limit in one of the three tax years before the calendar year (defined as running from the first Sunday in January to the first Saturday in the following January) in which the claim is made. The claimant must also have paid, or been credited with, National Insurance contributions on earnings at least equal to 50 times the lower earnings limit in each of the two tax years ending before the calendar year in which the claim is made.

Claimants must also demonstrate that they are incapable of performing their own job in relation to a claim for short-term incapacity benefit at the higher rate, and in relation to long-term incapacity they must satisfy a personal capability assessment.

Long-term incapacity benefit is not payable once the claimant has reached state pension age. Short-term incapacity at the higher rate can continue until day 364 of a PIW which began before the claimant reached state pension age.

Appendix 5

Amount payable (rates in 2003/04)

Short-term incapacity benefit at the higher rate

£64.35 p w

£72.15 p w if paid beyond state pension age and state retirement pension has been deferred.

Long-term incapacity benefit

£72.15 p w

+ £7.60 p w if the claimant was 35 but under 45 on the first day of the PIW; or

+ £15.15 p w if the claimant was under 35 of the first day of the PIW.

Increases for dependent children of £9.55 p w for the first child and £11.35 p w for any other children are payable. An increase for an adult dependant is only payable if the dependant is aged over 60 or cares for the claimant's child. Increases for adult and child dependants are only payable if any adult dependant earns less than a specified amount. Note, however, that such increases for dependent children are to be abolished and replaced by provisions made under the *Tax Credits Act 2002*.

Abatement

Under the provisions of the *Welfare Reform and Pensions Act 1999* incapacity benefit is reduced by 50% of the slice of income above £85 p w that is receivable by the claimant from an occupational or personal pension scheme. This reduction does not apply if the claimant is a widow, widower or other dependant of a former pension scheme member and the occupational or personal pension is payable as a result of that former scheme member's death.

Bereavement benefits

The *Welfare Reform and Pensions Act 1999* introduced, in relation to deaths on or after 9 April 2001, a new system of bereavement benefits payable to widows and widowers. These benefits are payable on sex-equal terms. The predecessor regular pension benefits of widowed mother's allowance and widow's pension will continue to be paid, with annual upratings, to existing claimants in relation to deaths before that date.

Bereavement payment

A single tax-free lump sum of £2,000 is payable on the death of a spouse. Entitlement depends on the claimant being under state pension age at the time the spouse died, although the bereavement payment can be paid if the claimant is over state pension age provided that the deceased spouse had not begun to receive a Category A state retirement pension (i e a state retirement pension that had been payable to the deceased spouse in his or her own right).

Entitlement also depends on the spouse having actually paid National Insurance contributions on earnings of at least 25 times the weekly lower earnings limit in any tax year, or the self-employed or voluntary contribution equivalents.

Entitlement depends on the claimant not having lived together with a person of the opposite sex other than the spouse at the time of the spouse's death.

Widowed parent's allowance

Widowed parent's allowance is payable to a claimant with the care of young children whose spouse has died while still under state pension age. (Note that it is also be paid to a widower whose wife died before 9 April 2001, the date the new benefit was introduced, provided that he has not remarried since and is still under state pension age.)

Entitlement depends on the surviving spouse being entitled to child benefit from the state in respect of a child:

- of the surviving spouse and the deceased spouse; or

- for whom the deceased spouse was entitled to child benefit immediately before his or her death; or

- for whom the surviving spouse was entitled to child benefit at the time of the spouse's death provided that the surviving spouse and the deceased spouse had been residing together immediately before the death.

Widowed parent's allowance can become payable if the surviving spouse is a woman who was pregnant at the date of her husband's death.

Widowed parent's allowance ceases to be payable if the surviving spouse remarries and will be suspended during any period that the surviving spouse cohabits with a partner of the opposite sex. Widowed parent's allowance ceases when child benefit ceases to be payable by the state for all children in one of the categories described above. It also ceases if otherwise still payable when the surviving spouse reaches state pension age, and is replaced by state retirement pension.

National insurance contribution tests

Entitlement also depends on the deceased spouse (referred to here as 'the contributor') having paid National Insurance contributions for the required number of *qualifying years*. Since 1978/79, a qualifying year has been a tax year in which the contributor has either paid or been credited with Class 1 National Insurance contributions on earnings of at least 52 times the weekly lower earnings limit for the tax year concerned. For the three years 1975/76 to 1977/78, the required amount was 50 times the weekly lower earnings limit concerned. For tax years before 1975/76, the number of qualifying years is found by adding together the total number of flat-rate contributions paid by, or credited to, the contributor and dividing by 50 (but the person cannot be awarded more qualifying years than tax years in this part of his or her working life). The self-employed or voluntary contribution equivalents will also count.

The required number of qualifying years depends on the length of the contributor's *working life*. A contributor's working life begins with the tax year in which the contributor reaches age 16 and ends with the tax year before the tax year in which the contributor either died or reached state pension age.

Length of working life	*Required number of qualifying years*
10 years or under	Length of working life minus 1 year
11 years – 20 years	Length of working life minus 2 years
21 years – 30 years	Length of working life minus 3 years
31 years – 40 years	Length of working life minus 4 years
41 years or over	Length of working life minus 5 years

The number of qualifying years required can be reduced if the person had been entitled to home responsibilities protection (HRP) during a tax year. (HRP is the name given to the system whereby those who do not work because they stay at home to care for a child or a disabled person are helped, none the less, to qualify for a basic state pension.)

If the contributor's National Insurance record does not have the required number of qualifying years, the benefit can still be payable at a pro rata amount provided that the number of qualifying years is not less than one-quarter of the required number for a full-rate. No benefit is payable if the number of qualifying years is less than one-quarter of the required number for a full-rate.

As noted above, the National Insurance contributions required for the qualifying years test may have actually been paid, or been credited to the contributor's National Insurance record. However, there is a separate requirement that, in order for a benefit to be payable, the contributor must have actually paid in at least one tax year the required amount of National Insurance contributions rather than having had them credited.

Widowed parent's allowance (2003/04)

Basic allowance	£77.45 p w
Increase for first dependent child	£ 9.55 p w*
Increase for each other dependent child	£11.35 p w*
Inherited rate of additional pension	See 'SERPS' and 'S2P' below

* Note, however, that such increases for dependent children are to be abolished and replaced by provisions made under the *Tax Credits Act 2002*.

The rates quoted assume that the contributor has the required number of qualifying years, except that increases for children do not suffer any pro rata reduction in cases where the number of years is less than the required number, provided that they are not less than one-quarter of the required number.

Bereavement allowance (2003/04)

Bereavement allowance is payable to a surviving spouse with no dependent children provided that he or she is aged 45 or over, but under state pension age (SPA), at the date of the spouse's death.

Entitlement depends on the deceased spouse's National Insurance record satisfying the same National Insurance contribution tests as described above for widowed parent's allowance.

Bereavement allowance is payable for a maximum period of 52 weeks. It will end immediately if the surviving spouse remarries or reaches state pension age and will be suspended during any period the surviving spouse cohabits with a person of the opposite sex.

Age of claimant at date of death of deceased spouse

55 or over, up to SPA	£77.45 p w full rate quoted
54	£72.03 p w
53	£66.61 p w
52	£61.19 p w
51	£55.76 p w
50	£50.34 p w
49	£44.92 p w
48	£39.50 p w
47	£34.08 p w
46	£28.66 p w
45	£23.24 p w

There is no inherited additional pension component payable from SERPS or S2P with the basic bereavement allowance (unlike in the case of the predecessor benefit widow's pension).

State retirement pension

State retirement pension may be either a:

- category A pension, payable to claimants on the basis of their own National Insurance record; or

- category B pension, payable to claimants on the basis of the National Insurance record of their spouse but which is payable direct to the claimants and forms part of their taxable income; or

- category A/B pension, being a composite pension comprising both category A and category B.

A state retirement pension will also normally comprise two components:

- a basic state pension; and

- an additional pension payable from SERPS and/or S2P.

Basic state pension

Entitlement to a basic state pension depends on the pensioner having made a claim and having reached state pension age. The pension is then payable for life. Entitlement also depends on the claimant, or the claimant's spouse, having paid National Insurance contributions that satisfy the same tests as set out above for widowed parent's allowance.

A category B pension payable to a wife at the married person's rate is only payable if the husband has also reached state pension age and claimed his pension. A married man will in future be able to receive a married man's Category B pension at the lower married person's rate when he reaches state pension age provided his wife has reached state pension age and claimed her pension and was born on or after 6 April 1950.

If the husband has reached state pension age but his wife is still under state pension age, the husband may claim an adult dependant's increase in respect of his wife. This increase is payable to the husband and forms part of his taxable income. The increase is not payable if his wife/adult dependant has earnings above a specified amount. A married woman who has reached state pension age can claim an adult dependant's increase in respect of her husband if she was previously claiming Incapacity Benefit and was receiving an increase for him with that benefit. From 6 April 2010 a married woman will be able to receive an increase for her husband on her Category A basic state pension under the same conditions as already applying to a married man claiming an increase for his wife.

A category B pension is payable at the widowed person's rate immediately to a widow if her husband died after she had reached state pension age. If her husband died before she reached state pension age, she becomes entitled to the category B pension when she reaches her state pension age; provided that she was entitled to, or could be treated as being entitled to, a state bereavement allowance or widow's pension immediately before she reached state pension age.

A widower becomes entitled to a Category B basic state pension at the widowed person's rate if both he and his wife had reached state pension age before his wife died. However, in cases where a man reaches 65 on or after 6 April 2010 a widower's Category B basic state pension will be payable to him under the same conditions as apply to a widow.

Furthermore, widows and widowers who are still receiving widowed parent's allowance when they reach state pension age are entitled, provided they have not remarried, to a Category B retirement pension, on the basis of their spouse's contributions, at the same weekly level as their widowed parent's allowance.

Widows or widowers who were previously entitled to bereavement allowance or were aged over 45 when they ceased to be entitled to widowed parent's allowance, provided they have not remarried, also become entitled to a

Category B retirement pension when they reach state pension age on the basis of their spouse's contributions. Where:

- the pensioner was under age 55 at the time that his or her earlier entitlement to widowed parent's allowance ended; or

- there was no entitlement to widowed parent's allowance at the time that the spouse had died and he or she became entitled to bereavement allowance;

then the overall rate of Category B retirement pension (including the additional pension component) is reduced by 7% for each year or part of a year that the pensioner's age at that time was less than 55 – but with a maximum of ten years to count so that the maximum reduction will be 70%.

Amount payable (rates for 2003/04)

Category A	£77.45 p w	full rate quoted
Category B		
• married woman	£46.35 p w	
• widow/widower	£77.45 p w	
Increase for		
• adult dependant	£46.35 p w	
• first child dependant*	£9.55 p w	
• each other child dependant*	£11.35 p w	
Age 80 increase	25p p w	

* Note, however, that such increases for dependent children are to be abolished and replaced by provisions made under the *Tax Credits Act 2002*.

A composite category A/B basic state pension cannot be greater than a Category A pension payable at the full rate, and so only benefits claimants who do not have a full Category A entitlement. The actual amount payable is the claimant's own reduced rate Category A basic state pension plus the smaller of the following:

- the amount by which the reduced rate Category A basic state pension is less than a Category A basic state pension payable at the full rate; and

- th amount of Category B basic state pension derived from the spouse's contribution record.

Additional pension

Additional pension is the second component of the state retirement pension. It may be payable even if, unusually, the claimant has no entitlement to basic state pension. It is payable to claimants who have reached state pension age.

Additional pension is payable from the State Earnings Related Pension Scheme (SERPS) in respect of earnings in the period 1978/79 to 2001/02 and from the State Second Pension (S2P) in respect of earnings in the period 2002/03 onwards.

SERPS calculation

The employee's earnings between the National Insurance lower earnings limit (LEL) and the upper earnings limit (UEL) are calculated for each tax year from 1978/79 to 2001/02 (inclusive). The resulting figure obtained for each tax year gives the *surplus earnings* for that year.

The surplus earnings figure for each tax year is revalued in the year before the individual reaches state pension. The revaluation is in line with the increase in national average earnings over the period running from the tax year the earnings were paid until the tax year before the individual reaches state pension age. The surplus earnings figure in the tax year before the tax year in which the individual reaches state pension age is included in the calculation but is not revalued.

Stage A

The resulting revalued surplus earnings figures for the tax years 1978/79 to 1987/88 inclusive are added together, multiplied by 25% and then divided by the total number of years between 1978/79 (or, if later, the tax year in which the individual attained age 16) and the tax year ending before the tax year in which the individual attains state pension age.

Stage B

The resulting revalued surplus earnings figures for the tax years from 1988/89 to the tax year ending immediately before the tax year in which the individual attains state pension age or, if earlier, immediately before 6 April 2002 tax year, are added together and then multiplied by the relevant percentage in the table below depending on the year in which the individual attains state pension age.

Tax year in which state pension age is attained	*Percentage*
1999/2000	25
2000/2001	$24\frac{1}{2}$
2001/2002	24
2002/2003	$23\frac{1}{2}$
2003/2004	23
2004/2005	$22\frac{1}{2}$
2005/2006	22
2006/2007	$21\frac{1}{2}$
2007/2008	21
2008/2009	$20\frac{1}{2}$
2009/2010 or later	20

The resulting figure is then divided by the total number of years between 1978/79 (or, if later, the tax year in which the individual attained age 16) and the tax year ending before the tax year in which the individual attains state pension age.

Stage C

The two amounts arrived at in stages A and B are added together and divided by 52 to give the weekly rate of additional pension from SERPS payable to the state pensioner.

S2P calculation

S2P, introduced under the *Child Support, Pensions and Social Security Act 2000*, came into force on 6 April 2002.

From 6 April 2002, eligible employees stopped building up further rights to additional pension from SERPS and began instead to build up rights to additional pension from S2P. Rights to additional pension from SERPS which had already been built up will be calculated and become payable as set out above when the individual concerned reaches state pension age.

Additional pension from S2P is calculated on the amount of an employee's surplus earnings falling in three bands, lying within the overall earnings band bounded by each year's current lower earnings limit and upper earnings limit.

A new low earnings threshold (LET) has been introduced. In 2003/04 it is set at £11,200.

All employees paying National Insurance who earn less than the LET in a tax year are treated for the purposes of S2P as if they were earning at the level of the LET, as are those entitled to invalid care allowance, those looking after a child under the age of six and disabled people who have been in work for at least one-tenth of their working life if they otherwise would build up no entitlement through employment.

A second earnings threshold is in place above the LET so that the band of earnings between the LET and this second earnings threshold is approximately twice the range of the band between the lower earnings limit (LEL) and the low earnings threshold (LET). More precisely, the top of the second S2P earnings band is defined as follows (where the qualifying earnings factor (i e the annual value of the lower earnings limit) is abbreviated as QEF):

$3 \times \text{LET} - 2 \times \text{QEF}$

In calculating $2 \times \text{QEF}$, the result is rounded to the nearest £100 with any exact amount of £50 being rounded down (so, in 2002/03, the second earnings threshold is £25,600).

For each tax year from 2002/03, the amount of the employee's surplus earnings falling into each of the following three bands is calculated as follows:

Band 1:   at least the QEF but not exceeding the LET
Band 2:   above the LET but not exceeding 3LET – 2QEF
Band 3:   above (3LET – 2QEF) *

* Because an employee's surplus earnings in any pay period during a tax year do not include any earnings in excess of the UEL applying for that pay period, the top of Band 3 cannot exceed the annual value of the UEL during that tax year.

Each surplus earnings figure in each of the three bands is separately revalued in line with the increase in national average earnings over the period from the tax year in which the earnings arose until the tax year before the employee reaches state pension age. The surplus earnings figure arising in the tax year before the tax year in which the individual reaches state pension age is included in the calculation but is not subject to revaluation.

The three revalued amounts are then multiplied by the appropriate percentage given in the relevant table below.

Employee attains state pension age before 6 April 2009

Band 1 $(40 + 2N)\%$
Band 2 $(10 + \frac{1}{2}N)\%$
Band 3 $(20 + N)\%$

where N is $\frac{1}{2}$ for each tax year by which the tax year in which the pensioner reached state pension age before 2009/10.

Employee attains state pension age on or after 6 April 2009

Band 1   40%
Band 2   10%
Band 3   20%

The three resulting figures are then added together. After a total has been calculated for each tax year, all the totals are added together and divided by the number of tax years in the period beginning with 1978/79 (or, if later, the year the employee attains age 16) and ending with the tax year before the tax year in which the employee reaches state pension age.

The final total is divided by 52 to give the weekly rate of additional pension from S2P payable to the state pensioner.

S2P becomes flat-rate

At some stage in the future it is envisaged that from the beginning of a specified tax year, the earnings taken into account for the S2P calculation will be limited to the earnings lying in Band 1, i e everyone will be treated as having earnings at the then current level of the low earnings threshold, so that S2P will then provide a flat-rate pension. S2P rights built up before this date will not be affected. Furthermore, it is envisaged that this change to a flat rate S2P will be limited to those aged under 45 on the date of the change, with those aged 45 up to state pension age continuing to build up S2P rights as described above.

Contracting out implications

As explained above at **1.8**, an employee who was contracted-out at any time during the period 6 April 1978 to 5 April 1997 will have built up a guaranteed minimum pension (GMP) entitlement. (If the employee had been contracted out by the protected rights test, the pension to be provided by the protected rights is taken to be the same amount as the GMP the employee would have accrued if he or she had been contracted out over the same period by means of the GMP test.) A Contracted Out Deduction (COD) is subtracted from the claimant's weekly additional pension entitlement equal to the claimant's GMP entitlement. For periods of contracted-out employment from 6 April 1997 onwards, the employee accrued no entitlement under SERPS.

The amount of additional pension from S2P is reduced from the amount arrived at from the calculation described above if the claimant has been contracted out for any period on or after the day S2P came into effect. The amount of the reduction in the claimant's S2P entitlement differs depending on whether the employee in any tax year has been contracted out through membership of:

- a contracted-out occupational pension scheme; or

- an appropriate personal pension.

In either case, where employees are contracted out but earn less than the LET (£11,200 in 2003/04), there is a residual S2P entitlement. This is because, for the purposes of the S2P calculation, employees are taken as earning at the level of the lower earnings threshold itself, but the reduction due to contracting out is based on their actual earnings. The residual S2P top-up is based on the difference between their actual earnings and the LET.

Where the employees are contracted out by means of an occupational pension scheme, not only is there a residual S2P entitlement for those earning less than the LET, there is also a further residual S2P entitlement arising for those earning less than the second earnings threshold (£25,600 in 2003/04). This is because the rebates payable to occupational pension schemes are not enhanced to reflect the more generous overall accrual rate under S2P compared to SERPS. In consequence, the reduction that is applied is based on the lower SERPS entitlement that would have applied if S2P had not been introduced. The top-up for those earning less than the second earnings threshold is , in effect, the difference between the SERPS benefit that would have applied had S2P not been introduced and the S2P benefit they would have accrued if they had not been contracted out.

This adjustment is not needed for employees earning above the LET who are contracted out using an appropriate personal pension (including a stakeholder pension legally established as a personal pension). This is because the rebates that are payable to appropriate personal pension schemes reflect the more generous overall accrual rate under S2P compared to SERPS. There is therefore no need for any residual S2P entitlement to be paid in the case of these employees.

Inherited entitlement to additional pension

Additional pension from SERPS and S2P not only becomes payable to employees at state pension age as part of their Category A pension. It is also payable as part of the Category B state retirement pension entitlement of a widow or widower.

In cases where the spouse has died before reaching state pension age, the inherited additional pension from SERPS/S2P is calculated in the usual way except that the tax year in which the spouse died is used rather than the tax year in which a pensioner reaches state pension age.

When a married person of state pension age dies, and the surviving spouse is also over state pension age at that date, the surviving spouse immediately becomes entitled to the inherited additional pension from SERPS or S2P as part of his/her Category B state retirement pension.

In cases where the surviving spouse has not reached state pension age when their partner dies, he or she will become entitled to the inherited additional pension immediately if entitled to:

- widowed mother's allowance;
- widow's pension; or
- widowed parent's allowance.

This inherited additional pension will then eventually transfer to the surviving spouse's Category B state retirement pension. If the surviving spouse is not entitled to one of those benefits but is entitled to bereavement allowance or was aged 45 or over when they ceased to be entitled to widowed parent's allowance, the inherited additional pension becomes payable when the surviving pensioner claims state retirement pension.

The inherited rate of additional pension was due to fall from the full amount of the inherited rate, subject to a maximum cash ceiling, to one-half of that rate, subject to the same cash ceiling, on 6 April 2000. This change was made to legislation back in 1986, but the fact was not reported in the relevant information produced by the then DSS. This might have left the Government open to claims that pensioners had suffered financially after receiving misleading advice. Under a revised inherited SERPS scheme all men and women over state pension age on 5 October 2002 are exempt from the changes. They are able to pass on 100% of their SERPS entitlement to their surviving widow or widower. For men and women who reach state pension age after 5 October 2002 but before 6 October 2010, the reduction to the amount of inherited SERPS is being phased in. The 50% rate of inherited SERPS will apply to those who reach state pension age on or after 6 October 2010.

The table below illustrates how the revised inherited SERPS scheme will be phased in for people reaching state pension age between 2002 and 2010.

% SERPS passing to surviving spouse	Date when the late spouse was due to reach state pension age	Date of birth of late spouse	
		Men	Women
100%	5.10.2002 or earlier	5.10.1937 or earlier	5.10.1942 or earlier
90%	6.10.2002–5.10.2004	6.10.1937–5.10.1939	6.10.1942–5.10.1944
80%	6.10.2004–5.10.2006	6.10.1939–5.10.1941	6.10.1944–5.10.1946
70%	6.10.2006–5.10.2008	6.10.1941–5.10.1943	6.10.1946–5.10.1948
60%	6.10.2008–5.10.2010	6.10.1943–5.10.1945	6.10.1948–5.07.1950
50%	6.10.2010 or later	6.10.1945 or later	6.07.1950 or later

The *Social Security (Inherited SERPS) Regulations 2001 (SI 2001/1085)* were made on 20 March 2001 and came into force on 6 October 2002. They contain the legislative measures bringing the revised scheme into effect. Note that the change only applies to additional pension rights accrued under SERPS, not to any additional pension rights accrued under S2P. This is because *Reg 1* of the *Social Security (Inherited SERPS) Regulations 2001* defines for the purpose of those regulations 'additional pension' as additional pension derived from contributions or earnings in any tax year beginning after 5 April 1978 and ending before the beginning of the tax year commencing 6 April 2002.

A widow or widower whose spouse dies on or after 6 October 2002 but before 6 October 2010, and who becomes entitled to inherited SERPS with either widowed parent's allowance or a category B retirement pension at any time after 6 October 2002, will have that rate of inherited SERPS calculated by reference to the percentage applying at the date the deceased spouse was due to have reached state pension age, as set out in the above table.

Deferring state retirement pension

A claimant has the option of deferring receipt of state retirement pension, but if the pensioner's spouse is entitled to a Category B pension that spouse will have to agree to the deferral. At present, deferment can last for a maximum five-year period. At the end of the period of deferment the entire state retirement pension will be increased by $\frac{1}{7}$th of 1% for each week the pension is deferred, with a minimum of seven weeks to count. No increases are currently payable once the person deferring the pension is more than five years older than state pension age (i e currently not beyond age 70 for a man and age 65 for a woman). On 6 April 2010 the rate of increase will be $\frac{1}{5}$th of 1% for each week of deferment and without any upper age limit.

No increases are normally payable if another state benefit is being paid to the claimant during the period of deferral. The extra entitlement is expressed as an

additional percentage of the state retirement pension that is payable at the end
of the period of deferment. This takes into account annual upratings that would
have been made to the pension if it had been in payment.

In its December 2002 pensions Green Paper (Cm 5677) the Government
advances arguments for the encouragement of flexible retirement to avoid the
'cliff-edge' of a sudden work/retirement transition, and states that it intends to
ensure that those: 'who choose to work beyond state pension age and defer
taking their pension are properly rewarded by the state system'. The
Government has therefore proposed to bring forward the date of the increase in
the rate of deferment originally scheduled for 6 April 2010. The Green Paper
suggests that the increase could apply to all new cases from 6 April 2006.
Furthermore, the Government proposes to offer a choice of either an increased
regular state pension or a taxable lump-sum payment as compensation for the
deferment of the pension.

A pensioner couple with a combined state pension of £150 p w who both
deferred for five years would receive £206 p w under the current rules. With
the increased deferral rate already set by the *Pensions Act 1995,* the couple's
joint pension after deferral would be £228 p w. If the couple chose to take a
taxable lump sum instead of the £22 p w increase, they would receive a one-
off payment of just over £30,000, assuming that income tax is applied at the
basic rate, in addition to their pension of £150 p w.

Increases to state retirement pension

Once in payment the whole amount of the basic state pension and each
individual's additional pension entitlement is normally uprated in the week
beginning with the Monday after the start of the new tax year in line with the
rise in the retail prices index for the previous September.

Minimum income guarantee

The minimum income guarantee is the term given to describe the means-tested
income support benefit payable to those aged over 60. If, after taking into
account deemed interest from any savings in excess of £6,000 (2003/04), a
pensioner's or a pensioner couple's income is less than the amount given in the
following table, the pensioner or the pensioner couple will be entitled to
income support equal to the amount of the shortfall. State retirement pension,
occupational pensions and personal pensions count as income for the purposes
of the minimum income guarantee. The pensioner must be resident in the UK
to qualify for the minimum income guarantee. The minimum income
guarantee ceases on 6 October 2003.

Minimum income guarantee for 6 April 2003 until 6 October 2003

Single: £102.10 p w
Couple: £155.80 p w

Joint capital held by the pensioner or pensioner couple of between £6,000 and £12,000 is deemed to provide £1 p w income for each £250 (or part of £250) of capital over £6,000. If the joint capital exceeds £12,000 no minimum income guarantee is payable.

However, if the claimant is a permanent resident in residential care, the claimant and any partner are assessed for income support separately. The claimant's own savings between £10,000 and £16,000 are deemed to provide £1 p w income for each £250 (or part of £250) of capital over £10,000. If the claimant's savings exceed £16,000 no minimum income guarantee is payable.

Capital is deemed to include all savings, investments, assets (but not personal possessions unless they were acquired deliberately to reduce the claimant's capital) and shares. The capital value of the claimant's home is disregarded as long as the pensioner lives there. If the pensioner moves into permanent residential care, the capital value of the home will only be disregarded if a partner or close relative of the claimant who is either aged 60 or over, or is incapacitated, still lives in the home.

Income from certain kinds of social security benefits are disregarded in assessing the pensioner's income. Disregarded benefits are: Housing Benefit, Disability Living Allowance, Attendance Allowance, any Social Fund payment, Christmas Bonus and Winter Fuel Payments which are all disregarded in full. The first £10 p w from a War Disablement Pension or War Widow's Pension is also disregarded. £5 p w earned income is disregarded in the case of a single claimant and £10 p w in the case of a couple.

Other disregarded income includes any payment made by anyone living in the pensioner's home as a contribution towards living expenses.

Pension credit

The *State Pension Credit Act 2002* gained royal assent on 25 June 2002 and is due to come into force on 6 October 2003.

Pension Credit consists of two components: a guarantee credit and savings credit. The guarantee credit serves the same purpose as the minimum income guarantee which is to ensure that individuals from age 60 have the protection of a safety net income. The guarantee credit, like the current minimum income guarantee, is set higher than the full-rate basic state pension. However, over time it is expected that the combined level of the basic state pension and the additional pension from SERPS and S2P (or the latter's contracted-out equivalents from private pensions) that initially comes into payment to a single pensioner or a pensioner couple will generally exceed the level of this guarantee – although this will be far from universally the case.

The guarantee credit component brings the claimant's income, or the joint income of a couple, up to the guaranteed level. It will be payable from age 60 although the age threshold will rise to 65 for new male and female claimants between 2010 and 2020. It is intended that the individual's, or couple's, income will include any deemed income from savings capital calculated at a 10% rate of return. However, income is to be deemed only in respect to any slice of savings capital in excess of £6,000 (£10,000 if the claimant is in residential care or a nursing home). Any capital below £6,000 will not be taken into account and actual income will not be used in the calculations.

The savings credit component of the pension credit is a new form of state pension provision. The main features of the savings credit are:

(*a*)   The savings credit component of the pension credit is payable tax free to a claimant who has reached age 65 or who is a member of a couple of which the other member has reached age 65.

(*b*)   The claimant receives a savings credit worth 60% of his or her *qualifying income* above the level of the relevant *savings credit threshold* up to a *maximum savings credit* – but claimant's savings credit is reduced by 40% of the claimant's *income* above his or her *appropriate minimum guarantee*.

(*c*)   *Qualifying income* is defined by the *State Pension Credit Regulations 2002 (SI 2002/1792)* as all of the claimant's *income* (as defined by *section 15* of the *State Pension Credit Act 2002*), save for certain specified benefits and payments. *Section 15* of the *State Pension Credit Act 2002* defines income as including earnings, retirement pension income, income from annuity contracts, certain specified social security and foreign social security benefits and deemed income from capital. Certain amounts of the claimant's income listed in *Schedule IV* to the 2002 Regulations are to be disregarded, and similarly certain sums listed in *Schedule VI* are to be disregarded from the claimant's earnings. *Reg 17(1)* of the 2002 Regulations prescribes that, for the purpose of calculating a person's income, there shall be disregarded:

    (i)   any amount payable by way of tax; and

    (ii)   any amount deducted by way of National Insurance contributions.

(*d*)   The *savings credit threshold* is set out in regulations and is, in the case of a single claimant, the current full rate of the basic state pension (£77.45 in 2003/04). In the case of a couple, the savings credit threshold will be the current aggregate of the full rate of the single person's basic state pension and the full rate of the married woman's basic state pension (£123.80 p w in 2003/04).

(*e*)   The *appropriate minimum guarantee* in most cases will be the same as the *standard minimum guarantee* which is also set out in regulations and in 2003/04 is £102.10 p w for a single claimant and £155.80 p w for a couple. It is the maximum level of the top-up guarantee credit component of the pension credit.

(*f*)   The *maximum savings credit* will be 60% of the difference between the *standard minimum guarantee* and the *savings credit threshold*, and so is £14.79 p w for a single person and £19.20 p w for a couple.

To better explain how the pension credit will work, it is useful to consider two worked examples.

Example 1

A single person reaches age 65 in 2003. She receives a basic state pension of £70 p w, additional pension from SERPS of £9 p w, and a personal pension of £11 p w. Her *qualifying income* is therefore £90 p w. (She has no other income except from savings of less than £6,000.)

She will also be entitled to a guarantee credit of £12.20 p w to take her income to her *appropriate minimum guarantee* of £102.10 p w.

Since her *qualifying income* is more than the single person's *savings credit threshold* of £77.45 p w, she will be entitled to a savings credit calculated as 60% of the difference between *qualifying income* and the single person's *savings credit threshold*, subject to a cap set by the *maximum savings credit*.

60% × (£90 p w–£77.45 p w) = £7.53 p w

Since £7.53 is less than £14.79 her savings credit is not capped by the *maximum savings credit*.

Since her *income* is less than her *appropriate minimum guarantee*, the savings credit is not reduced.

Her total income is therefore £109.63 p w.

Example 2

One partner of a couple reaches age 65 in 2003. This partner receives a basic state pension of £77.45 p w, additional pension from SERPS of £8 p w and an occupational pension of £27 p w. The other receives a basic state pension of £46 p w and deemed income from savings of more than £6,000 of £12 p w. Their *qualifying income* is therefore £170.45 p w. They have no further income.

Since their *qualifying income* is above their *appropriate minimum guarantee* of £155.80 p w they are not entitled to any guarantee credit.

They will be entitled to a savings credit of 60% of the difference between their *qualifying income* and the level of the couple's *savings credit threshold* (subject to the limit set by the *maximum savings credit* for a

---

couple of £19.20 p w) but as reduced by 40% of the difference between their *income* and the couple's *appropriate minimum guarantee*.

60% × (£170 p w–£123 p w) = £28.20 p w This exceeds the relevant *maximum savings credit* and so is capped at £18.60 p w.

This is reduced by 40% of the difference between their *income* and the couple's *appropriate minimum guarantee*.

40% × (£170.45 p w–£155.80 p w) = £5.86 p w

Their savings credit is therefore £19.20 p w–£5.86 p w = £13.34 p w.

Their total weekly income is therefore £170.45 + £13.34 = £183.79 p w.

US Department of Labor Interpretative Bulletin

The following reproduces the box insert in paragraph 5.89 of Paul Myners' review *Institutional investment in the UK*.

US Department of Labor Interpretative Bulletin 26

Interpretative bulletin relating to statements of investment policy, including proxy voting policy or guidelines, *Code of Federal Regulations Table 29 Chapter XXV*, 2509.94–2, 1994:

'The fiduciary act of managing plan assets that are shares of corporate stock includes the voting of proxies appurtenant to those shares of stock.'

'The fiduciary obligations of prudence and loyalty to plan participants and beneficiaries require the responsible fiduciary to vote proxies on issues that may affect the value of the plan's investment.'

'An investment policy that contemplates activities intended to monitor or influence the management of corporations in which the plan owns stock is consistent with a fiduciary's obligations under ERISA* when the responsible fiduciary concludes that there is a reasonable expectation that activities by the plan alone, or together with other shareholders, are likely to enhance the value of the plan's investment, after taking into account the costs involved. Such a reasonable expectation may exist in various circumstances, for example, where plan investments in corporate stock are held as long-term investments or where a plan may not be able to easily dispose such an investment.'

'Active monitoring and communication activities would generally concern such issues as the independence and expertise of candidates for the corporation's board of directors and assuring that the board has sufficient information to carry out its responsibility to monitor management. Other issues may include such matters as consideration of the appropriateness of executive compensation, the corporation's policy regarding mergers and acquisitions, the extent of debt financing and capitalisation, the nature of long-term business plans, the corporation's investment in training to develop its workforce, other workplace practices and financial and non-financial measures of corporate performance. Active monitoring and communication may be carried out through a variety of methods including by means of correspondence and meetings with corporate management as well as by exercising the legal rights of a shareholder.'

* ERISA = *Employment Retirement Income Security Act 1974.*

The bulletin also articulates the fact that managers must not allow themselves to be influenced by conflicts of interest:

'fiduciary duties ... require that, in voting proxies, the responsible fiduciary consider those factors that may affect the value of the plan's investment and not subordinate the interests of the participants and beneficiaries in their retirement income to unrelated objectives.'

The UK Government in its February 2002 consultation paper *Encouraging shareholder activism* made the following comment about the Department of Labor (DOL) Interpretative Bulletin 94–2:

'The essence of the guidance is that although within the corporate structure, the primary responsibility to oversee corporate management falls on the corporation's board of directors, active monitoring of, and communication with, corporate management and the exercise of shareholder votes is consistent with a fiduciary's obligations where the fiduciary concludes that there is a reasonable expectation that such activities by a scheme (either by itself or with other shareholders), are likely to enhance the value of a scheme's investment, after taking into account the costs involved.

Typical actions of fund managers will include considering a variety of aspects of companies in which shares are held, including:

- The independence and expertise of nominees to the board of a company.

- The appropriateness of executive remuneration.

- Financing and capitalisation issues.

- A company's M&A policy.

- A company's long term business plan.'

Index

Breach of trust *contd.*
  protection of trustees
    legal aid 22.1
    Trustee Act 1925, under 22.2
  unintentional 21.2
Company accounts
  pension costs, accounting for
    15.10
Contributions
  employee
    age-related 9.11
    payment over to scheme 8.4
    reporting requirement 8.4
  employer
    money purchase schemes 8.6
    payment of 8.3
    schedule of 8.5
  late arrival of 8.6
  personal pension schemes. to 2.2,
    8.7
  unpaid, payment by Government
    23.4
Corporate governance
  issues 16.25
  Statement of Best Practice 16.25
Data protection
  principles 11.6
  responsibility for 11.6
Deferred pension (*see also* Early
    leavers)
  death before retirement, pension to
    survivor 9.18
  revaluation of 9.16
Discrimination
  age 9.5
  disability 9.5
  sexual orientation, on grounds of
    9.5
Dispute resolution
  collective 20.1
  court, in 20.14
  internal mechanisms for
    excluded disputes 20.5
    first stage of 20.3
    reform proposals 20.6
    scheme, establishment of
      20.2
    second stage of 20.4
  Pensions Advisory Service 20.7

Dispute resolution *contd.*
  Pensions Ombudsman. *See*
    Pensions Ombudsman
  tribunal, in 20.14
  trustees, involvement of
    20.1
Duties of trustees
  advice, to take 10.1
  benefit redesign 9.11
  differing groups, to act fairly
    between
  bulk transfer, treatment on
    9.8
  discretionary powers, defence of
    9.1
  discrimination, forms of 9.5
  early retirement programmes
    9.6
  European law, equal treatment
    under 9.2
  interpretations and exceptions
    9.3
  senior executives, augmentation
    of benefits to 9.7
  trust law and social security law,
    provisions of 9.1
  women on maternity leave,
    treatment of 9.4
early leavers, rights of. *See* Early
    leavers
employees with personal pensions,
    to 9.13
general principles 5.1
information, disclosure of. *See*
    Information, disclosure of
main 5.2
new employees, to 9.9
opting-out, attitude to 9.12
pensionable earnings cap,
    information on 9.10
proper care, exercise of 5.1
reporting requirements 8.4
statutory 5.10
Early leavers
  death before retirement, pension to
    survivor 9.18
  deferred pensions, revaluation of
    9.16
  pension entitlement 9.15